D1605238

HEMINGWAY

HEMINGWAY

UP IN MICHIGAN PERSPECTIVES

Edited by Frederic J. Svoboda and Joseph J. Waldmeir

Michigan State University Press
East Lansing

Copyright © 1995 Michigan State University Press

All Michigan State University Press books are produced on paper which meets the requirements of American National Standard of Information Sciences—Permanence of paper for printed materials ANSI Z23.48-1984.

Printed in the United States of America

Michigan State University Press
East Lansing, Michigan 48823-5202

03 02 01 00 99 98 97 96 95 1 2 3 4 5 6 7 8 9 10

Library of Congress Cataloging-in-Publication Data

Hemingway : up in Michigan perspectives / edited by Frederic J. Svoboda and Joseph J. Waldmeir
        p.   cm.
    Includes bibliographical references and index.
    ISBN 0-87013-383-7 (alk. paper)
    1. Hemingway, Ernest, 1899-1961—Criticism and interpretation—
  Congresses. 2. Hemingway, Ernest, 1899-1961—Knowledge—Michigan—
  Congresses. 3. Michigan—In literature—Congresses. I. Svoboda, Frederic
  Joseph, 1949-   . II. Waldmeir, Joseph J.
  PS3515.E37Z6197 1995
  813'.52—dc20
                                                    95-11028
                                                    CIP

CONTENTS

ACKNOWLEDGMENTS

Jackson Bryer, University of Maryland
Maury Cohen, North Central Michigan College
Audrey Collins, Stafford's Perry Hotel, Petoskey
Richard Davison, University of Delaware
Tony Dunaske, North Central Michigan College
Candance Eaton, Little Traverse Historical Museum, Petoskey
Jerri Gillett, Michigan State University
Michael Gow, North Central Michigan College
Lorraine Hart, Michigan State University
Donald Junkins, University of Massachusetts at Amherst
J. Gerard Kennedy, Louisiana State University
Brad Leech, City of Petoskey
Kenneth Marek, Northwestern Michigan College
James McCullough, North Central Michigan College
Lisa Middents, Hemingway Collection of the John F. Kennedy Library,
    Boston
Roberta Schwartz, Oakland University
Stafford Smith, Stafford's Perry Hotel and Bay View Inn, Petoskey
John Waldmeir, University of Mary
The Students and Staff of North Central Michigan College
The Staff of Stafford's Perry Hotel, Petoskey
The Hemingway Society

Up in Michigan II sponsored by:
The Michigan Hemingway Society

Institutional sponsors for the conference:
English Department, Michigan State University
North Central Michigan College

Permissions to print or reprint granted by:

The Hemingway Review for Kelli Larson's "Stepping into the Labyrinth: Fifteen Years of Hemingway Scholarship."

Basil Blackwell, Ltd. for Michael Reynolds's "A Half-Slain Knight's Gambit: Or A Little Information on the Last Unpublished and Partially Unfinished Hemingway Novel You Are Ever Unlikely to Read," which is expanded in Reynolds's *Hemingway: Homeward Bound*, Basil Blackwell, 1992.

Studies in Short Fiction for Paul Strong's "The First Nick Adams Stories" from *Studies in Short Fiction* 28 (1991): 83-91. Copyright © 1991 by Newberry College.

The Ernest Hemingway Foundation for photograph of Hemingway as a young man.

Excerpts from the unpublished work of Ernest Hemingway published by permission of the Ernest Hemingway Foundation, Copyright © 1995, The Ernest Hemingway Foundation.

"The Ballad of the Goodly Fere" by Ezra Pound from *Ezra Pound: Personae*. Copyright © 1926 by Ezra Pound. Reprinted by Permission of New Directions Publishing Corp.

INTRODUCTION

WALKING INTO THE COUNTRY

FREDERIC J. SVOBODA

> I cannot write beautifully, but I can write with great accu-
> racy . . . and the accuracy makes a sort of beauty. . . . I
> know how to make country so that you, when you wish,
> can walk into it. . . .
>
> —Ernest Hemingway to Bernard Berenson,
> 20-22 March 1953.

EVERY ONCE IN A WHILE the students of Hemingway gather
to walk into the country that he experienced and then made again in his
fiction: in Traverse City, in Madrid and Pamplona, in northern Italy, and
in Schruns, Austria. As I begin to write this introduction some of us are in
Pamplona again, but I am in Michigan, thinking of Michigan; for in
October of 1991 we scholars gathered in Petoskey, Michigan to pay tribute to but, more, to work to understand that sometimes exasperating man
and great American writer, and to understand what his work said of his
time—and of our own. Admittedly, we tend to gather in pleasant places,
and Petoskey is a pleasant place. We do not, however, go just for the
pleasantness or for the good company, though one organizing a conference
of Hemingway scholars would be well advised to look to the quality of the
hotel rooms and the restaurants.

A little more than a year ago, Joe Waldmeir and I were in the basement
bar of Petoskey's Perry Hotel, organizing. It was unusually hot outside for
northern Michigan, over ninety, but the bar was cool and pleasantly dim.

"Do you think it'll be big enough, Joe?"

"Oh, sure, Fred. It's a good place. The dining room upstairs is nice,
too."

Hemingway scholars, Hemingway dialogue. We did not quite call the
bar well lighted, but we did notice that it was *clean*, and after a drink we

1

walked back out into the streets of Petoskey, two-story brick store fronts atop the bluff overlooking Little Traverse Bay.

A highway has been cut through between the business district and the waterfront since Hemingway's day, the two railroad stations have become a museum and an office building, yet much has not changed, and it was not hard to imagine a young Ernie Hemingway come to town from Walloon Lake with his parents, or a slightly older Ernest home from the Great War writing not-so-good fiction in the boarding house at 602 State Street, trying to learn his craft, or walking downtown to have breakfast at what is now Jespersen's Restaurant. There is something magical in Hemingway's writing, or many things magical, one of which is the way that he manages to evoke a sense of place for his readers. And the place would add another dimension to our examination of his work and life as we gathered in a resort hotel that had been opened the same year Hemingway was born and that was operating still, a reminder of elegant days gone by with its bar, dining room, and front porch cafe, and live music in two different settings after dark. And so in October we scholars would stay at the hotel, and walk the downtown streets, and motor to the lakes where he had fished and swum. After he left and fame claimed him, he returned only once that we are sure of, but neither he nor we would have had any trouble recognizing the Walloon Lake cottage his parents built, even if his sister Sunny had not peeked out from its garage at us as we drove by, careful not to intrude on her. And we would also have recognized the general store at Horton Bay, even without Bill Ohle to walk us around it with reminiscences of Ernest, and we would have known the Point where Nick Adams and Marjorie broke up even without the tour organized by Ken Marek. Hemingway knew it as well in his memory as in reality, and wrote it as well, and we knew it through him even before we saw it.

We recognized the weather, too. By October the July heat was only a memory and it was pleasant one day, blustery cold the next, and raining the third. There had been no three-day blow yet to strip the leaves from the trees, but the leaves had turned to red and gold, with the lake effect warmth keeping them still on the branches along the shores. How the weather was always has been a part of the beautiful accuracy of Hemingway's prose, and those three days in October helped remind us of that. There are shining moments in his writing, too, however modest he seems, for the moment, in the letter to Berenson that I quoted above, and the papers presented at the conference reminded us of how he could evoke those moments, as in the moment quoted by Michael Reynolds from the never-finished manuscript of the picaresque novel that Hemingway abandoned in order to write *A Farewell to Arms*. Very early one fall morning a young man climbs to the roof of a summer cottage to cap its chimney against squirrels and then looks out over the lake as it is in the cold morning air. It is a part of the autumn ritual of closing up for the winter, a ritual known to all those who have ever kept a summer cottage, and the passage is full of memory. The boy looks at the lake and trees, he says, "to remember them and all around; at the hills in back and the woods far off on the other side of the house and down again at the woodshed roof and I loved them all very much, the woodshed and the fence and the hills and the woods and I wished we were just going on a trip and not going away." Then the boy begins to go down, but his father asks him to stay and climbs himself to the roof, and shares the view, and the father does not want to leave either. The boy seems transparently the young Hemingway, and behind the fiction it is his memory of the place and the father he would leave and immortalize that suffuses the passage with its emotional resonances.

And so in autumn we gathered at the place Hemingway had seen and then made in his fiction, and we remembered on many levels, and those memories and perceptions make up this collection.

Some of us had things to say of Michigan, as did Waring Jones in suggesting the lessons of perception and self-reliance that Hemingway might have taken away with him from summers on Walloon Lake, or Jack Jobst in charting the moment of childhood's end for Hemingway in Michigan's Upper Peninsula, in Seney. I examine the ways in which Hemingway's wild Michigan is as much a fictional creation as a historical transcription. Paul Strong discusses the ways that Hemingway sets off the so-called savage and civilized Michigans in several early stories; Will Watson brings his own experiences as a child watching his doctor grandfather operate to his reading of one of the same stories, "Indian Camp," in which young Nick Adams becomes an unwilling intern. Larry Grimes suggests the debt to William James's religious thought (via the influence of Gertrude Stein) in another story of the young Nick, "The Doctor and the Doctor's Wife." H. R. Stoneback corrects the record with respect to a daughter of Petoskey, Marjorie Bump, in reminding us of the differences between fact, fiction, and biography in "The End of Something." Frank Scafella suggests how "nothing" makes its appearance early in Hemingway's work, as he deals with "Big Two-Hearted River," while Erik Nakjavani returns to the theme of memory and commemoration of past experience in his study of the story of an adult Nick Adams, "Fathers and Sons."

Something of what happened as Hemingway moved away from Michigan—in his life and in his fiction—is evoked in an exchange between Michael Reynolds and Linda Wagner-Martin, as Reynolds reports on Hemingway's difficulties in composing the unpublished and unfinished novel, "Jimmy Breen," from which I quoted above, and

Wagner-Martin suggests how the lessons taught by Gertrude Stein influenced his decision to drop the work-in-progress.

If Michigan is one starting point, however, it certainly was not all of Hemingway's life or his fiction, and we also walked with Hemingway into the wider world. James Nagel examines narration and the character Robert Cohn in the novel of Lost Generation expatriates, *The Sun Also Rises*, and Wolfgang Rudat links anti-Semitism to the genesis of Cohn. Linda Wagner-Martin examines Hemingway's debts in this and other early works to Spanish novelist Blasco Ibañez.

Robert W. Lewis and Bickford Sylvester discuss Hemingway's novel of the First World War, *A Farewell to Arms*, Lewis examining the relationship of manners to morals and Sylvester discussing the opposition of sexuality to romance. Robert A. Martin explores the ways in which that novel moved Hemingway away from his boyhood home in Oak Park, Illinois and its idealistic view of the world.

Mark Spilka takes on the often-argued ending of the great African story, "The Short Happy Life of Francis Macomber" in his letter to Nina Baym, and Warren Bennett links the less-known "Today is Friday" to Ezra Pound's "The Ballad of the Goodly Fere."

Four of us examined Hemingway's novel of the Spanish Civil War, *For Whom the Bell Tolls*. Paul Smith shows the links between love and death in the novel's love scenes, and Allen Josephs discusses the ways in which love rather than death becomes the "undiscovered country" of Hemingway's favorite among the novel's working titles. Linda Miller traces surprising new role models for its characters, particularly the strong woman, Pilar, and her husband, Pablo. Thomas Gould finds Hemingway stressing the human costs of war and death as he examines Hemingway's revisions in the novel's manuscripts.

Michael Seefeldt discusses *Across the River and Into the Trees*, often considered a failure, and concludes that both realistic and allegorical readings of the work may raise it in our estimation.

Moving from discussions more concerned with specific places and specific works, Robert Gajdusek ties together a number of works in exploring women's isolation from natural processes in Hemingway's work. Finally, Kelli A. Larson moves us to a consideration of the critical context for our studies in examining the last fifteen years of scholarly study of the author and his work.

Like young Jimmy of the unfinished novel, we scholars looked about at the lakes and hills as we prepared to leave northern Michigan on a Sunday morning in October of 1991. The conference was over, but while it had gone on we had walked into the country, and felt the country and what Hemingway had made of it. In this collection we share the view.

HEMINGWAY AND MICHIGAN

A Moveable Michigan

A Talk Given in a Room on the Petoskey Harbor overlooking Lake Michigan

WARING JONES

NINETY-THREE YEARS AND three months ago, Dr. and Mrs. Clarence Hemingway arrived up here in northern Michigan looking for a spot on the shoreline to build a cabin.[1] Twenty-six years after this trip, their son Ernest published a story called "Indian Camp" in a little Paris magazine.[2] It starts invitingly—a rowboat is drawn up on the beach, two Indians are waiting. I have brought a photograph of a rowboat drawn up on the beach at the local Horton Bay.[3] Before we take a little ride or two, let us have a personal reminiscence of the context of summer vacations in the upper Midwest.

Sixty years ago, my parents drove me up to Grandpa's place on Woman's Lake in northern Minnesota—right over there to the West of us from here. My aunts and uncles and all their children came up, too. We learned to swim, fish, pitch tents, dig trenches, and make wars with flying corn cobs and gobs of mud. When the kerosene lamps were put out at night, we were frightened of sounds in the woods surrounding us. There were the burnt ruins of a Girl Scout camp out on the mysterious island. The channel into the next lake, Little Boy Lake, was scary with fallen trees and cattails. There was always safety back at the base camp, however.

Trouble came in the family—a maiden aunt jealous of her married brothers and sisters persuaded Grandma, who was growing senile, to secretly sell the property. My parents found another summer place—a farm near a lake only fifteen miles from our city home. Now I was older, time for chores, taking care of the chickens, planting and weeding that big garden, painting the fences. I used to keep an alarm clock on the fence post so I could see how many minutes were left before I could bike down to the lake and swim. And *read*. I was ten years old and my mother gave me Christopher Morley stories—one, "Thunder on the Left," was about a boy who never grew up—I liked that one. We moved through the summers and that meant finding new jobs. I took a train out to Nevada, pitched hay all summer, and when I came home for school in September, I discovered my

7

parents were no longer parents. They were older friends. I was an independent person.

Over here in America we have a great advantage. In Europe, the summer vacations are only a few weeks long, too short for someone to hire a youngster for a full-time job. Here, in the school year we learn study habits, we are invited to widen our knowledge. In the summers, we learn to escape, relax, and work. This year I read a letter in Oak Park that Ernest wrote Mary Welsh when he was beauing her. He told her that all individuals who endure have an ability to completely relax and be terribly lazy, but such folks also have it in them, after lazy spells, to get up and work like real champions.[4]

Over these summer vacations, I also learned to make independent choices. I did not know it at the time, but these were choices that changed my life. Looking back, I call what happened "great, great luck."

I went back to that first summer place, Grandpa's, a couple of years ago. A large family from Kansas City had put in year-round city houses with a little jet landing field on the site of the cabin where we used to chase the bats with brooms. The little shed we had built for our war games Red Cross hut was now a dog house. Has all that I knew up there gone? I close my eyes and see it all just the way it was sixty years ago. "We're coming Mom, we're coming! Just one more dive!"

Let me throw a little hook in here. A bit ago a Danish friend and I walked around Walden Pond one sunrise. He got very angry and shouted, "We've been cheated—this isn't the Walden Pond I read about!" "You're right," I said. "The author wrote it in some mysterious way so that the real Walden Pond is the one you see when you read the book."

Let us take a contextual boat ride and see where the emerging patterns of summer vacations up here in Michigan take us. First of all, there are lots of boats (and train rides). To get up here, the Hemingways took a lake steamer from Chicago, then two little trains to the lake, and at last a little steamer to the cottage. Here they had two rowboats of their own, and a little later Poppa bought an inboard motorboat.[5]

In a few years Momma built a separate cottage across the lake where she could go to be herself, sometimes for several days. There was a lot of rowing across and back, and hiking over the hill to fish and camp by Walloon Lake. There were chores and reading. Ah, reading. Ernest read whenever he could, secret hours in the day or by lantern in a tent at night. Let us estimate very roughly: he spent some eighteen or so summers up here—from his babyhood to his marriage on 3 September 1921. We can bet most of these summer days he took time to read.

Reading makes for solitary happiness, and there was also the communal happiness—it made a strong base. A strong base in fresh territory when one is young makes for more confident exploring in the surrounding country. There were lots of "This is the last time I'm going to call you in!" and "Have you finished all your chores?" but it was not until later that Poppa began to exhibit moods and Momma occasionally grew difficult. One cannot emphasize enough the importance a happy childhood—the first one to fifteen years—provides a growing boy. Plus, a little unhappiness (providing the parental love holds, and it did) deepens one. Difficult stretches create a more human being. One can make something of Ernest coming home from the war and being told after a while to "get a job." Is not that common for a young man coming home just at the age most of his contemporaries have left or are leaving? Which would you rather have had, a childhood with no pain or one with a bit of strain?[6]

Let us row our little boat further out onto the lake and watch the patterns, the circles, widening. See the family move up from Oak Park, summer after summer, to this "safe" place in Michigan where one can be oneself. On with Ernest via ship and train to Italy, and there from the battlefield to the safety of the hospital. After the war, up here again from Oak Park. The family goes back to town and Ernest chooses to stay up here all winter. Cold weather comes, and he moves over to the upstairs room in the Petoskey boarding house run by Mrs. Evan Potter on 602 State Street. In his emerging confidence at being on his own, Ernest, with his charm, made friends and "took the town." Maybe not all the townspeople thought so, but he did. He was to have this confidence in making friends in new places all over the world, along with an eagerness to open up new opportunities. How did he get that first job after the war? That winter he gave a lecture on his war experiences at the little Petoskey public library here. A woman heard him and offered him a job in Toronto looking after her son.

Let us watch the pattern widen. Taking a job in Chicago, coming back up here with his fiancee to get married, on over to Paris with his separate scribbling room around the corner on the third floor of the "house where Verlaine died," and then off to Switzerland. (That was not a first. Ernest's older sister tells us of the Bible Dr. Hemingway bought in Switzerland when he was over there, years before.[7]) On to an Austrian inn with a separate little workroom. Back to Paris, over the mountains to Spain, off to Key West with a separate workroom there. (Remember his Poppa's motor launch up here? Ernest rented one in Key West, and later built one of his own.) Now off to fish the Gulf Stream and over to the upstairs room in the Ambos Mundos Hotel in Havana. Fishing and writing. No kerosene lamp now; he could read as late as he wanted by an electric lamp. Just like his Momma, they would not hear from him for many days. Hot summer came, then out to Cooke City, Montana with a separate work cabin, back to Havana, and out to Sun Valley to work. He even seemed to find some kind of peace in the hospital room at the Mayo Clinic in Minnesota near the end. Two friends of mine, George and Jean Waters, looked out the window one morning and there he was, walking by, whistling cheerfully. One can like being cared for, whether it is by Nurse Agnes or Nurse Mayo.

In the context of the above patterns, we can move in closer: his mother built a separate music room in their Oak Park family home, Poppa had his medical office in the home, and Ernest wrote his first high school stories at the desk in the room his parents gave him up on the third floor. A room of one's own. Insisted upon. What a gift this pattern was to be! Safe here, safe anywhere.

Let us hear from Ernest, "The writer who can't leave his country . . . is the local color writer . . . if he . . . deals with the human heart . . . then you may be sure he does not have to stay . . . for fear he will lose it. He can make the country . . . five thousand miles away from it looking at the whitewashed wall of a cheap room in any land you name and make it truer than anyone can who lives in it." That is item 754 in the Hemingway papers at the JFK Library. I think we can thank fellow Society member Frank Scaffella for pointing this out in his book, *Hemingway: Essays of Reassessment*,[8] at our Schruns conference. We can also thank Mrs. Potter for renting him that first room in Petoskey.

So how can we summarize this context of a "moveable Michigan"? Let us hear Ernest (writing about another place): "There's never any ending . . . this is how (it) was in the early days when we were . . . very happy."[9]

After his marriage up here in September 1921, did he ever come back in the remaining forty years of his life? Sometime after his father's death, his mother sent Ernest the keys to the cottage.[10] He paid the insurance on it for years.

William Ohle, a long-term resident up here who has written two books on the area, says, "No. Ernest never returned (to Walloon Lake)."[11] Petoskey citizens report that they saw Ernest in this town at least once, perhaps twice. If he did not move back to the area for extended stays, what could have been some of the reasons? He might not have wanted to return with a new wife because of his memories of his honeymoon with the first one here; he might have been too busy going back and forth across the country and overseas to take the time; he might not have wanted to joggle up memories of his father after the latter died; or perhaps Michigan was so clear in his heart that he did not have to. Maybe someone else was in the cottage? A mystery. We will ask our Hemingway Society private detectives to give us some more detailed answers. For some of Hemingway's written reasons for not returning, see chapter three in

Susan F. Beegel's *Hemingway's Craft of Omission* (UMI Research Press, Ann Arbor, Michigan, 1988). I know he did return to Oak Park years after his last visit at his Poppa's funeral. Twenty-five years ago, Ernest's jack-of-all-trades, Toby Bruce, told me he and Ernest were driving out West and they detoured to Oak Park and drove up and down the streets of the town one night, looking. Then they drove on.

Take another glance at this photo of the rowboat pulled up on the beach. Walk up to it. Then watch what Ernest does to us with the first sentence. "At the lakeshore there was *another* row-boat drawn up."[12] "Another" suggests there is room for us as well as the people in the story. What an invitational touch! Reminds one of Robert Frost's poem: "I'm going out to clean the pasture spring—You come too."[13] Now I do not believe for a second that Ernest sat down and consciously figured out that stroke. It was the spirit of life breathing through him and out of his right hand. We stay with the boy and his father for five pages, and in these pages we get a chance to enjoy a good relaxing cigar, land at a new place, almost simultaneously witness close-up a birth and a death, and then we are back in the boat and it is almost dawn, the sun is coming up, and in that great last sentence the boy tells us his only main overt feelings in the story. His Poppa is rowing, the air is cold, the boy puts his hand in the water. It is "warm." He feels "quite sure" he will never die.[14] We sense they will land on another beach and walk up to the home cottage and sleep, but the row-boat will go out again. We will cross to Paris and beyond, and, as Ernest rows us, a little bit each day, almost always in short little scenes, we will move up across half the world, up along the shores of Lake Maggiore, sweep down to peek at that Spanish bridge, go for a gondola ride in Venice, and have a wonderful, purifying swim in the Atlantic Ocean. And what a series of great openings: in that little rented room in Paris, Ernest will unfold his sectional map of the area right above us here—Michigan's Upper Peninsula—go over the *X*'s he marked where he caught fish, and start a story with the train's pulling out of sight and the boy sitting down on his camping equipment in a town totally burnt down.

When he writes about watching the fishermen on the Seine in the heart of Paris, we sense, looking backward now, how perfect life was to call him across the Atlantic over onto that very great river, the Gulf Stream.

How is this for an opening? "You know how it is there early in the morning in Havana. . . ." Usually when someone tells me, "You know how it is," I want to cry out, "No, I don't know!" With Ernest it is different—he rows us right into the experience with his details, and we are aboard and off. Then, when the story is over, we catch a glimpse of another ship, making its way up on the horizon.[15] So often as one trip ends he gives us these low-key evocations of a new one.

Sometimes we may feel extended, like the soldier who has just watched the crucifixion of Jesus Christ. "I feel like hell." "You've been out here too long, that's all."[16]

Here is a little six-and-a-half-page boat trip you can take some night when you are in a musing mood sitting on the cabin porch. A fellow tells us he has just had a fight about something that was not really "about anything." A big storm has occurred, the man learns he has unintentionally killed a person. Going out in his boat after the storm, he is the first one to discover a huge ocean liner that has just gone down with all hands trapped aboard. It is sitting on a reef just below the surface. Fish are already getting fat on the bodies of those drowned inside. He swims down and sees a dead woman floating behind a porthole. She has "rings on one of her hands." He fails to break the glass and reach the woman. At the end he says, "Even the birds get more out of her than I did."[17] We finish the story and wonder. Details have impressed us but we cannot connect them. Ah, the joy of these little boat trips. We have to make the connections. Let us see, here is a fight about nothing and we have to leave town? Come on, what was the fight really about? Did we leave a wife and a child? We discover a woman who has just drowned, and no matter how hard we try, we cannot break through to her. Are those rings she has on an engagement and a wedding ring? We get an awful feeling we are utterly alone out here; what have we done to create this? If the good God cares about birds, He will continue to watch over us, but we cannot go back to town, so what are we going to do now? In just six pages that is quite a little boat ride.

Let us let the circle close. Easily. Do not bend it! Relax and look at the last trip. Watch this one as it reaches back quietly and touches the first one. Again, here is a man, a boy, a boat on the beach. And we go out. Remember on the first trip the boy registers very few emotions, and these are mainly at the end. This trip the man offers us a steady stream of feelings, as we act and react with him. Again there is a sudden birth as a great fish explodes up out of the ocean, and again there is a death. We put our hands over the edge of the boat and heal them in the water. What was implicit at the end of the first story is explicit here as we come in from the Gulf Stream, beach the boat, walk up to the cottage, and at last go to sleep peacefully, gloriously.

What echoes here for the reader? Rowing back at dawn in the little boat toward the safety of the beach and cottage in "Indian Camp." It is the same shoreline Dr. and Mrs. Hemingway searched to find a spot on which to build the family cottage. Also, we remember Ernest's memorable passage in *Green Hills of Africa* in which he writes how our victories and defeats finally meld with the flow of the one lasting thing—the stream.[18]

Starting with his boyhood expeditions up in Michigan, Ernest's moveable fishing trips have come a long way.

Ernest really cared about his readers. About us. He knew the power and joy of beautiful sharing. That is one reason why he worked so hard. It is a lot of fun to take a look at the lists of stories he wanted to share with us but did not find the time for. The lists start in some of the early unpublished stories, and on page 98 in *The Torrents of Spring,* about experiences up here in Michigan.[19] They go on in *The Snows of Kilimanjaro* and, of course, in the great list at the end of *Death in the Afternoon.* As he begins that last chapter, he writes, "If I could have made this enough of a book, it would have had everything in it."[20] Then he gives us an eight-and-a-half-page list, like a compressed fishing diary. He mentions a "boy eight feet six inches tall." We might say that is the height the little child grew up to be— the boy whose parents brought him up here when he was only seven weeks old that September in the last year of the last century. The ship went right past this window.

I had an aunt who passed on in 1980, when she was one hundred and five years old. If her mother lived the same number of years, that mother might have been born in 1786—before there was a Chicago, a Seattle, a San Francisco, Denver, or Petoskey. (As we know them; of course, there may have been centers of Indian civilizations in those places.) The rocks over by my cabin on Lake Superior and on the shores around us are among the oldest in the world, sitting here for millions of years, exposed. In the context of time, real historical time, the Hemingways first came up here on that first boat trip a few minutes ago, about the start of this talk. My gosh, there they are out the window now, on the good ship *State of Ohio.*[21] It is August 1898. Let us all rise and with our invisible cups full of fresh, pure apple juice from that Horton Bay orchard, give Ma and Pa a toast. "Sköl, Grace. Sköl, Clarence. Thank you, thank life, for guiding you to come up here." Ernest will not be born until next summer. That is okay. We can wait. It will only be a second. "Hello! Hello! Hey, Ernest! Hello!" Look at him, he is too young to know his name. Yet. I will bet he grows up and fills out that name.

NOTES

1. Marcelline Hemingway Sanford, *At the Hemingways* (London: Putnam and Co., 1963), 68.
2. Ernest Hemingway, "Work in Progress," *the transatlantic review* 1, no. 4 (April 1924): 230. (There are at least fifty-six changes between this version and the version published in book form, *In Our Time* [New York: Boni and Liveright, 1925]. The changes are in capitalization, commas added, and other grammatical corrections, with no changes in content.)

3. David F. Scherman and Rosemarie Redlich, *Literary America* (New York: Dodd, Mead and Co., 1982), 152-53.

4. Ernest Hemingway to Mary Welsh, t.l.s., San Francisco de Paula, Cuba, September 1945, 1.

5. Sanford, *At the Hemingways*, 77.

6. Being told to leave home was a great catalyst. Ernest was free to establish new homes and seek new retreats for the rest of his life, with wonderful results in his work; that is, if he had kept the pattern of returning to Michigan, he might not have organized those several-day pack trips up into the Wyoming-Montana mountains. The climbing, the horses, the stalking, lying on the forest floor sighting down his rifle—all these were so easily transferable to Spain for his subsequent three-day mountain thriller.

7. Sanford, *At the Hemingways*, 195.

8. Frank Scaffella, *Hemingway: Essays of Reassessment* (New York: Oxford University Press, 1991), 91.

9. Ernest Hemingway, *A Moveable Feast* (New York: Scribner's, 1964), 211.

10. The keys are in the Oak Park Hemingway Foundation Collection.

11. William H. Ohle, *How It Was in Horton Bay* (Boyne City: the author, 1989), 109.

12. Hemingway, "Work in Progress," 230.

13. Robert Frost, "The Pasture," *Collected Poems of Robert Frost* (Garden City, New York: Halcyon House, 1942), 1.

14. Hemingway, "Work in Progress," 234.

15. Ernest Hemingway, *To Have and Have Not* (New York: Scribner's, 1937), 262.

16. Hemingway, "Today Is Friday," in *The Fifth Column and The First Forty-Nine Stories* (New York: Scribner's, 1938), 457.

17. Hemingway, "After the Storm," in *The Fifth Column and The First Forty-Nine Stories*, 476.

18. Hemingway, *Green Hills of Africa* (New York: Scribner's, 1935), 150.

19. Ernest Hemingway, *The Torrents of Spring* (New York: Scribner's, 1926), 98.

20. Ernest Hemingway, *Death in the Afternoon* (New York: Scribner's, 1932), 270. (To be sure he will not leave too much unwritten, Hemingway adds at the end of the narrative a sixty-four-page illustrated glossary, a four-page list of reactions to bullfights, a three-page estimate of one matador, a six-and-a-half-page list of bullfighting dates on several continents, and a final one-half-page signed bibliographical note to the book.)

21. Sanford, *At the Hemingways*, 68.

FALSE WILDERNESS

NORTHERN MICHIGAN AS CREATED IN THE NICK ADAMS STORIES

FREDERIC J. SVOBODA

IN HIS NICK ADAMS STORIES, Hemingway creates a fictional Michigan that is not quite the same as the Michigan he actually experienced as a boy and young man. Nick's Michigan is still essentially a frontier, both physically and morally. It is often prosaic in feel, yet it is sometimes romanticized as well. Hemingway's Michigan was far more civilized, an environment shaped, sustained, and simultaneously degraded by technology and by genteel nineteenth- and early twentieth-century American culture. Understanding the differences between the fictional and historical Michigans gives us an increased understanding of the stories, and of the nature of Hemingway's art.

We all know that Hemingway never really wrote of Oak Park. He explained this to Charles Fenton in 1952, writing that too many people might be hurt who were then alive.[1] Reportedly, in the late 1940s or early 1950s he cruised the streets with Toby Bruce late one summer night, remembering. We may be less conscious that, similarly, he never really wrote of Walloon Village or of Petoskey, which he also revisited—very quietly—in 1947.[2] As some commentators have pointed out, these locales may have been filled with ghosts for him.

Also, however, like the unexamined Oak Park, both Walloon Village and Petoskey were clearly "civilized" locations. They had thriving shops, movie theaters, pool rooms, hotels, and even various forms of manufacturing.[3] Hemingway avoided them in his published fiction of quality. (The comic treatment of Petoskey in *Torrents of Spring*, a work of lesser quality, certainly does not mark a departure from this general principle.) Instead, he set stories at Horton Bay, nearly a ghost town as he presents it in "The End of Something," and in the fictionalized, deserted Seney of "Big Two-Hearted River." He uses a similarly fictionalized saloon of "frontier" lumbering town Kalkaska in "The Light of the World," the "wilderness" north of Kalkaska in "The Battler," and an Upper Peninsula Michigan lake in "Indian Camp."

In itself, this selection of smaller, more isolated settings already departs from the full reality of northern Michigan as the young Hemingway experienced it. Further, of course, none of these stories are quite historically accurate in the fictional impressions they give, even of the Michigan places that Hemingway appropriates as settings.

As he grew up during summers at Walloon Lake, the young Hemingway hunted and fished in Michigan, but he really did not know a Michigan wilderness. That was long gone by the time he came there. Historian Bruce Catton, a renowned native of Petoskey, has suggested that the beginning of the end of the wilderness really dates to a change in the Michigan Indians' lives as fur trapping became more lucrative than their previous hunting and fishing existence. As early as 1761, when the British acquired what would become Michigan from the French, according to Catton, "the Indian only seemed to be living in the stone age. He really was a part of eighteenth century Europe," a part of a nearly worldwide pattern of production, trade, and consumption.[4] This caution about wider connections might equally be applied, slightly updated, to an examination of Hemingway in Michigan.

To continue the review of relevant Michigan history, in the eighteenth century civilization encroached only a little on the visible face of the land. By most estimates, there were only ten or fifteen thousand Indians in Michigan, and their European-inspired exploitation of the fur-bearing animals might only have been discerned by a sensitive ecologist, a creature not existing in that Michigan or in the young Hemingway's Michigan. Yet the pattern of outside exploitation had been set, and just as the Indians' stone age life was altered by the allure of manufactured guns, axes, kettles, blankets, and the like, life in northern Michigan would again and again change in response to new opportunities, perhaps not always for the better.

In northern Michigan, lumbering shaped the economy and scarred the land in what now seems an orgy of cutting that began slowly about 1840, accelerated after the Civil War, and then died back for lack of raw material between 1900 and 1910, just as the Hemingways were arriving. The seemingly inexhaustible white pine forests had gone to build towns and farms on the prairie frontier of America, including the town of Oak Park, Illinois. That village's near neighbor, Chicago, had been a major lumber shipping point. Much of the lumber trade had taken place by water, taking advantage of Michigan's lakes and streams.

Like many of the others, Walloon Lake was eventually plied by lumber steamers towing rafts of logs, including the now-famous *Magic* of "The Doctor and the Doctor's Wife." The biggest local conflict did not involve the Indians, however. From 1877, the homeowners' association battled lumberman W. L. McManus over the lake level. At times homeowner sentries patrolled the dam, which several times was knocked down by dynamite, leaving cottagers' docks standing high and dry. Only in 1917 was a legal lake level established.[5]

Great Lakes port cities had their sawmills and lumber docks, and innumerable temporary dams had been thrown up throughout Michigan, both to power sawmills and to float giant logs downstream to the mills. There was a limitation, though. Huge logs could be moved no more than a few miles overland by oxen or, later, horses, necessarily downhill and on the ice-slicked roads of winter, to be collected for the spring lumber drives. Thus, lumbering was a part-year activity, and many lumberjacks were family men who returned to their farms in the summers and falls.

As easily accessible timber was cut, the railroads were seen as the next solution to northern Michigan's problems. There were sturdy, well-engineered main lines equipped for high speed travel, as well as branch lines that snaked through the woods, powered by ingeniously flexible steam locomotives that sometimes ran on wooden rails.[6] The main lines were intended to last, the branches to be picked up and moved here and there as new lumbering grounds became available, or, if uneconomical, simply to be abandoned, a pattern of behavior that has marked many northern Michigan ventures over the years and that has been reflected in Hemingway's stories.

The railroads extended the scope of lumbering, making it possible for it to become somewhat more of a year-round activity. Of course, this accelerated the removal of the pines and brought nearer the end of logging. More importantly to the student of Hemingway, at the same time the railroads further opened the state to tourists, who would become the basis of a new and more lasting northern Michigan economy. Great resort hotels were developed, often by the railroads themselves, to stimulate traffic and to take further advantage of the vast land grants that had subsidized the laying of the rails.

The Grand Rapids and Indiana Railroad, which in 1899 carried the Hemingway family and six-week-old Ernest from the Harbor Springs lake steamer dock to the village at Bear Lake, punningly advertised itself as "the fishing line." It had helped finance Mackinac Island's Grand Hotel, built of white pine and opened in 1887 with what is still billed as the longest front porch in the world.[7] The island had been a summer resort even before 1850, and it became *the* destination for well-to-do midwestern vacationers by late in the century. At the same time, religious denominations were building their retreats, the Bay View Association on Little Traverse Bay being merely the most notable example near the Hemingways' more isolated lot on then-named Bear Lake. So even in the later nineteenth century, side by side with the lumbering frontier, there existed considerable leisure and wealth. By the turn of the century, more and more former lumbering towns were turning into resorts, and as transportation continued to improve, the woods of Michigan became more and more accessible to vacationers of more modest means, such as the Hemingways.

Thus, northern Michigan was not simply a lumbering frontier. It participated in much of late nineteenth-century American culture, both material and genteel. As resorts became increasingly important, northern Michigan came to seem to be a refuge from civilization, a refuge from the world of technology. Of course, this was in large part only an illusion. In fact, without the technology of steel and steam—or the soon-to-develop steel and gasoline technology of the automobile—the so-called Michigan wilderness could not have been reached. It was a false wilderness, an environment shaped, sustained, and simultaneously degraded by technology to a greater degree, yet in some of the same ways that the eighteenth-century Indians' Michigan had been shaped.

By the time Hemingway was old enough to hike and fish throughout upper Michigan, it was in a condition that has lasted more or less to the present. Just as the pines that had been expected to be inexhaustible disappeared, the railroads proved to be evanescent. Their history from about 1910 to the present has been one of mergers and abandonments, and the automobile has risen in importance. The roads that crisscrossed upper Michigan even in Hemingway's time have been paved and added to; and mobile tourism has to a certain extent replaced the more static resort economy of the century's turn, although in the 1980s and 1990s posh resorts are again on the rise.

In some ways, Michigan has returned closer to wilderness over the years; in others it has become more civilized. In any case, we must remember that upper Michigan has not been a real wilderness or frontier for more than a century, certainly not for many years before Ernest Hemingway happened on the scene. Rather, it was a place of bustling commerce (although somewhat slowed by Hemingway's time), of rising recreational use, and of the *memory* of the frontier. This should critically alter one's sense of what Hemingway experienced in northern Michigan, of the material he is working with as he writes of Michigan, and of what he is doing in his Michigan stories.

To take one example of how Hemingway adapts his material, examine the unpublished draft of "The Killers."[8] There, we find as setting the eminently civilized town of Petoskey in winter. We share with Nick Adams his view across Little Traverse Bay and with him enter the Grand Rapids and Indiana Railroad Station (now Penn Plaza, across from the Perry Hotel). In

Hemingway's revision, description of Petoskey disappears, and the story's setting becomes the fictional "Summit," which has been variously identified by scholars with Summit, Illinois, and with the tiny railroad junction, Summit City, Michigan. The Park Hotel lunch room of the early draft becomes a grittier-seeming place, almost something out of the Wild West—though with the tensions between frontier and civilization obvious, as in the persons of the vaudevillian killers, Al and Max.

Take another example mentioned earlier, the town of Horton Bay. Horton Bay in Hemingway's time was hardly the ghost town of "The End of Something." While the lumber mills indeed had been moved away, "everything that had made . . . Hortons Bay a town" had not really been carried away on the lumber schooners mentioned in the story's introductory paragraphs: the village was not abandoned. It was rather a small summer resort particularly noted for restaurants serving fried chicken dinners. Their renown drew vacationers to drive from Charlevoix and Petoskey for dinner (by reservation only at Elizabeth Dilworth's "Pinehurst").[9] It may be, however, that all of interest to Ernest Hemingway, writer, had been carried away when the village made the transition from frontier town to resort.

Take Seney, in Michigan's Upper Peninsula. It never was completely burned over, as Nick Adams "sees" it in "Big Two-Hearted River." The thirteen saloons Nick expected to see as he got off the train had been long gone by the end of the Great War, when Nick arrived for a little psychological R and R. Those saloons, the bawdy houses in the woods to the west, and all the roughnecks and shady women had been made notorious in articles describing the lumbering frontier in newspapers including the *Detroit Free Press* and the *National Police Gazette*. But this notoriety had not been achieved in the early twentieth century. By then the real Seney was a not-quite ghost town, as it still is today. The wide open frontier town existed in the 1880s and early 1890s, before the fictional Nick or the actual Ernest were born. Hemingway makes that wide open, anachronistic Seney something Nick expects to see in order to link his character to the frontier, to a rougher yet purer American past. "Long ago good, now no good." He also makes Nick's experience a little more pleasant than it might actually have been in Seney: there is only one mosquito in the story—I think it is the only mosquito in all of his Michigan stories—and Nick gets it before it gets him. This may be a romanticized Michigan, indeed.

Take "The Battler," set on the Grand Rapids and Indiana main line running north from Kalkaska through Mancelona (and eventually to Petoskey). Tossed off the freight, Nick lands in the midst of a swamp that really does not exist there. (The swamp is more like that near Seney.)[10]

Nick walks in the seeming wilderness between Kalkaska and Mancelona, "trying to get to somewhere." Finally he reaches Bugs and Ad Francis's camp near the outskirts of Mancelona. Some things disappear in the process, including the several flag stop stations he would have had to pass through—Leetsville, Westwood, and Antrim. These disappear, as do the roads he would have crossed; this in the service of the mood of wilderness isolation that Hemingway creates for Nick and for the reader.

Other examples might be cited. We know that Dr. Hemingway vacationed on several occasions at the Upper Peninsula's Brevoort Lake, and that there is some link to the setting of "Indian Camp." Yet the actual Indian camp was a short walk from Windemere cottage on Walloon Lake, and when at Brevoort Lake, the doctor stayed at the civilized Massey House, billed on its letterhead as "The Great Brevoort Lake Fishing and Hunting Resort," offering the "Finest Bass, Pickerel and Muskallonge [sic] Waters in Michigan," with "Boats, Guides, Fishing Tackle and Bait for Hire." (Rates were two dollars a day in the early years of the century.)[11] So the original Americans of the story appear on an isolated lake only courtesy of Hemingway's imagination.

I only briefly mention the posthumously published novella fragment, "The Last Good Country." I do so to point out that in it Nick and his sister, Littless, "light out for the territory" in a somewhat Freudian *hommage* to our greatest frontier novelist, Mark Twain. This so I may say something more of frontiers and of how writers may use them.

We all know of Hemingway's boyhood desire to be an explorer on the three "last great frontiers[,] Africa[,] Southern Central south [sic] America or the country around and north of Hudson Bay." He was born many decades too late, of course. His affinity for the frontier Rough Rider and big-game hunter, Teddy Roosevelt, as discussed by Michael Reynolds, is well known as well.[12] It may be that his reading misled young Ernie into imagining explorations possible that had already been accomplished. Still, the frontiers that seemed so alive in popular fiction and history were already closed in fact when at age fifteen he wrote in a notebook of his urge to explore.

What was he to do? Twain perhaps helped provide him with a model for the exploration of a lost frontier: among other things, *Adventures of Huckleberry Finn* is a great historical novel, set about forty years before its date of publication. Of course, Twain had experienced American frontier life, as Hemingway really had not. Perhaps another American classic suggested a solution. Stephen Crane had demonstrated that it was possible to write well about what one had not experienced: *The Red Badge of Courage*, whatever else it is, is the world's greatest research paper, written out of no direct knowledge of humans at war.

With no frontier left to explore physically, the solution seems obvious. We see it with 20-20 hindsight, although we need not think that Ernie Hemingway, would-be writer, necessarily ever thought it through in any systematic matter. To explore what one cannot explore: Read. Imagine. Invent from experience, adding what seems germane of one's own experience. Thus, in Hemingway's fiction we do not see civilized, upscale Petoskey. We find no description of bustling Walloon Village. We have to study northern Michigan carefully to find it significant that Methodist Bay View (founded in the 1870s) never appears to lift up our souls. The lumber barons, industries, resorts, and church camps disappear. These are things left out.

What is left in is the frontier, both physical and moral. Nick confronts death and courage in "Indian Camp." Dr. Adams faces the Indians in "The Doctor and the Doctor's Wife," which has more of gentility in it than almost any other Nick Adams story—and which does not much like gentility. Potential violence lurks, surprising, in places that by all rights should be refuges: the saloon of "The Light of the World," the lunchroom of "The Killers." The anachronistic, seemingly virgin pines of "Big Two-Hearted River" provide solace to a veteran Nick Adams returned from the war. An older Nick *remembers* Michigan in "Fathers and Sons."

In all of these works, we travel not to the civilized, real Michigan of Hemingway's time, but to an older, purer Michigan created in Hemingway's memory and imagination.

NOTES

1. Carlos Baker, *Ernest Hemingway: A Life Story* (New York: Bantam, 1969), 637.
2. Ibid., 586.
3. Roy L. Dodge, *Michigan Ghost Towns* (Oscoda, Michigan: Amateur Treasure Hunters Association, 1970), 1:56; Dorothy Munson Krenrich, *Muhqua Nebis: A Compilation of Legends of Walloon* (Walloon Lake: The Walloon Trust, 1984), 68-69.
4. Bruce Catton, *Michigan: A Bicentennial History* (New York: Norton, 1976), 40.
5. Krenrich, *Muhqua Nebis*, 80-83.
6. Ephriam Shay of Harbor Springs was the inventor of one such locomotive. It made him a millionaire.
7. Willis Frederick Dunbar, *All Aboard! A History of Railroads in Michigan* (Grand Rapids: Eerdmans Publishing Co., 1969), 490-91.
8. John F. Kennedy Library Hemingway Collection, Item #535.
9. William H. Ohle, *How It Was in Horton Bay* (Boyne City: the author, 1989), 66-68.

10. Frederic Svoboda, "Inventing from Experience in 'The Battler,'" in *Up in Michigan: Proceedings of the First National Conference of the Hemingway Society* (Traverse City: privately published, 1983), 43.

11. Clarence Edmonds Hemingway letter to Grace Hall Hemingway and children at Windemere, 15 July 1902, Harry Ranson Humanities Research Center of the University of Texas at Austin.

12. See Michael Reynolds, *The Young Hemingway* (New York: Blackwell, 1986), 24-30, for a discussion of Roosevelt and for the text of the 21 March 1915 notebook, which is in the John F. Kennedy Library Hemingway Collection. Reynolds's transcription of the notebook differs slightly from my own notes on it, which I have followed in the quotation above.

Hemingway Bids Goodbye to Youth

Childhood's End in Seney

Jack Jobst

In August of 1919, Jack Pentecost, Al Walker, and Ernest Hemingway left by train from Petoskey, Michigan for the four-hour or so ride to a small town in the middle of Michigan's sparsely populated Upper Peninsula. The trip to Seney would help Hemingway escape the frustrations of being a soldier at home by allowing him to celebrate the pleasures of bachelorhood with his friends. Although he remained only a week in the Seney area, Hemingway mentally returned to the small town many times in the early 1920s and used his memories for at least two literary works. The visit for him came to mean something more than a camping trip. The author collapsed memories from several trips into the short story "Big Two-Hearted River," and the Seney excursion came to symbolize the final act of his youth, the end of his childhood.

Of all the milestones we pass as humans, few are more poignant than the moment we realize that life is composed of age levels, and that each offers pleasures that are once enjoyed, then lost forever. Ernest Hemingway faced this realization during his early twenties, when he said goodbye to his bachelor friends, married Elizabeth Hadley Richardson, moved to a foreign city, and began studying the trade that would make his fortune and his reputation.

After his marriage Hemingway did not relinquish his interests in hunting and fishing, but he realized that the campfires he shared with other unattached males, and the boyish pranks from his teenaged years, would not occur again. He was not that old, but could have paraphrased the sentences he wrote in "Big Two-Hearted River," that life "was different though. Now things were done. There had been this to do. Now it was done."

The boys had traveled to Seney in hopes of finding a town like Dodge City, Kansas or Tombstone, Arizona—a throwback to the Wild West towns of the previous century, with loose women and free-flowing booze. Hemingway had probably heard about Seney from Chicago relatives or Petoskey friends of his parents who had heard of the town's reputation, or had read a colorful but inaccurate newspaper article filled with hyperbole about the small town and its rugged inhabitants. In an early draft of "Big Two-Hearted River" at the John F. Kennedy Library, three boys step off the train: "'This was the toughest town in Michigan,' Al said. They all three stood together looking around. The fire had effaced the town" (Item #279). Actually, fire had eliminated only one building, but Seney nevertheless was no Wild West town in 1919. It had not been wild since its brief heyday in the 1880s. The town was there to service lumberjacks from fifteen lumbering companies, and when the pine was gone the men left. Without them the town lost its major purpose, and subsequently, most of its population. In the 1880s, 3,000 people lived in Seney, and they were there for the men who worked for fifteen timber companies in the area. By 1919, however, only a few remained. Thus Hemingway correctly wrote in the published version of his story, "The thirteen saloons that had lined the one street in Seney had not left a trace."

Seney's railroad station in 1919 was still used, but its purpose had changed. No longer were there lumberjacks stepping off the train and looking for work. Instead, Seney became a shipping center, albeit on a small scale. The pine was gone but the chaff, the slash remainder of tree limbs and trunks unusable for lumber, remained. This was prime material for burning, and the resulting ash, in turn, was a perfect medium for blueberries and ferns. Both of these products were shipped out from the Seney station. The ferns, packed in 100 pound bales, went to flower shops and mortuary homes across the country.[1]

Although Seney was not what they had hoped, the boys obviously enjoyed themselves. In a letter from 1921, Jack Pentecost wrote to Hemingway, inviting him on another trip to the Upper Peninsula. Pentecost mentions a "justice loving deputy sheriff from Seeney [sic]," implying that the boys apparently met this individual on a somewhat professional basis. In a lengthy anecdote that sounds like one of Hemingway's tall tales, Pentecost describes a story he heard about recent events in the life of the lawman and his "circus queen wife." Pentecost implies that the deputy sheriff had harassed the three boys for undescribed offenses. The trip also was good for the boys in other ways: Pentecost ends his letter by saying that "I wish I were in the [healthy] condition we were in when we came down from the Fox" (JFK).

Although most people know of Seney from "Big Two-Hearted River," Hemingway's first published thoughts on the trip appear in a poem he wrote in early 1922. The theme here also seems to reflect the sense of a lost period in his life. Hemingway had just settled in Paris with Hadley. He had been married only six months, and we can assume that he was happily in love but also somewhat wistful about his concluded bachelorhood.

"Along with Youth"

A porcupine skin,
Stiff with bad tanning,
It must have ended somewhere.
Stuffed horned owl
Pompous
Yellow eyed;
Chuck-wills-widow on a biased twig
Sooted with dust.
Piles of old magazines,
Drawers of boys' letters
And the line of love
They must have ended somewhere.
Yesterday's Tribune is gone
Along with youth
And the canoe that went to pieces on the beach
The year of the big storm
When the hotel burned down
At Seney, Michigan.

The poem seems to consist of two sections: in the first part the narrator takes us for a tour, perhaps of an attic, noting such items as a poorly tanned porcupine skin, perhaps prepared by a young person learning this skill; this is followed by discarded taxidermy trophies. The narrator also sees old magazines and letters from boys, perhaps the narrator's friends. Since the first lines of the poem contain images of hunting and letters, we could surmise that these represent memories of shared hunting activities with one's boyhood friends. Also in this section the poet twice offers a refrain telling us that the items "must have ended somewhere," which could mean that either their existence or their importance to the narrator ended at some difficult-to-determine point.

In the second part of the poem the narrator tells us that yesterday's newspaper, perhaps the Chicago *Tribune*, is also gone, for such is the fate of old newspapers. It departed along with the narrator's youth, and this occurred during one eventful year: when a major storm battered a canoe, and a hotel in Michigan's Upper Peninsula burned to the ground.

The references in this poem are personal and specific; the only one we can identify with some certainty is the burned hotel. In "Big Two-Hearted River," Nick Adams gets off the train and looks down at the foundation of the Mansion House Hotel, which was actually the Philip Grondin Hotel, with its foundation "split and cracked by the fire." The Grondin was located immediately across the tracks from the depot. The hotel had burned the previous summer, in 1918.[2]

If we agree with the majority of critics who argue that the burned-over town of Seney represents a lost or scarred earlier segment of Nick's life, so the hotel might symbolize a more specific loss for Hemingway, that of his unattached bachelor youth—of the pleasures inherent in camping, hunting, and fishing with friends. In an early draft of the story, Hemingway describes the hotel in more detail: "Al went over and looked into the filled pit where the hotel had been. There was twisted iron work, melted too hard to rust. . . ." Hemingway then describes a gun cabinet, "the guns melted, and the cartridges a solid mass of copper" (JFK, Item #279). To the author, an ardent gun enthusiast, memories of the amorphous mass of twisted metal he viewed with his friends may have summarized his sense of loss. He may have recalled the broken bottles of alcohol and arrowheads from his father's collections that Grace Hemingway burned when she cleaned out the attic in Oak Park. Fire destroys, leaving only the memory. The melted guns and cartridges signified the end of a period in his life.

In a long moment of reverie, Nick Adams in "Big Two-Hearted River" remembers earlier camping trips and sadly recognizes the loss of boyhood friends. This occurs when Nick finally makes his camp the first night, eats supper, then sits back and relates in the longest paragraph of the story (347 words) his memories of Charlie Hopkins, with whom he once argued about the making of coffee. Hemingway did not bother to change the name of a journalist and camping friend, Charlie Hopkins, the afternoon assignment editor at the Kansas City *Star* and the author's companion on at least two northern Michigan fishing trips, although not the one to Seney.

Oddly, Hemingway gives Hopkins the background of someone we might find in pulp fiction rather than a realistic story. For example, the real Hopkins is from Oklahoma, but the fictional Hopkins is a Texas millionaire whose oil wells have finally produced, a man accustomed to playing polo and dating women of Hollywood-style beauty (we are told that he dates the "blonde Venus"). Possibly, in the description of Hopkins, Hemingway is trying to capture a sense of the adventure and tales of romance he heard while sitting with friends around a campfire during camping and fishing trips taken before his first marriage, and he borrows the writing style of boyhood adventure stories to produce the effect. He may also wish to emphasize Nick's solitary life on this trip with the colorfulness, albeit exaggerated, of his friends from previous excursions.

Although the fictional Hopkins's background is not entirely believable, the character nevertheless plays a key role in a biographical understanding of the story, as Hemingway uses him to express some of his own concerns. Besides Hopkins's Texas connection and his method of making coffee, he is remembered for two elements: his love life—he had several girlfriends, but he favored only one, whom no one dared kid him about—and his sudden departure when he received a telegram calling him away. When Hopkins left the group, Nick remembers, the enjoyment drained from the trip.

Hopkins's relationship to his girlfriend could reflect Hemingway's recent marriage. As Carlos Baker tells us in the biography, in 1921 "Ernest knew that marriage would destroy the kind of life he had been leading. During the spring, he 'damned near went cuckoo' dreaming of camping trips to the Sturgeon and the Black. All his life, he wrote Bill Smith, a man loved two or three streams better than anything else in the world. Then he fell in love with a girl and the 'goddam streams [could] dry up' for all he cared" (Baker 1969, 79). But, as Baker goes on to explain, Hemingway still missed the fishing trips. In an earlier draft of "Two-Hearted River" Hemingway writes that he had "lost them [boyhood friends—Odgar the Ghee and Bill Smith] because he admitted by marrying that something was more important than the summers and the fishing" (JFK, Item #274). Clearly, Hemingway shares with Hopkins the realization that women can cause a refocusing of priorities in a young man's life.

Hopkins the character leaves the group when a telegram arrives, calling him away, and this fictional description mirrors the telegram received by the author, and his own departure from his friends in 1918. Hemingway blends several experiences here, for although the short story refers to a trip on the Black River when the telegram arrives, he was actually fishing with Hopkins, Brumback and Carl Edgar at Horton Bay in the spring of 1918 when Dr. Hemingway forwarded the telegram calling Hemingway and Brumback to New York and their Red Cross training for World War I.

Hopkins also accompanied Hemingway on an end-of-bachelorhood camping trip with another friend, Howie Jenkins, before the author married Hadley in 1921. Hemingway could thus be thinking of two trips with Hopkins, both ending in major lifetime events.

When Hemingway was writing "Big Two-Hearted River," as Michael Reynolds points out in *Hemingway: The Paris Years*, the author was desperately learning his trade amidst excessive demands on his time and attention: from Hadley; from the baby, Bumby; and from Ford Madox Ford on editing the *Transatlantic Review*. Clearly, as Reynolds argues, Hemingway must have yearned for the cool banks of the Fox River in Michigan's Upper Peninsula. Even if the author did not use biographical elements in the short story, readers could sense the melancholy tone that Nick expresses for the past that is gone forever. Thus, from the camping trip in

Seney, Michigan Ernest Hemingway carved a piece of fiction that expresses his loss for the past, for his bachelor youth, and for his childhood's end.

NOTES

1. My source for Seney in 1919 is John J. (Jack) Riordan, who was the assistant depot-master at the time for the Duluth, South Shore, and Atlantic Rail Road.
2. The Seney depot was on the south side of the tracks; it was later moved to the north side, where it resides today as a storage building (Riordan). A pulp mill now stands where the depot once stood. For more information on Hemingway's visit to this small town in Michigan's Upper Peninsula, see my article "Hemingway in Seney," *Michigan History* (November/December 1990): 20-25.

WORKS CITED

Baker, Carlos. 1969. *Ernest Hemingway: A Life Story*. New York: Scribner's.
Hemingway, Ernest. 1923. "Along With Youth." In *Three Stories and Ten Poems*, Paris: Contact Publishing Company. Reprinted 1979. In *Ernest Hemingway: 88 Poems*. Edited by Nicholas Gerogiannis. New York: Harcourt Brace Jovanovich.
———. 1972. "Big Two-Hearted River." In *The Nick Adams Stories*. New York: Scribner's.
Reynolds, Michael. 1989. *Hemingway: The Paris Years*. Cambridge: Basil Blackwell.

THE FIRST NICK ADAMS STORIES

PAUL STRONG

HOW DIFFERENTLY THINGS would have worked out, had Hamlet and Othello traded places. "Othello in Hamlet's position, we sometimes say, would have no problem. . . ."[1] One ponders the result of an equally fanciful switch—that a more prolix, discursive writer than Hemingway, a Trollope or Richardson, had come up with the "iceberg theory" first. Would anyone really mind if Pamela had written shorter, subtler letters? For to have the master craftsman of stripped-down prose announce that what you see is less than what you should get is most disconcerting. Add the curious publishing history of *In Our Time*, and one is left with numerous difficulties.

Consider this: before publication of *In Our Time*, "Indian Camp" had its beginning, now known as "Three Shots," amputated; the coda to "Big Two-Hearted River," now known as "On Writing," received the same treatment. Five years later Hemingway made another change, placing "On the Quai at Smyrna" at the beginning of *In Our Time*. The reappearance of "Three Shots" and "On Writing" in Philip Young's *The Nick Adams Stories* had the salutary effect of clarifying several issues. Critics have pointed out, for example, that the addition of "Three Shots" accounts for the absence of anesthetic when Dr. Adams performs his "jack-knife Caesarian" (he, Nick, and Uncle George have been camping). Furthermore, the suicide in "Indian Camp" becomes ironic once we have read "Three Shots," for the earlier story shows Nick alone at night, overwhelmed by thoughts of death. One suspects Dr. Adams brings his son along to the Indian camp because the boy is afraid to stay by himself in the dark, yet the Indian's grisly suicide can do little to assuage Nick's fears. Perhaps there is even a connection between the hymn, "Some day the silver cord will break," and Nick's duty in the shanty—holding a pan for the afterbirth, with its severed cord.

Reprinted from *Studies in Short Fiction* 28 (1991): 83-91. Copyright © 1991 by Newberry College.

Yet while the added material in *The Nick Adams Stories* answers some old questions, it also raises new ones. For example, "Three Shots" makes one wonder how much time passes in "Indian Camp." In "Three Shots" Nick's fear is nurtured by the disquieting stillness of the nighttime woods; "Indian Camp" is permeated with the pregnant woman's screams, screams so disturbing they drive the Indian men "up the road . . . out of range of the noise she made."[2] Screams carry well over water. To read "Three Shots" before "Indian Camp" may lead one to wonder if the rowboat ride from campsite to shanty is longer than one had imagined, since no screams are heard. If so, what are we to make of a father and son who seem to have so little to say to one another? Given the way Hemingway sometimes works, this seems worth investigating.

What reader is not amazed at the end of "Hills Like White Elephants" to learn that thirty-five minutes have passed while Jig and her man wait for the train to Madrid, a detail that suggests long silences between sparse dialogue, and hints at the lack of connection between the two. In "The Battler," Nick sees the train, from which he has been dumped, round the curve at the story's beginning. Later, Ad tells Nick he saw the freight go through "an hour and a half ago" (131). The reader is surprised; so much time *seems* not to have passed. Nick, we realize, has been walking a long while, a detail that adds to his vulnerability—he is off in the middle of nowhere. No wonder Ad's fire looks attractive; no wonder the encounter is so frightening. It is likely, on rereading the opening pages of "Indian Camp," as we watch Nick and Dr. Adams walk from the beach through a meadow, into the woods, along a logging road into the hills before reaching the Indian camp, we will conclude that the Indian shanty is simply too far from the lakeshore for screams to be heard. Yet the question does not arise unless we read "Three Shots," with its absolute silence, first.

In his 18 October 1924 letter to Edmund Wilson, Hemingway wrote that *In Our Time* had "a pretty good unity," and most critics have agreed.[3] In the Plimpton interview, Hemingway remarked, "I should think what one learns from composers and from the study of harmony and counterpoint would be obvious,"[4] and while this—like his remarks about the influence of Cezanne on his work—may be an instance of being overtaken by what he sometimes called "the braggies," it seems counterpoint is Hemingway's favored method of ordering his work.

Sometimes beginning and ending are counterpointed: one thinks of the rain in *A Farewell to Arms*, or Jake and Brett's taxi rides, which envelop *The Sun Also Rises*. Sometimes settings are: the hot, dry, sterile plain on "this side" (273) of the Ebro; the trees, mountains, and fields of grain "on the other side" (276) in "Hills Like White Elephants." Occasionally the counterpoint is more formal, as in "Big Two-Hearted River," whose parts are indicated by roman numerals; some stories break in half less formally, as "Ten Indians" does; some pair off, like "The End of Something" and "The Three-Day Blow." Precisely because counterpointing was such a powerful habit of mind for Hemingway, our natural inclination in reading *The Nick Adams Stories* is to look for connections between "Three Shots" and "Indian Camp," yet to do so leads one away from what Hemingway was after when he cut "Three Shots"—the counterpointing of two of his most accomplished stories, "Indian Camp" and "The Doctor and the Doctor's Wife."

At first the pair seem quite different. "Indian Camp" is positively Dickensian: it is a smelly, noisy, crowded story. The barkpeelers' shanty appears to have two rooms, a kitchen and bedroom, and into them Hemingway has squeezed, at the very least, nine people, perhaps more. We can identify six with certainty: Dr. Adams, Uncle George, Nick, the woman in labor, her husband, and their newborn son. Beyond that, things are less clear. The story begins with "two Indians" (91), who row the Adamses to the Indian camp. One, the "young Indian" (91), rows George and laughs when the squaw bites him. Later, "Uncle George and the three Indian men held the woman still" (93). A third male Indian has arrived on the scene—assuming the other two are the rowers, which may or may not be the case. Including the husband in the upper bunk, then, there are at least four Indian men in the shanty. We also learn that "all the old women in the camp had been helping her" (92). Two are singled out: the "old woman [who] stood in the doorway holding a lamp" (92)—who may or may not enter the shanty—and, presumably, a different "woman in the kitchen" (92) who boils water for Dr. Adams.

What one learns about Hemingway's technique in "A Clean, Well-Lighted Place" from watching the nearly anonymous waiters at the story's beginning develop into the "unhurried waiter" (381) and the "waiter with a wife" (382) is that the smallest details of characterization always matter. One wonders, then, why Hemingway chose to single out the "young Indian" from the other rower, or from the third Indian who holds the screaming woman down, and why it is *he* who laughs at Uncle George's bite; why does he bother to distinguish between the woman with the lamp, an "old woman," and the "woman in the kitchen," boiling water? If nothing else, by establishing such small differences among them, he creates a fuller, richer canvas, and gives the feeling of crowding. The shanty, after all, is small. Barkpeelers are poor; bunkbeds conserve space. The room's bad smell adds to the sense of constriction, of closeness, even as the barking dogs who rush out at the Adamses, the squaw's screams, and, one assumes, the squall of the newborn boy, add a note of tension.

The contrast with "The Doctor and the Doctor's Wife" could not be greater, for the story is played off against its predecessor, point by point. A doctor's "cottage" replaces the "shanty." The cottage seems spacious: the doctor has "his room" (101) with his bed; his wife reads in "the room where she is lying" (101), which contains "her bed" (102). Presumably there is a kitchen and a room for Nick. From "Fathers and Sons" we know Nick has several sisters; perhaps they have rooms as well. Moreover, the decibel level could not be more different. Unlike the pregnant woman, whose screams drive the Indian men "out of range of the noise she made" (92), after some desultory conversation with her husband, the "wife was silent" (102). When the screen door slams the sound is thunderous; it then becomes so still the Doctor can hear his wife "catch her breath" (102).

Yet similarities overwhelm differences.[5] As Joseph Flora has remarked, "Whereas 'Indian Camp' portrayed the white man's entrance into an Indian world, 'The Doctor and the Doctor's Wife' shows the Indian coming into the white world."[6] In "The Doctor and the Doctor's Wife" the Indians return to the white man's camp to repay a favor—the Doctor has pulled Dick Boulton's squaw through pneumonia, a detail that recalls his saving the squaw's life in "Indian Camp." The Adamses who visit the Indian camp are father, son, and uncle. The Indians who visit the Adamses are father, son, and a third, older male.

"Doc" arrives at the Indian camp with his jack-knife to deliver a baby trapped in its mother's womb; unless he is successful, it will probably die. "Dick" arrives at the Adamses' with cant-hooks to free up logs trapped in the sand; unless he does, the wood will probably rot. "Doc" heats water, washes his hands, delivers the baby, and announces its identity—"it's a boy" (93). Eddie and Billy Tabeshaw deliver a log, wash it, and "Dick" determines its identity—"It belongs to White and McNally" (100). The cesarean ends with "Doc" "sewing it up" (94); because of the set-to, "Dick" never does "saw it up" (100).

The stories' central scenes occur indoors, and involve "sick" women in bed, in darkened rooms. We know why the Indian wife is in her bunk; it is not immediately clear why Nick's mother is abed. Perhaps like Grace Hemingway, whose scarlet fever during childhood prevented her eyes from adjusting to light, she too "was often bothered with headaches because of bright lights."[7] This explanation would seem to suit the Doctor's wife. Just as her Indian counterpart drives her men up the road, so Mrs. Adams drives husband and son to the woods. Moreover, the Indian woman's screams are matched by Mrs. Adams's silence. If we assume she *is* in bed with a headache, a slammed door might well be agonizing; Henry would know this when he hears "his wife catch her breath" (102). Like Dick Boulton purposely leaving the gate open, letting the screen door slam is a hostile gesture.

The two women in pain are paralleled by their equally unhappy men: the Indian husband with his razor, Dr. Adams with his shotgun. Both episodes are enigmatic. Arthur Waldhorn explains the Indian husband's suicide by noting, "In the bunk above, her husband, driven frantic by her screams, slits his throat."[8] Yet this leaves something wanting, for it does not explain why he becomes frantic *when* he does—after all, his wife has been "trying to have her baby for two days" (92) and relief, in the form of the Doctor's ministrations, has arrived. In fact, in a very few moments she will be quiet, at peace. Dr. Adams might even treat the Indian's foot and lessen his pain.

To the extent he addresses the reasons for the Indian husband's frustration, G. Thomas Tanselle's remarks are satisfying:

> The Indian father not only feels *de trop* but also guilty for causing so much pain in one he loves. He had "cut his foot very badly with an axe [*sic*] three days before"—surely a Freudian accident, a manifestation of an unconscious castration wish resulting from his guilt feelings. His frustration is increased because he can do nothing for his wife, while Dr. Adams and Uncle George, representatives of the complex civilization of the white man *and* intruders, can successfully take charge in this family crisis. Representative of a less developed culture, he feels more frustration than a white man over the unnatural birth and the necessity for outside intervention. His situation appearing unbearable, he kills himself.[9]

Yet this reading is problematical in other ways. Hemingway, as always, is precise with detail: as Tanselle notes, the husband "had cut his foot very badly with an axe three days before," yet we are also told she "had been trying to have her baby for two days" (92).

In short, when he cut his foot he had no reason to feel guilty—his wife's protracted, painful labor had not yet begun.

Hemingway writes in *Death in the Afternoon*, "If two people love each other there can be no happy end to it."[10] "Indian Camp" focuses on a husband who commits suicide after being driven frantic by his wife's pain, and perhaps his own. "The Doctor and the Doctor's Wife" anticipates another frustrated husband's suicide. Like birth and death, cesarean slice and neck girdling, the first Nick Adams stories announce the familiar Hemingway theme: for better or for worse, "once a man's married he's absolutely bitched" (122).

"Indian Camp," which began with father and son being rowed across the lake, ends with father and son rowing back; "The Doctor and the Doctor's Wife," which began with Indians entering "in through the back gate out of the woods" (99), ends with Dr. Adams walking "out the gate

and along the path into the hemlock woods" (103). The stories counterpoint one another as well: both end with father and son, men without
women, leaving shanty and cottage behind, screams and caught breath, to
find solace on the lake, in the woods. After the chaos of the shanty, Nick,
in the rowboat, trails his hand in lakewater that "felt warm in the sharp
chill of the morning" (95). After the tension in the cottage, father and son
wander in woods that are "cool . . . even on such a hot day" (103).

Such respite is momentary. In the counterpointed stories that follow,
"The End of Something" and "The Three-Day Blow," one has an uncom-
fortable sense of déjà vu. With Bill's unexpected appearance to ask how it
went, Nick and Marge replace Dr. Adams and his wife, and Bill replaces
Nick. Bill's questions recall the innocent son of "Indian Camp," and
reprise issues (Where was he? Did he overhear?) critics have debated in
"The Doctor and the Doctor's Wife." At the story's end when Nick lies
down, "his face in the blanket" (111), he assumes the prone position
Hemingway habitually uses to suggest man in agony, a pose we associate
with the Indian father, among others—"His head rested on his left arm.
The open razor lay, edge up, in the blankets" (94).

"The Battler" harkens back to life with father, while anticipating Nick's
wartime experiences: having to back down from a bellicose Ad Francis
recalls Dr. Adams's humiliation with Dick Boulton, even as Nick's experience with two hobos looks forward to his "separate peace" and the expatriate life to come. So, too, the apparent reference in the story's ambiguous
title shifts (at first we assume it refers to Nick, who has received a "shiner"
[130] from the brakeman; then to Ad, a former boxer); when we
encounter a seriously wounded Nick, "legs stuck out awkwardly" (139) in
Interchapter VI, its meaning changes again. At the story's center is Ad
Francis, who, like the Indian husband, serves as icon for both Adamses.
His gimpy leg ("The little man came toward him [Nick] slowly, stepping
flat-footed forward, his left foot stepping forward, his right dragging up to
it" [135]), like Nick's barked knee, anticipates the leg wounds of
Interchapter VI; like the Indian father's gashed throat, Ad's misshapen,
mutilated face anticipates our last view of Dr. Adams in "Fathers and
Sons," and the undertaker's "dashingly executed repairs of doubtful artistic merit" (491). No doubt about it, Bugs is right—Nick's got "a lot coming to him" (133).

In the last Nick Adams story, "Fathers and Sons," Nick thinks back to
the time when his father "gave him only three cartridges a day to hunt
with" (493), a detail that closes the circle by recalling "Three shots" even
as it shows Dr. Adams trying to impart one of his cardinal rules: self-con-
trol. Nick's break from his parents and their middle-American values is a
central theme of In Our Time; one senses that in place of Dr. Adams, Nick

will model himself after Bill's father—a painter—whose cabin is well stocked with whiskey and books, whose wife is nowhere to be seen, and who is free to go out and shoot his gun as often as he chooses, even in the high winds of a three-day blow. Indeed, one is tempted to read these first Nick Adams stories as Hemingway's *A Portrait of the Artist as a Young Man*. Rejecting his mother at the end of "The Doctor and the Doctor's Wife" is, after all, a somewhat muted *non serviam*, a prelude to exile. In his review of *In Our Time*, D. H. Lawrence saw the impulse to break free and stay loose at the very heart of the collection: "One wants to keep oneself loose. Avoid one thing only: getting connected up. Don't get connected up. If you get held by anything, break it. Don't be held. Break it, and get away."[11] The irony, of course, is that stories written so passionately about the need to "keep oneself loose" should form a collection as "connected up" as these are, stories that, as Hemingway was the first to admit, had "a pretty good unity."

NOTES

1. Maynard Mack, "The World of Hamlet," *Yale Review* 41 (1952): 502.
2. Ernest Hemingway, *The Short Stories of Ernest Hemingway* (New York: Scribner's, 1954), 92. Subsequent page references are to this edition and appear in the text.
3. In "The Complex Unity of *In Our Time*," *Modern Fiction Studies* 14 (1968): 313, Clinton S. Burhans, Jr. argues that *In Our Time* is "a consciously unified work." Jackson J. Benson counters the tendency, among detractors and admirers alike, "to think of Hemingway as a powerful prose stylist, but a writer incapable of sophisticated, complex design" in "Patterns of Connection and Their Development in Hemingway's *In Our Time*," *Rendezvous* 5 (Winter 1970): 103, reprinted in Michael S. Reynolds, ed., *Critical Essays on Ernest Hemingway's In Our Time* (Boston: G. K. Hall and Co., 1983). Harbour Winn's "Hemingway's *In Our Time*: 'Pretty Good Unity,'" *The Hemingway Review* 9 (Spring 1990): 125, 139, shows how Hemingway's "careful attempt over a period of years to combine previously published and new work into a structurally unified book" produced "a work too finely patterned to be described as a mere collection of stories and too dependent on individual components to be described as a novel." In *Hemingway: A Biography* (New York: Harper and Row, 1985), 83, Jeffrey Myers contends *Dubliners* "provided the model for the thematically connected and structurally unified stories of *In Our Time*." In some cases, individual stories are remarkably like their Joycean predecessors—"An Encounter" and "The Battler," for example.
4. *Paris Review* interview in *Writers at Work, Second Series*, ed. George Plimpton (New York: Penguin, 1963), 228.

5. Both stories break into three parts: (1) a meeting of whites and Indians away from the shanty/cottage; (2) a central scene indoors, where distressed husbands deal with ill wives; and (3) a coda, in which pressure is released, as Dr. Adams and Nick leave the shanty/cottage and retreat into a comforting natural setting.

6. Joseph M. Flora, *Hemingway's Nick Adams* (Baton Rouge: Louisiana State University Press, 1982), 35.

7. Marcelline Hemingway Sanford, *At the Hemingways* (Boston: Little, Brown and Company, 1961), 55.

8. Arthur Waldhorn, *A Reader's Guide to Ernest Hemingway* (New York: Farrar, Strauss and Giroux, 1977), 54.

9. G. Thomas Tanselle, "Hemingway's 'Indian Camp,'" *The Explicator* 20 (1962): Item 53.

10. Ernest Hemingway, *Death in the Afternoon* (New York: Scribner's, 1932), 122.

11. D. H. Lawrence, *Phoenix: The Posthumous Papers of D. H. Lawrence*, ed. Edward D. McDonald (New York: Viking Press, 1936), 366.

THE DOCTOR AND THE DOCTOR'S SON

IMMORTALITIES IN "INDIAN CAMP"

WILLIAM BRAASCH WATSON

WHEN I READ THAT Nick had to stand there at his father's side, holding that empty basin as his doctor father by lantern light cut into the very big stomach of the Indian woman with his jack-knife in order to deliver her baby and "it all took a long time," I, the son of a surgeon, could identify with Nick right away. I think I must have been a bit older than Nick when I saw my first operation, and my experience was hardly as brutal or as dramatic as his. Yet for me, too, before it was all over my "curiosity had been gone for a long time." I never forgot the experience, however, and it led to my first publication at the age of eleven or twelve, in the *AMA Journal*. "My First Appendectomy," I believe it was called.

Whether Hemingway's doctor father introduced him to the mysteries of surgery at an early age, as my surgeon grandfather (acting as proxy for my absent father in 1943) did me, or whether Hemingway's "first appendectomy" later became "Indian Camp," I do not know. Nor does it matter really, for the story he wrote so transformed any experience he could possibly have had as an impressionable doctor's son that he might as well have made it all up, as indeed he said he did (Hemingway 1972, 237-38).

Although I could imagine myself standing in Nick's shoes in all of that shouted pain and blood when I first read "Indian Camp," eventually it was not just with the young Nick that I felt an identifying bond. For the more I learned about the writing of "Indian Camp," the more I found myself identifying with the other doctor's son, the twenty-four-year-old Ernest Hemingway, writing this story in Paris in February and March of 1924. As I learned more about Hemingway at that critical point in his career, my interest in the story shifted from its dramatic action and brutal encounters with birth and death to the quieter, changing relationship between the doctor father and his son. In one way and another, the young Nick seemed to be taking the measure of his father, and in doing so he was taking the measure of himself as well.

37

I began to sense that this changing relationship between the two was either a powerful subtext or was itself the real subject of the story. I also began to suspect, as all of us biographically and psychologically oriented Hemingway scholars seem to do at one time or another, that Hemingway's exploration of this subject was of some matter to him personally at that moment in his life.

What prompted this last thought was not only the strained and ambivalent relationship between Hemingway and his parents, especially with his father, but the recognition that I, too, had once taken the measure of myself by taking the measure of my own doctor father at a rather critical time in my life. I suspect that any son or daughter of a doctor will know, without my telling them, that the time I am referring to is the time I decided not to become a doctor in order to pursue another vocation, one that I very much hoped would be equally worthy in my father's eyes. I was nineteen or twenty when I made that decision, a few years younger than Hemingway was when he wrote this story and when he, too, as I shall now try to explain, made an important decision regarding his future career. Although disappointed, my father supported my decision; Hemingway's never really did.

In the late months of 1923, Hemingway, who was a foreign correspondent for the *Toronto Star* and had recently returned to Toronto for the birth of his first child, made a decision that would have struck many as rash, if not irresponsible. Almost certainly it would have struck his parents this way had they been fully aware of its implications. The decision was this: no sooner had Ernest become the father of a baby boy than he and his wife, Hadley, decided that he should give up his newspaper work, the only paying job he had, and live off the modest income of Hadley's inheritance. They did so in order that Ernest could commit himself entirely to his fiction writing, a career that he had barely begun and whose financial rewards, let alone critical approval, were by no means assured.

We do not know how much Hemingway's parents knew about this unusual financial arrangement of their newly fathered son, but we can be fairly certain that Hemingway would not have felt obliged to ask their advice. For some time now, he had been earning his own way and setting his own standards. Still, it was a decision he knew they could hardly have approved had they been consulted.

Moreover, the strains in their relationship, which had been going ever since he got back from the war in Italy in 1919, took on new dimensions in the late months of 1923 as Hemingway became both a new father and a recently published author. What should have been a time of pride and joy for the Hemingway family was turning out to be something of a disappointment for Ernest's parents. The baby boy had been born on October

10th, but his grandparents were not going to have a chance to see him before Ernest and Hadley left Toronto in mid-January to return to France. Instead of bringing his family back to Oak Park, Illinois, to share the Christmas holidays with his parents, Ernest made a brief, one-day trip alone to see them just before the holiday (Reynolds 1989, 157).

As for his being a recently published author, that, too, was something he apparently kept to himself. Although he had copies of *Three Stories and Ten Poems* with him in Toronto, he chose not to give any to his parents, and for good reason. They would have been as shocked by the rape scene in one of the stories, "Up in Michigan," as his sister Marceline, to whom he had apparently given a copy, claims to have been when she read the story just after that pre-Christmas visit (Hemingway 1961, 215-16).

Despite these signs of strain in his relationship with his parents, Hemingway seems nonetheless to have wanted their approval of his writings. Copies of the Paris edition of *In Our Time* may have arrived too late in Toronto to take them with him to Oak Park, but he made sure his parents knew where to order them by mail. That his parents later returned most of their copies of the little vignettes to the publisher in Paris was deeply hurtful, a gesture he remembered for the rest of his life (Reynolds 1989, 198-99; Hemingway 1924).

Even with this kind of rejection, however, he kept trying to gain their understanding of his work. A year later, in March 1925, for instance, he wrote to his father explaining what he was trying to do as a writer. He was glad his father liked one of his stories (probably "The Doctor and the Doctor's Wife"), and he thought his father would like a long fishing story that was then just being published called "Big Two-Hearted River." He went on to mention that he had just received $200 advance royalties from his American publisher for his new book, that his other books were all sold out (not true, it turns out), and that negotiations were already under way to publish his new book in Germany as well. "Many things have been published there already," he added (Hemingway 1981, 153-54).

Although a letter like this makes it clear that Hemingway very much wanted his father's approval—and not just for a couple of his stories, but for his newly launched career as a fiction writer—he knew it would not be easy to win that approval. His father's view that literature should be uplifting and inspirational ran counter to his son's commitment to unflinching realism, a realism that often included violent and degrading human experiences. There was, moreover, a residual disappointment in their relationship that went back more than half a dozen years: Ernest had never gone to college and thus was never going to be a doctor.

So when Ernest and his own family returned to Paris in January 1924 to set out on his new career, he must have had to overcome any number of misgivings: Could he ever earn enough from his writings to support his family? Could he gain the critical approval of his literary mentors, Gertrude Stein and Ezra Pound, and others? Could he find the discipline and skill he needed to be a writer at all?

What is so interesting is that whatever misgivings Hemingway may have had, the ones that were first reflected in his fiction were framed in terms of his relationship with his father. As soon as Hemingway got his family settled in their new apartment, he returned in his imagination to his own childhood and wrote down his thoughts and feelings about Michigan, about the Indians and the lake, and about his doctor father, twisting and braiding them up into a violent story of a painful childbirth and a silent suicide.

The story, for all its surprises, is simple enough. Two Indians have rowed at night across the lake to ask the doctor's help in delivering the baby of an Indian woman. The doctor decides to take along his son, Nick, and his brother, George. Nick and his father get into the Indian's boat, and Uncle George gets into the family's camp boat, and the Indians then row them back across the lake in the two boats. They walk through the meadows and woods to the Indian camp and prepare themselves to deliver the baby by Caesarian section, with Nick serving as intern to his father. Despite the screams of pain and the difficulty in controlling the convulsions of the mother, the baby is successfully delivered and the mother's life saved.

The baby's father, who has been lying in the bunk above his screaming wife, has not said a word the whole time. At one point, however, he covers his head with a blanket and rolls over in the bunk to face the wall. When the delivery is successfully completed, the doctor decides to look in on the Indian father to see how he is doing. He pulls back the blanket and his lantern reveals—to the doctor and to everyone else, including the young Nick—that the father has slit his throat. "The blood had flowed down into a pool where his body sagged the bed." Nick is quickly ushered out of the shanty.

Later, as Nick and his doctor father walk back through the woods to their rowboat, the father apologizes to Nick. "I'm awfully sorry I brought you along, Nickie," he says. "It was an awful mess to put you through." As they walk along, Nick has some questions for his father about what he has just seen, and the father answers as best he can. The story ends as they row back to their camp across the lake in the cool of the early morning, the father at the oars and Nick sitting in the stern of the boat, trailing his hand in the warm water.

Despite the drama of these events, at the heart of this story is the changing relationship between a son and his doctor father. That relationship is crystallized in the final, peaceful passage that closes in upon the tumult of "Indian Camp."

> In the early morning on the lake sitting in the stern of the boat with his father rowing, he felt quite sure he would never die.

This beautiful passage has provoked a good deal of commentary, for the key to the story's largest meanings seems to lie with the question of whether Nick's feeling that he would never die is a childish illusion or not. In a sensitive reading of the story, Dick Penner argued that the father's love reinforces Nick's own sense of being, and thus Nick's feeling of immortality is neither illusory nor ironic (Penner 1975, 195-202). Paul Smith's observation that Nick's immortality is very precisely conditioned by time and place and by the reassuring presence of his father rowing and is not to be taken as a universal claim or a grand illusion on Nick's part is also persuasive (Smith 1989, 39).

These are acute and responsive readings, and I would be reluctant to disturb the beauty of that final scene between Nick and his father by suggesting that the healing power of love is not at work. The physician father, despite his shattered psyche, is ministering to the wounded son with the small reassurances he could still find in his own greater knowledge and broader experience. I do, however, have to point out that in the eyes of Nick this is surely a different father rowing back from the one that rode over.

I do not want to be too hard on the father, as some others have been. I, for one, do not blame him for being improperly prepared for this unforeseen emergency. He was living in a remote and still somewhat primitive wilderness, where he was on vacation and not expecting to be on call as an obstetrician, and he improvised rather brilliantly with the fishing gear he had at hand. Nor do I blame him for belatedly considering the Indian husband's suffering. He had his hands full trying to save the mother and her unborn baby under extremely difficult conditions. Nor can I hold him to be insensitive for ignoring his patient's screams, for had he allowed them to enter his consciousness, he could have lost his concentration and brought death instead of life to both the mother and the baby. Since at least the late nineteenth century, this equanimity (or "affective neutrality," as Talcott Parsons calls it) has been considered a virtue in attending physicians, especially in those who must cut open other humans in order to save their lives (Osler 1889; Monteiro 1973, 145-55). In all medical respects, therefore, the doctor performed professionally.

Yet, the father has in some important ways been diminished. He has been made smaller not by any failure of his medical skills, but rather by a world that is suddenly larger and more unpredictable and violent than the one he occupies and controls with his medical skills, his *techne*. It is a world he unwittingly demonstrates that he does not understand when, deciding to look in on the silent father in the upper bunk after the delivery, he says, half-jokingly to be sure, that it is the proud fathers who are "usually the worst sufferers in these little affairs." And, of course, it is a world that he cannot shield from Nick, who "had a good view of the upper bunk when his father, the lamp in one hand, tipped the Indian's head back." It is a world, moreover, that he cannot really explain to Nick very well either. At the end, coming back along the road from the Indian camp to the lake, "all his post-operative exhilaration gone," he tries to answer Nick's probing questions, but his answers either contradict something he had said earlier, or are vague, evasive, or simply minimal.

We see all too clearly that the doctor, no matter how fine an obstetrician he may be, is not really competent to tell us, or to tell Nick for that matter, about the world in which women have a hard time having babies, in which men and women sometimes commit suicide, in which dying can be hard, even violent. The doctor occupies a smaller world than that, and the doctor's son, I am quite certain, has found it out.

How could he not have found it out? The Indian father's suicide came as a complete surprise to his father, and its discovery immediately transformed a triumph of medical procedure into a series of questions about the nature of the world, and in particular about human suffering. Nick suddenly knows that the world is not as his father describes it or understands it, for his father does not allow human suffering to enter his world. It had entered Nick's world, however, and he saw it for what it was. He had a good view of it.

As a result of these experiences, the dynamic balance between the father and the son has gradually, almost imperceptibly, shifted by the end of the story. Although the doctor father is still answering young Nick's questions at the end as he had at the beginning, there are now more of them and their character has changed. So, also, has the quality of the father's answers.

In the opening paragraphs of the story, the father is authoritative in his knowledge and dominant in the way he uses it. Nick at this point knows nothing about how babies are born, but when he tries to indicate that he at least knows the Indian lady is going to have a baby, his father denies him even that knowledge, for Nick has a specified role to play here. He has to be the learner, the apprentice, the intern to his doctor father.

By the end of the story, however, Nick has learned the implications of his experience all too well. His questions go to the fundamental issues of life and death and to the differences between men and women, forcing the father onto the defensive. It is he, now, who is being forced to play a role, forced to be a teacher even when there is little he can teach Nick, even if Nick does not understand all that has happened and does not wish to deal with it.

These changes in the dynamic balance between the father and the son not only describe the changing relationship between the two in the story, they also advance a subtle but important claim on the part of the author. The story leaves the unmistakable impression that it is the son, despite his young age, who understands the world around him, a world in which violence and suffering exist, and that it is the father who cannot. The father is constrained by his preconceptions and limitations, some of which are prescribed by the requirements of his profession, and some of which, like violent suicide, are excluded from his narrowed moral universe.

In one sense, of course, such an impression seems inappropriate to the young Nick of this story, whose feeling at the end that he will never die is still, no matter how one frames it, a childish illusion. After the violent events of the preceding night, however, who could blame Nick for wanting to return to the stable, unchanging order that his own immortality would grant him and that his father's love would sustain?

There is another sense, however, in which Nick, who sees and partially understands the world as it really is, will in fact achieve immortality. That Nick is a character in many Hemingway stories in which, as in this one, parts of the world are revealed as they really are. Nick discovers something in "Indian Camp" that will remain true for him in other stories as well. He discovers certain truths about human experience, or rather, he is put up hard and violently against their unavoidable realities. Perhaps he does not understand all that is happening to him, but we, the readers, are made to see what is happening. We, in fact, return again and again to these encounters of Nick with the world because we find in them certain enduring truths about human beings and their experiences. Thus, Nick indeed becomes immortal.

This immortality of Nick, however, will only come later, after the writing of many Nick Adams stories. This is 1924, and this is just the first story in which Nick appears. The question, then, is not whether Nick eventually achieves immortality, but whether his creator, even at this early stage of his career, did not already believe in Nick's immortality? If he did believe in Nick's immortality, was Hemingway not making a claim to immortality of his own? It was a preposterous claim, perhaps, even if it was not a claim for himself personally or even for his own talent. It was a claim, rather, for his craft, for his chosen vocation, for the art of letters itself.

This claim emerged from the circumstances in which Hemingway wrote "Indian Camp." The son, the prodigal son one could say, returned to Paris to establish himself as a writer of fiction. The first subject he chose came from his own childhood experiences in Michigan and involved a relationship between a doctor and his son. The relationship was changed by events in the story in such a way that the boy, in losing his innocence, gained a new perspective on his father. He saw, perhaps for the first time, his father's limitations. As a result, the boy's understanding of the realities of the world seemed to grow as his father's understanding of them diminished.

In this first story of 1924, when it was not yet certain that he could be the writer he wanted to be, Hemingway set out to affirm, perhaps without reflection or conscious intent, the validity of his chosen profession by demonstrating, of all things, its superiority to medicine. He did not intend to, nor did he, in fact, demean the skills of his physician father, but he did want to show that the writer, in being able to see more of the world as it really was than his father could, had powers of understanding greater than those of even the most skillful and ingenious physician. He had to demonstrate the triumph of art over *techne*, the triumph of the artist's skills over those of the physician. It was his way of asserting the validity of his own calling in the face of his unsympathetic and uncomprehending father, a father whose love and approval he nonetheless still wanted.

Nick, at the end of "Indian Camp," believes he will not die. Whatever the multiple meanings of that affirmation within the story, the words carried with them genuine conviction because they were based on Ernest Hemingway's own belief in the power and necessity of art. It was this liberating belief that would sustain him through one of the most intensive and successful episodes of writing in his entire career. One day, the masterpieces created out of this conviction, of which "Indian Camp" was but the first, would grant both Nick and Hemingway immortality.

Works Cited

Hemingway, Ernest. 1981. *Selected Letters, 1917-1961*. Edited by Carlos Baker. New York: Scribner's.

_____. 1972. "On Writing." In *The Nick Adams Stories*. New York: Scribner's.

_____. 1938. "Indian Camp." In *The Short Stories of Ernest Hemingway*. New York: Scribner's.

_____. 1924. Letter to his parents, 7 May 1924. Lilly Library, Indiana University.

Hemingway, Marceline. 1961. *At the Hemingways'*. Boston: Little, Brown.

Monteiro, George. 1973. "The Limits of Professionalism: A Sociological Approach to Faulkner, Fitzgerald and Hemingway," *Criticism* 15 (Spring): 145-55.

Osler, Sir William. 1889. *Aequanimitas*. Philadelphia. [Many later editions.]

Reynolds, Michael S. 1989. *The Paris Years*. Oxford and Cambridge: Basil Blackwell.

Penner, Dick. 1975. "The First Nick Adams Story," *Fitzgerald/Hemingway Annual*, 195-202.

Smith, Paul. 1989. *A Reader's Guide to the Short Stories of Ernest Hemingway*. Boston: G.K. Hall.

WILLIAM JAMES AND "THE DOCTOR AND THE DOCTOR'S WIFE"

LARRY E. GRIMES

IF ERNEST HEMINGWAY WAS something of an autodidact, Gertrude Stein certainly was not. Her chief mentor at Radcliffe was William James. James's psychology shaped Stein's writing and she was mindful enough of this influence to send James a copy of her early work.[1] Since James was a very important influence on Stein's thought, it seems probable that she introduced Hemingway to James's work as part of her education of the young writer. However Hemingway came by his introduction, his interest led him to acquire some of James's works.[2] Evidence from the text of "The Doctor and the Doctor's Wife" suggests that Hemingway's lessons on William James included at least a synopsis of *The Varieties of Religious Experience*, the Gifford lectures for 1901-2. In that story, Hemingway contrasts the Christian Science, mind-cure philosophy of a doctor's wife with the doctor's dark, angry, guilt-ridden temperament.

James's Gifford Lectures provide excellent insight into this short story because they describe key tensions in the Protestant religious ethos of Oak Park from which the story takes its shape. Essential to James's description of religion is his distinction between "healthy-minded" religion and what he calls the religion of the "sick soul." He says that the healthy-minded religious temperament "has a constitutional incapacity for prolonged suffering, and . . . the tendency to see things optimistically." This temperament is

> the basis for a peculiar type of religion, a religion in which good, even the good of this world's life, is regarded as the essential thing for a rational being to attend to. This religion directs him to settle his scores with the more evil aspects of the universe by systematically declining to lay them to heart or make much of them, by ignoring them in his reflective calculations, or even, on occasion, by denying outright that they exist. Evil is a disease; and worry over disease is itself an additional form of disease, which only adds to the original complaint.[3]

47

James juxtaposes this modern, turn-of-the-century emphasis upon healthy-minded religion against what he regards as Christian orthodoxy. That orthodox tradition, beginning with Saint Paul and continuing through Augustine and Calvin to the Mathers and Edwards set the religious agenda for preliberal, congregational, Puritan America. On his father's side, Hemingway's religious heritage[4] bespeaks this orthodoxy. On his mother's side the orthodoxy takes an evangelical detour. The Hall family, though Episcopalians when Hemingway scholars meet them, came from a long line of Wesleyans. It is important to note, as this distinction is drawn, that orthodox Protestantism stood in militant opposition to both work-righteousness theology and mystical theologies of the inner light. Methodism embraced both, making it fertile ground for aspects of mind-cure religion and a rather sentimental mysticism. It is a sentimentalized mysticism that Grace manifests overtly in her later years and that Reynolds takes rather too seriously, I think, in his discussion of "The Doctor and the Doctor's Wife."[5] As James saw it, among Wesleyans, "you were saved now, if you would but believe it" (103).

More traditional, orthodox American Protestantism, on the other hand, still proclaimed the religion of the sick soul. At the heart of this religious perspective was the doctrine of the Fall and its horrible consequence—a death sentence on the human race. Unless remediated by a born-again experience or sacred rites (confession, penance, absolution), unless transformed through the "negative way" charted by saints like Teresa of Avilla or John of the Cross—a way almost inaccessible to Calvinist American Protestants—this theology could devastate the sin-sick soul. In James's argument, this bleak orthodoxy echoes the fatalism and naturalism of Ecclesiastes. He connects the temperament of the sick soul with the preacher's words in this passage:

> Make the human being's sensitiveness a little greater, carry him a little further over the misery-threshold, and the good quality of the successful moments themselves when they occur is spoiled and vitiated. All natural goods perish. Riches take wings: fame is a breath; love is a cheat; youth and health and pleasure vanish. . . . Back of everything is the spectre of universal death, the all-encompassing blackness—"What profit hath a man of all his labor which he taketh under the Sun? I looked on all the works that my hands had wrought and behold, all was vanity and vexation of spirit. For that which befalleth the sons of men befallest beasts; as the one dieth, so dieth the other; all are of the dust, and all turn to dust again. . . . The dead know not anything, neither have they any more a reward; for the memory of them is forgotten." (131)

Religious life and experience in Oak Park during the first decade and a half of the twentieth century was made tense by this dichotomy.[6] That tension manifest itself in the institutional life of Protestant churches and in the private spiritual lives of individuals. The Hemingway household and its individual members were not exempt from this disturbance of the soul. Grace Hall's religious temperament corresponds to what James calls "healthy-minded" religion, perhaps due to the Wesleyan roots of her family, and Clarence seems to practice the religion of the sick soul.

In October of 1899, Ernest Hemingway was baptized at First Congregational Church, Oak Park, Illinois by the Reverend William Barton, father of Bruce Barton, advertising man and author of the best-selling book, *The Man Nobody Knows*. Extant documents make it clear that Barton's church was a "healthy-minded," liberal church. James described churches like Barton's very accurately when he wrote:

> The advance of liberalism, so-called, in Christianity, during the last fifty years, may fairly be called a victory of healthy-mindedness within the church over the morbidness with which the old hell-fire theology was more harmoniously related. We have now whole congregations whose preachers, far from magnifying our consciousness of sin, seem devoted rather to making little of it. They ignore, or even deny, eternal punishment, and insist on the dignity rather than on the depravity of man. They look at the continual preoccupation of the old-fashioned Christian with the salvation of his soul as something sickly and reprehensible rather than admirable; and *a sanguine and "muscular" attitude*, which to our forefathers would have seemed purely heathen, has become in their eyes an ideal element of Christian character. (88, emphasis added)

However, it is a mistake to identify Hemingway's early religious life solely with Barton and First Church, for in 1899, the year of Hemingway's birth and baptism, his Uncle George was among a small missionary group from First Church who were dismissed from the mother congregation to form the Third Congregational Church of Oak Park. In 1903 Ernest's family also moved to Third Church. That move, I think, was a significant one.

While First Church was theologically liberal, evidence suggests that Third Church was not. Cornerstone remnants from Third Church shelved at Chicago Theological Seminary include educational materials from the conservative, evangelical publisher David L. Cook. Third Church also sponsored an active Christian Endeavor group, another mark of Third Church's discomfort with modernity and its evangelical, conservative leanings. Also important, I think, is a 17 April 1909 *Oak Leaves* article on revival meetings then being held at Third Church by the Reverend Henry

W. Stough. Stough, founding minister of Third Church, had apparently been something of an emotional, perhaps even a "sick soul" preacher, in his early years there, but now, according to the reporter, "Mr. Stough's sermon on 'Chaining the Giant,' based on the story of Samson, was a virile, forceful presentation of the fact that every man has his weak spot, and that fellowship with, and service of God, alone, can render his [sic] invulnerable." What the reporter suggests is that Mr. Stough has adapted his style and his content to the more "muscular" attitude James ascribes to liberalism. The emphasis on virility and muscularity is of utmost importance, for all this man talk is about the capacity to invent salvation out of strength and resolve. As I shall note later, it boils down to "Physician, heal thyself."

While, according to the reporter, Stough is still in the tradition of conservative, affective, "primitive" religion, he has at least "acted" in a way acceptable to the muscular, optative mood of progressive Oak Park in 1910. Grace must have felt comfortable in Third Church because it retained a nonintellectual, emotional, conservative piety and attendant sentimental spiritualism even as it adhered to the "virile," "muscular" Christianity that was transforming both evangelical and liberal congregations in Oak Park, placing the burden of salvation squarely on the broad shoulders of strong believers. Her letters of moral admonition to young Ernest, including her infamous twenty-first birthday letter, bespeak her comfort with this new muscular religion.

Clarence's relation to Third Church was more complex and distant. While he did participate in church life and provide leadership as a one-term deacon, he did not invest himself in Third Church with the energy and commitment of his wife or his brother George. It appears that he did his duty, then left church life to others. It also seems that his early religious experience in the stern world of preliberal, pre-Barton Congregationalism, registered heavily upon him, making him most mindful of human sin and error, and making him a melancholy, stern, and sober moralist. Perhaps his medical training and status as a devoted naturalist compounded the fatalism James notes in the temperament of those who practice the religion of the sick soul. Whatever the causal agent, Clarence saw life through the doubly dark lens of what I call Calvinistic Darwinism. As a Protestant naturalist, Clarence Hemingway was in a double bind—not only was he condemned to death biologically, he was also damned to hell with no way out but grace. As a perceptive man, it seems likely that the irony of his wife's name and her easy access to mind-healthy religion struck him hard. Further, the Catholic sacrament of penance that his son was to toy with later was not available to him, nor did he seem to have the temperament necessary to avail himself of the mind-cure offered either through the sentimental, evangelical fervor of Third Church (I'm saved right now and I know it—Praise the Lord) or the muscular, intellectual liberalism of First Church (God has blessed you with what you need to succeed right now— think positively, get tough, work hard, and you can succeed at life).

For the wider religious circle of Oak Park, it was the Reverend Barton who modeled and professed muscular, liberal religion. His theology was liberal through and through, as his sermons well illustrate. Throughout his work it is clear that he reduced Sin to a list of sins, sins that the "muscular" Christian could defeat. Because Sin had become sins, and because virile, muscular Christians could resist sin, practice goodness, and lead productive, progressive, happy lives, it was logical and practical for liberal Christians, like their pietistic, conservative evangelical counterparts, to identify these sins and drive them both from private life and from the very communities in which they lived.

Because of the way liberal theology and Victorian morality were mixed together in Oak Park, it was difficult to distinguish where church life left off and civic life began. Family, town, school, and church shared a single vision. The old Puritan theology of the "covenanted community" was alive and well in its prairie children. Being a good child, a good citizen, a good student, and a good Christian were all one thing. So *Oak Leaves* devoted many pages of each issue to news of the churches, to reprinting sermons, and otherwise reporting the "good news" of life in the village of God. Nor did anyone think this odd for a secular newspaper. *Oak Leaves* seemed almost a second pulpit for the Reverend Barton. His sermons, or excerpts therefrom, often appeared on its pages. Nor did it seem odd that Oak Park school superintendent, W. H. Hatch—a member of First Congregational Church, of course, should give a talk on "Moral Standards of Children" and that in it he would fuse liberal theology and Victorian morality. In the 20 May 1904 issue of the paper, one containing a picture of Grace Hall Hemingway and announcing her upcoming recital, Hatcher is quoted as saying,

It is difficult for us to conceive of truthfulness, honesty, or loyalty as abstract virtues. It is easy to think of a truthful, honest, or loyal person. God struggled through long ages to make himself known to man and was finally compelled to reveal himself in the form of a man in Christ. He found it difficult to realize virtues of character except when embodied in an individual. Hence the importance of keeping before the child the best in life. A few of the virtues in which the normal standards should be carefully formed are: Obedience to law, obedience to principle, obedience to outward promptings, obedience to inner impulses. Truthfulness. Honesty, property rights, a sense of mine and thine. Loyalty to friends, to principle, to conviction, to country. Uprightness, justice, and service.

It is hard to imagine Grace Hall Hemingway not pausing to take these words to heart and sense their spiritual rightness as she scoured the paper hunting for the announcement of her upcoming concert. To Clarence, on the other hand, the civil religion of Oak Park could only have been a cruel reminder of his own spiritual deviance, for religion of the sick soul had clearly become deviant by the religious yardsticks of both evangelical and liberal theology in Oak Park. Again an echo—"Physician, heal thyself—it's the manly thing to do."

Manly indeed. The civil religion of Oak Park was self-consciously assertive, healthy, virile, muscular. Glowing newspaper comments on the preaching of a Mr. Biederwolf who filled First Congregational Church to overflowing and preached his famous sermon on "White Life" provide an excellent example of this new masculine gospel. An *Oak Leaves* reporter writes in the 22 April 1904 issue: Mr. Biederwolf "disarmed all prejudice at once by announcing that he would say nothing that [would] insult a gentleman." He then went on to present his audience with five reasons for choosing the "White Life," a life free from the sins of sabbath desecration, intemperance, profanity, evil imagination, and impurity. Those five reasons are: "It is the manly thing, it is the responsible thing, it is the heavenly thing, it is the blessed thing, it is the way of service and salvation for others who follow one's example."

Clarence Hemingway deliberately, self-consciously, and quietly attempted to live the "Whitest" of lives. Hence his careful observance of the sabbath, his life of temperance, his insistence on strict honesty and accountability in all things. Whatever else we may wish to say about Dr. Hemingway, he lived a white life without blemish—a tough act to follow for any son—but an act without efficacy on the soul of the man who lived it. In the old theology of the Fall, works were not righteousness. Salvation came only through grace, and grace in the old theology was gift. However, one wants to understand the word, full-fleshed as it was in the Hemingway household, grace was not predestined to touch Clarence's soul and quicken it to life.

Clarence committed suicide in 1928 in spite of the "White Life" he led. At least a partial explanation for his suicide can be derived from his religious temperament in the Jamesian scheme. He was a person shaped by the religion of the sick soul. Those whose religion comes in this variety but who attempt to live healthy-minded religion only compound their religious problems. As official, public adherents of healthy-minded religion they assert that sins can be dealt with by truly muscular Christians. When sins are not, in fact, dealt with, when deep down inside they fester and explode, the obvious conclusion to be drawn is that one has failed as a Christian and a man. The penalty is something that can only be imaged as religious castration. For Clarence Hemingway, I suggest, this meant his unmanning as a health-minded religious person and confirmed what he truly believed deep down: that he was one of the lost, the damned, the despised. For Clarence this experience of religious castration was compounded by his wife's success as a healthy-minded religious person who could dabble in sentiment without despair, for she did not truly believe that there were any troubles in life that could not be overcome if one put some muscle into it. I suspect that it is a Jamesian, rather than a Freudian, knife that effects the "symbolic castration"[7] Joseph Flora sees in "The Doctor and the Doctor's Wife." In any case, at the religious level, as well as in their daily family life, Clarence and Grace Hemingway lived a series of sex role reversals which proved, finally, to be more than Clarence could bear. Clarence, in a doubly damnable way, knew what it meant to fall from grace.

Ernest Hemingway explores this Jamesian religious dichotomy quite directly in "The Doctor and the Doctor's Wife." There the doctor suffers dark, destructive doubts about his moral worthiness triggered by Dick Boulton's charge that he was a thief for claiming driftwood that bore the stamp of a lumber company. His wife gives him no comfort. She is only a dark presence in a separate room, inaccessible to him in this time of the "sick soul," partly because she lives in a religious world planets apart from his. She is a Christian Scientist, something Grace Hall Hemingway was not. So why this significant departure from autobiography? I think change is made to reinforce Hemingway's theme and that Christian Science was selected because, for James, it was the example par excellence of healthy-minded religion. As a Christian Scientist the wife can only assume that her physician husband should heal himself. She hears him out as he tries to share his sense of outrage, anger, and guilt. Her response denies the seriousness of his problem. She says, "I really don't think that any one would really do a thing like that." "No. I can't really believe that any one would do a thing of that sort intentionally."[8]

The doctor, of course, can believe humans are intentionally evil, capable of reducing order to chaos. What troubles him as he says is "*NOTHING MUCH*" (102, emphasis added). For him that nothing is dark and terrible. For his wife, darkness is no threat. She sits quietly in a darkened room, inwardly safe and enlightened by her Bible, her copy of *Health and Science*, and her *Quarterly*. True daughter of healthy-minded religion, it is easy for her to dismiss her husband's anguish with a biblical, mind-cure aphorism: "he that ruleth his spirit is greater than he that taketh a city" (101). He, on the other hand, does not believe that human power can do anything to heal the sin-sick soul. He has no Bible and his medical journals lie in a pile, unopened. For him there is neither a sacred nor a secular balm in Gilead to heal the sin-sick soul. There is only the shotgun in his lap, of which he is very fond, and an exit gate to and from the woods.

Sitting in silence with the gun on his lap, Dr. Adams faces radical and, therefore, violent, choices: he might shoot Dick Boulton, his wife, himself—commit murder and then suicide; or, he might accept religious castration and damnation, oblivion and nothingness. The presence of the shotgun is terrifying because it represents the only kind of power the doctor has left—the power to destroy. He is not a muscular one who can build the good life. His unmanning spiritually, ethically, domestically, sexually, has unfitted him for constructive acts. All he has within and before him is death and annihilation.

Yet the story ends neither in silence nor with a bang. However deep and dark the despair of Dr. Adams is, the structure of the story, the artistic grace of Ernest Hemingway, provides him with an exit. That exit is religio-literary in nature, for the story imitates traditional rituals of passage that move people through boundary situations to new realms of being. Formally, it is a series of scenes driven by a dialogue between the doctor and others that systematically reduce the doctor and his world view to "nothing much," then move him out through a fissure, a gate in his world boundary, to a new realm of existence. The gate allows chaos (represented by Dick Boulton and the other Indians) to enter into and assault his preestablished ethical, socioeconomic, and domestic life, and it also swings open to provide the doctor with access to another order of existence.

Hemingway's opening paragraphs are carefully written to accent the boundary situation at the heart of the story, making it, as Joseph DeFalco noted, an initiation/rite of passage story.[9] The initiate, however, is Dr. Adams and not young Nick. When the story opens Dr. Adams lives according to certain culturally predictable assumptions. With regard to drift logs that are to be cut into firewood, the doctor has assumed a proprietorship based on a series of buts and ifs. Experience tells him that no one else will claim the logs, and he "always assumed that this is what would happen"(99).

The doctor's assumptions, as the third paragraph of the story makes clear, are rational and logical. However, they are rational and logical assumptions based on the behavior of the crew of a steamer called *Magic*. The steamer's ironic, italicized name is rolled by twice in Steinian fashion before the short paragraph concludes, contrasting the doctor's logical assumptions with the world of magic and the irrational.

The doctor's story is not just about cultural contrast and ontological ironies, however. As a ritual drama, as a rite of passage, the story moves the doctor from one world to another, tearing down before it builds up, reducing the doctor to a childlike state before he reenters the world.

Cultural anthropologist Victor Turner has described the process of such a passage with particular care. He notes three phases: separation, margin (limen, or threshold), and aggregation.[10] In the case of Hemingway's story, separation is inflicted on the initiate. Boulton cuts the doctor adrift from his moral constructions as easily as the logs originally slipped from the boom. In the process, Boulton also severs the doctor from his carefully crafted rational self, leading him to the brink of violence. The Indians cause separation and move the doctor into a liminal state, which Turner describes as "betwixt and between the positions assigned and arrayed by law, custom, convention, and ceremonial."[11]

The Doctor is like other liminal, threshold people whom Turner studied, for after experiencing and contemplating great violence, the doctor adopts outwardly passive behavior and seems to accept his annihilation without serious complaint. His movement in the story is from high status to low as he bumps hard against the cultural challenge of Dick Boulton and the spiritual otherness of his wife. He is left, as he says so painfully when asked about his trouble, with "nothing much."

According to Turner, in a ritually responsive culture, this threshold state is desirable. The ritual humbling of a new chief, for example, is necessary if that person is to "have self-mastery thereafter in the face of the temptations of power."[12]

The art of Hemingway's story conforms to ritual. Although Dr. Adams is debased and humiliated by Boulton and by his wife, they do not destroy him. Quite to the contrary. As the cultural project that has been his life (scientist/doctor, patriarch, virtuous man, beloved husband—a man of the "White Life") is systematically dissembled, his impotency and his *nada* become the agents of his transformation.

Although preoccupation with his shotgun serves as counterpoint to the conversation he has with his wife about the Boulton affair, the doctor finally, as Hemingway writes, "stood up and put the shotgun in the corner behind the dresser" (102). With the act of standing up, Dr. Adams signals the end of his liminal period. No longer passive, he is ready to build himself, to walk across the threshold, out the gate, and into a new life. Once out the gate, he decides to ignore his wife's request to send his son home. Only moments before, he had slammed the screen door of the cottage shut with an explosion that is symbolically equivalent to the killing he had contemplated. The old world behind him is over and done with. Behind him "he heard his wife catch her breath when the door slammed" (102).

The ritual structure, the art of the story, deconstructs the no-exit, Protestant religious conception of the sin-sick soul and exposes within it the gate (fissure) to new life. Hemingway writes, Dr. Adams "walked in the heat out the gate and along the path into the hemlock woods. It was cool in the woods even on such a hot day" (103). The doctor has found comfort on the other side of the boundary of his existence. Decentered from his old world project, he now stands in chaos (represented by the woods themselves and the Indians who had acted as agents of chaos), apparently young again, experiencing an aggregation of the self around a new center with a new generation. His son leads him forward to where there are black squirrels in the woods.

In the world as it is ritually and artistically reconstituted on the other side of the border, Dr. Adams is no longer a threatened phallic self. His gun, we recall, is in the corner behind the dresser. Outside the gate, in the woods, black squirrels are to be observed, not shot. Nature/chaos, even the dark Nick Boulton side of the self can now be lived in and with. It need not be controlled. At story's end, life without grace or guts seems possible. No longer does the Bible echo, "Physician heal thyself." Rather, we hear at the edges, "and a little child shall lead them."

NOTES

1. Richard Bridgeman, *Gertrude Stein In Pieces* (New York: Oxford University Press, 1970), 20-22, 357-58.
2. James D. Brasch and Joseph Sigman, *Hemingway's Library: A Composite Record* (New York: Garland, 1981), 189; Michael Reynolds, *Hemingway's Reading, 1910-1940* (Princeton: Princeton University Press, 1981), 141.
3. William James, *"The Varieties of Religious Experience"* [1902], in *William James: Writings 1902-1910* (New York: Library of America, 1987), 121. Further references are to this edition of *Varieties* and page references are included in the body of this essay.
4. Aside from information available about the religious life of the Hemingway family in standard biographies, I have relied heavily on information provided by Grace Hall Hemingway in a typescript entitled "Heritage" [28 pages], The Hemingway Collection of the J. F. K. Library.
5. Michael Reynolds, *The Young Hemingway* (Oxford: Basil Blackwell, 1986), 131-32.
6. Material on religion in Oak Park is taken from documents at First United Church in Oak Park, issues of *Oak Leaves*, and the cornerstone file of documents from Third Congregational Church, now housed in the library of Chicago Theological Seminary.
7. Joseph Flora, *Hemingway's Nick Adams* (Baton Rouge: Louisiana State University Press, 1982), 38.
8. *The Short Stories of Ernest Hemingway* (New York: Scribner's, 1986), 102. All further references are to this edition and page references are included in the body of this essay.

9. Joseph DeFalco, *The Hero in Hemingway's Short Stories* (Pittsburgh: University of Pittsburgh Press, 1963), 25-39.
10. Victor Turner, *The Ritual Process* (Ithaca: Cornell University Press, 1969), 94.
11. Ibid., 95.
12. Ibid., 102.

"Nothing Was Ever Lost"
Another Look at "That Marge Business"

H. R. Stoneback

Marge Bump knitted it for me, and it is a peach of sweater.

–Ernest Hemingway to parents, December 6, 1917[1]

Inaccuracy, misstatement, and thoroughgoing confusion of fact and fiction have long been the rule in the biographical treatments of Marjorie Bump, as well as in critical discussion of "The End of Something" and "The Three-Day Blow." It is pretty to think that the matter of Hemingway's relationship with Marjorie Bump can be kept separate from his characterization of Nick and Marge in the fiction; yet the accumulated commentary—and a pretty mess it is—indicates that such a separation has not been possible for most biographers and critics. Biographers continue to read the actual Marjorie through the fiction, and critics compound the error, decoding the fictional Marge from the dim palimpsest of inadequate biography. Alas, the "low-class sexy waitress" tradition prevails. Tempting as it may be, given all this confusion, to head for some imagined aesthetic high ground, ignore biography altogether, and declare that the thrust and purpose of this essay is to see more truly two fine Hemingway stories on their own merits, this luxury (and laziness) will no longer suffice.

What have biographers told us about Marjorie Bump? Carlos Baker places the first meeting of Hemingway and Marge in the summer of 1919: "Marjorie and her friend Connie Curtis had come from Petoskey to wait on tables at Mrs. Dilworth's. She was seventeen, with red hair and freckles, dimpled cheeks, and a sunny disposition." Baker reports that the Dilworths thought that Marjorie was "much enamored of Ernest," that the two of them would go out "to the Point for long evenings beside a driftwood campfire," and that local "opinions differ as to the seriousness of their association."[2] He notes briefly that in the fall of 1919 Hemingway used to walk Marjorie home from school in Petoskey and that, on his honeymoon, he enraged Hadley by taking her into Petoskey to meet Marge,

59

"the hardware dealer's daughter" (81). This is about all Baker has to say
about what he calls Hemingway's "brief romance with Marjorie Bump at
Horton Bay in the summer of 1919" (132-33). Brief and innocuous as
Baker's version may seem, it is shot through with inaccuracy, imprecision,
and the first shadow of condescension regarding Marge, the "waitress,"
the "hardware dealer's daughter." Indeed, Baker's errors of fact and
unfortunate tone are still the primary source for the ever-more-muddy
stream of pseudoinformation regarding Marge.

First of all, Baker is factually wrong on these counts: (1) Marge's age—
she turned 18 in the summer of 1919; (2) Marge and Hemingway met long
before the summer of 1919; (3) Marge was not in Horton Bay as part of
some transient summer resort labor force; she was not a "summer waitress." I will come back to these matters of fact and nuance in a moment,
but we might consider Baker's image of Marge a decade or so later, by the
time of his *Selected Letters* volume, when he should have learned a good
deal more about Marjorie Bump and Hemingway. In a footnote he mentions that Hemingway had "befriended" Marge "during his stay in
[Petoskey] in the fall of 1919."[3] Elsewhere, he identifies a reference to
Pudge, i.e., Marjorie's sister Georgianna, as a reference to Marge (51). It is
obvious, given his failure to identify Hemingway's allusions to "Barge" and
"Red" (i.e., Marge) or Mrs. Graham (i.e., Marge's mother) in the letters, as
well as his misidentification of Pudge as Marge, that Baker had very little
factual grasp, let alone larger understanding, of Hemingway's relationship
with Marge. Yet his account has colored the report of all other biographers,
most of whom merely echo Baker and add a few graceless notes based not
on research, but on confusion of fiction with biography.

After Baker, we have Bernice Kert's *The Hemingway Women*—here, at
least, we might expect some precision, some real engagement with the
"Marge Business." After all, if we know the facts of the relationship and
its duration (longer, for example, than that with Agnes von Kurowsky),
Marge is clearly one of the more important of "the Hemingway women."
Yet this is what we get from Kert:

> In the evening [summer 1919] he waited for Marjorie Bump, a chubby high-
> school student from Petoskey who was a summer waitress, to get off from
> work. She had red hair and dimples and was softly vulnerable and good-
> natured, the right degree of woman for Ernest. She packed their picnics for
> long evenings in front of a driftwood fire and trolled with him for rainbow
> trout.

Also, in the fall of 1919, in Petoskey, he "waited outside the high-school
auditorium for Marjorie."[4] That is it. In this rather long book devoted to

"Hemingway's women," Marge rates less than one paragraph, even though it was a relationship that endured for many years. Kert simply repeats Baker's account, brings in a detail from the fiction about trolling for trout, and has her version of the "summer waitress" gain a little weight.

By the time Jeffrey Meyers comes along with his exercise in Hemingway biography, Marjorie is still "pudgy," "cute," "smiling," and "vulnerable." Repeating the errors of Baker, and compounding the unfortunate tonalities, Meyers writes: "In the summer of 1919, at Horton Bay near Walloon Lake, Hemingway met a seventeen-year-old, red-haired high school girl, suggestively named Marjorie Bump. She was the daughter of a hardware dealer in Petoskey and waited on tables during the summer." That is all Meyers has to say about what he calls Hemingway's "brief liaison with Marjorie," except for some off-the-wall comments that transform "The End of Something" into a "sour" treatment of Hemingway's "disintegrating" love for Hadley.[5] Meyers just echoes Baker, keeps the weight on Marge that she had gained in Kert's paragraph, throws in a little more condescension and sexism for good measure, and there you have it— Meyers's portrait of a lady "suggestively named Marjorie Bump."

We get more of the same from Kenneth Lynn. Marjorie here figures briefly in a few sentences that parrot Baker, Kert, and Meyers (although Lynn's Marge seems to have lost some weight). Lynn, like everybody else, places Hemingway's meeting with his "waitress," his "redheaded flame from Petoskey," in the summer of 1919, and he has Hemingway "hanging around Petoskey High School waiting for Marjorie," and taking her to dances. In addition, arbitrarily and absurdly, Lynn insists that the Marge of "The End of Something" is really Hadley, not Marjorie Bump at all.[6]

We also must not forget Peter Griffin, who devotes part of two sentences to Marjorie in the first volume of his exercise, *Along With Youth*, where we learn this, and only this: Marge was "a well-built red-headed waitress" with whom Hemingway flirted in the summer of 1919. Of course, if we care to turn to Griffin's even more curious second volume of biography, *Less Than A Treason*, we will discover that Hemingway knew that the characters of "Up in Michigan" "would seem awfully 'simple' to sophisticated readers. But he had known girls up in Michigan, girls with names like 'Marjorie Bump,' who lived and thought and felt just as Liz Coates did."[7]

I will not repeat what I wrote in the margin next to this comment by Griffin, but I will note that the genteel hint of condescension found in Baker's account, source for all the others, has, by the time Griffin writes, degenerated into the tackiest kind of sexism, the silliest patronizing tone, in dark complicity with misinformation and ignorance.[8]

Finally we have Michael Reynolds, from whom we have learned to expect fresh departures, new facts, more details. In *The Young Hemingway* we do get a little closer to the truth about the duration of Hemingway's relationship with Marge—he held her "in reserve" until the last minute in 1921, just before his marriage to Hadley. We get a glimpse or two of a more accurate image or an engaging insight in passing, for example: "With her red hair and freckles, [Hadley] looked like a taller version of Marge Bump."[9] Yes, it is a very true and most interesting fact. Unfortunately, however, we also get more of the same old business: for Reynolds, Marge remains that "cute summer waitress" that Hemingway met and flirted with in the summer of 1919 (68, 88). Most of the girls of summer, Reynolds writes, were like sisters:

> Except Marjorie was more than a sister, with her red hair, wide grin and firm little body. She was a nice complication; he could have her if he wanted. Maybe he could have her. There were some in Petoskey who thought he already had. She was two years younger than himself, and together they were special. (88-89)

What are we to make of such an account, rendered in such prose? Perhaps all that we can say is this: by the Iron Law of Hemingway Biography, people may lose or gain weight in the eyes of different biographers, but once a waitress always a waitress. In brief, Marge has been the victim of textual harassment.

So the core image, retailed from Baker on down, the dish this "waitress" is required to serve, is composed from a pinch of misinformation, a dash of disinformation, a tablespoon of sloppy transliteration from fiction into biography, and a recipe calling forth every sinister "-ism" in the careless biographer's cookbook. The critics then warm up the leftovers, reheat the stale, tasteless concoction in the crucible of fiction, and serve it up as literary analysis. Before we come to the critics and the fiction, however, let us now recite certain facts, most of them hitherto unexamined or unavailable.

Lucy Marjorie Bump was born on 24 August 1901 in Petoskey, Michigan, and she died on 29 March 1987. She was the granddaughter of one of Petoskey's "pioneer" businessmen, George Bump, and the daughter of Mate and Sidney Bump, founder of Bump & McCabe Hardware. By every account given by those who knew her, or knew of her, she grew up very much a "proper young lady" from a "good family," in a quite civilized place. (As a Michigan friend of mine says, Petoskey was not and is not Podunk.) How did she come to be in Horton Bay in the summertime? She was not, as one would gather from writers on Hemingway, drawn to

Horton Bay as part of some transient summer resort labor force—she *did
not come to Horton Bay as a waitress*. (Perhaps it should be said here that
even if she did, so what? Some of the best people, some of the very best,
have been waitresses. However, the sad, thin elitism of the Hemingway
biocritical tradition does not seem to allow for that possibility). Marjorie
Bump came to Horton Bay to visit with her uncle, Professor Ernest L. Ohle
of Washington University in St. Louis, who had his summer cottage there,
across the road from Pinehurst and the Dilworths. As one eyewitness
reports:

> When it appeared that the Dilworth evening guest list would number more
> people than usual, "Marge" and "Pudge" would phone a couple of
> Petoskey school friends, all of whom thought waiting tables for Aunty Beth
> was neat. . . . This went on for several summers.[10]

So much for the "waitress" identity. In fact, if class condescension had
been a factor in the Hemingway-Bump relationship, and I do not think
there is the slightest hint of it anywhere in the record (in fact, or in fiction),
it would have flowed in the other direction: the proper young lady at the
Professor's summer cottage looking somewhat askance at the summer
loafer-fisherman hanging around Dilworth's.

The next most engaging question, for the purposes of Hemingway
scholarship, is when did Marjorie meet Ernest Hemingway? Every biographer, every writer on Hemingway who alludes to the matter, has it wrong:
they met well before the summer of 1919. William Ohle, Marge's cousin,
recalls the dinners at the family cottage in the summer of 1917, with his
parents as the watchful chaperons of their niece's friend: "Ernest . . . sat
uncomfortably at the table speaking in monosyllables as my mother tried
to keep conversation going." Ohle gives this account of their first meeting:

> Ernest was bound for the Point one evening when he first met Marjorie
> Bump, age 13, as she was walking back from the creek to her uncle's house,
> a speckled trout on a stringer in one hand and a long cane pole in the other.
> Conversation about the fish launched a friendship that might have lasted a
> lifetime had it not been for the author's graceless lapse a few years later.
> (105)

Thus Ohle's account of the Hemingway-Bump relationship places their
first meeting in the summer of 1915, and indicates that their friendship
had developed considerably by the summer of 1917, with the chaperoned
dinners at the family cottage. Ohle's fine local history of Horton Bay
belongs in every Hemingway scholar's library, not just for the corrective of

the Hemingway-Bump relationship it provides, but also for the way it makes Horton Bay come alive as a *place*, far more concretely and tellingly than Hemingway scholarship has managed to do.

In addition to Ohle's account there is other remarkable evidence that clarifies the date of meeting and the subsequent relationship. In an unpublished manuscript, entitled "Another side of the story . . . Memory fragments about E.H. as told by Lucy Marjorie Bump," now in private hands, we have Marjorie Bump's account of their meeting: "The first time I saw Ernest Hemingway I was walking home from Horton Creek . . . where I had caught my first fish. I was not yet fourteen."[11] She places the meeting in August, so it would have been sometime shortly before 24 August 1915, when she turned fourteen. She continues:

> I was carrying my fish in my hands and was so excited that I forgot to be afraid to talk to a boy. Ernest stopped to admire the fish—a speckled trout— not too small. I was in Horton Bay visiting my uncle, Professor Ernest Ohle, who had a cottage there. EH was visiting his friend Bill Smith. . . .

What more perfect meeting, more apt symbolic scene to set the tone for an enduring idyll: creek, trout, innocent girl, and innocent boy on country road stopping to admire the trout. The idyll—that is Hemingway's word for it—lasted almost to the day he married Hadley six years later. Some Hemingway scholars know that Hemingway referred to his Horton Bay summer of 1919 as "idyllic"; yet all have ignored the fact that he also referred to the fall of 1919 as idyllic, that season when he lived in Petoskey so that he could be near Marjorie Bump.[12]

We also learn from Marjorie's "Memory fragments" that they wrote to each other while Hemingway was in Italy and that she knit him a sweater in 1917 to wear as he was preparing to go off to the war. Sadly, we also see that Marjorie was deeply hurt, all her life, by Hemingway's short stories, by his use of her real name in the fiction: "Ernest Painted a false picture under my true name."

Skeptical Hemingway scholars and biographers, reluctant to admit the false picture of Marjorie that has been painted in the Hemingway biocritical tradition, may hasten to point out that the new evidence I have presented here should be taken with a grain of salt because it is all *family* evidence, the other family, the aggrieved family. Maybe so; nevertheless it rings absolutely true, and it is confirmed by all other available evidence. Consider this, for example; on 6 December 1917, Hemingway, duly enlisted in the 7th Missouri Infantry, wrote to his parents from Kansas City:

I got another Army thing the other day too that is great. An Army slip on sweater. Khaki wool. Marge Bump knitted it for me, and it is a peach of a sweater.[13]

Is not it odd, then, that Hemingway went off to war wearing that "peach of a sweater" Marge knitted for him in 1917 and then, if we believe any or all of the Hemingway biographers, he finally met her for the first time, two years later, in the summer of 1919, when they had their so-called brief romance?

A good deal more remains to be said about the true identity of Marge Bump and her relationship with Hemingway. Yet, since I hold no brief here as biographer, and since the full biographical clarification that is needed is beyond the scope of this essay, I will consign to the notes certain facts and suggestions concerning Marge that should prove of value to future biographers and critics.[14]

&ξ   &ξ   &ξ

Nothing was finished. Nothing was ever lost. He would go into town on Saturday.
—"The Three-Day Blow"

Now we must turn to the critical tradition, insofar as it involves Marge and the two stories, "The End of Something" and "The Three-Day Blow." In brief, much of what has been said about these stories has been rendered irrelevant by the facts presented here. (Some of it was irrelevant to begin with). Arguments that dance around the matter of the date of the stories—1916? 1917? 1919?—are here rendered invalid inasmuch as they rely on the universally promulgated misinformation concerning Hemingway's meeting and so-called brief romance with Marge in 1919.[15] Likewise, all critical arguments which pivot on one aspect or another of what Sheridan Baker calls Nick's "waitress sweetheart," or what Jackson Benson describes as "Nick's break-up with a lower-class white girl" are herewith dismissed; indeed most critical discussions engage this question, implicitly or explicitly, as biography or fiction or some bastard version of the two modes.[16] To reiterate: there is no evidence in the stories that Marge is a waitress, and there is no evidence in the stories that she is "lower-class," just as the real Marge was neither lower-class nor a waitress.

Thus it would appear that it is about time to start all over again, with a clean slate, since, in large part, the very questions that have been asked of these stories have condemned the answers to insignificance. Of course, there are those critical discussions that focus on other matters, such as the place of the stories in the sequence and the overall design of *In Our Time*, or the still larger chronicle of Nick Adams. Most such discussion seems to me rather labored exegesis of obvious points: of course, "The End of Something" and "The Three-Day Blow" stand alone as stories; and, most certainly, they are richer taken together, and still richer in terms of whatever patterns of unity the reader may see in *In Our Time*, or in the complete corpus of Nick stories. As for those critics who are most engaged with what they regard as the latent homosexuality in the stories, well, perhaps "no comment" is the wisest response here. As I see it we have one, and one only, ample and insightful discussion of the stories, especially of Marge's role therein: to wit, Joseph Flora's. If I were to give a full-dress critical treatment I would find myself echoing and refining some of Flora's views, views that I have independently arrived at by different paths, though I am far from agreement with all of Flora's conclusions. Yet we are at least in the same ballpark. For example, Flora finds "unjustified" various negative critical versions of Marge's character and he stresses her *dignity*.[17] Delighted to read this, since I have been stressing her dignity in lectures for twenty-some years, I would add that not only does she possess dignity, but also competence, skill, discipline, humility, pride, and poise. Indeed, she may be, if we dare use these terms any longer, the tutor, the exemplar, the Hemingway hero of "The End of Something." Rather than dance around my points of partial disagreement with Flora's fine discussion, I shall sketch, in these concluding paragraphs, my design for completely new departures, for radically revisionist readings of the two stories.

Let us take the simplest one first, and do it in a few sentences, although we could belabor it and make a long chapter by talking on and on—as some observers have—about those opening paragraphs of "The End of Something." That beginning is a perfectly fine example of set-piece writing, of symbolic landscape or *paysage moralisé*, of machine-in-the-garden motif-mongering, and it serves the story sufficiently. Paul Smith and other lumberphobes may feel they could do without what they regard as this lumbering, "ponderous" opening;[18] yet, conventional and perfectly obvious as it may be, I rather like Hemingway's landscape-opening; the story—the story that I read—requires that opening. At one level, put most simply, "The End of Something" is an elegy for a *place*; this story, which some critics have found "pointless," is about the Point. The point is the Point. Six times in four pages we read "the point": "way to the point," "headed it for the point," "rowed up the point," "toward the point," "of the point," and, finally, as Marge tells Nick when she leaves: "You can walk back around the point."[19] We cannot get around the point, however, and it is, like it or not, a biographical one: Hemingway loved the Point at Horton Bay, and a few years after the "horrid" feeling that Marge and he had when it was sold in 1920, he celebrated the Point in this little elegy written in Paris, this fragmentary evocation of the idyll he had lived. So one something that ends in the story is the Point; it is that, and it is much more, since from the first day he had seen 13-year-old Marge Bump walking back from Horton Creek with that trout, she had been part of the Point, she had been a presiding numen, the *deus loci*, of that numinous place.

Now, at another level, and biographical parallels aside, we know from the story alone the depth and duration of Nick's feeling for Marge. We know, too, that it is nothing that she says, nothing that she does, nothing that she is, that causes Nick's hateful rejection of her. It is something as ancient as original sin, that radical insufficiency of human behavior, that proclivity for darkly inscrutable conduct, that pure orneriness that so frequently manifests itself in the conduct of teenagers and adults alike. What makes this instance of it in Nick's conduct significant is that he recognizes it: "I feel as though everything was gone to hell inside of me" (34). This core feeling, which generates the subtle power of the story as well as its emblazoned truth, has nothing to do with Bill, nothing to do with what has often been called Nick's choice of male camaraderie over female attachments, nothing to do with what some see as latent homosexuality. What happens happens because of the sudden overwhelming hell Nick feels inside. Bill may have provided a spur, may even have suggested or arranged the time and place of the actual event, but he has nothing to do with the deeper movement of the story. Indeed, as Hemingway writes toward the end of "The Three-Day Blow," "Bill wasn't there," an observation that echoes and underlines the concluding scene of "The End of Something": "Bill didn't touch him" (35, 47). Gerry Brenner, Paul Smith, Joseph Whitt, and others, to varying degrees, find this sentence about not being "touched" both curious and an indication of Hemingway's, or Nick's, "latent homoeroticism."[20] Yet there is nothing curious about it, nothing homoerotic about it. The variations on the theme of touch and being touched that Hemingway plays throughout *In Our Time* are obvious (almost as many and obvious as they are in one of his models, *Winesburg, Ohio*) and this is not the place to list them in detail. The pattern culminates, achieves its ultimate resonance in "Big Two-Hearted River" when Nick has made his camp alone—"in his home where he had made it"—and he feels at last that "Nothing could touch him" (139). There, in the wilderness, only animals and insects are near Nick—which, I hasten to add, is not to say that "Nothing could touch him" is an expression of Hemingway's, or Nick's, latent bestiality, latent animal, or ento-eroticism. It does, of course, mean what we say in the everyday expression for a variety of situations:

"nothing can touch me now, I'm home free." However, it also means that utterly alone, in the self-made home, is precisely when and where *nothing* can and will touch us, where nothingness and *nada* will touch all who are alive enough to feel it. Nothing could *touch* him. *Nothing* could touch him. The very "hell inside" of Nick that he first feels in "The End of Something" is the first touch of that nothing, that radical lonesomeness that has death and evil and pariahhood in it, which is why neither Marge nor Bill "touch" him.

On the evidence of the single story, then, can we say what has ended? It is inaccurate to say, with or without the evidence of "The Three-Day Blow," that the story depicts the end of Nick's feeling for Marge, or the end of his relationship with her; we cannot even say, without the details of "The Three-Day Blow," that the end of a season is depicted. Although all of that has been said many times over, we might just as well and more accurately say that Hemingway is writing about the end of Horton Bay (for him, for Marge), or the end of the Point. Yet, to be sure, what we most deeply and definitively feel is what we must call—in spite of the impoverishment of the phrase, the deprivation of its power and significance by loose usage—the end of innocence. Nick feels the hell inside himself and acts out of, and in strict accordance with, that hell. That strikes me as a pretty fair definition of the end of innocence, especially for a writer in his mid-twenties.

What does "The Three-Day Blow" add to the picture? A great deal, but nothing to change the core-feeling of the preceding story. Wonderful comic scenes, great boyish conversations, a damning characterization of Bill, and, for Nick, hope for a way out of his hell, a way back to Marge. Having mentioned Bill's character, I should pause to clarify, especially since some of the critical commentary reads as if Bill were the exemplar, or as if Bill had written the criticism. As I have argued elsewhere, "Bill's obtuseness, his insensitivity and condescension, is apparently shared by many readers of Hemingway who have generally failed to see that one central concern of the stories is the very insidiousness of Bill's patronizing attitudes."[21] At the time I wrote that sentence, I suppose I was emphasizing that it is not Nick, not Hemingway, but Bill alone who views Marge as not good enough for Nick. In saying that, I reckon I was at least partially agreeing with the prevailing tradition of commentary, that is, I was accepting some small part of the package of assumptions first expressed by Philip Young some forty years ago, and repeated by many writers since. From "The Three-Day Blow," as Young has it,

> we learn—learn why it was that Nick forced that break with Marjorie: she was of the "wrong" class for a doctor's son. It is again Bill who brings this

out. You just can't mix oil and water, he says; it's just like it was with Bill and "Ida that works for Strattons."[22]

This is not at all what we learn, however. We *may* learn that Bill thinks this, but now I rather doubt even that element of the assumption. Let us hear exactly what Bill says:

> Now she can marry somebody of her own sort and settle down and be happy. You can't mix oil and water and you can't mix that sort of thing any more than if I'd marry Ida that works for Strattons. She'd probably like it, too. (47)

In response to this, "Nick said nothing"; three times in less than a page, while Bill, windy and egregious, motormouths one cliché after another, "Nick said nothing." We could respond to Bill's misogyny, to his elitist and sexist clichés in various ways. We might say that it would do the silly snob some good to marry Ida, since elitist yuppie twits always stand to learn from working people, country people. Yet, however we respond to Bill, we cannot, from Hemingway's text, feel that Nick agrees with Bill. Indeed, I would now insist that we need to see further—and see very exactly—that Bill is *not* equating Marge with Ida, in class terms. He is making an analogy; analogy is not equivalence. What Bill thinks, I now believe, is that Marge is not *right* for Nick; she is too conventional, she wants to lead a too thoroughly "normal" life—home, family, children—and this is not, as Bill sees it, what Nick wants or needs. By "normal," I mean that contrasting quality, that opposite of the equally platitudinous notion of a "free," "creative," or "artistic" life; (in fact, I mean precisely the sense that my mother had of the word "normal," when she used to say to my father, a poet and musician by birth and vocation, "why can't you be normal?"). This, I repeat, is what Bill thinks, not Nick. I do not know, none of us will ever know, what Nick thinks about this, except that he disagrees with Bill. We do, however—to revert to biography—we do indeed know what Hemingway thought about it. In that "unmailed" letter that Hemingway wrote to Marge in 1921, there are suggestions of a tension between them that could be construed as a clash of conventional and creative personalities. There is also this: "Cheer up Red—I wasn't so bad for you—Except as Bill always said.—but I won't repeat that because I never agreed with him." *Whatever* it was that Bill Smith always said about Marjorie Bump and Hemingway never agreed with, there is not one shred of evidence that it had anything to do with "class," in any sense of that term.

To return, then, to the fiction, here is what we learn, Philip Young and all the others to the contrary, in "The Three-Day Blow":

1. Nick and Marge were not "engaged" but they were "going to get married."
2. Nick was planning to stay in town "all winter so he could be near Marge."
3. Nick does not like Marge's mother and stepfather.
4. Nick is "sorry as hell" over what he has done to Marge.
5. Nick will probably "go into town on Saturday," make up with Marge, and stay with and near her all that fall and into the winter, at least.

This last statement, I recognize, turns inside out the universally accepted reading of the Marge stories, since the one thing all observers agree about is that Hemingway is depicting the *end* of a relationship. I see little reason to make, and many reasons to resist, such a conclusion. That simply makes it a routine, very conventional story of the breakup of young lovers. Utterly conventional, too, is the way critics wax poetic about the key image of the "blow"—all those leaves stripped from all those trees—the three-day storm, and how it marks the end of something. However, the very point is that it lasts only three days. As Nick sees it, "there was not anything that was irrevocable. He *might* go into town *Saturday* night. Today was *Thursday*" (emphasis added). The emphatic point is that, by Saturday night, the storm will be over. Thus, Nick feels happy: "Nothing was finished. Nothing was ever lost. He *would* go into town on Saturday" (48, emphasis added). He may be drunk, but this is not just the drunken youthful illusion that some make it out to be, for his head is absolutely "clear." Paul Smith and others find Nick's hope of reunion with Marge "a vain and youthful thought"; "anyone," Smith writes, "with a smattering of tragedy in mind" will find it so, will find Nick's hope "fateful" (54). Yet, for anyone with more than a *mere* "smattering of tragedy in mind," the will and the effort to recover what you may have thrown away, to expiate; what may be the felicitous folly or the happy hope of reclaiming the lost innocence and the idyll which nourished it; and the vision of reconciliation, atonement, reunion with the love you have wounded and drawn into your own hell—all this is a far richer, far more fateful and tragic, far more mature design. Long before I ever heard of Marjorie Bump, or read any Hemingway biography or criticism, I remember reading these stories, fifteen or sixteen years old, and thinking, *knowing*, that Nick did go into town that Saturday night, and that, whatever else happened later, he did stay "near Marge" for another season. Then, much later— under the influence of the bumps and grinds of Hemingway exegetes and ecdysiasts—I dismissed such a reading. At least until I began to assign, every fall, an exercise for undergraduates that went something like this: "Assume that in some fashion Hemingway constructed this story on his so-called theory of omission. Write one sentence that you would add to the end of the story, a sentence that makes the thing omitted more visible."

Over the decades, I have had many responses, some of them both apt and hilarious; for example, one student wrote: "Nick saw what a jerk Bill was, what an insufferable snob and airhead, punched Bill out, ran all the way to town, half-drunk, half-crying, half-laughing, and even though Marge's mother locked him out in the storm that first night, he stayed and stayed and by Saturday night he'd made up with Marge and they were back together for a long time." The most eloquent single sentence that agreed with the prevailing critical interpretation of the story was this: "In the fall Marge was always there, but Nick did not go to her anymore." Yet, overwhelmingly, in approximately 90 percent of the responses, the opposite resolution was suggested. As one student wrote: "So Nick did go into town, he *had* to, and he stayed near Marge all that fall and into the winter." When I read this aloud to the class, I added: "And that's exactly what Hemingway did with the real Marge—but of course biography has little or nothing to do with fiction." They all smiled knowingly, winkingly.

No, nothing is ever finished, nothing ever lost, the past is never past, suffering and sin and innocence and betrayal and expiation vibrate and reverberate in the web and fabric of the world without end, and the story of Nick's teenage heart in conflict with itself is older than yesterday, fresher than tomorrow: his mind remains its own place, making in itself "a Heav'n of Hell, a Hell of Heav'n." "Oh, nothing is lost, ever lost: at last you understood—" and "there must be a new innocence for us to be stayed by": for a moment, I thought I remembered Nick saying this, a long moment, before I remembered that it was from that old Robert Penn Warren poem called "Original Sin: A Short Story." (Maybe the associative leap was in the names, Red Warren, Red Bump; but no, it is more, much more than just that.)

In conclusion, since one reason I went to Petoskey was that I harbored some secret hope that I might make some small act of atonement for the Hemingway biocritical tradition, for its sins of commission and omission with regard to a native daughter of that town, I will end in the biographical mode, on a note that some might call the "merely personal." It is truly sad, very sad, to think that the real Marjorie Bump was "plagued throughout her life" (as her cousin William Ohle writes[23]) by "The End of Something" and "The Three-Day Blow." For, however true to actual experience the fiction may be, one thing that some part of Hemingway, the writer and the man, wanted to make sure of in these stories was that nothing would be lost, not his Horton Bay idyll, not Marge, not his own obscure sense of betrayal, not his confession. In weaving the fiction, no matter how often the stories may be misconstrued by however many readers, Hemingway succeeded in creating a powerful image of a place he loved, and he made a delicate and enduring portrait of a Marge who possessed great dignity, discipline, poise, and a serene lyrical loveliness. Finally, since nothing is ever lost, and Hemingway saved everything, I wonder just where that "peach of a sweater" Marge knitted for him in 1917 might be. Is it in a thrift store somewhere around Petoskey, hanging on a Salvation Army rack? Or is Nick wearing it, in that place where nothing can touch him?

NOTES

1. This letter is in the Lilly Library, Indiana University; portions of the letter have been published in Henry S. Villard and James Nagel, *Hemingway in Love and War* (Boston: Northeastern University Press, 1989), 202.
2. Carlos Baker, *Ernest Hemingway: A Life Story* (New York: Scribner's, 1969), 64. Subsequent citations in text.
3. Carlos Baker, ed., *Ernest Hemingway: Selected Letters, 1917-1961* (New York: Scribner's, 1981), 32. Subsequent citations in text.
4. Bernice Kert, *The Hemingway Women* (New York: W.W. Norton, 1983), 73-74.
5. Jeffrey Meyers, *Hemingway: A Biography* (New York: Harper and Row, 1985), 48-49.
6. Kenneth S. Lynn, *Hemingway* (New York: Simon and Schuster, 1987), 101, 113, 254.
7. Peter Griffin, *Along with Youth: Hemingway, The Early Years* (New York: Oxford University Press, 1985), 122; Peter Griffin, *Less Than A Treason: Hemingway in Paris* (New York: Oxford University Press, 1990), 89.
8. It is curious that Hemingway's biographers—with the exception of Reynolds—seem to have overlooked or simply ignored evidence regarding Marjorie Bump and her relationship with Hemingway, evidence readily available (at the Kennedy Library) and clearly contradictory of the accounts given in the biographies. Such documentary sources (the correspondence of Marge and Hemingway) clearly suggest, to any reader, let alone biographer, the need to investigate the matter further and to correct the false image of the "Marge business" that has been retailed through the decades. It is even more curious that the biographers have failed to employ the technique of family and local interviews; one exception is Peter Griffin, who lists an interview with William Ohle among his sources. Most curious of all, given this interview, is the fact that Griffin—who apparently did not realize he was talking to Marjorie Bump's cousin—failed to turn up any new information regarding the matter, information that was there, waiting to be told. As far as I am able to discern, none of the other biographers have talked with Ohle. Have they even been to Horton Bay? It seems most unlikely, given what they have written. For his invaluable contributions to my research and understanding of the matters treated in this essay, through interviews and correspondence (1988-91), I record here my gratitude to William Ohle.

9. Michael Reynolds, *The Young Hemingway* (New York: Blackwell, 1986), 148. Subsequent citations in text.

10. William H. Ohle, *How It Was in Horton Bay* (Boyne City: the author, 1989), 104-5. Subsequent citations in text. Other sources: obituary of Marjorie Bump Main printed in the *Petoskey News-Review*, 23 April 1987; interviews and correspondence with Ohle and with Petoskey-area natives who wish to remain anonymous; Constance Cappel Montgomery, *Hemingway in Michigan* (New York: Fleet, 1966)—this volume, which predates all of the biographies dealt with here, remains by far the most complete and most accurate presentation of Marjorie Bump to date, in spite of the fact that there are errors of fact and certain skewed readings. I have not treated this volume in detail since, strictly speaking, it is neither biography nor literary criticism. It is, however, especially as it regards our concerns here, very valuable local history.

11. This manuscript is in the hands of a private owner who wishes to remain anonymous.

12. Ernest Hemingway to Marjorie Bump, April 1921, Kennedy Library [this letter is regarded as unmailed]. All unpublished letters cited hereafter are at the Kennedy Library.

13. Villard and Nagel, *Hemingway in Love and War*, 202.

14. The following matter, presented in appendix form, contains material concerning Marge Bump that has been hitherto unexamined and/or unavailable:

A) Marjorie Bump, Dramatics Editor, member of the Girls' Literary society at Petoskey High School in 1919 when Hemingway moved there to be near her, spent much time reading, studying, and discussing books with Hemingway. Together, they read many things, from books on etiquette to Hewlett's *Forest Lovers*, Together, they read Hemingway's early stories. When Hemingway left Petoskey for Toronto, Marge, still in high school, wrote to him about reading *Les Misérables* in French. She also wrote to him *in* French. (The very reason Hemingway got his live-in companion job in Toronto was because *Marjorie's grandmother* "prevailed upon him" to deliver that war talk to the Petoskey Ladies' Aid Society.) Given the stress that some biographers have placed on Hadley's role in Hemingway's education and literary apprenticeship, on Hadley's role in helping him with French, and so on, is not it odd that nothing has been said about Marjorie's analogous role in Hemingway's formative years? (See Montgomery, *Hemingway in Michigan*, 132; Ohle, *How It Was in Horton Bay*, 106, Ernest Hemingway to Marjorie Bump, April 1921; Marjorie Bump to Ernest Hemingway, 7 February 1920 and 28 February 1920).

B) Marjorie planned to go to Wellesley. Instead, she attended Washington University for two years. Thus, Marjorie was better educated at a better university than most of "Hemingway's women." Given the fact that this was a relationship that lasted as long, or longer, than some of

Hemingway's marriages, Marjorie Bump's intellectual and educational identity does indeed signify (See Marjorie Bump to Ernest Hemingway, 28 February 1920 and 14 January 1921).

C) Over a period of six years, Hemingway and Marge shared many things—books, stories, dances, dates, fishing, gossip, idyllic summer days by the lake, and cold winter days in the library (or in Hemingway's words, "moonlight swims," "fishing for rainbow off the point," "dances at the Bean house," "working in the orchard," the books they "studied together," etc.). They also shared a sense of place, a love of place, Horton Bay, and especially the Point. When the Dilworths sell the Point in 1920, the news makes Marge feel "horrid" and, writing to Hemingway in Toronto, she knows that he will probably feel even worse about it. "Everything," she writes, "will be different now." Thus she senses, in February 1920, the end of something (Marjorie Bump to Ernest Hemingway, 2 February 1920).

D) In January 1921, Hemingway writes to his new girlfriend Hadley, in St. Louis (where Marge was, too, where she and Hadley knew the same people), to suggest that maybe they should get married. Until that letter (and probably after it) he had clearly been keeping Marjorie, as Reynolds writes, "on the string right there in St. Louis" (173). Hadley got her letter on January 13. On the 14th, Marge wrote one of her last "Dear Stein" letters. She is tired, exhausted by preparation for her exams and it is not much of a letter; but it is clear that Hemingway has not told her about his plan to marry Hadley. Reynolds's account of this seems on target. However, he adds—with no evidence—the following: "Two months after what he had thought to be his last letter to Marjorie Bump, he got her reply, which stung him to the quick." Then he quotes (or misquotes, omitting Marge's punctuation) part of this letter and assumes that Marge's stinging letter is a response to a missing Hemingway farewell letter sent two months earlier. However, given the language and situational terminology of these supposed last letters, Marge's and Hemingway's "unmailed" response, the clear possibility exists that Marge, after her exams were over in January, journeyed north on term break and met with Hemingway somewhere. His comments about her "grand outburst" and his assertion that "it was the shape of [Marge's] mouth" that parted them forever suggest, in the absence of contrary evidence, just such a meeting, at which time Hemingway may have told her about his plans to marry Hadley, thus causing a "grand outburst." (Marjorie Bump to Ernest Hemingway, 14 January 1921 and 7 April 1921; Ernest Hemingway to Marjorie Bump, April 1921). Of course, even this would not have been their last meeting; Hemingway invited Marge to his wedding, and when she would not attend because her mother was not invited (Ohle, *How It Was in Horton Bay,* 108), the

honeymooning Hemingway took Hadley to meet Marge. They also
saw each other again, years later.

E) In 1935 Marge wrote to Hemingway, sending a Christmas greeting
with a photograph of her family, husband, two daughters, and son; she
expressed what sounds like a reiterated invitation to bring his family
and visit them. Key West and Daytona Beach, where Marge lived, were
not that far apart. Hemingway's response, if there was a written one,
has apparently not survived (Marjorie Bump to Ernest Hemingway, 26
December 1935). He did go to see her, however, and he got along well
with her husband (Lucy Marjorie Bump, "Memory fragments").

F) Given the fullness, the complexity, and the duration of the
Hemingway-Bump relationship here delineated for the first time, it is
quite natural that Marge haunted Hemingway's fiction from the beginning to the end of his career, not just in the two early stories. Joseph
Flora is probably right, in seeing Marge as Nick's unnamed girl in
"The Last Good Country": "'She was a beautiful girl and I always
liked her,' Mr. John had said. 'So did I,' Nick said . . . 'None of it was
her fault'" (Ernest Hemingway, *The Complete Short Stories of Ernest
Hemingway,* The Finca Vigía Edition [New York: Scribner's, 1987],
523-24). Flora sees this as a "tribute" to Marge, to "a vibrant character" (Joseph M. Flora, *Hemingway's Nick Adams* [Baton Rouge:
Louisiana State University Press, 1982], 53-54). Perhaps, too, the critics and biographers who deal with Hemingway's Petoskey book, *The
Torrents of Spring,* and those who see so much of Hadley and Pauline
in that "society of the friendly waitress" and in the tension between the
older waitress and the younger waitress, had better take another look
at that text. Diana, the literary-waitress-wife of the writer, Scripps, tells
him she would not mind if he used her story sometime: "'Not if you
find it interesting,' the waitress smiled. 'You wouldn't use my name, of
course'" (Ernest Hemingway, *The Torrents of Spring: A Romantic
Novel in Honor of the Passing of a Great Race* [New York: Scribner's,
1972], 19). Or perhaps even more to the biographical point is the
image of Scripps, standing in the snow, staring "up at the lighted windows of the High School," thinking of his daughter Lucy there in the
school, studying and learning. Although Lucy is identified as his
daughter, there is a curious resonance of that pattern in Hemingway's
later life and work: the shifting, oscillating image of the daughter-soul-
mate-lover figure. "'Lucy!' [Scripps] called, and again 'Lucy!' There
was no answer" (6-7). The first name of Red, of Barge, of Marge
Bump, I repeat, was Lucy. There may also be other echoes and glean-
ings from the rich and enduring idyll of Hemingway's first love still to
be identified, for we have all been so blinded by the myth of the brief
fling with the summer waitress that we have not known what to look
for, if look we must.

15. For a recent example of this kind of argument see Mark Spilka, *Hemingway's Quarrel with Androgyny* (Lincoln: University of Nebraska Press, 1990), 265-355; for a much earlier and paradigmatic instance see Philip Young's argument for the dating of the Marjorie stories in "'Big World Out There': *The Nick Adams Stories,*" *Novel: A Forum on Fiction* 6 (Fall 1972): 5-19.

16. Sheridan Baker, *Ernest Hemingway: An Introduction and Interpretation* (New York: Barnes and Noble, 1967), 29; Jackson J. Benson, *Hemingway: The Writer's Art of Self-Defense* (Minneapolis: University of Minnesota Press, 1969), 12.

17. Flora, *Hemingway's Nick Adams*, 56-57.

18. Paul Smith, *A Reader's Guide to the Short Stories of Ernest Hemingway* (Boston: G.K. Hall, 1989), 53.

19. Ernest Hemingway, *In Our Time* (New York: Scribner's, 1970), 31-35. Subsequent citations in text.

20. Gerry Brenner, *Concealments in Hemingway's Works* (Columbus: Ohio State University Press, 1983), 20-21; Smith, *A Reader's Guide*, 53-54; Joseph Whitt, "Hemingway's 'The End of Something,'" *Explicator* 9 (June 1951): Item 58.

21. H. R. Stoneback, "[Review] *How It Was in Horton Bay,*" *The Hemingway Review* 10 (Fall 1990): 77-79.

22. Philip Young, *Ernest Hemingway* (New York: Rinehart, 1952), 7.

23. Ohle, *How It Was in Horton Bay,* 120. In addition, my correspondence with Marjorie's daughter, Georgianna Main Dickinson, confirms the view that Marjorie was "plagued" by the stories.

"NOTHING" IN "BIG TWO-HEARTED RIVER"

FRANK SCAFELLA

"NOTHING" SURFACES EARLY in Hemingway, most interestingly perhaps in "Big Two-Hearted River" when Nick Adams, having set up his camp by the river, crawls inside his tent to place some things at the head of the bed.

> Inside the tent the light came through the brown canvas. It smelled pleasantly of canvas. Already there was something mysterious and homelike. Nick was happy as he crawled inside the tent. He had not been unhappy all day. This was different though. Now things were done. There had been this to do. Now it was done. It had been a hard trip. He was very tired. That was done. He had made his camp. He was settled. *Nothing could touch him.* It was a good place to camp. He was there, in the good place. He was in his home where he had made it. Now he was hungry. (Hemingway 1972, 165, emphasis added)

"Nothing could touch him"? What about the light through the brown canvas? The light touches Nick. What about the canvas smell? He is touched by it, too. Or what about the something mysterious and homelike, to say nothing of happiness, the feeling of being settled and at home, and his growing hunger? All of these touch Nick. Are these sensations nothing? If not, then "nothing" must represent something extra- or suprasensory. What can that be?

Consider that the idea, "Nothing could touch him," comes to Nick in the very moment when he feels himself most fully "settled," at "home," "in the good place," and beyond "the need for thinking," "the need to write." These needs cannot touch him in his tent at the river. At the same time, however, in the good place at the river the idea, "Nothing could touch him," actually touches Nick in thought beyond need. So the double significance of "nothing," at once an absence and a presence in Nick's thinking, means that "nothing" is "something" that Nick is free to enter-

77

tain conceptually—beyond need and beyond fear—in his tent at the river. How, then, do we determine just what this "something" is? Let us go back to the beginning of the story and make our way to the river with Nick, watching for features of his thought and action that might throw light on the "nothing" that could (or could not) touch him in his tent by the river.

When Nick jumps down from the train at Seney, "he had *expected* to find the scattered houses of the town" and the thirteen saloons that had lined its one street. Instead, he finds nothing but a "burned-over stretch of hillside." His expectation shattered, Nick responds not in curiosity, as one might expect, but with alarm, in fear: what if the river, too, has been burned away?

Immediately, he turns from the burned-over stretch of hillside and

> walks down the railroad track to the bridge over the river. *The river was there*. It swirled against the log spiles of the bridge. Nick looked down into the clear, brown water, colored from the pebbly bottom, and watched the trout keeping themselves steady in the current with wavering fins. . . . Nick watched them a long time. (159, emphasis added)

"The river was there"? Why should it *not* be there? What forest fire could burn so intensely as to dry up a river at its source, *unless* that source were Nick Adams's very expectations themselves? For where, logically, could this river go but out of Nick's mind and heart, out of memory? It may be that in the burning of Seney and in the river we are dealing with images that are symbols of Nick's inner world. Nick's spontaneous responses to the burned town and the river, guided in both instances by his expectations, alert us to the possibility that he looks less *at* than he looks *out for* certain things. He sees, that is, *in anticipation of* finding what he looks forward to, out of prior experience, from memory. In Nick, I am suggesting, *seeing* manifests a desire to confirm realities known in memory rather than factual objects in external nature.

Take Hemingway's own inner world, for example, that mine of memories from which he extracted the ore of which Nick Adams is made. For decades we have known that Hemingway's wounding on 8 July 1918 had a profound effect on and figures directly in his fiction. Moreover, we now know that the correspondences between Hemingway's life and art often show more factually in manuscript than in the published works—in manuscript fragments, for example, like Item 721 in the JFK Library, called "A Story to Skip: A Badly Organized Story of No Importance."

In this manuscript fragment on war and wounding, Hemingway begins narrating the wounding experience of a young man very like himself whose heart has been broken in battle: "And every July they took him out and broke his heart," the narrator begins, but try as he might he cannot follow through with his thought. The reason? He comes to see even as he writes that "A broken heart means that never can you remember and not to be able to remember is very different from forgetting" (JFK, Item #721). Not to be able to remember, he discovers, means nothing less than that you have become an inactive soul, a psyche in which *nothing* moves. Yet not to be able to remember "is not a question of anybody's fault," he sees: "Always they make it a question of somebody's fault and it is nobody's fault except your fault." Which is to say, a broken heart is *itself* the fault; it leaves you without—outside of—memory. It leaves your innermost self, it may be, a black grasshopper in a burned-over land.

If the inability to remember comes with a broken heart, then memory might be restored with the restoration of wholeness of heart, might it not? What magical object might restore wholeness of heart, once it has been broken? Can a trout stream mend a broken heart and restore memory? With Seney burned and his initial expectation shattered, Nick walks down the railroad track to the bridge over the river:

> Nick looked down into the pool from the bridge. . . . It was a long time since Nick had looked into a stream and seen trout. They were very satisfactory. As the shadow of the kingfisher moved up the stream, a big trout shot upstream in a long angle, only his shadow marking the angle, then lost his shadow as he came through the surface of the water, caught the sun, and then, as he went back into the stream under the surface, his shadow seemed to float down the stream with the current, unresisting, to his post under the bridge, where he *tightened*, facing up into the current.
>
> Nick's heart *tightened* as the trout moved. He felt all the old feeling. (160, emphasis added)

Not only is the river there, if Seney is not, to meet and fulfill Nick's deepest expectation, but by looking into it and seeing trout Nick's heart "tightens" into new wholeness with the surge of an anticipated feeling. The trout and the river mend his broken heart. He *felt* all the old *feeling*. A deep expectation fulfilled, Nick now knows that the river, too, has not been burned away. It has not been burned clean out of memory. For in the moment of his wounding, "there had been a flash and then a red roaring and [my soul] had gone out of me," says Nick, "with the rushing air" (JFK, Item #638). A trout stream, too, might dry up in heat like that, but with the feeling of the trout tightening his heart (the first significant action of "Big Two-Hearted River") and in his mind the idea of a trout on a tightening line, Nick walks back up the railroad track to Seney, gathers his pack and leather rod-case, and strikes out across the burned country toward that part of the river he will fish. He turns and leaves Seney behind him, as he puts it, "in the heat" (179).

"It was a hot day." How can Nick leave Seney behind him "in the heat" unless Nick himself walks out of the heat? And how can this happen on a hot day unless, as with Seney and the river, "heat" refers to an atmosphere not in the outer world of the senses but in the inner world of Nick's psyche? Seney he leaves behind him "in the heat" of memory's consuming fire, the fiery blast of war in the country of his psyche, where this part of the story takes place.

So Nick walks out of the heat with the feeling of the trout tightening his heart, because things were different now. "Seney was burned, the country was burned over and changed, but it did not matter. It could not all be burned. He knew that" (179). He has seen the river and has felt the trout in his heart. Now, having set his mind on getting to that part of the river where the trout and his heart can be united on a tightening line, Nick walks along "*feeling* the *ache* from the pull of his heavy pack," every sensation conscious, like being awake and dreaming. It is in this state of mind and heart that Nick finds himself at that demarcation between the burned-over land and the living land where he picks up and examines the black grasshopper. In the black grasshopper, our meditation on the "something" that can or cannot touch Nick in his tent at the river comes first and most fully to "nothing."

At the top of the range of hills that separates the railway from the pine plain Nick sits down to rest by a logging road that separates the burned country from the living land of the pine plain. Ahead of Nick lies the living country; behind him, the burned country. He sits and leans back against a charred stump to smoke a cigarette:

> As he smoked, his legs stretched out in front of him, he noticed a grasshopper walk along the ground and up onto his wollen sock. The grasshopper was black. As he had walked along the road, climbing, he had started many grasshoppers from the dust. They were all black. They were not the big grasshoppers with yellow and black or red and black wings whirring out from their black wing sheathing as they flew. These were just ordinary hoppers, but all a sooty black in color. Nick had wondered about them as he walked, without really thinking about them. Now, as he watched the black hopper that was nibbling at the wool of his sock with its four-way lip, he realized that they had all turned black from living in the burned-over land. He realized that the fire must have come the year before, but the grasshoppers were all black now. He wondered how long they would stay that way.
>
> Carefully he reached his hand down and took hold of the hopper by the wings. He turned him up, all his legs walking in the air, and looked at his

jointed belly. Yes, it was black too, *iridescent* where the back and head were dusty.

"Go on, hopper," Nick said, speaking out loud for the first time. "Fly away somewhere."

He tossed the grasshopper up into the air and watched him sail away to a charcoal stump across the road. (Hemingway 1972, 161-62, emphasis added)

The grasshopper's jointed belly is "iridescent where the back and head were dusty." Iridescence is no surface hue; the grasshopper participates wholly in the blackness to which it owes its being. In its iridescent blackness it appears part and parcel of the burned-over land where nothing thrives, where (as Nick had earlier observed of the town of Seney) even the surface had been burned off the ground. Nothing takes root in country like that. There the black grasshopper has nothing to live on. There it loses touch in its very nature with every instinct or inclination for the living land of the pine plain that begins in sweet fern growing ankle deep just across the road. For when Nick tosses the hopper up into the air with the command, "Fly away somewhere," it sails away not into the sweet fern but to a "charcoal stump" in the burned country.

Now, the naturalist will argue that a grasshopper of the small brown variety could never actually turn up with an iridescent belly, so this black grasshopper calls into question all that we know about the nature and habits of this creature. However, iridescence becomes a problem only if we think of the black grasshopper as a creature of external nature, which it is not, rather than as a symbol of Nick's inner world, which, in its iridescence ten times black, clearly it is. In the black grasshopper Nick faces an outward and visible symbol of the inward and spiritual condition of his soul—the soul that, when it returned into his body after his wounding, felt like "nothing at all" (JFK, Item #638). Thus the black grasshopper calls into question, as does the burned town of Seney at the very beginning of the story, Nick's guiding expectation that a fishing trip to the Big Two-Hearted River will permit him to leave behind the need to think, the need to write, other needs. The iridescent blackness of the grasshopper's belly challenges Nick's very expectation of gaining the "good place" where "nothing" can touch him.

From the vantage of Nick's soul, then—the soul that had, at the moment of his wounding, sailed out of him and gone a long way off and then come back ("Now I Lay Me"); the soul that he had held within him "brilliantly," by sheer force of will, immediately following its out-of-body journey (Hemingway 1970, chapter 6); the soul that had tried unsuccessfully, during Nick's convalescence in Milan, to think about itself in images of stricken fields of battle, the bloated dead, or a body coughing its life onto a rock as enemy soldiers rushed past him (the dramatic tension in JFK, Items #240, #723, #263, #260, #671, and "A Way You'll Never Be"); the soul that was double-crossed by God, Who had not permitted it to follow through with its rendezvous with death (JFK, Item #670b); the soul in dread of perishing alone in the dark ("In Another Country"); the soul that had recently found itself, quite unexpectedly one night, brooding on trout streams in memory with the undiminishing hunger of silk worms feeding in racks of mulberry leaves ("Now I Lay Me")—the black grasshopper personifies Nick's psyche itself, victim of a fiery blast that burned away everything but the river alone, leaving his soul, the imagining power of the psyche, like the grasshopper, blackened, in a parched land, directionless, hungry, and for dead.

In the black grasshopper Nick's soul fully personifies its spiritual condition for the first time since Nick's wounding. In the hopper Nick's soul wants to dream his conscious self awake to its deepest psychic state. Yet all that Nick can acknowledge consciously at this juncture of his journey is an insect blackened by having lived in a burned-over land. Nick's mind cannot see past the natural object; nor can he, at this point, think anything of it but that it should be somewhere else than in the blackened dust of the burned-over country: "Go on, hopper," says Nick. "Fly away somewhere." But the hopper only sails away to a charred stump, as Nick's war-blackened soul, bound by memories of war and wounding, retains its dread of "nothing" until, once having arrived at, camped by, and fished the river, Nick will choose to return into the blackened land where, by writing the river as he pictures it in his mind, he faces in himself the possibility that his soul has not only died but has been "permanently scared" by the fiery blast of his wounding at war (JFK, Item #746a, an early-1920s draft of "A Way You'll Never Be"). At the moment when Nick picks up and contemplates the black grasshopper, his soul is just discovering a living world where it can "be" in the full symbolic solidity of that world itself.

Nick stands up, slips his arms through the straps of his pack and settles it on his back, then strikes down the hillside away from the burned land toward the pine plain and the river. "Underfoot the ground was good walking" (180). Where else would the ground be good walking but underfoot? To whom is such a reminder necessary but to himself? What purpose does it serve but consciously to confirm a deep feeling of satisfaction in Nick himself? Here again Nick *feels* a *feeling*.

> Two hundred yards down the hillside the fire line stopped. Then it was sweet
> fern, growing ankle high, to walk through, and clumps of jack pines; a long

undulating country with frequent rises and descents, sandy underfoot and the country alive again.

And Nick alive in it, consciously and unconsciously, in mind and in soul, "I" and "myself" together occupied in the living land: "He broke off sprigs of the heathery sweet fern, and put them under the pack straps. The chafing crushed it and he smelled it as he walked" (181), smelling the smell of the sweet fern as he feels the feel of his pack.

It is almost dark when Nick walks down through the meadow to the silent, smooth, fast-flowing river. In the river swim the trout whose movements will tighten Nick's heart with all the old feeling. As Nick comes down to the river, all up and down it he sees trout feeding on insects that come from the swamp directly across the stream; the insects fly low over the water, some trout leaping far out of the water to take them. "Now as he looked down the river, the insects must be settling on the surface, for the trout were feeding steadily all down the stream. As far down the long stretch as he could see, the trout were rising, making circles all down the surface of the water, as though it were starting to rain" (182). Watching them, Nick finds that he is very hungry.

How simple it would be for Nick to unpack his fishing rod from its leather carrying case and cast for a trout for supper. Casting for and hooking trout had been his primary aim in fishing rivers in memory, in Italy. Here at the Big Two-Hearted, however, things are different. Fishing here is not a matter of hooking trout after trout to pass the time of night. Here it is a matter of tightening the heart into wholeness again, of feeling all the old feeling, even of feeling the feeling of disappointment that would come with the inevitable loss of the big trout. Here, therefore, it is a matter not of casting for trout but of conserving time, the time of the heart tightening with all the old feeling. For heart time is sacred time, time that is reversible, primordial, ontological, neither changing nor exhaustible, and endlessly reintegratable by performing those rites that actualize the world in which he can enter the flow of this time. The reversible time Nick seeks is the time when "all the love" in him went into fishing, as fishing stirred to life all the love there was in him. To cast for a trout at this point and to eat it for supper without first establishing himself in this "good place" where heartfelt fishing can occur, would be for Nick to barge into the sanctuary and wolf down the host at the altar. Here the trout is primarily food for the heart and soul, and he must be as honest as a priest of God in preparing for this meal.

The extent to which Nick's establishment of his camp aims not merely for convenience but for the consecration of space and time to the uses of his heart and soul becomes evident in Nick's thoughts when he crawls inside his tent to put those things at the head of his bed. To settle in his home "where he had made it" is to consecrate this terrain to the uses of his innermost self. Yet the tent and the space it encloses do not merely conform to a preexisting idea in Nick's mind. There had been this to do, an obligation he had foreseen. Unforeseen was the coming of that something "mysterious" that had entered the tent with its making—something not of this physical place merely, but resident here because the tent opens on a dimension beyond historical time. Inside the tent is a homelike space, different from the undifferentiated space outside the tent. Inside the tent, Nick finds himself open to communication on a vertical scale, from above and from below: "Nothing could touch him."

On the level of physical being, as we have seen, this assertion is ridiculous. Many things might and will touch Nick. "Nothing" must refer to something inside Nick and to those things, like thoughts of his dead soul, that *can* touch him in the good place. On the one hand, nothing of the surrounding world can alter the happiness, the homelike feeling, and goodness of being in this tent, "in his home where he had made it." On the other hand, "nothing" *can* touch Nick here, in the good place, because here his soul is wholly at one with his expectations. Here he lies down in the dark and willingly "goes to" sleep. Here he need not fight sleep to hold off its coming. Then, when Nick "goes to" sleep, willingly, they hang Sam Cardinella. (Hemingway inserted interchapter 12 between parts 1 and 2 of "Big Two-Hearted River" where Nick sleeps; Philip Young removed this interchapter from his edition of *The Nick Adams Stories*). For in the good place by the river, in his home where he had made it, thoughts of his blackened soul can touch Nick without driving him to drink, fear, or panic. The question, then, is will Nick's heart, tightened into new wholeness by the feeling of a trout on the line, break again with the rush of disappointment sure to come when he fails to land the big trout? Will his newly tightened heart, beating with the pulse of the big trout on the line, be a conduit of emotions that last? The answer, of course, is implicit in Nick's actions.

When Nick crawls out of his tent after having placed the things at the head of his bed, he finds himself more hungry than ever: "He did not believe he had ever been hungrier." For he has now made his home. He feels the mystery of being in the good place. He knows that nothing can touch him here. *Now* when he eats, food will satisfy the hunger in his soul. He must neither rush his preparations for his meal nor take short cuts, however. He starts a fire, sets up a grill, and puts on the frying pan, opening and emptying and stirring and mixing and then pouring the bubbling beans and spaghetti onto a tin plate, his actions slow and methodical like a priest's at an altar. Then, "There was a good smell" (184). There was not merely the distinct, olfactory aroma of beans and spaghetti, an aroma on the air discrete and strong and identifiable; there was, deep within him, confirmation of his expectation of "a good smell." "He was very hungry" (184):

> All right. He took a full spoonful from the plate. "Chrise," Nick said. "Geezus Chrise," he said happily. He ate the whole plateful before he remembered the bread. Nick finished the second plateful with the bread, mopping the plate shiny. He had not eaten since a cup of coffee and a ham sandwich in the station restaurant in St. Ignace. *It had been a very fine experience*. He had been that hungry before, but had not been able to satisfy it. He could have made camp hours before if he had wanted to. There were plenty of good places to camp on the river. But this was good. (185, emphasis added)

Why had it been a very fine "experience" rather than a very fine "meal"? For the same reason that there had been a very good "smell" rather than merely the pleasing "aroma" of spaghetti and beans, and for the same reason that he had felt the feeling of his heart tightening before he walked "out of the heat" of Seney. There *had* been the aroma of food, a sensation unabstracted, but to call it "a good smell" and the eating of it "a very fine experience" is to render the aroma an abstraction unfelt except in his soul. It is to deepen an event into an experience. Nick had fixed the meal and his soul was the guest who came to dinner. Then, with his hunger satisfied in body and soul, Nick welcomes sleep when he feels it coming. He crawls inside his tent and "goes to" sleep before it arrives to take him, Sam Cardinella and all.

When Nick crawls out of the tent in the early morning and stands, his shoes and trousers in his hands, looking around him, he finds everything in perfect accord with his expectations: "There was the meadow, the river and the swamp. There were the birch trees in the green of the swamp on the other side of the river" (187), a habitat, precise ecology of forms, within and without, and Nick very excited by what he feels in accord with what he sees.

He knows that he must hold his excitement in check until he has made preparations for fishing or it will become *just* fishing. "He was really too hurried to eat breakfast, but he knew he must." He dare not upset the balance of motion and fact that produce the soulful sensations of the good place; he must not let sheer excitement of hooking a trout dictate his actions or the resulting sensations will be ephemeral and fleeting. For it is not trout as game that matters to Nick, as we have seen. It is "feeling" the "feeling" of the trout in his heart; it is harboring the love of that sensation forever in his soul. That is a sensation not to be rushed into or rushed through from sheer excitement. It is a sensation that he must be fully prepared for when it comes. Then he will lose none of it. Nor will he lose himself to it.

When Nick has prepared himself for fishing in the early morning, he goes down over the bank of the river and steps full into the stream. "It was a shock. His trousers clung tight to his legs. *His shoes felt the gravel*. The water was a rising cold shock" (190, emphasis added). Nick's "shoes" feel the gravel on the bottom of the stream. Factually, this is quite impossible, like "nothing could touch him." How can shoes feel? The meaning seems clear enough: through the soles of his shoes, Nick feels the gravel of the stream bed. Then why does not Nick say that? He is very precise about other things. Why does not he describe this event as it actually happens? Perhaps he does. The question might be, what does it mean for shoes to feel?

Nick lives at the bottom of the stream as consciously as he lives above it. He sees and feels and knows the stream from inside himself. On the one hand, he wants the stream in unabstracted feelings, through his physical sensations, so he steps into the river at a point where the water is thigh deep. He has no rubber hip boots or heavy wool socks to blunt the sensation of the smooth rushing, spring-cold water. It is a rising cold shock up his thighs. In the same instant, on the other hand, his shoes feel the gravel because everything is sentient in the world of imagination, as in a dream. Nothing is a mere implement. The river is a living land, a land of symbols. Hence, ritual enactment is the means of gaining access to it; forget or forego one step, or ignore one thing, and the spirit of sacrality is dispelled.

Once in the river, Nick wades with the current toward the middle of the stream. He knows there will be small trout in the shallows and he wants to feel one of them in his heart before he casts for the big one. So he threads a hopper on the hook and drops him into the current. The hopper floats down stream, Nick letting out line, watching him, then he disappears under water and the rod comes "alive" in Nick's hands.

Nick comes "alive" with the rod, pulling and lifting, unhooking and dropping the trout in response to the trout's jerking and pumping, thumping and flashing in the sun. Yet this is a trout hooked, played, and brought in by Nick not for eating but for feeling, for warming up in preparation for the big trout. When the trout drops back into the stream,

he hung unsteadily in the current, then settled to the bottom beside a stone. Nick reached down his hand to touch him, his arm to the elbow under water. The trout was steady in the moving stream, resting on the gravel, beside a stone. As Nick's fingers touched him, touched his *smooth, cool, underwater feeling* he was gone, gone in a shadow across the bottom of the stream. (191-92, emphasis added)

First, Nick's shoes feel the gravel. Then Nick's fingers touch not the trout but its "underwater feeling." What is it to touch an underwater feeling? It is to feel what is in accord with your deepest expectations. It is to feel with the heart. In this first trout Nick has at once feeling with his fingers and feeling with his heart and soul. The trout is a conduit of feeling between body and soul.

However, he does not want this feeling repeatedly. Nick is not there to catch fish after fish. He wants the big trout, the biggest trout he has ever heard of, and with that trout the sensation that transcends all feeling. After feeling the underwater feeling of the first small trout, therefore, Nick wastes no time in going for the big trout under the logs downstream from his camp where the mink had crossed earlier in the day.

Nick "wallows" downstream with the current into water that deepens up his thighs sharply and coldly. He stops at the upper edge of the dammed-back flood above the logs, just where the water becomes smooth and dark. Leaning back against the strong current, he threads a hopper on the hook and spits on him for luck then tosses the hopper out ahead on the fast, dark water. "There was a tug. Nick struck and the rod came alive and dangerous, bent double, the line *tightening*, coming out of water, *tightening*, all in a heavy, dangerous, steady pull" (193, emphasis added). At the railroad bridge, it was the trout that had tightened and Nick's heart that had tightened in response. Now the trout and Nick's heart are joined by a dangerously "tightening" line. The trout holds Nick by his heart on the line with a "dangerous" pull—dangerous in a twofold sense. Either Nick lands the trout and all feeling is drawn out of the river, or the trout breaks free and all feeling is drawn out of Nick's heart.

The trout had the bait and was running with it. Nick's heart feeling stopped with the intensity of emotion on the tightening line, the reel ratcheting into a mechanical shriek, the core of the reel showing as the line runs out, Nick feels the moment when the pressure is too great: "the line tightened into sudden hardness and beyond the logs a huge trout went high out of water" (193). (Why "out of water" rather than "out of *the* water"? Is it because this is a "picture" rather than an actual stream?) The leader had broken, the line went slack, and Nick's tightened heart spun loose from the heightened pitch of feeling to which it had risen on the tightening line. "The thrill had been too much." It left Nick feeling just a little sick and wanting to sit down. He was falling into disappointment. This would be a test of the restorative power of being in the good place. Now Nick's heart would also beat in unison with the other heart of the river.

The disappointment was inevitable because the big trout, like Old Ben of Faulkner's "The Bear," can never be caught and is not meant to be held but momentarily by the hand of man. For it is the feeling of that momentary connection, not the killing of the animal, that is everything. The feeling, if it is of enough intensity, lasts forever. It serves the heart of the innermost self as a power against emotions that threaten disintegration, like disappointment. So when disappointment floods Nick's heart with the loss of the big fish and his heart is in danger of breaking under the intensity of that feeling, his heart holds firm in the "tightening" it has received from the trout on the line.

Nick will not rush the sensation of disappointment either. Nothing *can* touch him here at the river, in the good place. So he sits down on a log across the stream and reorients himself to the good place. There downstream was the sunlight glittering on the ripples of the shallows. There nearby were the big, water-smooth rocks. There along the bank were the cedars. There in the green of the swamp were the white birches. There under him were the logs smooth to sit on, warm and gray to the touch. Under the influence of these sensations, "slowly the feeling of disappointment left him. It went away slowly, the feeling of disappointment that came sharply after the thrill that made his shoulders ache. It was all right now" (194). Nothing *could* touch him. His heart, tightened into wholeness by the big fish, did not break with the "touch" of disappointment when Nick lost the trout. His heart had held firm against the intense downward pull of that emotion.

So there was magic in this river. Here he could wade in the water while he moved in the picture. Here he could fulfill his desire to bathe his head and heart in atmospheres unknown to his feet, even in disappointment of the deepest love in him. From happiness to disappointment, that is, and from landing a trout to losing the big one, Nick's heart had held steady in love. He had felt both hearts of the river, the comic and the tragic, beat in his own, in happiness and in disappointment. At just this point in the narrative Nick notices the swamp, that heart of the river to which he was formerly "dead," as a place where he also must fish in writing—the kind of writing that will "kill" Nick in other ways than disappointment at the loss of fish. In these ways, too, he will find himself that much more "alive again."

In the picture without "On Writing" in it, in place of the conclusion that "On Writing" provided, the swamp appears, that place where the fishing was always tragic. In the story with "On Writing" excluded, rather than follow the desultory flow of his reflections on writing, Nick, his soul holding steady in a tightened heart, now whole, two-hearted, in joy and in sorrow, like the river itself, sits on the logs over the stream and contemplates the picture of the river with the swamp, its other heart, in it:

Ahead the river narrowed and went into a swamp. The river became smooth and deep and the swamp looked solid with cedar trees, their trunks close together, their branches solid. It would not be possible to walk through a swamp like that. The branches grew so low. You would have to keep almost level with the ground to move at all. . . . He did not feel like going on into the swamp. . . . He felt a reaction against deep wading with the water deepening up under his armpits, to hook big trout in places impossible to land them. . . . In the fast deep water, in the half light, the fishing would be tragic. In the swamp fishing would be a tragic adventure. Nick did not want it. (198)

Notice that Nick calls it *a* swamp rather than *the* swamp: "Ahead the river narrowed and went into a swamp." The indefinite article is curious since this is the very swamp that Nick looked across the river into from his camp by the meadow. It is the same swamp against which the birch trees stand out white in the early morning. It is the same swamp the mink crossed into over the logs just below Nick's camp. Yet it becomes *a* swamp as Nick, in the story and walking in the picture, contemplates fishing in it. "It would not be possible to walk through *a* swamp like that."

The swamp is at once an idea and an actuality, like the river, a factual memory in Nick's life and a feature of the terrain of his psyche that he must fish out of love. So, in the stories that logically follow Nick's experience in "Big Two-Hearted River," it is in the tamarack swamp that the brakeman on the freight train knocks Nick into the cinders beside the track, and at the edge of the tamarack swamp that Nick meets Ad Francis and Bugs in "The Battler." It is in the swamp on the far side of Horton's Bay that the limestone foundations of the abandoned saw mill stand up white against the green of the second growth timber as Nick and Marjorie row across the bay in "The End of Something." It is in the swamp that Bill's father hunts, the afternoon of "The Three-Day Blow," when Nick and Bill cut down through the orchard with their shotguns to join him. The swamp is that "flooded ground," that frightening different width of the river, in Nick's recurrent dream of Fossalta in "A Way You'll Never Be." The swamp in the picture of the Big Two-Hearted foreshadows these events in Nick's life.

In the afternoon of fishing the Big Two-Hearted, it seems safe to say, the swamp indicates Nick's recognition of the necessity of making his soulful return into time, of going back to the Illinois shore, and of the need to write, the need to think, other needs, especially to thinking seriously about the war. The swamp is an indefinite presence at the river because the sensations to be had fishing in it all lie ahead of Nick. For him it is no longer a question of avoiding the swamp; it is a matter simply of choosing not to fish it that day: "There were plenty of days coming when he could fish the swamp" (199), as in writing the stories from "Indian Camp" to "A Way You'll Never Be." On another day he would cross the river and go into those trees.

WORKS CITED

Hemingway, Ernest. 1972. *The Nick Adams Stories*. Edited by Philip Young. New York: Scribner's.
Hemingway, Ernest. 1970. *In Our Time*. New York: Scribner's.

THE FANTASIES OF OMNIPOTENCE AND POWERLESSNESS

COMMEMORATION IN HEMINGWAY'S "FATHERS AND SONS"

ERIK NAKJAVANI

IN "FATHERS AND SONS," NICHOLAS ADAMS tells us that "at thirty-eight, he loved to fish and shoot exactly as much as when he first *had gone* with his father. It was a passion that *had never slackened* and he was very grateful to his father for bringing him to know it" (emphasis added).[1] I would say that Nicholas Adams's desire to *commemorate* this enduring passion for fishing and hunting in its close connection with the memory of his father causes him to make the subtle shift from the simple past to the pluperfect past, that is, *the past of the past*. This temporal shift finds its parallel in the change from simple recollection to a past reconstituted through the act of *commemoration*, whose goal is the potentially unlimited evocation of this past. Within the boundaries of what I call Nicholas Adams's own "autobiographical consciousness," Nicholas Adams's mind moves within the interstices of a mode of recollective free association. He compares his father's extraordinary eyesight to a bird of prey, "the eagle" (489), and connects it with his father's superior ability to instruct him in fishing and hunting. So the transcendent ability of Nick's father to see "much farther and much quicker than the human eye sees," a "faculty that surpasses human requirement" (489), is the foundation of his father's initial superior knowledge. As Jean-Paul Sartre discerns, "To know is to devour with the eyes."[2] In other words, to see is one of the foundational constituents of any extensive epistemology.

COMMEMORATION AND THE FANTASY OF OMNIPOTENCE

To know how to fish and to hunt is to become *empowered* in a wholly atavistic and primal sense. This is so because knowledge and power comprise the two sides of the same coin. I would therefore urge that a *specific*, as opposed to exhaustive, reading of Nicholas Adams's passion for hunting and fishing would reveal it as the conscious analog of the subconscious

91

fantasy of omnipotence. As Hemingway clearly states in *Death in the Afternoon*, the killer "has pleasure in taking to himself one of the Godlike attributes; that of giving it. This is one of the most profound feelings in those men who enjoy killing."[3] Hemingway's statement focuses on a particular moment of what Sartre designates as the fundamental project of human individual: "to be God" (Sartre 1956, 566). Similarly, English psychoanalyst Wilfred R. Bion also observes that "references to God betray the operation of 'memories' of the father. The term 'God' is seen to indicate the scale by which the magnitude, wisdom and strength of the father is to be measured."[4]

This universal fantasy of omnipotence as identification with the father points to its own dialectical pole in an absolute "lack," that is, the self (the ego), as Sartre expresses it. "Fundamentally man is *the desire to be*," writes Sartre (Sartre 1956, 565). He goes on to add that this "desire . . . is identical with lack of being" (*manque d'être*) (567). This lack is the dialectical antithesis of the fantasy of omnipotence and its subjacent primary narcissism, whose traces remain and pervade the adult psyche.

I would suggest that what Freud termed the "omnipotence of thoughts" in *Totem and Taboo* reveals its double in the "thoughts of omnipotence" that are only quasi-conscious.[5] Such thoughts no doubt carry an enduring trace of narcissism, because they overvalue the self over the nonself, the world of external reality. This powerful fantasy of omnipotence surges up in conscious human life as passion(s), which is one of the localized and sharply focused modalities of desire in its purest form. The fantasy of omnipotence makes itself manifest in fishing and hunting, as well as in literature and the arts. Both are entwined in Nicholas Adams's life as a writer.

"Fathers and Sons" provides a sharply drawn and convincing if microcosmic example of this control when, bitten "clean through the ball of his thumb" by a squirrel he has wounded, Nick can immediately get rid of "the little bugger" for good by smacking its head against a hemlock tree (490). The killing of the squirrel *magically* stops the threat of its intrusive reality. The power to kill changes the direction of the possibility of *reciprocal violence* into an absolutely *unilateral one*. In this sense, one may indeed claim that the world of the successful hunter (killer) is a *magical* world of total mastery over the hunted. The animal symbolically stands for food and reproductive sexuality. To kill it is, then, to seize and incorporate into the self its powers of survival and continuity. The killer conquers and takes all in the act of killing and enters the fantasy of Godlike invincibility and endless accumulation of power. In this sense, he who kills is permitted to dream limitlessly of the mysteries of *absolute power* and its destructive and creative potentials.

Thus the fantasy of omnipotence seeks the fulfillment of the desire of the self (ego) as the self-sufficient master of the world in identification with the Father, the powerful One. In turn, the fantasy of omnipotence finds its counterpart in the overwhelmingly negative fantasy of powerlessness that external realities draw forth. The former acts as an antidote for the former. Consequently, the power of seemingly untamable outside realities is greatly diminished in and through the fantasy of omnipotence. For Nick, fishing and hunting provide the *first* experience of this fantasy of omnipotence. For him, the realm of fantasy intrudes upon reality in this clearing to halt its rapid, cancerous, paralyzing spread. Later, for Nicholas Adams as a writer, it is within this clearing that the magic of desire as emotion, imagination, myth, and fiction firmly inscribe themselves as the sources of human power within human speech and culture. French phenomenologist Paul Ricoeur tells us that "magic is a technique of desire" and that "the quasi-hallucinatory satisfaction of desire marks the primitive encroachment of desire over reality; henceforth the true meaning of reality is to be achieved in and through this false efficacy of desire."[6] If one places Nick's early passion for fishing and hunting in this context, as I have done, it is easy to comprehend why he eventually becomes a writer as Nicholas Adams. In their largest possible sense, these two enterprises, fishing-hunting and writing, unfold within the same psychic space of the fantasy of omnipotence and mastery of the world and produce their miraculous effects.

In the specific areas of knowledge and instruction of fishing and hunting, Nick's father shows ample evidence of being able to cope with his son's expanding psychic universe while his own appears to be contracting rapidly. The son profoundly appreciates the knowledge he receives. In psychoanalytic terms, one may theorize that Nick internalizes the power his father possesses inasmuch as he learns from him how to fish and hunt. For me, this crucial moment of Nick's recollective appreciation of his father is *memorial*, but not at all in the sense that he memorializes his father as such. He rather *memorializes* and *commemorates* the first instance(s) when, through the mediation of his father's tutelage, his subliminal fantasy of omnipotence is limned in the conscious activities of fishing and hunting. I use commemoration here in its "most ancient" sense of "an *intensified remembering*."[7] I find Nick's mode of commemoration to be the result of a dialectic between commemoration and what Edward S. Casey refers to as "intrapsychic memorialization" (Casey 1987, 218). The "primary operative factor within such memorialization is *identification* understood in Freud's sense of the term" (239), as Casey has remarked, which signifies an identification with the father. I would say that this psychic identification with the father represents the reverse side of the Freudian castration complex.

Nick's commemoration is an evocation of his father's memory to the extent that the father as a knowledgeable and skillful man can initiate his son to the psychical and physical intricacies of fishing and hunting. Through the agency of intrapsychic identification, Nick acquires his father's knowledge and the considerable power that issues from it. "*Knowing*," as Sartre points out "is a form of appropriation" (Sartre 1956, 577) that fills the "lack" that constitutes the divided and beleaguered self. To follow Sartre's formulation, knowing as potentially unlimited appropriation makes it possible to say that "To be man means to reach toward being God" (Sartre 1956, 566). Accordingly, Nick's commemoration of his father as expert fisherman and hunter is also simultaneously a reappropriation of the magical mysteries of the fantasy of omnipotence that dwell in the vestiges of the memories of his father. To remember the dead father-hunter is to make active the latent source of an original endowing psychic power.

The narrative of "Fathers and Sons" begins with the description of a town and its surroundings, presumably in the southern part of the United States. The mnemonics of the southern countryside serves Nick, the *commemorator*, as a substitute for *commemorabilia*, to use Casey's terminology (Casey 1987, 218). However, it is the memory of the father itself that serves as the *commemorandum* (Casey 1987, 218) for Nicholas Adams. Nicholas Adams's complex mode of commemoration (memorialization-identification) ensures in two clear and distinct ways one of the distinguishing characteristics of all commemorative acts: their ceaseless cyclical repetition, in every one of which the past, present, and the possibility of future are integrated, in every one of which the diachronic and synchronic dimensions of commemoration crisscross one another. Nick's commemorative passage fully demonstrates this fundamental cyclical and repetitive pattern. Nick writes that

> His father came back to him in the fall of the year, or in the early spring when there had been jacksnipe on the prairie, or when he saw shocks of corn, or when he saw a lake, or if he ever saw a horse and buggy, or when he saw, or heard, wild geese, or in a duck blind; remembering the time an eagle dropped through the whirling snow to strike a canvas-covered decoy, rising, his wings beating, the talons caught in the canvas. His father was with him, suddenly, in deserted orchards and in new plowed fields, in thickets, on small hills, or when going through dead grass, whenever splitting wood or hauling water, by grist mills, cider mills and dams and always with open fires. (496)

This is a rather long passage, but one can easily locate and point out its commemorative features. The passage as a whole is as solemn as a funeral oration, and essentially yields a ritual of *thanksgiving* as well. All this is as it should be, because, as Casey points out, "*commemorating solemnizes by at once taking the past seriously and celebrating it in appropriate ceremonies*" (Casey 1987, 223). Nick evokes the memory of his father in this passage as a long list of sensual mnemonic elements. They associate his father with the animal and natural worlds and depict him as a kind of Rousseauist character. Nick loves this part of his father's personality and has passionately endeavored to make it his own. Each sensual mnemonic detail of the passage implies a series of commemorative cyclical recurrences, whose evocation honors the dead father to the extent that the son finds it acceptable to identify simultaneously with him and with the fantasy of omnipotence that his memory generates.

It is obvious that Nick's commemoration of his father initially takes place on the *intrasubjective* plane. However, through the alchemy of writing that Nick as the writer-narrator exercises, this commemoration raises itself above the intrasubjective plane and subsequently works on the level of the *intersubjective*. To put it more technically, Nicholas Adams subsequently *textualizes* the original commemorative event and through the mediative role of this textualization he then makes it surpass the limitation of its intrasubjective origin; henceforth it can be *reanimated* and *reenacted* at will by anyone who can read.

The father as "commemorandum" finally reaches his full and permanent status when Nick's own son participates in the commemorative narrative. The fundamental question of hunting arises again when Nick's son asks the salient question: "How old will I be when I get a shotgun and can hunt by myself?" (498). This question is no doubt another way of asking: When will I be the master of *my own world*, the powerful One? Inevitably this inquiry leads to the question, "What was my grandfather like?"

After admitting that his father is "hard to describe," Nicholas Adams unhesitatingly locates the loci of his father's strength and responds: "He was a great hunter and fisherman and he had wonderful eyes" (498). Presently he adds, "He shot very quickly and beautifully. I would rather see him shoot than any man I ever knew" (498). In the context of the notions that I have so far developed, the smoothness of the transition from Nick's praise of his dead father as a hunter to his son's next inquiry, "Why do we never go to pray at the tomb of my grandfather?" (498) is quite natural and expected.

The mythic circle of this cycle of memory and continuity completes itself when Nick, responding positively to his own son's desire to visit the grave of his grandfather, declares: "We'll have to go . . . I can see that we'll have to go" (499). This promise salvages the past by making intelligible its natural link in memory with the present and the future. The pluperfect past of the introductory passages of the short story will now find their complementary counterpart in a promised future perfect. Thus ends the attribute to the man who is *instrumental* in initiating his son into the Godlike mysteries of the hunter's mode of being, "for someone has to give you your first gun or the opportunity to get it and use it" (490). The rest is up to nature *and* society—within whose womb and fold we are born, live, struggle, and make our ontological journey toward death.

SEXUALITY AND THE DIALECTIC OF OMNIPOTENCE AND POWERLESSNESS IN "FATHERS AND SONS"

At the very moment that Nick's fantasy of omnipotence intersects with reality, at the very instance of his experience of "one of the Godlike attributes," the killing of the offensive squirrel, the specter of the father's lack of *total* knowledge and its consequent powerlessness imperceptibly slides into the father-and-son dialogue. Nick's habitual use of the slang expression "the little bugger" (490) pushes the dialogue away from the naturally *empowering* province of hunting to the murky region of sexuality as socio-cultural taboo.

The father explains to Nick, who is unaware of the precise meaning of the word "bugger," that "a bugger is a man who has intercourse with animals" (490). The father's explanation quite reasonably elicits from his son the query, "Why?" The father, who shares the eyesight of the bighorn ram and the eagle, who lives very close to nature as a hunter and a fisherman, can merely reply, "I don't know," but he concludes that "it is a heinous crime" (490).

Nick's father is a man close to nature. He is also a physician, a man of science. His reasoning, however, appears to be far more ethical and religious than scientific. He would certainly have agreed with St. Thomas Aquinas that "the principles of reason are those that are in accordance with nature" and that zoophilia on that basis "is the most serious sin," because "in the case of unnatural vice man violates what has been determined by nature concerning sexuality. . . ."[8] Animals are to be killed, not to have sexual intercourse with. The former establishes unlimited superiority while the latter confirms the social taboos of weakness, perversion, criminality, and sin. Nevertheless, none of this in any way whatsoever answers Nick's authentic and precise question of "why" anyone in fact would have sexual intercourse with an animal. Perhaps the father fears that an answer to this question may well imply an unconscious connection between the violence of the hunt, sexuality, and death.

Nick acknowledges that "that was the sum total of direct sexual knowledge bequeathed him by his father except on one other subject" (490-91).

That other subject is the arrest of Enrico Caruso on the charge of "mashing." To Nick's question, "What is mashing?" comes his father's incantatory reply, "It is one of the most heinous crimes" (491). Finally, the father sums up "the whole matter by stating that masturbation produced blindness, insanity, and death, while a man who went with prostitutes would contract hideous venereal diseases and that the thing to do was to keep your hands off of people" (491). The father's approximation of sexuality, violence (now done to oneself), and death, which has until now been suppressed, is clearly verbalized.

If imparting true knowledge and information prepares a terrain where the knowledgeable and the informed gain power to the extent that they are knowledgeable and informed, providing pseudoknowledge and misinformation creates a void, a negative space, as it were, where power is diminished or lost. The ability of Nick's father to fish and hunt well and to instruct and initiate his son in their ritual performance is a gift that Nick treasures. For Nick, the power to take life, to destroy, is tantamount to a realization of the fantasy of omnipotence. Now, however, the father is unable to guide Nick toward that other source of Godlike attribute, the sexual potency, the power to create and to procreate. Here, Freud's remark that "sexual desires do not unite men but divide them" (Freud 1963, 144) comes readily to mind in its largest and most profound sense.

One may very well claim that the destructive component of the fantasy of omnipotence is less threatening to the father than its sexual and creative one. For him there is no complementarity between the two faces of the fantasy of omnipotence. The Freudian theory of the Oedipus complex would bear witness to the validity of such a conclusion. Pushing the Freudian argument even further, sexologist John Money argues that "it is part of our cultural strategy to obtain children's overall obedience and conformity via all-out veto on eroticism and sex. There is no corresponding all-out veto on aggression and violence. Sex and violence are traded off against one another as negative and positive, respectively."[9] One can define the world of Nick's father as that divided land where a cluster of cultural ethos and religious ethics struggles to maintain its uneasy coexistence with pagan reverence for sexuality as a sacred natural force. If nature represents free play of natural forces, ethics constitutes precisely its radical dialectical pole of restrictions, constraints, and control of such a freedom. Nick's father, operating from within the culturally sanctioned confines of sexual morality and ethics exercises his authority in delineating the limits of his son's freedom to fantasize. Correspondingly, he weakens his son's confidence in him as the bearer of Godlike enabling gifts.

At the very crucial point where Nick's father crosses over from being "sound" on fishing and hunting to being "unsound" on sex, a critical moment emerges that I would characterize as the beginning of a "negative dialectic" in the father and son relationship. Their relationship suddenly begins to *devolve* in ambivalence, even hatred, rather than to *evolve* in filial love. Even though Nick clearly balances his scorn for his father by stating, "on the other hand his father had the finest pair of eyes he had ever seen and Nick had loved him very much and for a very long time" (491), it is quite clear that a profound break or discontinuity occurs in their relationship. In direct defiance of the father's warning that "mashing" is "one of the most heinous crimes," the son resolves "with considerable horror, that when he was old enough he would try mashing at least once" (491). Understandably, Nick then makes it clear that "after he was fifteen he had shared nothing with him [his father]" (496). Something is irrevocably lost between the father and the son. It is truly "the end of something," a "something" that has considerable significance for both.

What is lost forever is no more and no less than the son's illusion of identification with the father as omnipotent. The discovery of the inadequacy of the father is a lasting menace to Nick's own fantasy of being in control of the world around him. It is the father as ethical man, as man in alliance with society's taboos rather than instinctual forces, who fails. The failure of the father makes his absent presence in memory "not good remembering" (491) for the writer Nicholas Adams. A fundamental illusion is shattered for Nick. In its wake the loss of this illusion carries serious threats to Nicholas Adams's fantasy of omnipotence as a writer. This threat has significant consequences for his whole life project; that is to say, for his self-image as a Godlike fisherman-hunter, writer-to-be, and writer. In conjunction with identification with his father, remembering him as a failure is not merely "not good remembering," it potentially spells disaster for Nicholas Adams, the writer. It is *punitive remembering*. A series of memories that depict the father more and more disparagingly now unfolds in the narrative of Nick's relationship with his father. The visual images of his father abruptly give way to pervasive olfactory images. Nick—who has a remarkable sense of smell and only likes the smell of his sister Dorothy in the family—recalls that his father "sweated very much, in hot weather," that he "loved his father but hated the smell of him" (496). He confesses that "it made him feel sick" when he was forced "to wear a suit of his father's underwear" (496). Ann Edwards Boutelle speculates that, at least partially, "It is the smell of sex, of adult paternal sex" that Nick smells in the father's underwear and that makes him sick.[10] The connection she makes between the father and adult sexuality is on the mark because sex constitutes a veritable problematic for Nick in relationship to his father. The father's so-called sexual knowledge and authority translate for Nick into hyperbolic proscriptions *against* sex rather than simple prescriptions *for* enhancement of its potency, its safe use, and its fulfillment; in short, the father's sexual knowledge at best inhibits and at worst negates Nick's own sexuality. The narrative of the story of Nick's being forced to wear his father's malodorous underwear, his claim of having lost it, his being punished for it in the woodshed, reaches its climactic intensity in Nick's patricidal declaration: "I can blow him to hell. I can kill him" (496). This is clearly a dramatic moment of Nick's Oedipal fantasy as an omnipotent hunter-killer.

This remarkably Oedipal moment, for me, however, is more a matter of *tyrannycide* than of patricide. Perhaps these two desires share the same psychic origin. In any case, it is the *tyranny* of a father who denies his son the sexual and creative part of the fantasy of omnipotence who has to be eliminated in and by the same fantasy. Put more precisely, it is the father perceived as *arresting* the growth of his son's fantasy of omnipotence in its most extensive (read destructive as well as creative) sense that has to be blown to hell, with the very gun that his father has provided him. Significantly, Nick acknowledges that he feels "a little sick about it being the gun his father had given him" (497). The Oedipus complex would lose its considerable tragic sense without its deep ambiguities and ambivalences.

Indeed, the expression of love for his father constitutes the constant in Nick's narrative in "Fathers and Sons." It is in no way a seamless love, a whole and indivisible love, but love, nevertheless. This filial love, which we have no reason to find insincere or bogus, is consistently, however, coincidental only with the father's memory as the sound fisherman-hunter-tutor. Since Nick gives equal weight to his father's soundness on fishing and hunting and his unsoundness on sex, it is justifiable to conclude that the latter for him represents an equally strong and enduring passion. To round off the argument advanced earlier, one may assert that this is the reason his love for his father carries in its innermost being a dark and relentless resentment. What Nick cannot share with his father after the age of fifteen is precisely his *other* passion, his sexuality.

The "unsound" father represents, then, the Other to Nick, the symbolic sum of all that withholds sexual potency. Nick equates the "unsound" father with powerlessness and emasculation. He portrays his father as sentimental, unlucky, trapped, and betrayed by all. Ironically, the hunter-father dies "in a trap that he had helped only a little to set . . ." (489-90). Nick's final image of him is that of the absolute powerlessness of his face in death, an object for an undertaker's art, a still life (in French, interestingly, *nature morte*). Nick reveals to the reader that "The undertaker had only made certain dashingly executed repairs of doubtful artistic merit. That face had been making itself and being made for a long time" (491).

The undertaker's skill in mortuary arts manages sheerly to complete a funereal mask that had been in the molding stage "for a long time."

As Jackson J. Benson has perceptively put it, "The father's life in ["Fathers and Sons"] emerges as an archetypal pattern, a design for man's fate—even a prediction, personally, socially, and metaphysically."[11] If the saying that "power corrupts" is true, one may also justifiably claim that the obverse side of that saying is also true: powerlessness equally corrupts. In a certain sense, human powerlessness becomes total in death. In his father's life and death Nick finds an intimation of the elusiveness of potency in its absolute sense. It is exactly this impossibility of the realization of the fantasy of omnipotence that makes Sartre declare that "man is a useless passion" (Sartre 1956, 615). The world is badly made for those who desire to be God—except, perhaps, for the truly great creative artists who reign in the created universe of their imagination as omniscient and omnipotent. This is precisely the world where Nicholas Adams lives.

NOTES

1. Ernest Hemingway, *The Short Stories of Ernest Hemingway* (New York: Scribner's, 1954), 496. Further references to this work appear in the text.
2. Jean-Paul Sartre, *Being and Nothingness: An Essay On Phenomenological Ontology*, trans. Hazel E. Barnes (New York: Philosophical Library, Inc., 1956), 578.
3. Ernest Hemingway, *Death in the Afternoon* (New York: Scribner's, 1932), 233.
4. Wilfred R. Bion, *Second Thoughts: Selected Papers on Psycho-analysis* (London: William Heinemann Medical Books, 1967), 144.
5. Sigmund Freud, *Totem and Taboo: Some Points of Agreement between Mental Lives of Savages and Neurotics*, trans. and ed. James Strachey (New York: W. W. Norton and Company, Inc., 1963), 85-86.
6. Paul Ricoeur, *Freud and Philosophy: An Essay on Interpretation*, trans. Denis Savage (New Haven: Yale University Press, 1970), 237.
7. Edward S. Casey, *Remembering: A Phenomenological Study* (Bloomington: Indiana University Press, 1987), 217.
8. St. Thomas Aquinas, *St. Thomas Aquinas on Politics and Ethics*, trans. Paul E. Sigmund (New York: W. W. Norton and Company, 1988), 80.
9. John Money, *Love and Lovesickness: The Science of Sex, Gender Difference, and Pair-Bonding* (Baltimore: The Johns Hopkins University Press, 1980), 152.
10. Ann Edwards Boutelle, "Hemingway and Papa: Killing the Father in the Nick Adams Fiction," *Journal of Modern Literature* 9 (1981-82): 145.
11. Jackson J. Benson, *Hemingway: The Writer's Art of Self-Defense* (Minneapolis: University of Minnesota Press, 1969), 14.

WORKS CITED

Casey, Edward S. 1987. *Remembering: A Phenomenological Study.*
Bloomington: Indiana University Press.

Freud, Sigmund. 1963. *Totem and Taboo: Some Points of Agreement between Mental Lives of Savages and Neurotics.* Translated and edited by James Strachey. New York: W. W. Norton and Company, Inc.

Sartre, Jean-Paul. 1956. *Being and Nothingness: An Essay On Phenomenological Ontology.* Translated by Hazel E. Barnes. New York: Philosophical Library, Inc.

LEAVING MICHIGAN BEHIND

HEMINGWAY AND THE LIMITS OF BIOGRAPHY

AN EXCHANGE ON THE "JIMMY BREEN" MANUSCRIPT BETWEEN MICHAEL REYNOLDS AND LINDA WAGNER-MARTIN, WITH AUDIENCE COMMENT

Frederic J. Svoboda: I am supposed to somehow introduce Mike Reynolds and Linda Wagner-Martin to you. It makes me want to run for cover. But I will tell you a little about where they're coming from and the format of what we're going to do this evening. You probably know that Mike Reynolds writes biographies, and he has very nearly completed the third volume of his continuing biography of Hemingway. What he is going to do tonight is to talk about an aspect of that biography and tell us something about the "Jimmy Breen" manuscripts. He will lead us through that, and then Linda Wagner-Martin, who also knows something about biography—has dealt with the difficulties of biography, including Olwyn Hughes—is going to give a response, and then we'll throw things open if we have time at the end of the meeting for discussion. So, with no further ado, Michael Reynolds.

[applause]

Michael Reynolds: There's always that panicky moment when you look under the podium to see if your paper is there where you left it. It is appropriate of course that we are here this evening at this place, with this audience, to discuss Ernest and his work. It is also appropriate, I might add, that we are here with Bob Martin and Linda, his wife, who met at the first of the Michigan conferences. Is that not correct?

Linda Wagner-Martin: Yes.

Reynolds: And subsequently got married. [applause] And they're still married. So. . . .

Permission to reprint Michael Reynolds's "A Half-Slain Knight's Gambit: Or A Little Information on the Last Unpublished and Partially Unfinished Hemingway Novel You Are Ever Unlikely to Read," which is expanded in Reynolds's *Hemingway: Homeward Bound* (Basil Blackwell, 1992), granted by Basil Blackwell, Ltd.

I am working on the last chapter of volume three of the ongoing saga of Ernest Hemingway becoming the writer that he became, and what this is this evening is a work in progress. But before I tell you about it, before I read it, I want you to know how I came to read the so-called "Jimmy Breen" manuscript, because I don't want everybody bombarding the Kennedy Library with requests, because you've got to understand first of all what you have to do in order to read that manuscript. First of all, between *The Sun Also Rises*, published in 1926, and *A Farewell to Arms*, published in 1929, we all know that Hemingway began and then set aside a novel variously referred to as the "Jimmy Breen" novel or, *A New-Slain Knight*. The name Jimmy Breen does not appear in chapters one through twenty or in the revised chapter nineteen, I think it is. It only appears once in the entire manuscript and that is in one revised chapter, chapter two. How this got to be called the "Jimmy Breen" manuscript, I do not know. The kid's name is Jimmy Crane to start with. I don't know what the father's name is, because he is never named. Maybe Stevie. I don't know. And then it's changed to Jimmy House, as you'll see as we go through it. Most of us know that this manuscript has remained closed at the Kennedy Library by the Hemingway estate. Well I, "pleading my belly" as it were, I appealed to the Hemingway estate that I could not leave out five months of Hemingway's creative life and do a literary biography. I just couldn't do that. The other biographies have finessed it one way or another or said something about it. Much of it hasn't helped a whole lot. Let me say right off by the way—I've heard this somewhere—this is *not* an Oak Park novel. It has nothing to do with Oak Park. Period. It does briefly end up in Chicago, but not in Oak Park.

In reply I got a letter from the family lawyer saying that sure I could read the manuscript if I would sign the enclosed legal agreement. And he advised me to consult a lawyer before I signed the enclosed legal agreement. I read it five times and then I—I'm in Santa Fe this year writing—and I got ahold of one of the best copyright lawyers in the United States, in Santa Fe, unlikely, and also with the unlikely name of Sol Cohen. From Queens . . . who has been living there for twenty-five years, and so I talked to him on the phone and he said that for a hundred and eighty-five dollars and sixty-four cents, he would tell me. He would give me an hour of his time (that includes the tax) and explain to me what it was that I was or was not signing. And essentially what the legal document was . . . by signing it I made myself financially liable if by reading the manuscript I in any way reduced its financial value. How one would determine what its financial value would be to start with I do not know. But that's what I signed. Sol said, if it's not crucial don't sign it. He said, "There's a risk involved." [laughter]

I got an hour's lecture, history on copyright law, invaluable. He said, if it's really important, sign it. Take out an insurance policy. So that is what I'm doing. If you want to read the manuscript, you could probably write the estate and take out an insurance policy and read it. I'm not sure that it's absolutely worth it.

That is my preamble. And like Huck, I'm not going to tell you everything, but what I'm going to read to you in my amble is an excerpted portion of the chapter in the biography volume three that'll be out next fall that deals with the writing of the manuscript. You'll have to forgive my rhetoric. This is written to be read with your eye, not with your ear, and so it sounds a little overstated at times.

To set out the framework, the year is 1927, Ernest has just divorced Hadley and married Pauline. They have returned to Paris from their honeymoon followed by their long summer in Spain. He has written only one short story in the preceding ten months and he's now worrying about what the next book is going to be, which he knows has *got* to be good. And he is smarting under the criticism that he doesn't write fiction, that he doesn't create characters, but he only writes down what his acquaintances say and do. That's irritating. Pauline is worried, because he hasn't written anything but "Hills Like White Elephants," and that was on their honeymoon. You can visualize that breakfast scene:

"Sweetie, I want to read you this story I've just finished."
"Oh, Ernie, it's a lovely story, just what a new bride wants to hear."

She is worried that he's not writing, because he was before he married her, and now he seems to have stopped and he's having trouble getting started. Therefore . . . that's where they are in the biography . . . so return with me now if you will to those daring days of yesteryear when the franc was twenty-five francs to the dollar, when a Paris apartment was thirty dollars a month, and when college professors on average made less than three thousand dollars a year. I'm calling this (Phil Young would love this), I'm calling this:

A Half-Slain Knight's Gambit
Or
A Little Information on the Last Unpublished and Partially Finished
Hemingway Novel You Are Ever Unlikely to Read

In the fall of 1927, there were plenty of violent signs pointing to political unrest across Europe, but traveling Americans were not interested in the message unless it interfered with their private lives. Taking a break from manipulating the stock market, Charley Mitchell, the brains behind National City Bank, discovered "little tension" while visiting in Italy, and declared Mussolini to be much admired in the States.[1] Whenever possible, you left politics at home, where there was only one burning question: what did presidential incumbent Calvin Coolidge really mean when he said, "I do not choose to run"?

On the first of October, having spent the previous week entertaining another of Pauline's rich uncles, Ernest read back through the novel he started two weeks earlier. It was going "very well," he told his mother-in-law, Mary Pfeiffer. "I think [it] will keep me going every day until we will go to the mountains and ski and rinse out the head on the inside if possible and then start re-writing in a couple of months. Whether to go to America before or after that is finished is sort of a problem. You see when you are not working for anyone, but only in your head, and not writing down something that has happened but making it all up entirely, you get careful about going to new places while the work is going on because if one morning the head doesn't work and you can't make anything up, you are through."[2] Not knowing where the novel was going, he was serious about keeping to a set routine. Each morning he sat down in his new writing room, putting pencil to paper, creating what he first called "A New Slain Knight."

In March of the previous year, when he thought he would next write "a picaresque novel for America" about Red Ryan's escape from the Kingston prison, that was the title he chose. It was going to be a story of a "tough kid lucky for a long time and finally smashed by fate." In his notebook he told himself, "Criminals are not diseased men. We are all criminals. The criminal is simply a more normal, better coordinated man. In the old days he was the professional fighter." Then in parentheses he reminded himself that "This is horseshit."[3] He still liked "A New Slain Knight" well enough to use it nineteen months later on his opening page, but he crossed that out early to call the new book simply:

A Novel

Chapter One
In Which Goodbye Is Said To The Old Places in the First Person[4]

It began at Walloon Lake, the heart of his first mature fiction and some of his best stories, began in the cottage where he lived every summer of his early years. Only now it was fall, when his father closed Windemere for the season, capping the chimney to keep out the squirrels, boarding up the windows for winter. Ernest did not know that routine, for his father always did it alone. Now in Paris, exactly when Clarence Hemingway was closing the family cottage, Ernest was with him in his fiction, making it up lovingly, remembering all the sounds and smells of lake and woods, saying goodbye to a part of his life he missed deeply.

The invented story was of father and son, the best kind of story he knew, one he returned to frequently, trying to make up for his own father who disappeared from his summer life when Ernest most needed him. Dr. Hemingway's long and losing battle with his "nervous condition," as the children called it, began early, making him an increasingly moody and sometimes dark person, remote and demanding. By the time Ernest was twelve, the best days with his father were passed, leaving the son to wonder what had gone wrong and the father to wrestle with the demons of depression and paranoia.[5] In early October when he received his father's latest letter, Hemingway must have smiled. The Doctor, writing about Bumby's visit to Oak Park, said, "Surely hope you can bring him up with the love for Nature and fine ideals. How we would rejoice to have him with you at Windemere some summer."[6] That's what he was doing all right, there on the penciled pages, letting father and son say goodbye to the lake. Only the invented father was part of himself and so was the son. He liked having it both ways, doubling himself up, then and now; at least here he could be sure of why things were happening.

The imagined boy, Jimmy Crane, grew up on the lake, never having to go back to Chicago and never knowing much about his strange father or his missing mother. Now the boy was leaving the lake for a road life which he did not understand and which his father did not explain. They close up the cottage, load their meager belongings into the motor boat, and push off from the dock with Jimmy running the boat. "When I looked back," he said, "the dock and the boat house were out of sight and there was only the point with three crows walking on the sand and an old log half covered in the sand and ahead the open lake."[7] That was the same point where Marge left Nick in "The End of Something," the same log Dick Boulton started to saw up in "The Doctor and the Doctor's Wife;" the crows were the same hungry three stropping their beaks in the "Twa Corbie," the source of his title:

> In behint yon auld fail dyke
> I wot there lies a new-slain knight
> And naebody kens that he lies there
> But his hawk, his hound, and his lady fair.
> His hound is to the hunting gane,
> His hawk to fetch the wild-fowl hame,
> His lady's ta'en anither mate,
> So we may mak our dinner sweet.[8]

That's the kind of story it was going to be, Jimmy's father against the world with no one but the boy for support, no hawk, no hound, no wife— a curious story for a newly remarried man to be writing.

All that October, he held to his routine, writing in the mornings, biking in the afternoons, seeing almost no one, answering as few letters as possible, saving everything for his fiction. It was like the summer of *The Sun Also Rises*, when pages piled up so easily that his moments of self-doubt seemed foolish. A few name changes as usual, a blotted line or two, but he made no substantive revisions as the story line followed the train tracks from northern Michigan to Chicago to New York. It was a story of double focus: the education of the young boy, Jimmy Crane, who knew little of the urban world, and the survival of his father, a professional revolutionist of such repute that the State Department would no longer allow him an American passport. Jimmy, the tyro, narrated the story while his father and other male tutors taught him rules of the road.

Mostly what his father taught him was to pay attention to significant details, memorizing the scene. "Notice everything you can," he says. "Remember everything you see. Draw any conclusion you want. But never know anything when a thing is going on."[9] On the train to Chicago there were two detectives, each with a criminal handcuffed to his wrist. Jimmy watched them carefully, but at the Cadillac lunch stop, he missed the significant action. When the one prisoner irritated his captor enough that the detective began to cuff him about the face, Jimmy did not keep his eye the criminal's hands.

> "Well," my father said. "While the sergeant hit him in the face with the handcuff on his right hand he picked up a steel-bladed knife off the table with his left hand and put it in his pocket."
>
> "I didn't see."
>
> "No," my father said. "Every man has two hands, Jimmy. At least to start with. You ought to watch them both if you're going to see things."[10]

As they go forward to the smoker where the two detectives are holding their prisoners, the question is whether to say anything about the knife. Jimmy says "No." His father allows that it is "an ethical question," but keeps silent. When the prisoner knifes his captor in the men's room and escapes through the window, Jimmy says he doesn't know what to think about their silence. His father replies, "Neither do I."

Jimmy and the reader do not know what to think about a lot of things, but particularly about a father who feels more akin to criminals than the police, a father who regularly and religiously drinks too much, a father who cannot tell his son or anyone else the complete truth. Jimmy thinks they are going to Canada, but instead it's New York via Chicago. In Chicago his father tells the cab driver they are going to Europe, which is news to Jimmy. His father also says they are going to a hotel, but instead they arrive at the butler-attended house of a rich aunt. "It's a hotel in the French sense," his father tells him. "Hotel de Crane." From his Aunt Ruth and his father, Jimmy learns that he was born in Paris and that his mother still lives there: curious information for a fourteen-year-old not to know about himself. His father, carefully and at regular intervals decanting his apparently bottomless bottle of Scotch into a pocket flask, sips his way through the afternoons and evenings, a man with a murky past and vague future. Having lived too long on the losing side of revolutions, he trusts no one, not even his son. He explains to Jimmy that he does not tell him more "because someone might question you sometime in a very nasty way they have of questioning people and what you don't know you can't tell."[11]

The father is full of advice, some of it less than helpful. "Thinking," he tells his son, "ruins a boy. Thinking and masturbation." Jimmy, again somewhat strangely, does not know what masturbation is. "It's something like thinking," his father tells him. When his father finds Jimmy kissing the secretary in the family lawyer's office where he has gone to raise money, he becomes angry, forgetting he told his son that he had to learn more about women. "If you want to please me don't kiss anybody at all for a while yet," the father says. Three days later when Jimmy tries to kiss his aunt's maid, he gets his face slapped.[12] The further Hemingway developed the story, the more Jimmy began to age, until he finally sounded more like a teenager and less like Bumby, but something remained fundamentally wrong about his voice and the naive questions he asked. Reading back over the first eight chapters, Hemingway wrote himself a note: "Re-write all Chicago stuff after arrival—eliminate all the shit."[13] The next day he took time to write Archie MacLeish:

Papa has been working like a son of a bitch and has nine—count them but don't read them—chapters done. Is going well, reaping the results of the long layoff. Been back three weeks or so, haven't been in bed later than 10 o'clock—seen nobody—working all the time.[14]

That he was writing was more important than any flaws in the fiction, and unlike *The Sun Also Rises*, he was making it all up. Jimmy and his dad were living the secret, male road-life that Ernest, at fourteen, never had with his own father. Here he was able to imagine both fictive father and son, creating his revolutionist from his reading and his acquaintance with Charles Sweeney, a soldier of fortune for whom war and revolution were money in the bank. Hemingway's fictional father was a homeless road man, on the move and unencumbered by wife, property, or conventional morals, a man without fixed political allegiance who could accept family money from the lawyer without accepting the system that produced the money.

Mr. Crane, still without a first name, was a recognizable product of his creator's penchants and the political times. All his life, Ernest read about and admired secret codes, clandestine operations, and clever spies. He lived in the age of the provocateur, when it took only three to make a Russian revolution, or one to light a fuse. That summer in Boston, Sacco and Vanzetti were held guilty of armed robbery and murder but were executed largely for their socialist/anarchist beliefs. In Spain, while touring bull rings and cathedrals, Hemingway could not avoid talk of revolution, which reappeared in the *Herald*'s October 3 headlines:

POLITICAL COUP FAILS IN SPAIN
Two Army Officers Charged With Launching Attack on De Rivera
Within the next week, bungled revolutions appeared daily in the *Herald*.

October 5
BULLETS HALT MEXICAN COUP
General Sarrano and Fifteen Followers Shot by Federal Firing Squad

October 8
BULGARIAN BANDS ATTACK SEVERAL SERBIAN VILLAGES
Soviet Spy Plot Bared In Vienna As Doctor Is Held

In Nicaragua, American Marines relentlessly pursued General Sandino's guerillas, the Sandinistas, who opposed the conservative, pro-American government. By 1927 the twentieth-century agenda was well in place: the socialist/communist Left in conflict with the fascist/capitalist Right. With graffiti obvious on broken walls throughout the hemisphere and political unrest increasing, Hemingway's revolutionist was an astute choice for his fiction. The only question was, could he imagine the fugitive life fully enough to make it plausible?

The day after he wrote MacLiesh, Hemingway took Mr. Crane and Jimmy to a west-side Chicago kitchen where six Italian men are eating pasta and drinking Chianti. Jimmy learns to roll his pasta on his fork and listens to the men argue about the best way for his father to slip back into Italy. One says to go by way of Modana. Another says it is better to come down the lake by boat from Switzerland and on into Milan. Finally they ask Mr. Crane if he wants to see "the old man," which he does. Jimmy follows his father into a bedroom where a white-haired old man with

dark skin and "a purple bulge like a small grape" on one side of his nose
is lying in bed. Crane apologizes for Jimmy's stare, telling the *capo* that
he has taught his son to be observant. "You're not going to Italy are
you?" the old man asks. Crane says he isn't. "It's a country I no longer
care about." But when asked where he will go, Crane is noncommittal.
"Quite right," the old man tells him. "I wouldn't mention it in your
place. I only asked from curiosity." When asked how many revolutions he
has seen, Crane says "Twelve." At conversation's end, Crane gives the old
man $100 cash for a false passport. As he and Jimmy leave, the old man
says, "I hope you have a long life, settle down and stop all this nonsense."[15]

For six weeks the story flowed effortlessly. Then one morning it began
to lose its energy, and he did not know why any more than he knew how it
started. Several weeks passed before he completely lost its pulse, but looking back over the pages, he could see it turning away from the central issue
of Crane the revolutionist. "Cut out all the shit in these last two or three
chapters," he told himself in the margin.[16] Changing the name from Crane
to House did not help. Each day he went into his surgery, trying to save it,
and each day the patient grew worse. There was too much talk and not
enough action as the narrative weight fell more and more on the boy
whose sometimes precocious remarks were wearing thin. On the New
York train Ernest had the night porter and the dining car chef do a little
minstrel show routine, a little buck and wing, ending with slapstick echoes
from Hamlet. "But my God, Jimmy," the porter said, "the only thing that
saves a man is to have a view point."[17]

On October 14, *Men Without Women* was published in New York. By
the first of November, when the New York reviews began to appear in
Paris, Ernest's writing had come to a halt. Most did not see what he was
doing in the stories, or did not appreciate it if they did, damning him either
roundly or, worse, with faint praise. Hemingway wrote Fitzgerald that he
had seen the reviews of Burton Rascoe, Virginia Woolf, and a couple of
others. "These goddamn reviews are sent to me by my 'friends,'" he com-
plained, "any review saying the stuff is a pile of shit I get at least 2000
copies of. . . . Am thinking of quitting publishing any stuff for the next 10
or 15 years."[18] The reviews, he said, were ruining his writing. To
Fitzgerald, he bravely maintained that his novel was alive and well at
50,000 words when it was actually stalled at about 30,000 since late
October.

During the first week of November, he and Pauline went to Berlin for
the six-day bike races, stayed ten days, bought a painting at Alfred
Flechtheim's gallery, and shared a meal with Sinclair Lewis and Ramon
Guthrie.

When the Hemingways returned to Paris, he reread the sixteen chapters of his novel, which seemed "all right part of the time" and at other times seemed like "horse manure."[19] On Thanksgiving day, while Americans in Paris were eating their turkey, Hemingway wrote Max Perkins that he had about a third of the book—seventeen chapters—done. "I'm putting it in the third person now—got tired of the limitations of the bloody first person—always thinking in one person's head, etc. and the changing is difficult but I think will improve it very much."[20] The shifting voice improved the narrative flow, but it could do nothing for Hemingway's basic dilemma about the story's direction. If Mr. Crane, who was now Mr. House, was the story's center then Ernest needed more information about revolutionists than he had at hand. If the story was about the education of Jimmy House/Crane, then he needed to get on with his schooling.

On the streets of New York and in the third person, he had Jimmy's father giving his son dubious advice about how to recognize and deal with homosexuals, a subject about which he seemed to worry a good deal. Testing out his father's wisdom, Jimmy found it of little practical use when approached by the very gay Mr. Elwyn, who had none of the characteristics Jimmy had been warned against: mincing walk, plucked eyebrows, and elongated face. The interlude then took Hemingway further afield to Glenway Wescott and homosexual writers. Jimmy's father, who knew far too much about writers for any soldier of fortune, said that homosexuals made good interior decorators but second-rate writers because they had to fake the love scenes between men and women. Even good American writers did not last long due to crossbreeding. "Sometimes you get one that . . . doesn't go ga-ga at forty five. But lots of American writers are through before they're thirty and most of them are finished by forty five."[21] As Jimmy says about his father,

> If he ever got started on writers and books he was liable to go on forever and I could never change him. He was interesting about wars or hunting or fishing or fairies or people or places but he was never interesting about writers or books.[22]

Trying to amuse and please his father, the boy falls back on proven topics: how to talk to whores and how to recognize homosexuals, none of which was getting them any closer to a revolution. Hemingway stopped at Chapter Twenty, boggled, unable to get his characters on the boat to Europe.

The less than ecstatic reviews of *Men Without Women* did not kill the new novel, but coming as they did when Hemingway's confidence was shaky and his story bogged down, the critics were more influential on his career than they knew. As Ernest was packing the pencil manuscript into his bags for the Christmas trip to Gstaad, a letter arrived from Max Perkins enclosing an ad for *Men Without Women* filled with great quotes and headlined somewhat mendaciously: "Not one harsh note in the critical chorus." At the center of the ad was the silhouetted bull from the dust jacket, only his phallus seemed to glow with incandescent virility. "Only ten thousand bulls got loose in this heated condition," Max said, "and those in the provinces. Heaven protect simple minded cattle there. And it seems to be a fact that the divinity that so strangely shaped *this* end was chance."[23] A second letter came from Hemingway's old war buddy, Bill Horne, whom he had not seen since 1921. Bill said:

> I wish you would do over again, now, some of those early stories you wrote right after we got to Chicago. . . . The world is reading war stuff now, nine years afterwards, as we decided long ago they would. . . . Give it a whirl again.[24]

It was good advice but bad timing, what with Christmas shopping, last minute crises, and Ernest's customary sore throat, all of which left his writing lurched and left him less than receptive to literary advice. On December 13, with all of Paris frozen in its sleep, Ernest, Pauline, and Bumby boarded once again the night train to Switzerland. Included in his entourage were Mr. House and his boy from Horton Bay, fathers and sons a long way from home.

As soon as he and his family got on the overnight coach, nothing went right. Within a week he wrote Fitzgerald that he was suffering from blindness, piles, flu, and a toothache which combined to bring his new novel to a halt.

> Had 20 chapters done . . . then got sick . . . just grippy in the head so I couldn't write—then came down here with Bumby and Pauline to get healthy and at Montreux on the way down Bumby when I picked him up in the night to put him on the pot stuck one of his fingers in my right eye and the nail went in and cut the pupil . . . it was my one good eye and I've been in bed and shot to hell one way or another ever since.[25]

It was essentially the same letter he wrote to Waldo Pierce, Ezra Pound, and Guy Hickok; in fact he wrote so many letters from Gstaad that their very number made light of his proclaimed inability to write. Hickok was not impressed with the excuses. "I didn't know Ernest had only one good eye. I know he had only one good leg and I suspected that maybe some of his other organs that are ordinarily found in pairs had been reduced by half, but I never suspected that he had a bum eye."[26]

By the time Hemingway returned to Paris in mid-February, 1928, his frozen radiator pipes were not fixed and neither was his mind, which continued to struggle with the story of the revolutionist and his son. Mr. House and Jimmy remained in the New York hotel looking no different than when he left them there. He fiddled with the manuscript, making minor ink corrections and a few excisions, but nothing of consequence. When it would not write, he caught up on old news and read *Lawrence and the Arabs*, *Recollections of the Irish War*, and *The Riddle of the Irish*, looking desperately for some help on his stalled fiction.[27] A residue from the ski trip was a lovely head cold which in Paris deteriorated into the grippe. "Have been trying to work every morning," Hemingway wrote Perkins, "but all my production seems to be from the nose."[28] The operative word was "trying," for there was little to show for his efforts.

"I should have gone to America two years ago when I planned," he confessed to Perkins. "I was through with Europe and needed to go to America before I could write the book that happened there."[29] Quite defensively, Hemingway ticked off several good reasons that his new novel would not be finished for the fall season. But he was talking to himself, not to Max, for the only pressure to finish the novel was self-generated, and the remorse he felt resulted from his own need to reestablish continually his identity as a writer.

That is when, quite literally, the roof fell in. The *Herald* reported:

Hemingway Cut In Skylight Crash

Mr. Ernest Hemingway, author who was wounded about the head when a skylight crashed on him at his home Sunday [March 4] morning, yesterday was recovering, according to officials at the American Hospital at Neuilly. Mr. Hemingway's wound, which required three stitches inside and six outside, is healing and he was able to pursue his usual life.[30]

What the paper could not report was the odor of his blood as it streamed across his face, or the pricking of the surgeon's needle closing the wound. He had not seen so much of himself exposed since the night in Italy when the mortar blast turned his right knee to jelly, filling his boot with blood. Giddy with shock, he tried to explain to Archie in the night cab streaking to the hospital how the blood tasted and how the smell of it was like being in the ambulance again with the men dripping in the back, but it all came out wrong. The stranger's face in the hospital mirror was too white to be his own, and the bandage swathing his head too large for civilian times.

Pauline met him at the street door, his bandaged head glowing in the dark, took him in hand and put him to bed, from which he arose early that Sunday afternoon a new man. There was no explanation for it, no logical reason that his blood had set him free. It simply did. When the pain dulled to the opiate's control, he knew exactly what he should be writing. The story had been there all along, ever since the manuscripts disappeared in the Gare de Lyon. The story was the war, the wound, the woman. He knew part of the story by heart, and better yet, he knew exactly where it started looking out on the dusty road with troops marching past the window and the dust rising and the leaves falling. Two weeks later he told Perkins that he was suddenly getting "a great kick out of the war and all the things and places. . . . My wife says that she will see that I'm bled just as often as I can't write—judging by the way it's been going this last week."[31] For nine months while the magic was elsewhere, he struggled doggedly with Jimmy and his father. Now that was over. Without regret and never looking back, he abandoned them there in New York, waiting for a boat that never came.

Wagner-Martin: The line between life and art is often faint, and just as often blurred; in the business of Hemingway criticism and biography, that line sometimes disappears entirely. As Professor Reynolds's paper has proved, knowing the "Jimmy Breen" manuscript is crucial to our comprehending what Hemingway's concerns were in those late-twenties years, the time period between *The Torrents of Spring* and *The Sun Also Rises* and *A Farewell to Arms*. I agree with Professor Jobst from yesterday's program that Hemingway was probably most comfortable writing about a male world, uncomplicated, unmuddied, by the presence of women. This *is* the "Jimmy Breen" story. Let me quote a passage from the manuscript of "Big Two-Hearted River" to show an early image of that conflict, Hemingway's love for the male world unable to exist simultaneously with his love for a woman—here, his "loss" of his fishing buddies after his marriage to Hadley, here named "Helen":

> When he married he lost Bill Smith, Odgar, the Ghee, all the old gang. He lost them because he admitted by marrying that something was more important than the fishing. They were all married to fishing. He'd been married to it before he married Helen, really married to it. It wasn't any joke. So he lost them all. Helen thought it was because they didn't like her.

This male world *was* the Hemingway subject: the "Jimmy Breen" story *should* have worked.

Admittedly, if we read Hemingway only for "technique," if we isolate him as the quintessential modernist who created our tense, ironic, yet poetic contemporary "voice," then the "Jimmy Breen" manuscript is an example of a narrative that doesn't get anywhere. The pattern of the aimless journey reminds us of Hemingway's problems with "Hills Like White Elephants," also written in this time. The early versions of that story put Jig (Hadley) and the American man (Hem) on the train for which they only wait in the finished version. The dialogue which now *is* the story hadn't yet arrived. Without the "white elephant" simile to characterize the woman speaker, and make her more sympathetic than the male, the reader has no indication of authorial privilege—the same technique Hemingway had used with less dramatic effect in Marge's dialogue—ruins like castles—in "The End of Something." Going back to "Hills Like White Elephants," which was more than likely a story of the group of "Cross-Country Snow," "Out of Season," and "Cat in the Rain," the pregnancy-abortion group, Hemingway was able to save it, through focusing on the early image which gave him the theme and title.

The "Jimmy Breen" manuscript needs more of that metaphoric genius, more of the dialogue or event that struck sparks to illuminate the fictional world. While some of the writing is as good as anything Hemingway had written, the work in "Jimmy Breen" had this "aimlessness" that signaled artificiality, contrivance, and forced the reader (and the writer) to ask, Why keep going with this? "Writer's block" is the wrong label, though; stopping the "Breen" manuscript was more of an editorial decision.

The "Jimmy Breen" manuscript shows some important things about what Hemingway had learned in the early Paris years, but it illustrated what he had learned from Gertrude Stein, not from Ezra Pound. Now we must think past "modernist technique." *How to write* in a narrow sense was the province of the Imagist poets led by Ezra Pound; *how to write* in a grand, inclusive sense was the interest of Gertrude Stein. (There was never anything small about Gertrude.) What Stein cultivated in Hemingway was his capacity to write from the center of himself—from the centers of his life as his consciousness (or subconsciousness) incorporated his life memories. What Stein dealt with was the human investigation of feeling and intimacy, or, in Virginia Woolf's term, those "moments of being" that shaped human lives.

Not for nothing had Stein at Radcliffe been the loving student of William James, whose wholistic theories had forced the narrow "scientism" of late Victorian thought to expand to embrace his integrative field of "psychology." From Stein's work on attention and fatigue in two projects that were written up as essays for *The Harvard Psychological Review*, her specialization in brain anatomy as both a medical student at Johns Hopkins and as a research assistant to Lewelys Barker, not to mention her being such an avid reader of Henry James that she quoted from Kate Croy

(*The Wings of the Dove*) in her own first novel, *Q. E. D.* Stein was aware that writing was a mystifyingly complex process, the opposite of the "automatic writing" that B. F. Skinner later attributed to her.

Stein and Hemingway, on their long walks through Paris, and perhaps during evenings at Lipps, talked about this mystery. They talked a lot about it. The way Stein had arrived at her varied styles through the more than twenty years she had been a serious, though largely unpublished, or self-published, writer, was through her meditative sensing of what for her were the *essential* subjects. Once she had found the truly meaningful subjects, she trusted that appropriate form would follow.

Luckily for Hemingway, *his* meaningful subjects, and their uniquely appropriate forms, were more accessible for readers than were Stein's. Readers cared about Hemingway's essential subjects—fathers and sons, women who loved but interfered (even mothers), men still boys and fearful, men thrown into life without knowing the rules. Yes, Hemingway learned a great deal about the way *The Making of Americans* was essential for Stein, and about the way a family story could refocus "literature"— and his readiness to risk writing family stories may have come from his enthusiasm for Stein's *The Making of Americans*. What Hemingway really learned, however, from Stein, was how to TRUST what his whole self— not simply his mind—gave him as subject.

This is one explanation for the nearly perfect early manuscripts of, especially, the *In Our Time* stories, and of a later work like *The Old Man and the Sea*. Many of us have been amazed at how close to the published versions these drafts are, and some comments have wondered at what point Hemingway produced these "early" versions. My conclusion now, after these years of being immersed in Stein's writing and manuscripts, as well as her beliefs about the writing process, is that Hemingway had learned well the Stein method—of letting the power of meaningful subject trigger rhythm and form, of being so *in touch* (though not simply rationally or intellectually) with such essentials, with the origin of all language (i.e., heart, soul) that he could write the fiction that he has been revered for.

Hemingway knew "Jimmy Breen" was going nowhere, and one reason he could not save it by going back to revise was that it contained a contrived character, that of the father, a man who could never have existed. The father in "Breen" was wise, confident, and very sexual. He was also morally indecisive, much like that other early father from "My Old Man." Parts of this character grew out of Hemingway's anger with his own father, and parts out of his wish that his father might be something different. By making the father an enigmatic man of mysterious profession, a chameleon of necessity, Hemingway hoped to avoid what were inherent contradictions within the man—but the ruse did not work. The real problem was that Hemingway as author could not go into his deepest self and find the man he was creating, anywhere.

One reason the Breen manuscript is so important, I think, is that it prefigured Hemingway's need and desire to create some idealized world as a male world. In *The Sun Also Rises* he had, with its ending, abandoned the pretense that heterosexual romance was an answer: it wasn't even pretty to think so anymore. In *The Torrents of Spring*, heterosexual romance was travesty. The idealization of Catherine Barkley in *A Farewelll to Arms* three years later is one way around having to deal with the primary plot of the conventional romance; and even as F. Scott Fitzgerald warned him that Catherine didn't sound "real," that he wasn't "listening" to women any longer, Hemingway certainly knew what Fitzgerald told him. He wasn't trying to depict realistic women any longer, and the character of Catherine Barkley became the "B" response to the dilemma of how to write the "Jimmy Breen" story. If Hemingway could not create a believable male world, at least not then, which was his aim in "Jimmy Breen," then he would stay with romance but he would create his own fictional beloved to make that heterosexual world as palatable as possible. The "A" choice of the author of "Jimmy Breen," of course, was to keep writing the story of the idyllic all male existence. As Hemingway wrote the stories and novels that culminated in *The Old Man and the Sea* and *Islands in the Stream*, he created the father-son story over and over—Santiago and Manolin, Thomas Hudson and his three sons, the son and father shifting places, melding, merging. That world was not without conflict, however, as Thomas Hudson said in the manuscript of *Islands in the Stream*:

> He had replaced everything except the boys with work and the steady hardworking life he had built on the island. That is, he thought he had. I would rather love a good house and the sea and my work than a woman, he thought. He knew it could never be true. But he could almost make it. . . .

By recovering the place of "Jimmy Breen" in Hemingway's writing life, Professor Reynolds enables us to see how well—and how early—Hemingway had learned to write about his essential subjects, and thereby write with all his ability, wisdom, and passion.

Now my question for Mike is what does the biographer do when he has the demands of the estate, the demands of his publisher, the demands of commercial reviewers, his own demands, and the world of the Hemingway scholars looking at him, how does it feel to be poised, pitted at that position? And you know it's you we want to hear from.

Reynolds: The reason that Linda had a little difficulty reading that is because it is in very tiny handwriting in pencil. She didn't see my work until the night before last and she did that in twenty-four hours while this conference was going on. So now you know how it's done.

The question's a good one, and I wish she hadn't asked it because I try not to think about it in those terms. I've decided that I'm never going to make a lot of money doing this, and there's always going to be somebody who is unhappy with what I write, and the only joy I get out of it really is the doing of it, and so I guess I'm writing this to please myself and my own writing needs. But there is a problem in dealing with a—I haven't had the problems that Linda's had dealing with a literary estate, and if I'd had to go through what she went through with the Sylvia Plath book I might have given this up and taken up bricklaying or something. I mean, just sort of incredible problems and difficulties. I haven't had, I haven't faced that, and so it hasn't been quite that discouraging. I don't know what's going to happen about publishing this. They just said they'd let me read it. They didn't say they'd let me write about it. And that's going to be a different problem altogether. But I don't know, maybe the insurance policy will cover it. I mean the bottom line is, yeah, I am going to publish something about Hemingway's writing of "Jimmy Breen" in this period as I go, because it is important to understand what's happening in that period.

What does a biographer publish and what does he not publish? How much does he/she put in? What do you leave out? Do you give in to the pressures of the literary estate? Sometimes you don't have any choice, I mean, Linda didn't have any choice. What is good taste? Somebody asked me—I used to have a flip answer for Carlos Baker's biography, as much as I admired it—was it a good book and I said, "Well, there weren't any lawsuits." And people would go away shaking [their heads saying], "I wonder what he meant by that?" If he'd really told the truth there would have been lawsuits, that was what I was saying. If he had said everything, there would have been lawsuits. There have been things that I haven't put in, probably simply because I thought they were in bad taste. Nick Gerogiannis is bringing out a new edition of the Hemingway poems right now as we speak and he's adding three poems that I know of that I suggested that he might like to look at that he hadn't seen before. There was a fourth poem that he's not putting in the book. It's a really scurrilous poem and when it comes to light as it's going to in the next six months—not in Nick's book but someplace else—when it comes to light you're going to hear "Hemingway the racist" in a way that you've never heard it before. And the newspapers will pick it up and they'll just beat him to death with it for a day and a half or six minutes or whatever it lasts. Actually, it's not a poem about Hemingway the racist. It's about Hemingway and how much he really disliked his sister-in-law when he married Hadley Richardson, but that's not the way it's going to come out. A number of us have known about the poem for a long time and simply have not really used it because it was just in bad taste. It was not did I do injustice to the Hemingway literary biography by leaving it out? I don't think so. I don't think it's going to add a lot to it. Unless you know the context of the poem and why it was written, it's certainly misused. But it is a problem, and it's a problem that . . . trying to find a balance. I know that Scott Donaldson—Scott's not here, that's too bad—the problems that Scott had with the Cheever biography and having that cut out from underneath him. I guess ideally what I'd really like is the author who's a really good author who left lots of manuscripts and letters who's as dead as he'll ever be and has no children. That's what I'm looking for. Unfortunately [unintelligible].

Jackson Bryer: Mike, you know you could take the position with regard to the Jimmy Breen manuscript—you ought to ask your lawyer about this—that if you write about it tantalizingly enough you're increasing the commercial value of it.

Reynolds: Yeah, and I. . . .

Bryer: You understand what I mean. In other words, no one knows anything about it, and if you write anything about it that may increase, increase its commercial value by convincing Scribner's or somebody to want to publish it.

Reynolds: That's a good point.

Audience, unidentified: But that's not what you've done here.

Reynolds: You don't think I've made it more tantalizing?

Audience: [Unintelligible.]

Reynolds: Well, I'd be dishonest with you if I said I thought it was really great. I think it is important and I think it is fascinating. I mean, to pick up a Hemingway manuscript that no one has read written in pencil and there it is on the page . . . let me tell you, it's bloody exciting. Even on a bad day, it's exciting. But it's objectively, I can't. . . . Linda, you saw some of my notes. Am I misjudging it?

Wagner-Martin: But, Mike, I think everybody wants every scrap. I mean, when I was out near the Waltham [(Massachusetts) Federal Records Center] collection before the JFK Library was built, I was out there to do a book on John Dos Passos. Every morning I took my youngest to kindergarten, I got in the car and I rode out to Trapelo Road. Jo August [then Curator of the collection] would say, "I've just catalogued the Pauline letters, do you want to see them?" I wasn't even working on [Hemingway]. I was all done with my book on Hemingway. And I think we all just want to know what it all is. I do find some of that, the early sections I think, very interesting. And yes, very . . . you know, he's not . . . he hasn't changed his ability to hang on to your interest as reader. It's just that where it was going, I think, was the real problem and that's why it was never. . . .

Reynolds: And you realize that part of it has been published as those two stories ["A Train Trip" and "The Porter"] in the Finca Vigía edition, so-called complete stories, with things excised from those stories that are not marked by ellipses. And some terrible—a couple of terrible misreadings of words in the manuscript. For example, his father fills a "granite bucket" if you can imagine such an item as a granite bucket. It was a graniteware bucket, which—anyway, things like that. But, yeah, I guess we do want it. We want to know everything. And eventually it'll probably be published, and there are portions of it that are quite well written. With the sections in New York, I think they're not going to add to the literary reputation. Other questions? Jim?

James Steinke: I had a couple of quick questions. I thought in your writing about it of "The Revolutionist" as a literary precursor of that.

Reynolds: Oh, yeah, yeah. This chapter that I read to you is half of the chapter. I mean, I cut out half of it because I didn't think you'd want to sit here for an hour listening to this. Yeah, it ties in very, very neatly with Thomas Hudson, well with Thomas Hudson, yes. It ties in very neatly with Robert Jordan in *For Whom the Bell Tolls.* He's connected with him, pretty obviously.

Steinke: The other thing that I was wondering about was that there's a strange catalogued item [in the Hemingway Collection of the John F. Kennedy Library] where Hemingway is writing to himself about bringing the novel's father to Key West or Cuba as [a] dope runner.

Reynolds: On this one? For "Jimmy Breen"? I haven't seen that. Maybe I've missed it, but that wouldn't surprise me. He'd just—he'd been in Key West. He'd picked up just a little bit of information about Key West. Clearly he didn't know enough to write that one then either. But he comes back to that in the *To Have and Have Not* manuscript, in the excised section where the gunrunner is running guns into Cuba. I don't think the literary estate even knows about that. I wish they'd publish that section. It does connect. There are patterns and he never gives it up completely. He keeps coming back to things.

Steinke: One last quick one. What about the two stories, Italian stories, that he wrote, "In Another Country" and "A Way You'll Never Be" as kicking in that *Farewell to Arms* material?

Reynolds: Oh, yeah. I've got a long—I've got a buildup in here leading up to it. He's been working with that opening section of *A Farewell to Arms* before he started working on "Jimmy Breen." It just didn't lead there at that point. There was another question?

Svoboda: I've got something for you. You mentioned, Mike, he puts some emphasis on the piece that's published as "A Train Trip" where Jimmy goes up on the roof to put the bucket over the stovepipe and then his father says—Jimmy's starting to come down—and his father says, no, wait, and his father climbs up to him and they look around. And then they go on to start the boat to leave behind the Point, the sunken log and the three ravens, which seems to me to be leading in an interesting direction, something of the interesting direction that Linda suggested. It makes me think a lot of "Fathers and Sons." It's a sort of a radiant moment. Is there anything else in here that's as much a radiant moment, or do you just hit it in the first three and a half pages?

Reynolds: I can't think of any other moments that are that . . . radiant's a good word. And when he called that opening chapter "Saying Goodbye to the Old Places in the First Person" that was clearly the impetus. But it never gets . . . after that there's never that, never even a closeness. But there is an interesting passage. There's a revision of one of chapter twenty or chapter nineteen in which Jimmy says the thing that worries him most is that his father's going to send him away to boarding school. He says ever since he gave me a copy of *Tom Brown's School Days* I've been worried sick about this and maybe that he was sending me a message. And so he tries very hard to please his father and not bother him and not worry him and only talk about things that his father is interested in, and Jimmy tells us, I was never interested in talking to whores, but I knew that Dad thought that was funny, so I would bring it up. He said, and I would go out, and I wouldn't talk to whores at all, and when I came back he would ask me how it was and I would make up something. And it's a very curious perspective. He sees his father drinking too much and doesn't particularly like it. And when he starts talking about writers I thought that that was just from Hemingway's own—not problems—but own behavior patterns during the times it is: I think he's seeing himself very clearly, he's able to do that. He does it again in *Green Hills of Africa*. He does it, getting that perspective, distance on himself, seeing himself as someone else would see him and almost satirizing it. But no, there's no radiant moments like that. That part of it seemed radiant. That one did.
Thank you.

NOTES

1. "American Banker Discovers Little Tension In Italy," *New York Herald*, 18 September 1927.

2. Ernest Hemingway-Mrs. Paul Pfeiffer, 1 October 1927, Patrick Hemingway Collection, Firestone Library, Princeton University.

3. Hemingway notebook dated March 1926, owned by Toby Bruce and copied in the Baker Files, Firestone Library, Princeton University.

4. The "New Slain Knight" working title is crossed out on the pencil manuscript, Item 529b, JFK Library. The manuscript runs twenty chapters with minor revisions in ink. There are two alternate chapters, one from a shifted point of view, both done apparently as revisions. This manuscript, previously closed to scholars, was opened to me by the Hemingway Estate under special permission.

5. See Michael Reynolds, *The Young Hemingway* (New York: Blackwell, 1986) for more detailed information on Dr. Hemingway's gradually deteriorating condition.

6. C. E. Hemingway-Ernest Hemingway, 28 September 1927, JFK Library.

7. MS-14; there are two pages numbered 14. At page 142, Ernest Hemingway renumbered all previous pages sequentially. At some later point in revision, he added this page, which he also numbered 14.

8. "The Twa Corbies," *The Oxford Book of English Verse*, edited by Authur Quiller-Couch (Oxford University Press, 1939), 450. Hemingway first came to know and love this poem in high school. In his March 1926 notebook, he transcribed the second verse while making notes for a novel about an escaped convict.

9. Item 529b, chapter 6, 6/89.

10. This portion of the unfinished novel was published in the Finca Vigía edition of the short stories as "A Train Trip," 565. A typo on page 565 should read Ad Wolgast, not Moegast.

11. Item 529b, chapter 6, 6/89.

12. Item 529b, chapter 7, 17-18/110-11.

13. Item 529b, chapter 9, 1/127.

14. Ernest Hemingway-Archibald MacLeish, 8 October 1927, in *Selected Letters, 1917-1961*, ed. Carlos Baker (New York: Scribner's, 1981), 262.

15. Item 529b, chapter 10, 1-12.

16. Item 529b, chapter 13, 14.

17. Item 529b, chapter 13, 10.

18. Ernest Hemingway-F. Scott Fitzgerald, ca. 3 November 1927, JFK Library.

19. Ernest Hemingway-I. S. Godolphin, 5 December 1927, Firestone Library, Princeton University.

20. Ernest Hemingway-Max Perkins, 24 November 1927, Scribner Author File, Firestone Library, Princeton University. Chapter 17 is fewer than two

pages, breaking off for the shift in point of view. He tried the same shift to no purpose when rewriting *The Sun Also Rises*.

21. Item 529b, chapter 19, 5.
22. Item 529b, chapter 20, 1.
23. Max Perkins-Ernest Hemingway, 30 November 1927, JFK Library. The advertisement in the *New York Times Book Review* for 27 November 1927 announced the book was in its "Third Large Printing."
24. William Horne-Ernest Hemingway, 29 November 1927, Baker Files, Firestone Library, Princeton University.
25. Ernest Hemingway-F. Scott Fitzgerald [ca. 18 December 1927], JFK Library. This letter was torn up and then pieced back together with a brief cover to explain it.
26. Guy Hickok-Ernest Hemingway, 22 December 1927, JFK Library. Hemingway did, in fact, have congenitally defective eyesight.
27. Hemingway's borrower's card, Beach Collection, Firestone Library, Princeton University. Card notes he returned the January *Dial* on 13 February.
28. Ernest Hemingway-Max Perkins, 12 February 1928, in *Selected Letters*, 271.
29. Ernest Hemingway-Max Perkins, 17 March 1928, in *Selected Letters*, 274.
30. *Herald*, 6 March 1928.
31. Ernest Hemingway-Max Perkins, 17 March 1928, in *Selected Letters*, 274.

HEMINGWAY IN THE WORLD

NARRATIONAL VALUES AND ROBERT COHN IN *THE SUN ALSO RISES*

JAMES NAGEL

THE SUN ALSO RISES is a first-person, retrospective novel told by Jake Barnes shortly after the conclusion of the festival of San Fermin in Pamplona. As such it has an inherent temporal duality (the time of the action rendered from the time of the telling) and a corresponding thematic doubling, for things have a different significance in each of the time schemes. Jake is not the same person after the fiesta as before, and his assessments of himself and his friends have altered, in varying degrees, as have the values he places on even common events and observations. Indeed, Jake, one of the most vulnerable figures in American literature, has lost much that is important to him during his holiday in Spain, and his recounting of it seems motivated by a need to come to terms with his altered circumstances, with his diminution of self-esteem, and with his sense of guilt. As he reflects at one point, the world can be a good place, but "all I wanted to know was how to live in it. Maybe if you found out how to live in it you learned from that what it was all about."[1] Telling the novel is part of the process of learning how to live in the special circumstances of his world.

Jake has much to deal with. What he reveals about himself, largely through indirection, is that he was a pilot in Italy during World War I when he was wounded and sent to the Ospedale Maggiore in Milan, where he fell in love with Brett Ashley, a British V. A. D. After he learned that he was impotent, they separated, only to meet again in England, where their relationship deepened. In material Ernest Hemingway cut from the galleys, Jake explained further that he left London in 1916 and went home to America to work on a newspaper in New York. In due course he started the Continental Press Association with a friend and moved to Paris in 1920 to head the European office of the firm.[2] Although Jake is silent on these details in the published version, that would still seem to be his position when he sees Brett in Paris in 1925.

In the nine years between London and Paris, Jake has struggled to live with his condition, finding meaning in work (he is one of the few characters

in the novel who takes work seriously), in friendships, and in sports, where
his interests lie in boxing, bicycle racing, fishing, and, especially, bullfighting, for which his sensitivity and perception make him not only an expert
observer but an aficionado, part of Montoya's sacred group of insiders. He
loves Paris, enjoys his profession, makes friends easily, and knows how to
value the simple things in life, the avenues and restaurants and historic
monuments near his apartment. It has not been easy for him, however: he
has dealt not only with his physical wound but with its implications for his
life as well, the loss of romance and family. It is not for nothing that he
notices and records, without special emphasis, the intimacy of young lovers
walking with their arms about each other on the streets of Paris (77), or on
the raft in San Sebastian (234), or the husband and wife and young son on
the train to Bayonne (85). As Robert E. Meyerson has pointed out, Jake's
restraint and humane nobility have given his situation special qualities:
"Where the others are pathetic . . . Jake is tragic; where the others have lost
their nerve, Jake has lost his manhood."[3]

Everywhere around him there are reminders of what he and Brett can
never have. As Jake says in the first draft of the manuscript, where
Hemingway's tendency was to make explicit much that is only implied in
the novel, "there was a time once when I had loved her so much that it
seemed there was nothing else. There could never be anything else."[4] But
Jake has made a life for himself, and he explains that although "such a
passion and longing could exist in me for Brett Ashley that I would sometimes feel that it would tear me to pieces and yet in the intervals when I
was not seeing Brett, and they were the greater part of the time, I lived a
very happy life."[5] The novel he tells is about how all of that changed, how
after seeing Brett in Paris he regressed to depression and insomnia, to fits
of crying and self-pity, to the turmoil of attempting to establish some emotional stability again.

That all of these events have happened before Jake tells the first page of
the novel has important implications for the meaning of what is told, for
he does not tell everything and, after the passage of time, either cannot
remember or is unsure of certain details.[6] What he includes would seem to
be events that mean something special to Jake at the time of the telling,
even if they seemed unimportant at the time of the action. That he has
established an orderly and comforting routine of work and pleasure in the
opening scenes has a special poignancy after the turmoil to come, for
example, as does all of the anticipatory pleasure of the fiesta in Pamplona.
By the time he tells the novel, Jake is all too painfully aware that everything went wrong in Spain, and that he will never fully recover from it. An
informed reading of the novel requires the recognition that there is an
irony from the narrative perspective that is not inherent in the active past.

All of this is especially true of the portrait of Robert Cohn, a figure who has given rise to a great deal of scholarly speculation, as though Hemingway used this novel simply to savage some of his friends, most commonly Harold Loeb, who was a Jewish friend from Princeton,[7] or, most recently, and less plausibly, Gertrude Stein, a mentor he needed to reject.[8] However, Robert Cohn is a figure in a novel with only a speculative reference to actual persons. What is important about him is his relationship with Brett and his role in the destruction of Jake's therapeutic construct. In this regard, there is a clear distinction between the kinetic and narrational values in the novel.

At the time of the initial action of the novel, it is clear that Robert Cohn and Jake Barnes are quite good friends, unencumbered by what some readers have come to regard as Jake's anti-Semitism.[9] Robert calls him his best friend (39), and Jake asserts, more than once, that he likes Robert (7). There is a good deal about him to interest Jake, for he is good at things Jake admires: he was a boxing champion at Princeton; he is a good tennis player, and an even better sport when he loses; and he keeps himself fit. In his relationships with men, he shows admirable restraint in responding to taunts and insults, for he is clearly the best fighter in his circle of friends. With women, Robert is sincere and considerate, failing with Brett primarily in his assumption that because she was willing to spend a holiday with him, there must be some special emotional bond between them.[10] He is naive, but never vicious: to him, Brett at first appears "fine and straight," when in reality she has been, to some extent, "coarsened and twisted by life and war."[11] Jake has yet to attempt his first novel at a time when Robert has actually published a good one and is working on his second, although suffering from writer's block. Indeed, he resembles Jake in many respects, not the least of which is that he can be a genuinely nice guy and is capable of deep affection, as is soon revealed by his obsessive love for Brett. The friendship between Jake and Robert is implicit from the beginning, when Robert drops by Jake's office unannounced to go to lunch, and later naps in Jake's office, implying that they are so close he feels free to do so. Jake also reports that Robert was a husband and father who left the States for expatriation and a writer's life in Paris.

The central dilemma that critics have not confronted is why, in the context of an established friendship between the two men, Jake presents such a devastating portrait of Robert, making him the most negative character in the novel, more pathetic, hopeless, obtuse, and impossible than any other member of the lost generation. Anti-Semitism does not present a viable explanation, in that Robert was just as Jewish in Paris before the fiesta as he is in Pamplona during the bullfights: Jake does not suddenly discover Robert's ethnicity and turn against him. Nor are Robert's personality traits indicative of any specific ethnic group. A more plausible answer is that, in his relationship with Brett, Robert has hurt Jake deeply, in the most vulnerable part of himself, and at the time Jake tells the novel he is deeply bitter. The devastating portrait of Robert Cohn in Paris, in effect, derives as much from the retrospective imposition of Jake's feelings after the fiesta as it does from the events themselves. When Jake reflects that "somehow I feel I have not shown Robert Cohn clearly," it is evident that he is speaking retrospectively after the events in Pamplona, when objectivity and accuracy would not be his primary obsessions. Many of Jake's negative observations about Robert are petty, as in the suggestion that he did not think much about his clothing, that his tennis went all to pieces when he fell in love with Brett, that in social situations his conversation was unremarkable (45). From another perspective, these traits might even be seen as admirable. Indeed, if Robert were truly an ass of the first water from the very beginning, Jake and his friends would never have permitted him to come along.

If, at the time of the telling, Jake is disgusted by Robert, he is also, clearly, disappointed in Brett and not at all pleased with himself. Indeed, as negative as the comments about Robert are, Cohn has not transgressed as grievously as has Jake, violating fundamental, sacred principles that define him as a person. At the center of it all is Brett. Even the structure of Jake's narrative stresses his vulnerability: during his first encounter with Brett at the *bal musette* Jake handles his emotions well until he goes home to his apartment on the Boulevard St. Michel and discovers the wedding announcement from the mysterious Kirby family. The document triggers his first psychotic episode, as his mind races ("to hell with Brett. To hell with you, Lady Ashley" [30]) and he cannot sleep. He dwells on his wound ("of all the ways to be wounded. I suppose it was funny"), even though he has had nearly a decade to reconcile himself to the fact of his condition. When he thinks back to meeting Brett in Milan and seeing her again in England, he loses control and begins to cry. This is not macho posing that Jake would be proud of at the time he recounts it, but it is part of the reality he must learn to face. He pulls himself together, but when Brett drops by his flat he has a bad time again. As he reflects: "It is awfully easy to be hard-boiled about everything in the daytime, but at night it is another thing" (34). His problems surface again after Brett and the count visit him, but his deepest despair does not begin until he learns that Robert had an affair with Brett on their trip to San Sebastian. When Brett asks if Robert is going to Pamplona with the group, Jake answers:

"Yes. Why?"
"Who did you think I went down to San Sebastian with?"
"Congratulations," I said (83).

Jake's question seems to imply that at that moment, before he knows about the affair, Jake can think of no reason why Robert should not be included in the trip. Once he knows the truth about them, this revelation shatters Jake's defenses against the world, and in response he destroys nearly everything that has meaning for him.

Jake's explanations of all of this were more direct in the first draft of the novel than in the published version: "When she went off with Cohn it hurt me badly again. As badly as in the worst days."[12] Jake's preoccupations are not with striking out at Robert, for he never harms Robert physically in Pamplona, but with introspection: "I was through with hurting myself. Somewhere I must have registered it all though because of the way I hated Cohn now."[13] His hatred seems to derive not simply from Robert's sexual liaison with Brett, for Jake does not hate Michael, who has an ongoing relationship with Brett, nor the Count, who propositions her, nor Pedro, who runs off with her. The problem is that, as Jake progressively discovers, Robert acts outside of the codes of behavior that give Jake's life an ethical foundation. Jake did not fully realize this at the time of the initial action, when Cohn's transgressions seemed harmlessly "frank and simple" (4); he is all too aware of it by the time he narrates his story.

Jake derives meaning from simple friendships and proper conduct, from his work, his city, his principled life. As Jake comes to realize, Robert violates all of it, and he has no instinct for the values that guide Jake and his friends. He is, from the very beginning, an outsider, the only central character in the novel who was unscathed by the war, who retains his idealism and illusions, and who seems utterly incapable of recognizing tragedy.[14] He hates Paris, neglects his writing, intrudes on the activities of others. Just when it is most called for, as in the abuse Frances gives him in Jake's presence,[15] he has no substance, and he takes what no one with self-respect should ever permit; to compound the issue he attempts to pay off his ethical obligations to Frances with money.[16] He sleeps through the Spanish countryside that fascinates Jake and Bill, and his only concern in viewing his first bullfight is that he not be bored. He assumes a superior air in knowing the schedule of Brett and Mike, and he irritates Jake immensely with excessive barbering, as though Brett will be attracted to him based on his appearance.[17] When she shows no romantic interest in him in Spain, he pursues her relentlessly, and when even that fails he resorts to violence, although it should be remembered that the only account of the fight between Robert and Pedro Romero comes to Jake through Mike Campbell, hardly an objective reporter of the incident.[18]

Robert's ultimate impact on Brett is even more devastating, as Jake is acutely aware, for their brief affair has changed her. This is more subtle in the novel than in the manuscripts, where Jake makes the point directly:

"She had never been that way before. She was ashamed, that was it. She had never been ashamed before. It made her vulgar where before she had simply gone by her own rules."[19] Beyond what it does to Brett, it also destroys something precious in Jake, his unconditional love for Brett. In going off with Robert, he explains, "she had wanted to kill off something that was in her and the killing had gotten out of her control. Well she had killed it off in me. That was a good thing. I did not want to be in love with any woman. I did not want to have any grand passion that I could never do anything about. I was glad it was gone. The hell I was."[20] Even though it is clear that Jake continues to love Brett, something valuable has been destroyed.

It is Robert's incessant pursuit of Brett that inspires Jake to introduce her to Pedro, a step that causes additional damage: it violates Jake's sacred code of bullfighting, and it costs him his long-standing friendship with the revered Montoya; it puts Brett through a destructive and disorienting relationship in which she discovers that Pedro is ashamed of her iconoclasm.

It destroys Robert in his fight with Romero, against whom his boxing prowess is not effective and not appropriate; and it costs Jake yet again, for he abandons his palliative sojourn in San Sebastian to go to Madrid to assist Brett. Jake says: "Send a girl off with one man. Introduce her to another to go off with him. Now go and bring her back. And sign the wire with love. That was it all right" (239). In the manuscript, he has an even more difficult time: "I had certainly acted like anything but a man. . . . Well I could not apply the rules to myself. I was not a man anyway. Oh stop that stuff. There was not going to be any of that stuff."[21] Jake's emotions are more submerged in the published version, but it is still clear that seeing Brett again may well engender yet another bad time for Jake.

Indeed, the narrative stance of the novel suggests that *The Sun Also Rises* is Jake's attempt at cathartic synthesis, his effort to face the painful realities of his condition and construct the best life he can for himself. It is an exercise in self-definition, and he does not portray himself to advantage nor spare his own feelings. What he reveals is that he has corrupted his most sacred values, violated the codes that gave his life structure, and compromised his relationship with the one person he truly loved. He tells of his episodes of psychological instability and leaves little reason to expect that he will ever be entirely healthy. He can never go back to the Hotel Montoya and the cult of aficionados he so treasured, and he will have to live with what has happened to Pedro Romero. Far from showing himself as a man who is strong despite his wound, he portrays himself as a passive figure, a spectator who is not an active suitor for Brett, a rotten dancer who does not box or race a bicycle or wade the Irati to fish for trout or run with the bulls, who is knocked out by Robert and rendered helpless, weeping in the night, when he attempts to face his condition. As Michael Reynolds has said, "Jake Barnes is no tough guy."[22] As negative as he has been in his portrait of Robert Cohn, he is even harder, in retrospect, on himself. Yet, in the rendition of the harsh reality of it all, he exhibits his one act of extreme bravery, for his story is essentially a confession[23] and a confrontation, and whatever cathartic virtues are inherent in relating this painful narrative will help form the basis for the rest of his life.

NOTES

1. Ernest Hemingway, *The Sun Also Rises* (New York: Scribner's, 1926), 148. All quotations are from this edition.
2. The most readily available record of Hemingway's excisions from galley proof is Frederic Joseph Svoboda's excellent study *Hemingway and The Sun Also Rises: The Crafting of a Style* (Lawrence: University Press of Kansas, 1983). The passage regarding Jake's move to Paris is on page 134.
3. See Robert E. Meyerson, "Why Robert Cohn?: An Analysis of Hemingway's *The Sun Also Rises*," *Liberal and Fine Arts Review* 2, no. 1 (1982): 65.
4. My quotations from the first draft of the novel are from *Ernest Hemingway, The Sun Also Rises: A Facsimile Edition*, ed. Matthew J. Bruccoli, 2 parts (Detroit: Omnigraphics, 1990). This quotation is on page 398. Since the pagination is consecutive throughout the two volumes, I will give only page numbers for citations.
5. *Facsimile Edition*, 617-18.
6. For Jake's lapses of memory, see pages 90-91.
7. Harold Loeb has given his version of the events portrayed in *The Sun Also Rises* in "Hemingway's Bitterness," *Connecticut Review* 1 (October 1967): 7-24. A consideration of his perspective is essential to an understanding of the biographical background of the novel.
8. See Linda Wagner-Martin, "Racial and Sexual Coding in Hemingway's *The Sun Also Rises*," *Hemingway Review* 10, no. 2 (1991): 39-41.
9. Michael J. Hoffman argues that it is precisely Robert's Jewishness, particularly his intellectualism and need to verbalize his feelings, that make him out of place in the undemonstrative and disillusioned social circle of the lost generation. See "From Cohn to Herzog," *Yale Review* 58 (Spring 1969): 342-58.
10. I am indebted here to Arthur L. Scott, "In Defense of Robert Cohn," *College English* 18 (March 1957): 310.
11. S. A. Cowan, "Robert Cohn, the Fool of Ecclesiastes in *The Sun Also Rises*," *Dalhousie Review* 63 (Spring 1983): 103.
12. *Facsimile Edition*, 402.
13. Ibid.
14. See Meyerson, "Why Robert Cohn?" 66.

15. One of the best scenes in the novel is the conversation among Jake and Robert and Frances Clyne in which she punishes Cohn verbally for his treatment of her. Her comments are so vicious that Jake comments, in retrospect, "I do not know how people could say such terrible things to Robert Cohn. There are people to whom you could not say insulting things. They give you a feeling that the world would be destroyed, would actually be destroyed before your eyes, if you said certain things. But here was Cohn taking it all" (49). A more positive reading of the scene would give Robert some credit for his gentlemanly restraint.

16. See Michael S. Reynolds, *The Sun Also Rises: A Novel of the Twenties* (Boston: Twayne, 1988), 53. Reynolds' study is a valuable introduction to the novel.

17. Robert McIlvaine, in "Robert Cohn and *The Purple Land*," *Notes on Modern American Literature* 5, no. 2 (1981): Item 8, suggests that Robert is basing his actions on Richard Lamb, the protagonist of W. H. Hudson's *The Purple Land*, who is a noble and courageous fighter among men and irresistible to women.

18. Scott makes this point on page 312.

19. *Facsimile Edition*, 397-98.

20. Ibid.

21. Ibid., 590.

22. Reynolds, *The Sun Also Rises*, 52. Reynolds also offers an excellent discussion of Jake's role as an anti-hero.

23. For alternative approaches to the meaning of Jake's confession, see Svoboda, *Hemingway and The Sun Also Rises*, 102, and Reynolds, *The Sun Also Rises*, 29.

ANTI-SEMITISM IN *THE SUN ALSO RISES*

TRAUMAS, JEALOUSIES, AND THE GENESIS OF COHN

WOLFGANG E. H. RUDAT

NUMEROUS STUDIES HAVE BEEN written on anti-Semitism in *The Sun Also Rises*, with many of those studies at least implicitly accusing Hemingway himself of anti-Semitism. In his 1988 book entitled *The Sun Also Rises: A Novel of the Twenties*, Michael S. Reynolds made the following reply to those charges:

> Some readers will want to use the *Sun*'s text to charge Hemingway with anti-Semitism. True or not, the charge is irrelevant to the reading of the novel. Jake Barnes is not Ernest Hemingway. To confuse the author with his narrator is to misread the novel and to relegate Hemingway's insights into his age to the same level as Jake's. . . . [Yet] It would be most remarkable if [Hemingway] were not anti-Semitic. . . . Ernest Hemingway is a historical result, no better or worse than the America in which he was raised. We should not, therefore, shoot the messenger who sends us over the decades such a clear picture of our national values.[1]

I agree of course with Reynolds's cautions not to confuse Hemingway with his narrator, and not to let Hemingway's possible own anti-Semitism interfere with our appreciation of a work of art created when the *Zeitgeist* was radically different from our own. I disagree, however, with Reynolds's contention that the charge of Hemingway's possible anti-Semitism is irrelevant to our reading of the novel. I disagree precisely *because* "Jake Barnes is not Hemingway." Hemingway's portrayal of Robert Cohn, in Roger Whitlow's words, as "the complete ass,"[2] is too complex to be attributed to the narrator alone.

To be sure, as critics on one side of the fence have claimed, Jake is untrustworthy as a narrator. Some of those critics may not even be aware of the fact that *the narrator* is being a "complete ass" when, in an attempt to prejudice the reader against Cohn from the very beginning, Jake-the-narrator opens the novel with anti-Semitic wisecracks, which include a dissertation on how Cohn's nose was "certainly improved" (3)[3] by being flattened in a boxing match at Princeton. The narrator, who had never seen Cohn's nose in its original state, betrays his bigoted assumption that Cohn, being Jewish, must have had a nose that was stereotypically Jewish and therefore not good, and thus betrays his anti-Semitic bias by equating *Jewish* and *not good*.[4] Here Hemingway is satirizing his narrator for racism in the satirical remarks about Robert Cohn, and thus presenting his narrator as a satirist satirized.[5]

This is exactly where I see a danger: Hemingway's dissociating irony toward his narrator's anti-Semitism could be a smoke screen. I suggest that the observations that Kenneth G. Johnston made in 1987 in his introduction to *The Tip of the Iceberg: Hemingway and the Short Story* should also be applied in examining *The Sun Also Rises*:

> Despite his many claims to the contrary, the majority of Hemingway's stories are biographical fragments, which, when pieced together, constitute a truthful, rather complete record of his inner and outer life. Hemingway's theory of "omission" permitted him to tell the real story, to bare the soul, yet at the same time mask the truth. Herein lies the central paradox: Hemingway the writer felt impelled to reveal, although obliquely, what Hemingway the private man wanted to obscure.[6]

I wish to argue that Hemingway created the Robert Cohn of *The Sun Also Rises* because as a writer he "felt impelled to reveal, although obliquely," what as "a private man [Hemingway] wanted to obscure," namely his unfair real-life treatment of his Jewish friend and fellow writer Harold Loeb, "bar[ing] his soul, yet at the same time mask[ing] the truth."

In his 1987 biography, Kenneth S. Lynn observed, concerning Cohn's portrayal:

> The author of *The Sun Also Rises* took sadistic delight in degrading the fictional stand-in for Harold Loeb, only to become ashamed of himself in the process and ambivalently sympathetic with Cohn as a result. Through Jake Barnes, Hemingway gave voice to his on-again, off-again feelings. . . . [At one point Jake] says, speaking directly to the reader, "Somehow I feel I have not shown Robert Cohn clearly." Perhaps it was Ernest Hemingway that he was unable to show clearly.[7]

I submit that one part of the Ernest Hemingway that the narrator was unable to show clearly was the Hemingway who resented Loeb for coming from a wealthy family. As Lynn notes,

At a time when he and Hadley were strapped for money, Hemingway was extremely envious of people who had never had that problem—and all around him in the expatriate community he saw such people. Even though Loeb had run through most of his initial inheritance, it still galled Hemingway to remember that this Princeton Jew was the grand nephew of one of the founders of *Kuhn, Loeb and Company* and that his mother was the second daughter of Meyer Guggenheim, the legendary copper king.[8] (emphasis added)

The author of *The Sun Also Rises* is sublimating his personal resentment through a series of linguistic games. In one sense Hemingway is reinstating into the novel the real Harold Loeb, who in the first draft had become Gerald,[9] when he gives him the name Cohn: in "Cohn" Hemingway is re-Hebraicizing the Germanized version of the Hebrew word for "priest,"[10] *Kuhn,* and thus identifying Robert Cohn with Harold Loeb.[11] Hemingway is giving us a signal that the name Cohn carries a special significance for the novel when he has Bill Gorton ask about Cohn's Spanish telegram, "Vengo Jueves Cohn" (127), a telegram in which Cohn announces his arrival in Pamplona, "What does the word Cohn mean?" Through Bill's seemingly gratuitous question, Hemingway is alerting the reader that the name Cohn can take on surprising meanings when used in other languages. Robert's last name explains why this "priest" possesses "that incapacity to enjoy Paris" (42). The explanation is that the French are likely to pronounce the name Cohn the same way they pronounce *con,* the most common French slang term for the female pudendum.

His last name makes it extremely difficult for Robert, who is a rather shy and self-conscious person to begin with, to introduce himself to French people. Just imagine Robert first pronouncing the name "Cohn" in English (especially a New York Jew's), where the diphthongization makes it sound closer to the nasal pronunciation of "con," and then adding, "Je suis trés enchanté á faire votre connaissance." Here the juxtaposition to the infelicitous name not only gives rise to a pun in "*con*naissance," but also associates "connaissance" with "knowing" in the Biblical-sexual sense. As James Hinkle demonstrated in his article on "What's Funny in *The Sun Also Rises,*" a groundbreaking study in close-reading Hemingway, understanding some of the jokes in the novel requires a certain amount of familiarity with foreign languages.[12]

While we can assume that the dephallused Jake[13] is gleefully aware of Cohn's awkward situation in the capital of *l'amour*—it is interesting to note that the narrator usually refers to his other close friends in the novel by their first name but to Cohn by his last—the narrator has nothing to do with the naming of the novel's characters. What, then, does it mean for our understanding of the novel that the author transforms Harold Loeb, whose fictional stand-in he portrays as the most manly of all the characters (with the exception of Romero) in *The Sun Also Rises*, into a *con*? First of all, since at the time of the composition of *The Sun Also Rises* Harold Loeb was better off financially than Hemingway was, the following possible scenario emerges. Possession of money means the power that Hemingway does not have. This kind of power can be substituted to make up for "im-potence," that is, for the lack of the male's sexual "power." Hemingway therefore might have wished to punish Loeb, alias Cohn poetically by presenting him as sexually impotent. However, that would hardly have been poetically effective because, in addition to being financially potent, Loeb had managed to bed Duff Twysden, something Hemingway never did. I would therefore suggest that, in a departure from the castration threats that, real or imagined, permeate a novel whose heroine is explicitly associated with the archetypal castrating female Circe,[14] Hemingway is transmogrifying the Harold Loeb of the Kuhn-connection into the part of the female anatomy that the French call *con*. An essential theme in the novel, then, is the vaginification, or *cunnification*, of Harold Loeb into Robert Cohn.

This is not a nice thing to do to one's friend, but from a satiric point of view it is very effective: if we believe in the archetypal killing-power of satire as Robert C. Elliott describes it in *The Power of Satire: Magic, Ritual, Art*,[15] then Hemingway is killing his rival writer when he transforms Harold Loeb into a *con*. This wordplay is certainly distasteful but, at least from the stance of Hemingway the private man, it is meaningful.[16] The transformation of Loeb into a *con* is meaningful in the sense that it neuters Loeb as a writer, since Hemingway equates the pencil with the phallus.

Hemingway indicates such an equivalence by having Bill refer to pencil and sexual potency when Bill uses Jake's mention of coffee to begin the free-associating game in Burguete about the would-be writer Jake's war injury. Bill starts out with a bizarrely twisting allusion to the popular belief that caffeine, as Hinkle expresses it, "puts lead in your pencil,"[17] that is, gives a man sufficient potency, again in Hinkle's words, "[to be] an easy rider":[18]

> "Good. Coffee is good for you. . . . *Caffeine puts a man on her horse and a woman in his grave.* You know what's the trouble with you? You're an expatriate. . . . Nobody that ever left their own country wrote anything worth printing. Not even in the newspapers."
>
> . . .
>
> "You don't work. One group claims women support you. Another claims you're impotent." [Bill said]

"No," I said. "I just had an accident." (115, emphasis added)

The first joke intended by Bill is that while caffeine is supposed to have a beneficial effect on a man's potency, it would not do the physically maimed Jake any good. Regardless of whether there is the additional irony that Jake lost his "pencil" because he and/or his plane were hit by a piece of lead, which caused Jake, in his own words, "to be wounded . . . [in] a rotten way and flying on a joke front like the Italian" (31), Bill is cracking a second joke which is downright brutal: through the gender exchange in the portion I italicized, Bill is suggesting that Jake's loss of his "pencil" has transformed him from a man into a woman.

Bill subsequently tries to soften the suggestion of a sex transformation by citing some people's claim that Jake is "impotent," but when Jake responds, "No . . . I just had an accident," Jake himself is deliberately returning to the notion of a man-into-woman sex transformation.[19] Thus Jake is not only acknowledging that his war "accident" caused direct physical damage to his "pencil," rather than impotence, which could be psychologically based. He is also acknowledging that having left his country had a negative effect on his writing—with Jake's status as an "expatriate" actually extending backward seven or eight years to the point where, as a result of his hubris of enlisting in a foreign airforce,[20] he suffered damage to his "pencil." In other words, Hemingway is presenting us with the cunnification of a would-be novelist who is currently a Paris-based foreign correspondent for an American newspaper. Therefore, since Hemingway modeled Jake Barnes's experiences in Paris and Pamplona after his own, the cunnification of Jake Barnes tells us more about Hemingway himself than about Harold Loeb alias Robert Cohn, especially since Hemingway, an ambulance driver during the Great War, received a wound that temporarily caused a sexual disability.[21]

As has been noted, Hemingway is presenting Cohn, "whose coat [Jake] wears and whose bed he sleeps in and who holds his seat for him on the bus to Burguete," as "Jake's alter ego companion," whom Jake tries to cast off by replacing him with Romero.[22] On the other hand, while Jake Barnes is not Hemingway, the novel's first-person narrator is a fictional stand-in for the author himself in a sexual sense. Readers have always wondered what induced Hemingway to write a novel, narrated in the first person, about a young man whom the Great War had deprived of his penis. I wish to argue that *The Sun Also Rises* is a special abreaction on the part of the author, the abreaction of a man who was obsessed by fears of what might still happen to him (even years after his own war injury), and that some of the novel's jokes are an attempt on the author's part to overcome residual war anxiety that had not quite been assimilated. The dynamics behind the composition of the novel is what Lynn calls Hemingway's "horrific image of phallic loss."[23]

The foundation for such a fear of phallic loss must have been laid by something that occurred long before the war. Lynn discusses such an occurrence, but he does not try to establish a *synergistic connection* between the early event and the effects of Hemingway's wounding. Lynn does connect the earlier occurrence that caused the fear of phallic loss with what *The Sun Also Rises*' narrator calls an "accident":

> At Walloon Lake in 1900, the summer of Ernest's first birthday, he and Marcelline had played naked on the narrow beach in front of their parents' newly completed cottage. Dr. Hemingway's snapshots of them in the buff, duly pasted into scrapbooks by Grace, are charming. But . . . it can be presumed that Ernest had ample opportunity to notice—if he had not done so already—that he and his sister were not built identically.
>
> Did the infant boy take pride in the equipment that set him apart from Marcelline? *Or did the sight of her smoothness make him think that she had suffered some sort of a dreadful accident which might soon befall him as well?* Or were pride and fear intermingled in his turbulent imagination? Familiar Freudian speculations these, which acquire extra force in this case because *Ernest would soon become aware that he and Marcelline were being treated like twins of the same sex.* And in years to come, the horrific image of phallic loss would be . . . dealt with . . . in two anguishing works of fiction, "God Rest You Merry, Gentlemen" and *The Sun Also Rises*.[24] (emphasis added)

The young Hemingway must have *seen* himself as the victim of some horrible accident when, about a year after the bathing scene, Grace Hemingway, who raised the two siblings as "twins" of the same sex, dressed Ernest in girl's clothes, and alongside a scrapbook photograph showing her son in such an outfit wrote "summer girl."[25] In Hemingway's "turbulent imagination," the twinning not only dephallused him—it cunnified him. In *The Sun Also Rises* Hemingway explicitly projected his own imaginary cunnification in terms of textual statement onto Jake, onto the de-Jacobed man who carries the "sissified name of the Biblical patriarch, Jewish and prolifically potent," who fathered the tribes of Israel.[26] But then, since Hemingway himself chose the name "Jake" for his own fictional stand-in, he himself was already setting a stage for contexts with possible anti-Semitic undertones, and Hemingway's fictive use of the Loeb-Kuhn connection was a natural follow-up. This natural follow-up, however, would eventually include Hemingway's implicit projection of his imaginary cunnification onto the fictional stand-in for Harold Loeb.

How does awareness of such an implicit projection of Hemingway's own cunnification onto his character Robert Cohn help us better understand *The Sun Also Rises*? The answer, according to Johnston's model, is that it is helpful to be aware that in his portrayal of Robert Cohn "Hemingway the writer felt impelled to reveal, although obliquely, what Hemingway the private man wanted to obscure." Hemingway is trying to avenge himself in sexual terms on his friend, not so much for having slept with the model for Brett Ashley as for publishing a novel before Hemingway did. Hemingway retroactively takes the lead out of Harold Loeb's pencil by removing the pencil altogether and replacing it with a *con*.

This literary transaction on the part of the author is only thinly disguised: after making the reader privy to what he thinks of Cohn's boxing career, the not-yet-published narrator treats us to the following gem of literary criticism in commenting on Cohn's first novel: "it was not really such a bad novel as the critics later called it, although it was a very poor novel" (5-6). At first reading, we probably disregard the narrator's criticism of Cohn's novel, a criticism voiced without offering any concrete evidence, as belonging in the same category as the immediately preceding anti-Semitic wisecracks, which seem to establish a barrier of dissociating irony between Hemingway and his narrator. That is to say, we do not originally attach any authorial significance to the would-be novelist Jake Barnes's attempt to put down his rival. However, once we have discovered that Hemingway is playing an anti-Semitic word game with the name of Harold Loeb's family connection, a word game in which the author "depencils" his Jewish friend because Loeb is a literary rival, we become inclined to equate the narrator who throws out digs at the novelist Robert Cohn with the author himself.

The narrator's racially couched wisecracks against Robert Cohn now appear to have become wisecracks on the author's part against the Harold Loeb who, much like the Robert Cohn whom Jake introduces as "a *member* . . . of one of the richest Jewish families in New York*" (4, emphasis added), went to Princeton (whereas Hemingway never went to college) and managed to publish a novel before Hemingway did. Since in his college days Harold Loeb engaged in wrestling rather than boxing, that is, engaged in a sport that was less likely to flatten and thus "improve" a presumably Jewish-looking nose, Hemingway has to poetically attack Loeb in another region of his anatomy: performing a poetic cunnification of Harold Loeb, Hemingway satirically kills a "member" of one of the richest families in New York—but, within the context of his novel's anti-Semitic aspects, Hemingway is excising that which according to the Biblical account Jake's namesake was so good at using that it produced the tribes of Israel.

If my foregoing interpretation of what Hemingway did to Harold Loeb is correct, does it not mean that the Hemingway of *The Sun Also Rises* was "racist" even by the standards of the 1920s, standards that were much lower than today's sensitivity toward ethnic diversity? My answer is yes, which is why I disagree with Reynolds's contention that the charge of Hemingway's possible anti-Semitism is irrelevant to our reading of the novel. According to Reynolds, and according to Hinkle, the anti-Semitism in the *Sun* reflects "one of the ways the game was played."[27] If Reynolds, the historio-biographical Hemingway critic par excellence, had combined his method with Hinkle's close-reading method,[28] he might have been able to put the Cohn-Loeb-Kuhn connection to interpretive use, especially since by his own account Reynolds reads the *Sun* as a roman à clef.[29] Yet even if a critical reader *had* suggested that Hemingway might be using his character, Robert Cohn, to cunnify his literary rival, Harold Loeb, he/she still would have had to be able to relate such a reading to Hemingway's portrayal of Jake Barnes—a relation that eventually would have to address both the name "Jake" and the spoofing equivalence that, in the novel's most extensive discussion of Jake's war injury, Bill establishes between pencil and penis.

The combination of Hemingway's "summer girl" experience and his war trauma led to both his creation of the character Jake Barnes and the most viciously racist ingredient in his portrayal of Robert Cohn, that is, Hemingway's use of that character in an attempt to get back at Harold Loeb. This ingredient invites the suspicion that the author's presentation of his narrator as a "complete ass" in his early anti-Semitic wisecracks may merely be a smoke screen that Hemingway sets up to dissociate himself from the anti-Semitism practiced in the novel, practiced both by the narrator and by some of the characters. Then, however, the object whose obscuration might thereby be intended does not really have to be Hemingway's general anti-Semitism; it could be something else.

The object that Hemingway the writer wanted to both expose and hide could be the fear of a pencil-loss of sorts—the fear that Hemingway might lose the ability of which he poetically stripped his rival Harold Loeb, namely the ability to write. If that is the case, then Hemingway's anti-Semitism *as displayed in this novel* is the direct, although for the most part unintended, result of a combination of unresolved inner conflicts, including the pain caused by his ambitiousness—pain that could be eased by finding a scapegoat: one of the personal rivals of the budding writer Ernest Hemingway happened to be Jewish, and Jews traditionally have been handy scapegoats.

This is not to say that we should absolve Hemingway from the anti-Semitism he perpetrated in *The Sun Also Rises*. We should, however, credit to what Reynolds so aptly calls "Hemingway's insights into his age" the fact that, in its very form, the racism that Hemingway perpetrates in the novel exposes itself and self-destructs—which I would argue indicates that he was not exactly proud of the anti-Semitism he and his contemporaries were practicing. The insights into his age and his consummate artistry enabled Hemingway to satirize not only that age, but also himself—so that we have a case of the author voluntarily joining his narrator as a satirist satirized.

NOTES

1. Michael S. Reynolds, *The Sun Also Rises: A Novel of the Twenties* (Boston: Twayne, 1988), 54. Unless otherwise indicated, all Reynolds citations are from this study.
2. Roger Whitlow, *Cassandra and Her Daughters: The Women in Hemingway*, Contributions in Women's Studies, no. 51 (Westport, Connecticut: Greenwood Press, 1984), 56.
3. Citations are from the 1954 edition of *The Sun Also Rises* (New York: Scribner's). I am using this rather than the first edition of 1926 because it was not until 1953 that Charles Scribner Jr. reinstated Mike Campbell's "bulls have no balls" (175-76) for the bowdlerized version, "bulls have no horns"; cf. James Hinkle, "'Dear Mr. Scribner': About the Published Text of *The Sun Also Rises*," *The Hemingway Review*, 6 (Fall 1986): 46. All other Hinkle citations are from "What's Funny."
4. I offer a more detailed discussion of Jake's wisecracks in the opening paragraphs in particular and his anti-Semitism in general in my book, *A Rotten Way to Be Wounded: The Tragicomedy of The Sun Also Rises* (New York: Peter Lang, 1990). In the present study, I am approaching the question of Hemingway's anti-Semitism from a somewhat different angle.
5. For the satirist satirized idea I am indebted to Robert C. Elliott, *The Power of Satire: Magic, Ritual, Art* (Princeton: Princeton University Press, 1960). (Elliott does not mention Hemingway within the context of that concept.)
6. Kenneth G. Johnston, *The Tip of the Iceberg: Hemingway and the Short Story* (Greenwood, Florida: The Penkevill Publishing Company, 1987), 4.
7. Kenneth S. Lynn, *Hemingway* (New York: Simon and Schuster, 1987), 62.
8. Ibid., 63.
9. Cf. William Balassi, "The Writing of the Manuscript of *The Sun Also Rises*, with a Chart of Its Session-by-Session Development," *The Hemingway Review* 6 (Fall 1986): 65-78.
10. In "*The Sun Also Rises*: I: The Jacob Allusion II: Parody as Meaning," *Ball State University Forum* 16 (Spring 1971): 53, Manuel Schonhorn discusses the name Cohn and observes: "The reader should consult *The Dictionary of the Bible*, ed. James Hastings (New York: Scribner's, 1898-1904), IV:

67-100"; Schonhorn also refers to the relevance that *The Jewish Encyclopedia* may have for our understanding of *The Sun Also Rises*.

11. That Hemingway intended from the very beginning of the composition of the novel to link by the name Kuhn the character who eventually became Robert Cohn to the Loeb-Kuhn connection seems to be suggested by the comical near-rhyme Gerald-Harold.

12. James Hinkle, "What's Funny in *The Sun Also Rises*," *The Hemingway Review* 4 (Spring 1985): 37. Independently of each other, the late Professor Hinkle and I had come up with the Cohn-*con* explanation for Robert's "incapacity to enjoy Paris," and for a number of years debated the pros and cons for such a reading. In a letter dated 23 August 1987 Hinkle informed me that he was abandoning that reading, because a native of France had advised him of the implausibility of such an interpretation on the grounds that already in the 1920s the French had an inoffensive standard pronunciation for the name Cohn. I would argue that, even if Hemingway was aware of the inoffensive French standard pronunciation, he would have still wanted to make the pun for those *American* readers who knew the common French term for the female pudendum and therefore might catch and even appreciate the pun. (*Con* is also used in the nonsexual meaning of fool, just as in English a person can be called a "prick," with that word being used in a nonsexual sense.) Hemingway seemed to have a penchant for creating multilingual puns on slang terms for the female genitalia; see my article, "Hemingway's Rabbit: Slips of the Tongue and Other Linguistic Games in *For Whom the Bell Tolls*," *The Hemingway Review* 10 (Fall 1990): 34-51.

    I first offered the Cohn-*con*-joke reading in my book, *Alchemy in The Sun Also Rises: Hidden Gold in Hemingway's Narrative* (Lewiston, New York: The Edwin Mellen Press 1992), where I do not use the joke nearly as much for purposes of biographical criticism as I do in this study.

13. As Robert E. Gajdusek notes in *Hemingway and Joyce: A Study in Debt and Payment* (Corte Madera, California: Square Circle Press, 1984), in a letter to Philip Young, Hemingway would "indicate that his model [for Jake] was actually a young man whose penis had been shot away but whose testicles and spermatic cord remained intact" (45n.73). Since the idea of Jake's much-debated wound as a shot-off penis could have been an afterthought of Hemingway, we have to find clues in that direction in the novel's text itself. I believe I provide the evidence to clinch that perennial argument in my *A Rotten Way to Be Wounded* book; but see also note 19.

14. Cohn's reaction to Brett having dumped him after a short-lived affair draws the following comment from Mike Campbell: "[Cohn] calls her Circe. . . . He claims she turns men into swine. Damn good. I wish I were one of these literary chaps" (144). For an intriguing discussion of Hemingway's use of Brett as a Circe figure, see Milton A. Cohen, "Circe and Her Swine: Domination and Debasement in *The Sun Also Rises*,"

Arizona Quarterly 41 (1985): 293-305. I further elaborate on Brett as a Circe figure in my *Rotten* book, but I would like to raise here the following question: did Hemingway present the literary chap Cohn as calling Brett "Circe" and thus as making an allusion to classical literature because the family of his Princeton-educated rival had founded the Loeb Classical Library?

15. Elliott, *The Power of Satire*, 64.

16. Jackson J. Benson cautioned in 1969 that the novel is full of wordplay that is "so . . . distasteful . . . that much of it will never be discussed in print" (*Hemingway: The Writer's Art of Self-Defense* [Minneapolis: University of Minnesota Press, 1969], 68). The question today, after Hinkle has opened the floodgates to close textual reading, is not how much will actually be discussed in print but, instead, how much distasteful wordplay *exists* in *The Sun Also Rises* that is also meaningful.

17. Hinkle, "What's Funny in *The Sun Also Rises*," 40.

18. Ibid.

19. Bill's gender-exchange joke would seem to provide additional evidence that the novel itself suggests that Jake's mysterious injury is the loss of his penis. It also reflects Hemingway's concern with androgyny; for discussions of this concern see Mark Spilka, *Hemingway's Quarrel with Androgyny* (Lincoln: University of Nebraska Press, 1990), and, with respect to *The Sun Also Rises*, the final chapter of my *Alchemy* book, "Androgyny and Parental Influence: Gender Roles and Battles between the Sexes."

20. Wirt Williams, *The Tragic Art of Ernest Hemingway* (Baton Rouge: Louisiana State University Press, 1981), 41, has suggested that Jake's accident could be read as a classic case of "*hubris*: Jake's wound is the consequence of his flying in the Italian air arm, and it was patently a romanticism, a thrust towards the ineluctable, to enlist in a foreign force in the first place."

21. Benson, *Hemingway*, 56.

22. Gajdusek, *Hemingway and Joyce*, 15.

23. Lynn, *Hemingway*, 53.

24. Ibid.

25. Cf. the caption to the photograph on page 289 in Lynn's *Hemingway*.

26. Jesse Bier, "Jake Barnes, Cockroaches, and Trout in *The Sun Also Rises*," *Arizona Quarterly* 39 (1983): 170.

27. Hinkle, "What's Funny in *The Sun Also Rises*," 36.

28. It should be noted that Hinkle possessed a tremendous knowledge of the historical background of *The Sun Also Rises*.

29. Reynolds, "The *Sun* in Its Time: Recovering the Historical Context," in *New Essays on The Sun Also Rises*, ed. Linda Wagner-Martin (Cambridge and New York: Cambridge University Press, 1987), 44.

THE SECRECIES OF THE PUBLIC HEMINGWAY

LINDA WAGNER-MARTIN

WE HAVE ALL BENEFITED from John Raeburn's study of Hemingway as a public personality, and even more recently from Leo Braudy's *The Frenzy of Renown, Fame and Its History*. I want today to suggest a new dimension to one quality that is reasonably well known about Hemingway's public persona: the secretiveness of it, the fact that Hemingway did not really talk a lot about his knowledge and his sources, did not ever quite "level" with his fellows, even though Braudy notes that Hemingway seemed to worship what he called the fellowship of writers and artists together, some "lost Eden of artistic camaraderie, always situated somewhere in the past" (546). One possible source for Hemingway's writing during the 1920s is the work of Blasco Ibanez, the Spanish-Argentinian author who was both writer and man of action, a writer Hemingway never mentioned, so far as I know.

In 1919-20 the Spanish author made a triumphal tour of the United States. He lectured, made public appearances, was welcomed in the House of Representatives, and was given an honorary doctorate from George Washington University; he became the center of attention for many American writers, readers, and moviegoers. Not only were his more than two dozen novels translated into English and made available in United States bookstores (such novels as *The Cabin*, 1898, *Reeds and Mud*, 1902, *The Naked Maja*, 1906, and the 1908 *Blood and Sand*), but his 1916 worldwide best-seller, *The Four Horsemen of the Apocalypse*, became the 1921 film that made Rudoph Valentino a star. Sold to U.S. filmmakers for $200,000, Blasco's antiwar novel became the prototype for antiwar fiction. Eventually it became the most widely read book ever printed, next to the Bible. Later in 1920, Gertrude Stein borrowed it from Sylvia Beach's Shakespeare and Company. It seems doubtful that Hemingway could have avoided knowing about either that novel or others that were filmed (*Blood and Sand*, 1922, with Valentino and Lila Lee; *Enemies of Women*, in 1923, with Lionel Barrymore and Alma Rubens; *Mare nostrum*, in 1926, with Alice Terry and Antonio Moreno; and *The Torrent*, 1926, with Greta Garbo)—or about Blasco himself.

Michael Reynolds points out in *Hemingway's Reading* that all of Hemingway's "first-hand experience was supplemented by research" (27) and that his personal aim of leading an adventurous life meant that he read quantities of biography of romantic figures (Byron, T. E. Lawrence, D. H. Lawrence) who "had led monumental public lives" (24). Blasco Ibanez fits this category. Born in 1867, the survivor of more than a dozen duels with monarchist firebrands, a radical reformer, Blasco—already a published author—was educated at the University of Valencia in law. In 1890 he exiled himself to Paris to escape prosecution as an antimonarchist conspirator, but in 1891 he returned to Valencia and married his first cousin. While there he also founded and edited *El pueblo*, a republican daily newspaper that serialized his first novel, *Arroz y tartana* (Rice and a carriage). In 1896 he was self-exiled to Italy. In 1898 he was elected for the first of 6 terms as deputy from Valencia to the National Congress— and then began his serious writing career. In 1910, he lived in Argentina and farmed; during World War I he lived in Paris, supporting the Allied cause; and in 1919 he was living at Monte Carlo. John Dos Passos criticized Blasco in one of the essays in his *Rosinante to the Road Again*, 1922, for his incredible public successes and his easy, fluid writing; yet Hemingway says nothing about him.

He did own copies of Blasco's novels. According to both the Brasch and Sigman *Hemingway's Library* and Reynolds's *Hemingway's Reading* and its supplement, Hemingway owned *Arroz y tartana*, *La barraca*, *A los pies de Venus*, *Blood and Sand*, the essays on South America, a collection of stories, and *The Four Horsemen of the Apocalypse*. Because Hemingway's borrowing records from Shakespeare and Company are lost for the years 1922-25, although we know that he borrowed extensively, I am assuming that his pattern with Blasco Ibanez was similar to that with other authors that he found useful. In Reynolds's words, "when Hemingway liked an author, he read him in depth" (16).

Reading the fiction of Blasco Ibanez suggests a number of similarities between his work and Hemingway's. In the best of the fiction, for example, in *La barraca*, the reader is convinced that the work is lyric, of a piece, tonally keyed to reflect the emotion in every narrative movement, descriptive detail, and choice of word. From beginning to end, the tapestry of language pounds away at the desired effect—here, pathos, courage, inevitable doom. (One is reminded in some ways of a novel that Hemingway admired so much that he recommended it to Hadley during their courtship, Knut Hamsun's *Hunger*; but the Blasco text is richer.)

The Spanish author cared about real people, both men and women, and while many of his works were "political," in that they spoke to the poverty in which these Spanish characters endured, they also emphasized the power of character with which people did the enduring. Santiago would fit well into Blasco's fictional world. An irrefutable part of that complex world was the characters' sexual life. For the late nineteenth century, this fiction is dramatically outspoken, doing on the scale of novel what many of Guy de Maupassant's shorter fictions had done for readers (and we know that Hemingway read Maupassant). In several of his novels, Blasco creates women who very much prefigure the Brett Ashleys of modernism; and his 1919 novel, *Los enemigos de la mujer*, creates a group of men who decide to exist without women. The novel proves these "enemies of women" foolish, but may have given Hemingway the title for his second collection of fiction, *Men Without Women*. (Published in the United States by Dutton, *Los enemigos de la mujer* went through twenty-one printings in two months of 1920.)

Some quotations or characters from Blasco's fiction suggest uses Hemingway may have made of this body of work:

1. This comment from Blasco's story, "Sunset" (*The Old Woman of the Movies*): "The death of the sun is not death at all. That sun knows that he will rise tomorrow morning in the east, and retraverse the path of glory he has followed for thousands and thousands of centuries. I imagine that is why, each evening, he bids us farewell so gloriously. He reminds me of a great actor who does a death-scene on the stage, with his mind on the midnight supper he is to have in the cafe an hour later" (172). (This is more than a little reminiscent of the epigraph to Hemingway's *The Sun Also Rises*; and one might speculate that his epigraph from Ecclesiastes might be as big a false lead as the "lost generation" quote attributed to Gertrude Stein).

2. To the far end of Hemingway's oeuvre, this passage about sharks from *Mare nostrum* (which saw twenty-four printings in August of 1919 alone): "The superior glutton is the shark;—that mouth with fins, that natatory intestine which swallows with equal indifference the dead and the living, flesh and wood, cleanses the waters of life and leaves a desert behind its wriggling tail" (68).

3. Ibañez's fiction includes an immense amount about the bullfight, which may have sparked Hemingway's short fiction, *The Sun Also Rises*, and *Death in the Afternoon*. This representative passage from *Blood and Sand*, a 1908 narrative of bullfighting, complete with footnotes of explanation for readers who were not aficionado:

Garabato pushed small wads of cotton-wool between his master's toes, and put a layer of it over the insteps and soles; then taking out the bandages he began to wrap them round in tight spirals like the bindings of an Egyptian mummy. He finished this operation by securing the ends with tiny stitches, with a needle and thread from his sleeve. . . . he now pulled on pink silk stockings to hide the white ones, and Gallardo slipped his feet into a pair of pumps selected from several which his servant had laid out for him on a chest, all quite new with white soles.

Then began the real business of dressing. The servant held out his knee-breeches of tobacco-coloured silk heavily embroidered with gold at the seams, and Gallardo pulled them on, leaving the thick cords with their gold tassels hanging loose. These cords, pulled tight below the knee, would constrict the legs and give them extra strength; they were called *machos*.

Gallardo told his servant to pull them as relentlessly tight as he could, and at the same time he swelled out his leg muscles. This was an operation of vital importance, for a matador must always wear his machos extremely tight, and Garabato quickly and skillfully rolled up and fastened the cords out of sight under the breeches, with tassels hanging. (21-22)

Blasco's message in *Blood and Sand* is that the crowd watching the bullfight is "the real beast," showing inhumanity toward the deaths of horses, bulls, and matadors as vividly as the reader can bear— Hemingway's "The Undefeated" resembles this fiction. Here Blasco's narrative of the matador Gallardo coming to the end of his career, fighting to keep his reputation despite his weakening body and will, ends with his being disemboweled in the same way countless horses are throughout the novel. (The persistent bull "had unseated three picadors, who were waiting for it with their lances ready, and of the horses two lay dying with dark gouts of blood gushing from the holes in their chests. The other was galloping round the arena, mad with pain and terror, with its saddle flapping loose and its stomach ripped open, showing the blue and red entrails like enormous sausages. As it dragged its intestines on the ground and trod on them with its hind feet, they gradually became disentangled as a skein is unravelled" [290].)

4. Blasco's women characters are modern, sexual, and outspoken: of the Duchess Alicia de Delille, in *Enemies of Women*, the author wrote, "she has lived life just as she pleased. . . . She has seen almost as much of it as I have. She has as much of a reputation as I. They even accuse her, just as they do me, of love affairs with people she has never seen" (25). When Alicia speaks for herself, she vaunts her differentness:

You know me too well ever to imagine that I believe in love as the majority of women do. I know that a certain amount of illusion is necessary to color the material aspect of love . . . but way down deep, I laugh at love as the world understands it, just as I laugh at so many things which people venerate. . . . I don't want lovers, I want admirers. I am not looking for love; I care more for adoration. . . . I am not afraid of what people say. (80-81)

Of the Princess Lubimoff, "an aggressive young woman, capricious and inconsistent in both words and deeds . . . smoking and drinking . . . and taking a hand in their exercises in horsemanship" (30-31), Blasco shows her erotically attracted to a Spaniard, demanding as her first act of flirtation to see his frightful wounds. In keeping with the plot of *Enemies of Women*, women like these are admired—because they are like men in many ways; but primarily they are feared because they become tyrants over men's lives, taking their privacy, desires, and money ("There is a glitter of gold at the bottom of every passion . . . . Love invariably ends by giving or taking money" [21].) In the words of the male protagonist, women

work their way into our lives, and finally dominate us, and want to mold our ways to suit their own. Their love for us after all is merely vanity, like that of the conqueror who loves the land that he has conquered with violence. They have all read books—nearly always stupidly and without understanding, to be sure, but they have read books—and such reading leaves them determined to satisfy all sorts of vague desires, and absurd whims, that succeed only in making slaves of us, and in moving us to act on impulses we have acquired in our own early romantic readings. (20-21)

The Hemingway reader will recall Jake Barnes's meditations on the cost of love, Count Mippipopolous's wounds, and some of Brett Ashley's contradictory qualities.

5. Blasco's attitudes were objectionable as he privileged these free-living women (especially in the 1906 *The Naked Maja*, a story of the passion of Josefina, the jealous wife of an artist who works from nude models), and many readers criticized the "morality" of his fiction. In his 1920 preface to the publication in English of *The Naked Maja*, he wrote about the role of the subconscious, which he called "the novelist's principal instrument," and criticized the attitudes of "a certain part of the Madrid public, unduly evil-minded" who persisted in reading the novel as a roman à clef, a story of real people. Blasco discussed the

way writers create characters, drawing from life but "only in a very fragmentary way . . . using the materials gathered in my observations to form completely new types which are the direct and legitimate off-spring of my own imagination. . . . As a novelist I am a painter, not a photographer." The issue of the source of fiction aside, he then concluded that "Far from believing it immoral, I consider this one of the most moral novels I have ever written. . . . Morality is not to be found in words but in deeds and in the lessons which these deeds teach" (vi-vii). We remember Hemingway's choice of wording as he claimed that *The Sun Also Rises*, the novel of his most sensational and most often criticized woman character, was his most "moral" novel. Ironically, though he had published a reminder of the fictionality of characters in the preface to *In Our Time*, his first commercially published book, he did not repeat that injunction in *The Sun Also Rises*, leaving its roman à clef character undisputed.

6. The most interesting set of suggestions garnered from reading Blasco Ibanez's fiction is the way combining stories of love and war is possible. In *The Four Horsemen of the Apocalypse*, the love story of Julio Desnoyers and Marguerite—who meet in the Garden of the Chapelle Expiatoire—is set within the World War I story, and is instrumental in making the foreign-born Desnoyers a part of that conflict. When Marguerite is caught up in the war and becomes a nurse, she finds her blinded husband (from whom she is separated) and realizes that she cannot leave him. In the anguish of his loss of the woman he loves, Desnoyers joins the army and witnesses all the terrors of wounding and death. "Desnoyers saw approaching along the high road the last stragglers from the infantry. They were not walking, they rather appeared to be dragging themselves forward, with the firm intention of advancing, but were betrayed by emaciated legs and bleeding feet. Some had sunk down for a moment by the roadside, agonized with weariness, in order to breathe without the weight of their knapsacks, and draw their swollen feet from their leather prisons, and wipe off the sweat; but upon trying to renew their march, they found it impossible to rise. Their bodies seemed made of stone. Fatigue had brought them to a condition bordering on catalepsy; so, unable to move, they were seeing dimly the rest of the army passing on as a fantastic file—battalions, more battalions, batteries, troops of horses. Then the silence, the night, the sleep on the stones and dust, shaken by most terrible nightmare" (258).

Violence, here and in some of the stories of *The Old Woman of the Movies*, is described graphically yet laconically: "the fantastic flash of the cinematograph;—the officer's head suddenly disappeared; two jets of blood spurted from his severed neck and his body collapsed like an empty sack" (373); "He saw men pierced through the middle by gun points whose reddened ends came out through their kidneys" (375); the village water supply contaminated because the head of a German was found in it (380). Desnoyers dies at the end of the novel, but before he does, he is faced with killing a man he knows, the German captain from the Atlantic crossing that had opened the novel, the German captain—"a corpulent, moustached man making speeches in the style of the Kaiser"—whose wife became one of Desnoyer's lovers: "The two men, during the interminable second in which they had confronted each other, had showed in their eyes something more than the surprise of an encounter, and the wish to overcome the other. Desnoyers knew that man. The captain knew him, too" (453).

Some of the war stories in the 1925 collection, *The Old Woman of the Movies*, published individually from 1919 to 1925, also provide vivid and succinct descriptions. The surviving soldier of "The Monster" returns home by ambulance, "horribly disfigured, his cheeks furrowed by the livid arabesques of terrible scars." Worse, he was "a mere trunk. . . . He ended there. He had no arms and no legs . . . a mutilated shred of human flesh with a living head" (365). In "A Serbian Night," Blasco depicts a retreat. "The long columns of women, children, and old people, intermingled with the pack animals . . . swallowed up in the night" (346), a retreat that leaves the hospitalized soldiers—fifty of them—to the enemy. Rather than be captured, they ask the captain of their troops to kill them, giving "honor" to their deaths. "With the blade of his sword turned outward, he thrust the point into their throats, seeking to cut the jugular vein with one stroke. . . . They came, crawling on all fours; they emerged like larvae from the shadows" (348). The story is about the effects this mass slaughter has on the captain, now a civilian, but the reader is left, as is he, with the image of the bloody bodies, "slowly emptying like red wine bags" (349). The war vignettes of *In Our Time*, *A Farewell to Arms* and *For Whom the Bell Tolls* all resonate with suggestions of these descriptions and plot lines.

If one of Hemingway's tendencies was to keep what he valued as important information to himself, even while seeming to share everything in his typically ingenuous Midwestern pattern, then we might infer that the writing of Blasco Ibanez was of some importance in the development of Hemingway's oeuvre, from its early configuration in stories of bullfighting, love, and war to its later appearances in treatises on a man's honorable life and death, and his relation to the sea.

WORKS CITED

Blasco Ibanez, Vicente. 1919. *The Cabin* (La barraca). Translated by Francis Haffkine Snow and Beatrice M. Mekota. New York: Alfred Knopf.

———. 1920. *The Enemies of Women* (Los enemigos de la mujer). Translated by Irving Brown. New York: E. P. Dutton.

———. 1919. *The Four Horsemen of the Apocalypse* (Los cuatro jinetes del apocalipsis). Translated by Charlotte Brewster Jordan. New York: E. P. Dutton.

———. 1920. *La Maja Desnuda* (Woman triumphant). Translated by Hayward Keniston. New York: E. P. Dutton.

———. 1919. *Mare nostrum* (Our sea). Translated by Charlotte Brewster Jordan. New York: E. P. Dutton.

———. 1925. *The Old Woman of the Movies and Other Stories*. Edited by Arthur Livingston. New York: E. P. Dutton. Includes "A Serbian Night," first published in *Hearst's International*; "The Monster," first published in the *Chicago Tribune*; and the title story first published in *McClure's Magazine*.

Brasch, James D., and Joseph Sigman. 1981. *Hemingway's Library, A Composite Record*. New York: Garland.

Braudy, Leo. 1986. *The Frenzy of Renown, Fame and Its History*. New York: Oxford University Press.

Day, A. Grove, and Edgar C. Knowlton Jr. 1972. *V. Blasco Ibanez*. Boston: Twayne.

Hamsun, Knut. 1920. *Hunger*. New York: Alfred Knopf.

Raeburn, John. 1984. *Fame Became of Him, Hemingway as Public Writer*. Bloomington: Indiana University Press.

Reynolds, Michael S. 1981. *Hemingway's Reading. 1910-1940, An Inventory*. Princeton: Princeton University Press.

———. 1986. "A Supplement to Hemingway's Reading: 1910-1940," *Studies in American Fiction* 14, no. 1 (spring): 99-108.

Stein, Gertrude. Borrowing Records from the Sylvia Beach Shakespeare and Company Bookstore, 1920, Beach Collection, Princeton University Library.

MANNERS AND MORALS IN
A FAREWELL TO ARMS

ROBERT W. LEWIS

A great traveller, [Herodotus] doubtless brought back . . . not a few travellers' tales; but the knowledge of men he acquired in the course of his travels made him value them not by reference to a preconceived standard, but for what they were. Foreign manners awake his interest, never his antagonism. If a man, he remarks, were given the chance to choose any system of beliefs and practices in the world, he would invariably choose those of his own country as the best; for custom is all. . . . It is a primitive philosophy—but it goes deep.

—Aubrey de Selincourt
Introduction to Herodotus, *The Histories*

MULTICULTURAL AWARENESS AND political correctness are catchphrases, but they nevertheless denote profoundly important educational principles. As Herodotus long ago perceived, so some recent intellectual travelers repeat his observations in a vastly different context—that of our schools. We go to school to acquire information and to learn how to judge and think. These activities provide us access to our culture. What we are, we have learned to become, to become "acculturated." Without resort to Emily Post or Miss Manners, we can play with the terms *cultured* and *mannered* and make the connections between knowing and thinking, on the one hand, and on the other, the social intercourse that from society to society is governed by attractive, curious, or incredible manners. Perhaps schools, from nurseries to universities, should be places where one not merely learns, but also acquires the *manners* enabling one to join in the many conversations of culture.[1]

Elsewhere, I and others have written about Ernest Hemingway's *A Farewell to Arms* as a bildungsroman (literally, an education novel or story of one's maturation.)[2] Many of his tentative titles alluded to such a novel, and three of them had the very word *education* in them. Clearly the

157

theme is pertinent, and if manners are a kind of instrumentality of education, tracing the presence of matters related to them may reveal interesting
connections.

Furthermore, the great subject matters of the realistic novel are the
manners and morals of the characters and classes written about. One reason we read novels, whether consciously or not, is to learn how to live well
and rightly. Thus, the direct pertinence of the false-true, nonessential-
essential, disguised-real themes in *A Farewell to Arms* or any other novel.[3]
(Obviously, we may also read novels to discover *how* such themes are present and artfully woven into the tales.) Manners, the prevailing modes of
social behavior, may not seem to be as equally important as the great
moral questions of right and wrong, as if one were to equate the knowledge of which fork to use with the ability to choose good and not evil. But
neither the realistic novel in general nor *A Farewell to Arms* in particular
reduces the treatment of manners to the trivial. Indeed, Hemingway ele-
vates manners to a kind of substitute for morality as he reveals the ambiguity of the important moral questions in the two spheres of the novel, the
public and the private. In the former, the war itself can only be believed in
as right and just by the naive and innocent. In the latter, Frederic's behavior is judged as totally immoral by the conventional wisdom of Helen
Ferguson. ("The Scotch are such a moral people" Catherine says of her
[246].) Ferguson too is as naive and innocent about their love as the chau-
vinist Gino (184-85) and the hero Ettore (119-24) are about the war.

In a world in which moral distinctions and clarity have been lost, knowing *how* to live fills the moral vacuum. This alternative is central to per-
ceiving how much of Hemingway's work is about a morally ambiguous
world in which the existential hero must learn a code of behavior, must
learn *manners* of profound value. The tyro-tutor distinctions among
repeated characters that Earl Rovit named and the code hero as distinguished from the Hemingway hero that Philip Young named have been
useful perceptions for many Hemingway readers. The tutor "teaches" the
tyro; the code hero sets a model of behavior for the Hemingway hero.
Usually the tyros and the Hemingway heroes are the protagonists, however, whereas the tutors and the code heroes are secondary or even minor
characters.

In *A Farewell to Arms,* Frederic's obvious instructors are the priest and
Count Greffi, but the attentive student learns from a wide range of other
characters who behave either well or illy, and chief among his teachers by
her manner of living is Catherine. Throughout the novel, then, Frederic the
narrator includes details of etiquette, not of the sort like choice of cutlery,
but of those conventions that are arbitrarily chosen and that define our
culture. On the one hand, if they are taken too seriously they become a

mockery, as illustrated in chapter 20 when Catherine and Frederic meet two Italians at the racetrack: "The Italians were full of manners." Two more Italians appear who "were also very mannered and matched manners with the two we had collected before. In a little while no one could sit down." Frederic is sardonic in this exaggeration, and Frederic and Catherine escape from the group with her saying, "Those last four boys were awful" (130-31). Catherine's use of *boys* suggests that fine manners do not convey maturity, and earlier Frederic makes a similar distinction in talking with the priest, whose values he has not yet embraced:

[Frederic] "Did you always love God?"
[Priest] "Ever since I was a little boy."
"Well," I said. I did not know what to say. "You are a fine boy," I said.
"I am a boy," he said. "But you call me father."
"That's politeness." (72)

That is, conventional good manners dictate filling the blank spaces in conversations, when one does "not know what to say," with polite if insincere remarks.

Similarly, the night before Frederic leaves Milan and Catherine to return to the front, it may be the somewhat obsequious behavior of the hotel manager as much as the whorehouse decor that saddens Catherine, seeing through his bowing and scraping behavior (151-52) as masking his real motive of gain (156). As another such illustration, just as there are real victories and then "victories in the papers," so Catherine and Frederic's behavior is divided between their real (private) love and their masked (public) behavior: "They would not let us go out together when I was off crutches because it was *unseemly* for a nurse *to be seen* unchaperoned with a patient who *did not look* as though he needed attendance." The head nurse would sometimes relax the unwritten rules of decorum, however, because "She thought Catherine came from very good people and that prejudiced her in her favor finally" (117-18, emphasis added; "good" in this context surely does not mean morally good, but cultured and "proper"). Frederic's weak excuse for having liquor and wine in his room is his appeal to head nurse Van Campen's sense of good manners. He tells her, "I have had Italian officers visit me frequently and I have kept brandy to offer them." Comically, the empty bear-shaped bottle of Kümmel "enraged her particularly," and she does not buy his rationalization. It *would* be good manners to offer guests a drink, but how could one politely offer an officer a drink out of a bottle absurdly shaped like a bear sitting on its haunches? When Van Campen berates Frederic for what she judges to be self-inflicted jaundice—"Pity is something that is wasted on you"—he satirically thanks her before launching a counterattack that infuriates her and drives her to drop the mask of good manners called for by the well-bred even toward someone rude or insulting (143-45).

Throughout the novel there are many examples of the superficial but socially important "good manners." The exchange between Frederic and the proprietor of a wine shop where he stops for coffee is marked by Frederic's polite evasion and the proprietor's polite but insistent inquiries as he seeks to sell Frederic his illicit services. He accepts the ten lire Frederic pays to buy off the prying barman; in contrast, the kind hospital porter subsequently refuses Frederic's ten lire. Good manners in the first instance makes buying the proprietor a drink acceptable, but good manners between true friends makes a payment of money in exchange for silence unneeded and possibly offensive (237-40).

Immediately after these episodes, Frederic seeks help from the American opera singer, Ralph Simmons, whom he had earlier disparaged. Frederic needs civilian clothing and information, both of which Simmons provides, but Simmons in turn needs sympathy for his singing failures:

> "I was a great flop at Piacenza."
> "I'm awfully sorry."
> "Oh yes—I went very badly. I sung well too. I'm going to try it again at the Lyrico here."
> "I'd like to be there."
> "You're awfully polite. You aren't in a bad mess, are you?" (241)

The wily Frederic uses his company manners to trade a guise of concern for what he needs, even aping his benefactor's speech pattern and twice following Simmons's use of *awfully* with the same word in language characteristic of his insincere persona: Simmons's "awfully early" and "awfully polite" alternate with Frederic's "awfully sorry" and "awfully busy." But Simmons is no fool, for right after calling Frederic "awfully polite," he guesses that the uncustomary language is motivated by need and connected with a "mess" (240-41). One might think that Frederic had gone to school with Emily Dickinson's "Tell all the Truth but tell it slant / Success in Circuit lies."

Other instances of manners in conventional forms include Frederic's choosing to arrive at the Stresa hotel in a carriage rather than on foot, knowing that the concierge would then be "very polite." Similarly, both he and Emilio, his barman friend, exchange white lies (of which there are many in the novel), whether they are about the promised tobacco (244, 266), the legal relationship of Catherine to Frederic (245), or the reason why Frederic is about to be arrested (264-65). Just as relationships with

servants tend to be governed by a code of behavior on the part of both the
server and the served—Kazuo Ishiguro's novel *The Remains of the Day* is
a fine recent narrative on the subject—so too are relationships with profes-
sionals, as illustrated by the stylized, polite dispute between the two Swiss
customs officers and Catherine and Frederic's equally stylized response to
it, ending with both of them saying, "Thank you very much," and the customs officials bowing them to the door, the one who had lost the argument bowing "a little coldly" (284). Similarly, the hospital personnel take
refuge in bedside manners to inspire confidence—for example, "'Things
are going very well,' the doctor said" (316)—and in conventional manners
after the death of Catherine and the baby. Three times the doctor asks
Frederic if he can take him to his hotel. The doctor needs to be allowed to
exercise some slight conventional act of good manners, but Frederic needs
to say goodbye to Catherine, and three times he says, "No, thank you."
With the nurses working in Catherine's room, however, Frederic reacts
rudely to their officiousness, ordering them out before he discovers the
futility of his desire (321-32).

As their relationship ends with ill manners, a slight breakdown of the
social lubricant, so too had it begun with Frederic transgressing and deceit-
fully using manners to attempt to seduce Catherine. On their first meeting
he uses the stilted and insincere "That's awfully nice" and "I'm awfully
sorry" (18), and he politely quizzes her in preparation for his next visit
when he makes his pass after Catherine informs him that the nurses are
"all on very special behavior" (25). "Please," he asks as he tries to kiss
her, and after she slaps him she says, "I'm so sorry" and "I'm dreadfully
sorry" and "I said I was sorry" as Frederic acknowledges she was right to
slap him and attempts to excuse his behavior and further advance his ultimate goal of seduction. His amorality is concealed by his superficially
good manners. Indeed, their next visit begins quite formally, moves
through further steps in their love game, and changes in their mutual
recognition that it is, in Catherine's words, "a rotten game" of mannered
moves. Frederic continues to play it, however, fantasizing about making
love to a pliant Catherine (37-38), yet also quickly forgetting her in his
drunken revelry (32) and being tardy for their date (41).

His manners with the two young sisters during the retreat are insensitive
to their fear and confusion (195-96), but with his men as well as his friends
Rinaldi and the priest and his fellow officers in the mess hall, he regularly
treats them kindly, albeit with situational manners, for instance, being the
bibulous joke teller in the officers' mess when the others are also (39-40).
Twice he backs down from confrontations, once on the crowded train,
where he recognizes that he was wrong to try to reserve a seat (158-59),
and later, again on a train, when "some aviators" treat him scornfully. The

latter incident is significant because Frederic is aware of a change within himself: "In the old days I would have insulted them and picked a fight," but, by implication, his manners are improving (243).

The episode in Stresa is full of revealing behavioral details, beginning with the rite of arrival at a good hotel, the cocktail rite, and the rite of the white lie. The barman Emilio tells his fish story: "Trolling this time of year you catch some beautiful pieces"—fish—but when they do go trolling they catch nothing (244, 255-56). Frederic and the barman also exchange white lies about the tobacco Frederic had promised and a thank-you card that of course the barman had not sent. Another white lie is understood as such by Emilio. Frederic tells him that one of the two nurses at Stresa is his wife, and the bartender replies jokingly, "The other is my wife." Emilio is as accurate as Frederic, but Frederic's response, "I am not joking," must then elicit an apology from Emilio: "Pardon my stupid joke. . . . I did not understand." Even though Frederic had lied, it was a different lie than the one about the unsent tobacco (245).

Frederic and Catherine's behavior vis-à-vis Helen Ferguson is problematical and instructive. Fergy is the moral barometer who loses in her moral argument to the greater power of love. Fergy's principle objection to their behavior is that they exercise all the privileges of marriage without the rite (and thus the right). Further, she fears that Frederic will not accept his responsibility to Catherine and the expected baby. Yet she eventually stands aside to allow them to impose the priority of love before friendship and situation ethics before absolute morality. Three years later, Hemingway would famously pronounce, "I know only that what is moral is what you feel good after and what is immoral is what you feel bad after. . . ."[4] Nevertheless, Fergy's belief in the wrongness of their behavior, past and present, does precede if not determine her friend's disastrous end. In this episode, and earlier in the Milan hospital, she fatalistically believes that her friend Catherine will suffer for her sins. She accurately predicts that they will not marry and that they will either quarrel or die. Frederic, on the other hand, is wrong on two accounts when he assures Fergy that he will marry Catherine and he will not "get her in trouble" (108).

Fergy is, finally, treated rather shabbily by Catherine and Frederic, but because it is Frederic's story to tell and not Catherine's, we do not know her feelings about their virtual rejection of Fergy. She, on the other hand, does little to deserve such ill-mannered behavior. Indeed, she makes a gesture of good manners even as she is upset by Frederic's sudden appearance and her intuition that the mufti-clad Frederic must be in some "mess." She and Catherine are at mess, dining, and even as Fergy's first words are challenges—"You're a fine mess. . . . What are you doing here?"—her next words are the somewhat humorously incongruous but absolutely polite

"Have you eaten?"—even her moral distress unable to displace the code of hospitality (246). Clearly, however, her morality rules her manners as surely as Catherine and Frederic's passion rules theirs. Frederic replies flippantly to Fergy's question as to why he is in mufti: "I'm in the Cabinet," and he does and says little to ease Fergy's distress. Indeed, he is willing to make matters worse by abandoning her in the middle of dinner and going off with Catherine to his room with its *letto matrimoniale* (marriage bed) and its satin coverlet. Catherine's manners are better than his, but she tends to patronize Fergy, patting her hand and comforting her as if she were a child: "There, there, Fergy. . . . I'll be ashamed. . . . Don't cry, old Fergy," while she plays footsie with and smiles at Frederic. Fergy is "sick" of Catherine and Frederic, and he is "sick of Fergy" in her crying, righteous anger. Yet Fergy does not want to be left alone by Catherine, her holiday spoiled, nor abandoned by them in the middle of dinner. They compromise, seeing dinner through but, in spite of Catherine's promise not to leave her afraid and alone at the virtually deserted resort, doing just that (244-49).

Catherine does visit Fergy the next morning and invites her to have lunch with her and Frederic: "I knew you wouldn't mind," Catherine generously says to him, but she also twice admonishes him to be "nice" to Fergy, to mind his manners (257). Frederic makes no mention of dinner, however. Do they leave Fergy to eat alone? They do utterly leave her in Stresa in the middle of the night when they flee to Switzerland. The last mention of Helen Ferguson reveals again that Catherine's sense of manners is stronger than Frederic's. As they are rowing across the lake, Catherine says to him, "Poor Ferguson. . . . In the morning she'll come to the hotel and find we're gone." Frederic's reply is not unexpected. He is not so much worried about poor Fergy or manners as he is about the practical matter at hand, their hazardous escape (271).

Between these references to Helen Ferguson are the episodes concerning that exemplar of fine manners, the 94-year-old Count Greffi. No doubt he functions in other ways too, but Frederic makes much of his manners, and they seem to have provided the Count an anchor throughout his long and cosmopolitan life. Neither state nor church, neither social philosophy nor religion, neither knowledge nor power—all of which he has known—has endured as guidance in his life. The young Frederic talks with, questions, and watches his venerable mentor, who reduces all conventional wisdom to good manners.

"An aged man is but a paltry thing," W. B. Yeats wrote the year before, in 1928, but this aged man is "younger than ever" and demonstrates the abilities that Frederic respects by drinking heartily and beating him in billiards. In a mad world, the pleasures of food and drink and the arbitrary precision of sport and game provide existential "meaning" precisely because they (like passion) ignore the world of ideas and beliefs.[5] The Count's billiard game is authentic and not fixed like the horse races at San Siro (chap. 20), and his drinking is not like that in the officers' mess (chaps. 3 and 7). He "was an old man with white hair and mustache and beautiful manners," no doubt complementing his profession as a diplomat who had been contemporary with the great Austrian statesman Prince Metternich. Frederic also knows that he was not a partisan nationalist, for he served both Austria and Italy, and in the same breath he notes that "his birthday parties were the great social event of Milan." The juxtaposition of his diplomatic career and his birthday parties is not as incongruous as it might seem, for both are highly mannered activities. Similarly, Frederic notes of his combining the drinking of champagne with the playing of billiards, "it was a splendid *custom*" (254, emphasis added). Good style, good form can do wonders to fill the voids of life, as the bowing of the distinguished Count impresses even the righteous and distraught Ferguson, who also is sufficiently impressed by the celebratory wine at lunch that she retires to her room to lie down.

Count Greffi, however, drinks two bottles of champagne with Frederic during and after their billiards game which the Count wins in spite of an eighteen-point handicap. The game and the drinking are the context for Frederic and the Count's conversation and the latter's impeccable manners. Even though he is much older than Frederic, he waits for him to sit down first and defers to him at every point, his good manners contrasting with Frederic's abrupt if not rude remarks in contradicting the Count, who transposes two words in the title of H. G. Wells's novel *Mr. Britling Sees It Through*. Frederic's unexplained contradiction of the little mistake fits with the theme of human ignorance (of not being able to see through apparent chaos), but here it also reveals Frederic's manners as rude in contrast to the Count's. Frederic's are those of the callow young man making a little joke. The Count, however, practices noblesse oblige and politely corrects Frederic's assumptions about wisdom. Nevertheless, the Count gives him some wisdom about religion and love before his last words, perfectly put to conclude the episode between this remarkably different pair: "We will walk up stairs together" (259-63).

Other episodes that nicely illustrate the public and private social lubrication of manners include the exchanges that Frederic and Catherine have with Emilio the barman and the hotel porter as they prepare their escape, and all subsequent interchanges with servants and waiters (267-69). Frederic is sensitive to and observant of such small rituals. In the rowboat crossing the big lake, the manners of Frederic and Catherine toward each other are a splendid illustration of the importance of knowing what to say and how to behave (chap. 37). "Grace under pressure" was Hemingway's definition of courage, and it is amply demonstrated here, as it was earlier by the Italian lieutenant colonel—arrested by the battle police—who is questioned and executed but who maintains his dignity and bearing. "I beg your pardon" and "please" he says in defiance of the cruel stupidity of the drumhead court-martial. He crosses himself and is ready to die (223-24). Also, of course, the ultimate in such courageous good manners are those of Catherine in labor and in her dying, when her one lapse, an abrupt "Don't touch me" directed at Frederic, serves to highlight her disregard of self and her concern for Frederic (chap. 41). Earlier Frederic had foreshadowed her death in his thoughts about the fate of the courageous, with whom he links the people of good manners. "The world breaks every one and afterward many are strong at the broken places. But those that will not break it kills. It kills the very good and the very gentle and the very brave impartially" (249). Catherine is that paragon, that nearly perfect exemplar of the good and brave gentlewoman. She epitomizes the transformation of what may at first glance appear to be merely superficial forms of social intercourse into radical behavior that demonstrates how one may live and die well and rightly.

NOTES

1. I am particularly indebted for these opening tropes to John Searle, "The Storm over the University," *New York Review of Books*, 6 December 1990, 34-42.

2. Ernest Hemingway, *A Farewell to Arms* (New York: Scribner's, 1929). References to the novel are cited parenthetically in the text, to the 1957, and still current, printing. My own development of the bildungsroman theme is in *A Farewell to Arms: The War of the Words* (New York: Macmillan, 1992).

3. See the chapter on *A Farewell to Arms*, "The Tough Romance," in my *Hemingway on Love* (Austin: University of Texas Press, 1965).

4. Ernest Hemingway, *Death in the Afternoon* (New York: Scribner's, 1932), 4.

5. For elaboration of the sport and game motifs, see my *A Farewell to Arms: The War of the Words*, 115-21, and my article "Hemingway's Concept of Sport and 'Soldier's Home,'" in *The Short Stories of Ernest Hemingway: Critical Essays*, ed. Jackson J. Benson (Durham: Duke University Press, 1975), 170-80.

HEMINGWAY'S *A FAREWELL TO ARMS*

THE WORLD BEYOND OAK PARK AND IDEALISM

ROBERT A. MARTIN

IN HIS DEFINITIVE STUDY of Hemingway's early years in Oak Park, Michael Reynolds in *The Young Hemingway* describes a boyhood that by all appearances would seem idyllic:

> In that world before the war, young Hemingway grew up in the heart of a secure, prosperous, educated and admired family, a family respected not for its wealth but for its integrity. Village life—for it was truly a village then—revolved slowly about church and family. . . . It was a world into which Chicago was not allowed to intrude, for the Oak Park founders, like the Hemingways, had built this haven to keep their families safe from the city's vice, filth, and hazard of fire. . . . For a young boy in those pre-war years, Oak Park was a world self-contained and entertained. . . . It was a world about which Hemingway never wrote a single story.[1]

Believing in the Victorian ideals of Oak Park and Teddy Roosevelt, Hemingway volunteered to man the American Red Cross Canteens at the Italian front in World War I. Soon afterward, on 8 July 1918, he was seriously wounded by shrapnel from a random Australian trench mortar. In order to come to terms with this painful experience, Hemingway had to find a realistic philosophy from which to understand the world and his own life. Eleven years later, in 1929, his new perspective appeared in his second novel, *A Farewell to Arms*.[2]

While *A Farewell to Arms* is not autobiographical in a literal sense, Hemingway drew heavily on his personal experience to portray Frederic Henry's world, and, according to Philip Young, to provide a catharsis for his own war trauma.[3] In addition, Hemingway became involved in a disillusioning love affair in Italy with a nurse, Agnes von Kurowsky. Frederic, who starts out as an idealistic volunteer on the Italian front lines, finally must face his devastating personal loss alone, and although *A Farewell to Arms* is not a religious novel, it deals with an important

167

theological problem of our time—the individual's search for ethics and values under modern conditions.[4] *A Farewell to Arms* is Hemingway's twentieth-century parable, describing his own and his romantic hero's gradual initiation into a chaotic, indifferent world—a world that is brutally stripped of illusion and controlled by fate.

Frederic Henry finds out about the world beyond Oak Park very gradually, through the people around him, the military action, and , above all, through his own subtle, internal development. Without any real experience in life at the beginning of the novel, Frederic listens intently to the opinions of the priest and Rinaldi, a surgeon. The priest, Hemingway's allegory for a good Christian man in our time, has "many tastes alike but with a difference between. . ."(14) him and Henry. In his advice to Frederic on the war he says: "It is never hopeless . . . I try always to hope but sometimes I cannot" (71). The priest's way to happiness is through unselfish love. He explains the ideal as "When you love you wish to do things for. You wish to sacrifice for. You wish to serve" (72). After Catherine dies, Frederic remarks with hindsight about the priest's understanding of love and his own reluctance to accept it. The priest "had always known what I did not know, and what, when I learned it, I was always able to forget. But I did not know it then, although I learned it later" (14). The priest has his love for God; Frederic finds his love with Catherine.[5]

In opposition to the priest, Dr. Rinaldi is Hemingway's representative of a man of science and reason in our time. Rinaldi argues against love and in defense of the inevitability of "nada."[6] Since nothing he does will have an impact, Rinaldi remarks, in a subtle play on words: "I don't think—I operate" (167). Like the priest, he tells Frederic, "really you are just like me underneath" (66); but there is also a difference between them. Applying existential values, Rinaldi prefers "the simpler pleasures" (41) of Villa Rossa and its whores to a complicated love affair. When Frederic returns to the front, Rinaldi teases him that love is one of Henry's "sacred subjects" (169). Rinaldi, however, is the knowledgeable "snake of reason" (170) who attempts to teach Frederic the truth about nihilism when he says: "You're dry and you're empty and there's nothing else. I know when I stop working" (174).

Frederic Henry also observes Rinaldi's pragmatic reality through the other characters, although he completely denies it until after he experiences military action at the front.

Catherine calls it a "silly front," and Frederic counters, "This is the picturesque front" (20). When Catherine exposes Frederic to a true picture of war, it becomes Hemingway's metaphor for life in the twentieth century.[7] Her fiancé did not die of "a sabre cut. They blew him all to bits" (20), but Frederic nevertheless insists that helmets in Gorizia are "too bloody theatrical" (28), believing that the war "seemed no more dangerous to me myself than war in the movies" (37). Before returning to his unit, he nonchalantly tells Catherine, "I am leaving now for a show up above Plava" (43). Catherine questions his description, "A show?" and immediately gives him her Saint Anthony medal, the saint for lost causes. On their way down the mountain, the ambulance driver reveals that he is doomed by showing Frederic a Saint Anthony medal he wears next to his heart. In contrast, Frederic Henry keeps his medal inside a capsule in his pocket and continues to ignore the omens around him, even after he gets to the front. Foreshadowing Frederic's experience in the retreat at Caporetto, Manera, one of the ambulance drivers, tells Henry how the Carabinieri randomly shot every tenth man of the Italian grenadiers and then left their families "without law to protect them" (49) because the grenadiers had refused to attack.

After Henry is wounded in a mortar attack, he experiences additional evidence of the chaotic, indifferent world around him. The nurse in charge of his care in Milan "can't do anything without the doctor's orders" (83), but the orders are in Italian, a language she cannot read. Later, again because of a miscommunication in language, the barber threatens him with a razor even though Henry is supposed to be a hero. Another hero, Ettore, "the boy they're running the war for" (121), confides in Henry that he has been awarded five medals for bravery, but the papers have only come through on one where the action was successful. Apparently, Italian medals are given only for military victories and not for heroism. Before he returns to the fighting, Henry begins to acquire some insight into the reality of the war, but has no real understanding of fate. He buys a secondhand pistol to wear, presumably to replace the rifle he keeps locked away in a trunk. The pistol "belonged to an officer who was an excellent shot" (148), but whose marksmanship evidently did him no good, since it was returned by his orderly after his death. Nevertheless, as John Stubbs has noted, Catherine and Frederic deny there is any real danger before Caporetto by role-playing together.[8] Catherine imagines that Frederic will be "a little hurt in the foot," and Frederic replies, "Or the lobe of the ear" (155).

In the same way that role-playing takes Frederic and Catherine away from their nihilistic world, the distant impersonal war at the beginning of *A Farewell to Arms* allows Henry to keep his romantic illusions. Step-by-step, however, the events of the novel teach him the meaning of his gratuitous fortune in an apathetic world.

Frederic, however, senses no danger from the war when his narrative begins. Before he actually sees combat, Henry remarks that the Austrians bombard "only a little in a military way" (5). Soon afterward, he makes his first nihilistic observation. He had imagined that the smooth running of his unit depended to a considerable extent on himself. Yet, he finds that, "Evidently it did not matter whether I was there or not. . . . The whole thing seemed to run better while I was away" (16, 17). Subsequently, when the action moves closer, becoming at once more realistic and nihilistic, during a mortar attack Frederic is seriously wounded and Passini is killed. True to fatalistic belief, this happens quite unexpectedly while they are eating cheese and drinking wine, even though they hide themselves in a dugout (54).

Once Frederic has actually experienced the terror of combat, the action depicts an even more devastating and senseless turmoil for him. When he learns that the Austrians have broken through at Caporetto, he is ordered to take the hospital equipment with him, but to leave the wounded behind (187). Although he observes that "There was no more disorder than in advance" (188), now advance and retreat are the same, and during the retreat, Frederic participates actively in the violence, adding to the confusion. Foreshadowing again the executions by Italian officers at the Tagliamento River, Frederic shoots a sergeant from his own side for desertion. Then, with an almost careless indifference, he shows Bonello how to fire his pistol to finish off the injured man in cold blood (204).

As the chaos increases on both sides, the Germans blow up a small bridge, but casually leave one on the main road intact for the Italians to use. German and Italian soldiers switch uniforms to confuse each other, and Frederic realizes, "We are in more danger from Italians than Germans (214). Although German bicycle troops clearly see Frederic and his men, they do not shoot. Nevertheless, like the sergeant, one of Frederic's drivers, Aymo, is saved from death from the Germans only to die a short while later under fire from his own side. Acknowledging the random violence of the action, Frederic comments: "No one bothered us when we were in plain sight along the railway. The killing came suddenly and unreasonably" (218).

Afterward, at the Tagliamento River, Frederic's personal survival is threatened, clearly providing a warning to him about nihilistic reality. Italian battle police randomly pull people out of the crowd for questioning, which automatically results in death by a firing squad. Frederic is selected by the battle police because he speaks with an accent; but, as he objects to the Carabiniere officer, "so do you, you—" (223). His objections, however, make absolutely no difference.

While order dissolves around him during and after his desertion, Frederic finds out that his own actions have no effect whatsoever on his destiny. For example, when he dives into the river in an effort to save himself from being executed, a random piece of timber in the fast-moving current rescues him, not his own actions. He later learns the same lesson in the boat on the way to Switzerland, as Catherine, who has always been closely attuned to reality, uses an umbrella as a sail while Frederic rests; he finds that doing nothing works better than all of his rowing.

Once they reach Switzerland, Frederic begins to act on his previous nihilistic experience. He tells Catherine to wave from the boat to a uniformed officer, who quite reasonably might decide to arrest them, because Frederic knows that nothing Catherine does will affect what happens to them. When he is questioned by German-speaking soldiers after they land in Switzerland, he observes that "you did not want something reasonable, you wanted something technical and then stuck to it without explanations" (281). Afterward, Catherine follows Frederic's lead, picking Montreux at random as the place they will stay. It is only at the end of the novel, when Catherine's life is in jeopardy, that Frederic forgets what he has learned, telling the doctor to "Operate as soon as you can" (321). He should know by this time that outside intervention will not change the outcome. Although Henry relies on a faulty instinct when he discusses Catherine's predicament with the doctor, he has already learned a great deal from the people around him—the rules of the combat game, and his own internal, growing awareness of nada.

Without any deliberate reflection, Frederic gradually discovers the truth through his own words. Frederic has a limited understanding of the world he lives in when he first encounters the opposing philosophies of Rinaldi and the priest. The priest wants Frederic Henry to go to the Abruzzi to find a religious love, so that Frederic can love and serve God and find happiness. When he returns from leave, however, he tells the disappointed priest that although he had wanted to visit the Abruzzi, fate had interfered: "we did not do the things we wanted to do; we never did such things" (13). Later, when he meets Catherine, Frederic explains that fate is also the reason why he joined the Italian army: "There isn't always an explanation for everything" (18). Then, in a scene with the priest after he returns to duty, Henry describes how he discovers values for himself when he confesses: "I never think and yet when I begin to talk I say things I have found out in my mind without thinking" (179).

Without any conscious effort, therefore, Frederic Henry and Hemingway continued to learn about the meaning of life beyond the mortal platitudes of Oak Park. In an internal monologue just before he learns that the Austrians have broken through at Caporetto, he recognizes the meaninglessness of empty forms that are invoked in the name of patriotism:

> I was always embarrassed by the words sacred, glorious, and sacrifice and the expression in vain. . . . There were many words that you could not stand

> to hear and finally only the names of places had dignity. . . . Abstract words
> such as glory, honor, courage, or hallow were obscene beside the concrete
> names of villages. . . . (184, 185)

As John Killinger has persuasively demonstrated, Frederic has finally
learned an important truth about his existential world: abstract words are
meaningless conceptions of complicated ethics, whereas he now determines
his existence in relation to the concrete objects around him.[9]

Because his vision of the world has become increasingly nihilistic, he
tries not to think. After his escape at the bridge, Frederic jumps aboard a
passing train, where he finds time to reflect. True to his existential belief,
he no longer feels anger or any obligation, and he does not care for outward forms. He longs for a simple life. He thinks, "I wished . . . I would
eat and stop thinking. I would have to stop" (232). Repeating this idea, he
decides, "I was not made to think. I was made to eat. My God, yes. Eat
and drink and sleep with Catherine" (233).

Faced with his awareness of nothingness, Frederic now has a clear
impression of how he must function. He has, finally, become wise, like the
cynical Rindali. Even Fergy notices the change in Frederic when they talk
in Stresa. She says, "You're like a snake" (246), the very word Rinaldi uses
to describe himself.

Frederic's philosophical understanding increases even more dramatically
during his time in Switzerland with Catherine. In his most eloquent monologue, he finally reveals what he has learned from the experience:

> If people bring so much courage to this world the world has to kill them to
> break them, so of course it kills them. The world breaks every one and after-
> ward many are strong at the broken places. But those that will not break it
> kills. It kills the very good and the very gentle and the very brave impartially.
> If you are none of these you can be sure it will kill you too but there will be
> no special hurry. (249)

Frederic here not only realizes that life is harsher on the good, the gentle,
and the brave, but also that some must suffer more and longer. In existential terms, Henry knows there is ultimately no hope. In the meantime, he
must continually attempt to recreate authentic life, gaining strength out of
suffering, to live to the full.[10]

When Catherine is in labor, Frederic applies what he has learned to the
present situation in an invective, internal speech: "This was the end of the
trap. This is what people got for loving each other. . . . So now they got her
in the end. You never got away with anything" (320). Six months earlier,
he had made a general comment, "You always feel trapped biologically"

(139). Experience has shown him that we are trapped in every way—by war, by love, and by death[11]—but immediately after his brave speech at the hospital he tries to deny what will obviously happen.

Once the dead baby is delivered, however, and Frederic is faced with Catherine's impending death, he recognizes his powerlessness to save her. Frederic's fine rhetoric about the impersonal "they" cries out with pessimism in a world without God.[12]

> Now Catherine would die. That was what you did. You died. You did not know what it was about. You never had time to learn. They threw you in and told you the rules and the first time they caught you off base they killed you. Or they killed you gratuitously like Aymo. Or gave you the syphilis like Rinaldi. But they killed you in the end. You could count on that. Stay around and they would kill you. (327)

Death is inevitable; Frederic Henry has studied the rules.

The rules, however, have nothing to do with violating moral conventions.[13] Catherine does not die from disease or as a result of her sexual promiscuity with Frederic, nor is her death the result of traveling with a deserter during wartime. Moreover, she receives entirely adequate medical treatment in the hospital, in sanitary surroundings, in spite of the war. Even the decision to go ahead with the Caesarean operation does not cause her death. Catherine dies of a spontaneous hemorrhage, which occurs randomly in women, having nothing to do with small hips or any medical procedure of the time.[14]

In the last minutes before Catherine dies, Frederic becomes terrified at the thought of losing her and sinking back into "nada." Panicked by fear, he momentarily forgets all he has learned and desperately reverts to repetitive praying. He forgets his vision of an indifferent Messiah allowing ants to steam to death in fire. He forgets his unreasonable injury. He forgets the stray mortar that killed Passini. He forgets how Aymo died at the hands of his fellow Italians. He forgets about Rinaldi's syphilis. He forgets that he killed an Italian sergeant without provocation. He forgets the battle police executions. He forgets his life was saved in the river by a stray piece of timber. He forgets how the wind carried the boat to Switzerland after he stopped rowing. He even forgets about his own son's death. But Catherine's last words bring him back sharply to reality—he knows she is right. Catherine's death, as she tells him, is "just another dirty trick" (331), with no rational explanation.

Hemingway's parable explaining how Frederic Henry finds out about his nihilistic world ends when he kisses Catherine just after she dies. He feels nothing: "It was like saying goodbye to a statue" (332). He walks out into the rain knowing, finally, that, as Killinger has observed, "the only peace of our time is the 'separate peace,' the nervous, tenuous half peace which can only be won over and over again."[15] Hemingway's romantic hero has learned what it means to be defeated by an indifferent fate in an indifferent universe. Frederic Henry's initiation is complete, and with it Hemingway, too, left Oak Park behind and everything it had taught him, everything he could never write about.[16]

NOTES

1. Michael Reynolds, *The Young Hemingway* (New York: Blackwell, 1986), 3-5.
2. Ernest Hemingway, *A Farewell to Arms* (New York: Scribner's, 1957 [1929]).
3. Philip Young, *Ernest Hemingway: A Reconsideration* (University Park: Pennsylvania State University Press, 1966), 27.
4. Ray B. West Jr., "The Unadulterated Sensibility," in *Twentieth Century Interpretations of A Farewell to Arms*, ed. Jay Gellens (Englewood Cliffs: Prentice-Hall, 1970), 16.
5. Bernard Oldsey, *Hemingway's Hidden Craft: The Writing of A Farewell to Arms* (University Park: Pennsylvania State University Press, 1979), 76.
6. Arthur Waldhorn, *A Reader's Guide to Ernest Hemingway* (New York: Ferrar, Straus, and Giroux, 1972), 120.
7. Joseph DeFalco, *The Hero in Hemingway's Short Stories* (Pittsburgh: University of Pittsburgh Press, 1963), 132.
8. John Stubbs, "Love and Role Playing in *A Farewell to Arms*," in *Fitzgerald/Hemingway Annual*, 1973, eds. Mathew Bruccoli and Frazer Clark Jr. (Washington, D.C.: Microcard, 1973), 275.
9. John Killinger, *Hemingway and the Dead Gods: A Study in Existentialism* (New York: Citadel Press, 1965), 49.
10. Ibid., 28.
11. Ray B. West Jr., "The Biological Trap: in *Hemingway: A Collection of Critical Essays*, ed. Robert P. Weeks (Englewood Cliffs: Prentice-Hall, 1962), 144.
12. Killinger, *Hemingway and the Dead Gods*, 47.
13. Norman Freidman, "Small Hips, Not War," 105-7.
14. For this information I am indebted to a former student who was an experienced surgical nurse in obstetrics, familiar with the history of caesarian deliveries and emergency procedures.
15. Killinger, *Hemingway and the Dead Gods*, 2.
16. To some degree, Agnes von Kurowsky, Hemingway's nurse in Milan and, he believed then, his future wife, was indirectly responsible for Hemingway's fictional representation of her as Catherine Barkley in *A Farewell to Arms*. From Italy, on 7 March 1919, she wrote to Hemingway

in Oak Park breaking their engagement, and saying that she expected "to be married soon" to an Italian officer, and that to her Hemingway was "just a boy—a kid." Catherine's painful death during childbirth was, consciously or unconsciously, Hemingway's method of resolving his anger and sense of betrayal toward Agnes. See Henry Villard and James Nagel, *Hemingway in Love and War* (Boston: Northeastern University Press, 1989), 163-64, for her "Dear John" letter and surviving correspondence with Hemingway.

I would also like to acknowledge the insights and perceptions contained in the essay in Scott Donaldson's *New Essays on A Farewell to Arms* (New York: Cambridge University Press, 1990), especially Donaldson's introduction, and also the similar insights derived from Robert W. Lewis' *A Farewell to Arms: The War of the Worlds* (New York: Twain, 1992). To Lewis, the novel "endures because its story of love and war, the old combination of subjects present in literature from the time of Homer's *Iliad* and *Odyssey* to today, touches us and helps us understand the human condition" (12). Further, Lewis concludes that "we are drawn to *A Farewell to Arms* not for what is says but for how it says it" (13). The opening paragraph of the novel that so enthralled F. Scott Fitzgerald may yet prove the authenticity of Hemingway's judgment on how a story is told, what can be left in and left out, and finally "how the weather was." Finally, I am greatly indebted to conversations over the years with Michael Reynolds and the factual information contained in his *Hemingway's First War* (Princeton: Princeton University Press, 1976), without which any study of *A Farewell to Arms* would be incomplete.

The Sexual Impasse to Romantic Order in Hemingway's Fiction

A Farewell to Arms, *Othello*, "Orpen," and the Hemingway Canon

Bickford Sylvester

Farewell the tranquil mind! *Farewell* content!
Farewell the plumed troops, and the big wars
That makes ambition virtue! O, *farewell*!
—*Othello*, III, iii (emphasis added)

℘   ℘   ℘

Othello's occupation's gone!
—*Othello*, III, iii (emphasis added)

I WANT TO SUGGEST AN interpretation of *A Farewell to Arms*, guided and informed by significant parallels, not only in the Shakespeare play that is the primary literary antecedent of the novel's title,[1] but in Hemingway's works as a whole, including an early apprentice tale. My interpretation supports the essential direction of recent readings by Solotaroff and Beversluis, readings indebted to Lewis in recognizing that the novel repudiates sexual love as a satisfactory substitute for worldly commitment.[2] Yet I will account for this basic thrust of the novel without depending upon speculation as to Hemingway's unconscious needs, as does Solotaroff, or upon textually unfounded Catherine-bashing, as does Beversluis. Rather, I will view the hero's attempted immersion in an emotional relationship as a conscious authorial strategy. I will see the novel's examination and rejection of sexual absorption as an experimental step in the author's progress toward his ultimate goal as an artist seeking—despite the harsh realities of the twentieth century—to realize some vestige of American romanticism's dream of perfectible human experience in a comprehensible universe.[3]

His immediate goal in this novel is to find a way in which his hero and heroine can satisfy the American romantic wish for culminative absorption in something, even though facing a world without convincing moral imperatives. The novel particularly asks what would happen if a man dealt with the hypocrisy and futility of all twentieth-century political, social, and professional endeavors by immersing himself in a relationship with an exemplary woman. Could this relationship yield fulfillment compensating for his retreat from the other kind of arms and from the world at large? As Solotaroff implies, and I will clarify, the answer is no; the price of this officer's "separate peace" is the sacrifice of his male need to do as well as to be. A twentieth-century Prince Prospero of sorts, Lt. Henry evades the adult's obligation to participate in the welter of worldly experience, and to do so without regard to practical success—an accomplishment that is the abiding benchmark of emotional and moral maturity throughout Hemingway's canon. (In this, Lt. Henry is like Wilson-Harris in *The Sun Also Rises*, stuck in the orderly insularity of Burguete, vaguely unfulfilled yet reluctant to return to the flux below.)[4] Consequently, as the prescient Catherine gently warns him by quoting Shakespeare, Lt. Henry becomes "Othello with his 'occupation gone.'"[5]

A glance at this line's meaning in the context of the play is instructive. The sentence Catherine adapts ("Othello's occupation's gone") refers not simply to a hero's abdication of his military/social/moral position; it refers also to his lost autonomy thereby—a loss of purpose leaving an "unoccupied" inner vacuum. In Othello's case that vacuum is occupied by Iago's chaos; in Henry's case it becomes an oppressive void, even before Catherine's death, and remains so at the novel's end. That void, I suggest, is the source of the emptiness criticism has attempted to define in seeking an objective correlative for the flatness of the conclusion. And the flatness is the point. It sets the stage for Hemingway's heroes to return, in the ensuing works, to principles of procedure rather than attachments, a reliance that had allowed Nick Adams and Jake Barnes to participate at last in worldly activity with dignity, despite the moral ambiguities of the twentieth century. The novel is thus a key work in a way we have not realized.

For Catherine, on the other hand, the situation is, to use her word, "different" (308)—or would be, if she did not love a male, and accept his needs because they are his. For her the emotional relationship and its biological fruits are sufficient "occupation," as she points out when she observes Frederic's lack of inner fulfillment. "I'm having a child," she explains, "and that makes me content not to *do* anything" (308, emphasis added). "But," she has just told Frederic, "you're different." She turns out to be right. In this regard, biology is destiny, here as elsewhere in Hemingway's fiction. *She* is overcome only by a fortuitous death. But if she and her child had lived, both she and Henry would have been thwarted by Henry's death-in-life. For by an adversity of nature, the circumscribed domestic stasis that would have been fulfillment for her would have been emptiness for the man she loved[6]—and also for the male child she envisions as a naval officer in the endless wars she foresees (147). For her to think only of the satisfaction she would derive from Frederic's endless absorption in their love would be to "ruin" him. That is the paradox of the desire she is willing to temper for him, but that he unwisely tries to share by denying his other needs: "Yes. I want to ruin you," she admits. "Good," he says, "that's what I want too" (315). And we hear, beyond the tenderness of his reply, his awareness that for him one "want" cancels out another, that his need to match her need inevitably implicates him in self-ruin. It has made him a man willing to say, "I'm no good when you're not there. I haven't any life at all any more" (310).

To turn now to "The Tale of Orpen," we see that *A Farewell to Arms* essentially re-examines the premise of this apprentice fantasy composed in Chicago in 1920.[7] Affirming the value of love over combat, the neglected tale is relevant not only to this novel, but to the rest of Hemingway's canon. Following a plot like that of Bierce's "Occurrence at the Owl Creek Bridge," the story presents the hallucinatory dream of a British soldier (formerly a pianist/composer), wounded while valiantly defending a bridge during WWI.[8] Between being hit by a shell fragment and regaining consciousness in surgery, the soldier dreams that he is in Valhalla—where the heroes are all secretly bored by the constant fighting they are supposed to enjoy—and then in Heaven, where his mother greets him in the music room where he used to compose at home. He confesses, to her joy, that he wants to compose there forever, rather than return to the war games in Valhalla. He is assured that he will not have to go back to Valhalla, first by his mother in the dream, and then by another woman's voice, a nurse's in the operating room as he awakes. Earlier in his dream, the soldier has overheard Lord Nelson, and other legendary warriors equally miserable in Valhalla, longing not for the battlefield, but for cloistered garden and homely business—and not for companions in arms, but for the arms and companionship of their wives.

Thus the young man's experience in the rest of his dream affirms his mother's assertion, just before he regains consciousness, that values traditionally considered female actually govern both sexes. A male's supposed love of combat is a pose, she indulgently explains, conditioned rather than innate; a man does not really want to do *anything* beyond participate in the domestic and artistic affairs that so satisfy the narrator's triumphant mother. This is, we note, almost exactly the initial premise developed by the plot of *A Farewell to Arms*, and then disproved by the tone and implications of Book Five. In the novel we see Hemingway the mature artist testing the revelation of his apprentice fantasy, and discovering in the process that the tale is wrong—that the traditionally feminine focus on home, the arts, and romantic attachments is, after all, totally satisfying only to the female—as Catherine instructs Frederic in the passage I have cited, as the youth in the tale had initially assumed, and as Western platonic tradition had taught.

From the perspective of the novel's conclusion, then, "Orpen" emerges as the narrator's imaginative trying-on of what might today be called his mother's "herstory," her revisionist interpretation of the past. Thrown into relief by Catherine's analysis of Frederic's incompleteness during their alpine idyll, Orpen's dream appears shaped by fear and by his unconscious wish to please his mother and surrender to values his mother has represented and encouraged. (Biographically, we think of Grace Hemingway's music room at 600 North Kenilworth Avenue.) The idea that male preoccupation with combat and glory is merely a social construct derives from Orpen's mother. The youthful Hemingway steals a march on some contemporary theorists in speculating that male aggression may be conditioned rather than innate, that the values of the hearth may be equally primary in men and women. It is this "herstory" that the novel's plot so sympathetically tests, before finding the dream-fantasy to be just that—a dream.

We could, certainly, view this early dream of a yonic universe, and Frederic Henry's subsequent attempt to live out that dream (together with the novel's ultimate rejection of the dream's universality), as demonstrating the author's ambivalent, personal struggle with androgyny. That would, of course, be consistent with Mark Spilka's recent approach[9] to what he and others see as Hemingway's fear of his own repressed identification with feminine values, an identification he could not acknowledge and thus unconsciously overcompensated for. Yet I am interested in the advertent craftsmanship of these thematic parallels; their psychosexual implications are clearly acknowledged by Hemingway's texts, rather than subtly encoded by his subconscious. Actually, the thematic continuity emerges as almost programmatic, when we think of novel and tale together (quite apart from the illuminating Othello analogues). Thus I resist the assumption that parallels so obvious to us, once we read "Orpen," were not intentionally developed by the man who composed both works.

Any artist of stature observes in human beings of both sexes paradoxically opposed drives for sexual absorption on the one hand and immolation in aggressive accomplishment on the other; both sexes feel at times both the need to cherish the temporal and the need to transcend it. Hemingway's work as a whole does affirm a difference in primary interests between the sexes: his women are more content to be, as Catherine says; his men have a greater need to sacrifice survival for values beyond the temporal. But "The Tale of Orpen" and its reexamination in *A Farewell to Arms* show how early Hemingway demonstrated the catholicity of spirit and the artistic openness of the later *The Garden of Eden* manuscripts. He is willing to toy creatively from the beginning with the chance that the values of hearth, bed, and music room (traditionally female values he himself had observed and intuited as primarily feminine) represent the deepest needs of both sexes—the fundamental needs of humanity.

In fact, *A Farewell to Arms* is not Hemingway's first major test of Orpen's dream. An unspoken premise developed and discarded in *The Sun Also Rises*, after all, is that love suffices for both man and woman. Jake (at first) and Brett (to the end) labor under the assumption that love itself— their great attachment, if it could be physically enhanced—would leave nothing lacking in the life of either. But having worked the issue through with a neurotically distracted, "bad" woman, Brett, and retested it with a devoted, "good" woman, Catherine, this literary artist affirms, ruefully, that the ideal unanimity of interests posited in the early tale is impossible for any male and female. Orpen's dream had mirrored his mother's unrealistic projection of female contentment with love and beauty and his own frustrated human yearning for discernible logic in nature. For many women the values of the hearth are primary, but for many men Valhalla's dominate; human nature is complex. Novel comments on dream fantasy, masterpiece upon apprentice work—as Hemingway's imagination grapples with the central threat to his rage for order.

Let us observe this continuing struggle in the rest of Hemingway's canon, and begin by tracing further the theme defined by the Othello allusions in *Farewell*. Much of Hemingway's fiction, we are seeing, is focused on the philosophical and creative attempt somehow to integrate a man's need for the love he can share with a woman and his need for aggression that she cannot share with him. The attractive folly of this attempted integration is an explicit, secondary theme in *Othello*, in a way that illuminates not only "Orpen" and *Farewell*, but also Hemingway's other major works. Othello's rash decision to take Desdemona to war with him at Cyprus contributes to his undoing. The issue of jealousy aside, one of the play's points is that Venus and Mars cannot be served simultaneously. That is what Desdemona's dying self-recrimination acknowledges, when she is asked who killed her: "Nobody—I myself" (V. ii. 122-23). As she earlier admitted, the "fair warrior," Desdemona (II. i. 179), has been "an unhandsome [inept] warrior," indeed (III. iv. 151), wishing to join her husband at the front, yet interrupting his martial duties with her womanly concern for Cassio's *personal* interests.

The play proclaims that men must sometimes subordinate domestic felicity to another primary need, must make a choice, and that Desdemona should have been left behind—as are all of Hemingway's major heroines after *A Farewell to Arms*: Marie Morgan, Maria, Renata, Tom Hudson's first wife, Catherine Bourne, and even Marita. They are "fair warriors" all, physically brave and wishing to share all of their men's commitments. Yet they are finally apart. That the heroine cannot share the competitive dimension of her man's life becomes a central issue in works like "The Short Happy Life of Francis Macomber"[10] and *The Garden of Eden.* When Margot Macomber finally respects her husband and personally enters into the danger of his new "life," she can, ironically, only shorten that "life." For had she hit the buffalo she aimed at, her aid would have been as inappropriate and intrusive to her husband's brain psychologically, as is her bullet physically. Acting, in an aggressive arena, on a need to protect (or assist)—a need released by her husband's newfound manhood—she can only lose. And twenty years later, in *Garden,* Catherine Bourne and Marita—serving as final test cases, we shall see—fail in the same arena.

The Mars/Venus conflict, made clear in his apprentice tale, plagues Hemingway's romantic sensibility to the end, then, as it does Lt. Henry's. But (revealingly) the apparent injustice of nature that defeats Henry becomes for Hemingway's ensuing protagonists the basis of a tragic, rather than pathetic vision. Their acceptance of the sexual impasse, heart-rending but undeniable, provides depth and poignancy in his portrayals of both men and women. The difference in primary interests between the sexes that Catherine selflessly invites Henry to see is for them a given: woman must temper her drive to share all parts of her man's life; to survive emotionally, man must temper his wish to reconcile his divided needs with her need.

In her tutelage, Catherine replaces the unrealistic mother of the "Tale of Orpen" and the similarly unrealistic Brett. She embodies the figure of the adoring sister-against-mother-and-"the others" of "The Last Good Country," *together* with maternal components of the feminine. In this, she prefigures Hemingway's most mature erotic heroines: Renata, the fictional/historical Hadley of *A Moveable Feast*, and Marita. Catherine Barkley possesses the necessary balance lacking in Catherine Bourne—that *anti*-maternal (competitive rather than sharing) sister, supplanted for a time by the balanced sharer/nurturer Marita. And it is a woman's wisdom, we note, that explicitly acknowledges the obstacle to coherence and bliss in Hemingway's world.

However, Henry does not respond to this "female ministrant's"[11] warning that he cannot find retreat from worldly activity as fulfilling as she can. He ignores her implication that he must deal with a side of his nature that she cannot share—with an irreducible inner conflict as a male from which there is no separate peace. For a contradiction of nature mocks not only the vanity of human wishes but, worse, of human logic: that is the burden of Catherine's wisdom that Henry cannot bear. His Hardyesque reflections on determinism show him in Book V intellectualizing still, belaboring the world at the very juncture where Hemingway's exemplary heroes are learning how to live in it. The novel's point, therefore, is not that an adverse cosmos deprives us of believable political and religious purposes in the twentieth century and then capriciously denies us the private satisfactions to which we retreat. The point is that it was folly for Henry (far more literally than Catherine) ever to have assumed otherwise. Having slipped into dependence upon a sexual relationship for "things he cannot lose"—as has the major of "In Another Country," he has placed "himself in a position to lose" the only thing a Hemingway protagonist need not lose: the resigned acceptance of inevitable material failure that allows a human being to be "destroyed, but not defeated."[12]

A *Farewell to Arms* is not the departure from Hemingway's vision some have seen, then; it affirms by omission the one point of view sustaining all his other major protagonists. The emotional flatness of the conclusion shows what happens to a protagonist who cannot accept Hemingway's only alternative to despair. That alternative, of course, is the satisfaction of mastering "the old thing" of *The Sun Also Rises*—of holding one's "purity of line" when facing "the maximum of exposure."[13] And the maximum of exposure for Frederic Henry, as for any Hemingway hero, is to commit himself to the plain of worldly struggle and perform *as if* material success were possible, yet with the full recognition that it is not. This paradox is what the major of "In Another Country" has grasped during his three-day withdrawal—his rebirth into "another country" of the mind that brings him back to physiotherapy without caring that the exercises are useless in any practical sense. He has "resigned" himself, as have the three heavily decorated soldiers, the "hunting hawks" with "detached" eyes, who have faced death enough times to "see" beyond the inevitability of material defeat. It is to that "country" beyond the material realm that the major directs his now-detached gaze "out of the window" at the end, beyond hope for a restored hand or wife. He is reconciled (as Henry never is) to the spare compensation of going through the motions of commitment in an apparently random world, simply because this is the "country" in which we have been placed and in which we must participate with resolution, if we are to demonstrate our full detachment from the dashed dreams of mortal life. Only thus can we prove our true "farewell" to all that men and women hope to gain by weapons or by embraces.

Immersion in the destructive element, Henry's one viable recourse, is the thing conspicuously left out when the lieutenant does *not* take this final step forward, as does the major. The published story of 1926 thus stands with "The Tale of Orpen" as the 1929 novel's twin imaginative precursor (we now see), and serves as the tale's corrective foil. The novel's ending, with Henry in a state of inconsolable adolescence (compare Joe's in "My Old Man"), dramatizes the dead-end awaiting those unable to look beyond mortal adversity and therefore destined never to become "strong at the broken places" (258-59). It is not surprising, after this reexamination, that for the male protagonist in the great remaining works the only way to satisfying "life" atop the mountain is through a commitment to timeless principles of action on the temporal plain below.

In the psychomachia "The Snows of Kilimanjaro," an example not yet mentioned, it is because Harry resumes his "occupation" (as he inwardly "writes" his true history) that he earns his mystically perceived passage from the plain to a mountain perpetually frozen—to a refuge beyond time, as Catherine and Frederic's mountain is not. In the middle and late works, this commitment to action in the world inevitably leads the hero apart from the heroine and to temporal death. But what matters more to both[14] is his life-in-death (signaled, even for Harry Morgan, by some kind of epiphany): the strange freedom of having performed "without hope but with resolution,"[15] an ethic as invulnerable and abiding as high snows that do not melt in the spring.

As for the already fulfilled female protagonist with child in *Farewell*, if she had to think only of herself, her temporal death would be merely a "hated" end (341) of achieved satisfaction.[16] But we have seen that the life of shared survival and fruition that might have made her "content"[17] is death-in-life to the man with whom she has "wanted" to merge. And hers is, with variations, the bitter paradox faced by the female protagonists in all the subsequent major works (a paradox much like that in *Women in Love*).[18]

Criticism should trace fully this continuity persisting from "Orpen" through the *Garden* manuscripts. The latter deal as centrally as the rest of the canon with the conflict between nurturing and aggression, love and objective accomplishment—with the male's need for togetherness and aggressive individualism, and the dilemma his divided needs create for the female. The manuscripts even reopen the nature-nurture question of "Orpen," to test a new, converse approach to the conflict. If cultural taboos were canceled, might aggression balance nurturing in women as well as men, so that all experience could be shared? "I want to hold the legs of the gun and love thee all in the same moment," Hemingway's heroine had begged in *For Whom the Bell Tolls* (1940); and his protagonist had come to believe (conveniently late) that the feminine is not alien to combat: that "her breasts . . . could know about the two of them in battle."[19] Accordingly, in the '46-

'58 *Garden* manuscripts Hemingway brings his "fair warriors" to the front once more, as Catherine and Marita approach the warrior-writer David's creative field of struggle. Catherine's androgyny serves there to reverse acculturation, in experiments heterosexual in purpose within the large context of the work. Their function is to determine, again, whether the ruthless, aggressive component of man's need to create form and/or take life is dominant by nature or conditioning, and (this time) whether or not woman can discover in herself the capacity to experience such aggression, so as to participate in man's endeavor rather than merely appreciate its necessity in another. But Catherine is in practice torn apart by needs simultaneously to compete and nurture. And though Marita incorporates both drives in a nearly incredible symbiosis with David's, not even their remarkable concord of interests holds them together. In a bold, final attempt to resolve creatively the impasse of differing primary concerns between the sexes, these speculative portrayals of sexual atavism push human nature beyond its limits. Catherine's insatiable narcissistic yearning for impossible fulfillment comments on the kindred obsessiveness of creativity—on the artistic impetus to reconcile all contradictions that is at once David's motive for taking part in her exercises and Hemingway's motive for having set this artist parable in motion. The sin in (and of) Hemingway's garden is humanity's rage to make where it cannot know. It is a necessary sin—nature's paradoxical response to natural paradox—but still a sin, the final bafflement that is perhaps his ultimate subject. For Catherine's madness, David's unending ambivalence toward her, and his unexplained separation from the ideal Marita mark the grand futility of a Faustian design—in the quests of characters and author. The doomed romanticism spanning a career is renounced as always; as always, its tragic implications prevail.

Patient study is needed to assess the full implications of these narratives for Hemingway's total vision. Some suspect a self-reflexivity canceling out all avenues to closure. But David's reappearance with his flawed Catherine in the "provisional endings" may imply something new and potentially affirmative: that without hope for perfectibility in human experience or comprehension, men and women can yet be sustained by living humbly, lovingly, with the sexual impasse that becomes Hemingway's donnée for an unfathomable cosmos.[20] We may construe in the fragments as a whole a thrust toward closure based upon classical resignation, beyond reliance even upon Hemingway's customary mysticism. This would be an advance. For the resolutions of his other mature works, profound as they are, sustain his muted romanticism by the reassurance of epiphany—by transcending those contradictions in the human breast that render all quests for concord in love "unfinding," and the maker's quest for intimations of order "unrealizable" in the end.[21] But wherever we come to see his epistemological search as leading, we can trace—from apprentice sketch to posthumous manuscripts—yet another record of Hemingway's unrelenting artistic tenacity and courage.

NOTES

1. Overlooking the *Othello* quotation and parallels discussed later, we have accepted Hemingway's misleading intimation (propagated by Carlos Baker) that he had solely in mind the title of George Peele's poem to Queen Elizabeth. See *Ernest Hemingway: A Life Story* (New York: Scribner's, 1969), 199, 430. For Hemingway's "leaking" half-truths to conceal his allusions, see my "The Writer as l'homme engagé: Persona As Literary Device in Hemingway and Malraux," *North Dakota Quarterly* 60, no. 2 (Spring 1992): 19-38.

2. Robert Solotaroff, "Sexual Identity in *A Farewell to Arms*," *The Hemingway Review* 9 (Fall 1989): 2-17; John Beversluis, "Dispelling the Romantic Myth: A Study of *A Farewell to Arms*," *The Hemingway Review* 9 (Fall 1989): 18-25; Robert W. Lewis, *Hemingway on Love* (Austin: University of Texas Press, 1965), 45-54.

3. For Hemingway's epistemology as essentially that of romanticism rather than realism, see C. Hugh Holman's important "Hemingway and Emerson: Notes on the Continuity of an Aesthetic Tradition," *Modern Fiction Studies* 1 (August 1955): 12-16; my "Hemingway's Extended Vision: The Old Man and the Sea," *Publications of the Moderern Language Association* 81 (March 1966): 130-38; Oliver Evans's "'The Snows of Kilimanjaro': A Revaluation," *Publications of the Moderern Language Association* 77 (December 1961): 601-7; my "Winner Take Nothing: Development as Dilemma for the Hemingway Heroine," *Pacific Coast Philology* 21 (1986): esp. 75.

4. Ernest Hemingway, *The Sun Also Rises* (New York: Scribner's, 1926), 125-30.

5. Ernest Hemingway, *A Farewell to Arms* (New York: Scribner's, 1929), 266. subsequent references are to this edition. In *Othello*, see III. iii. 354.

6. For Hemingway's romantic epistemology and the sexual paradox see Evans, "'The Snows of Kilimanjaro,'" and my "Winner Take Nothing."

7. John F. Kennedy Library Hemingway Collection, Item #445 (a seventeen-page, untitled, complete story typescript).

8. Sir William Newenham Montague Orpen (1878-1931) was a British painter, appointed Official War Artist in 1917, whose paintings and drawings presented the exploits and suffering of all ranks in WWI: *The Dictionary of National Biography, 1931-1940*, edited by L. G. Wickham Legg (London: Oxford University Press, 1949), 660-62.

9. Mark Spilka, *Hemingway's Quarrel with Androgyny* (Lincoln: University of Nebraska Press, 1990).

10. For Hemingway stories see *The Complete Short Stories of Ernest Hemingway* (New York: Scribner's, 1987).

11. The term is Peter Hays's: "Ministrant Barkley in *A Farewell to Arms*," in *Hemingway in Italy and Other Essays*, edited by Robert W. Lewis (New York: Praeger, 1990), 123-30.

12. Ernest Hemingway, *The Old Man and the Sea* (New York: Scribner's, 1952), 114.

13. Hemingway, *The Sun Also Rises*, 168.

14. The sole exception, Harry's well-intentioned wife, lacks the vision of Catherine and the other heroines; thus he must verbally shunt her survivalist illusions, as well as leave her apart from his inner struggle for vocational integrity that is beyond her interests.

15. Hemingway, *The Old Man and the Sea*, 113.

16. Catherine's death is a reversal, the only time in Hemingway's works when the heroine, free of the primacy of physical survival, leaves the hero behind with nothing to cling to. Cf. Joyce Wexler, "E.R.A. for Hemingway: A Feminist Defense of *A Farewell to Arms*," *Georgia Review* 35 (1981): 122. Wexler's approach needs adjustment to accept the sexual differentiation of Catherine's example. Catherine has demonstrated, as a woman, the full human potential Henry could have emulated by accepting his corollary commitment, as a man, that she tactfully acknowledged.

17. In the *Othello* passage Catherine quoted earlier, the words "Farewell content!" (l. 343) subtly link contentment with "the plumed troops, and the big wars" (l. 344) in the warrior's mind, and by extension here in Henry's, as opposed to hers.

18. D. H. Lawrence, *Women in Love* (New York: The Viking Press, 1920).

19. Ernest Hemingway, *For Whom the Bell Tolls* (New York: Scribner's, 1940), 270, 456. See also Renata to Cantwell: "I would wish to be a soldier if I could fight under you" (Ernest Hemingway, *Across the River and Into the Trees* [New York: Scribner's, 1950], 231).

20. "World very complicated . . . as long as they have mens and womens, will have plenty problems": Hemingway on *Garden*, letter to C. T. Lanham (7/14/46), Princeton University Library (C0067).

21. Ernest Hemingway, *The Garden of Eden* (New York: Scribner's, 1986), 193, an accessible but misleading condensation. My remarks refer to the unpublished manuscripts at the J.F.K. Library (KL 422.1-422.9c, 609).

NINA BAYM'S BENEVOLENT READING OF THE MACOMBER STORY

AN EPISTOLARY RESPONSE

MARK SPILKA

LATE THIS SPRING I received from Nina Baym an unsolicited xerox copy of an essay she had contributed to Jackson Benson's 1990 anthology, *New Critical Approaches to the Short Stories of Ernest Hemingway*. Under the editor's rubric, *Feminist Perspective*, the essay was entitled "Actually, I Felt Sorry for the Lion." On the cover sheet, a copy of the title page of the anthology, the author had written: "for Mark Spilka— no rest for the 'purely benevolent view' after all! Sincerely, Nina Baym." She was plainly quoting back to me a sentence from one of my own essays, "A Source for the Macomber 'Accident': Marryat's *Percival Keene*," which had originally appeared in the *Hemingway Review* in Spring 1984, but which has since become available in slightly modified form as Appendix A in my own book of 1990, *Hemingway's Quarrel with Androgyny*. In both versions of that essay I had shown that Hemingway's famous story, "The Short Happy Life of Francis Macomber," had been influenced by aspects of Marryat's novel, including the thrice repeated lines from Shakespeare, "We all owe Heaven a Death"; a comic incident of a cowardly man running before a charging cow; and, shortly afterward, a nearly tragic shooting accident during hunting season by which the hero receives a shotgun blast in the back of the head, which later proves to have been a deliberate attempt to kill him. After displaying these suggestive items I had provisionally held that the concluding evidence of murderous intent in Marryat's novel "might help to settle a long-standing dispute about the ending [of Hemingway's story], now in its third decade. For if Hemingway had been storing up since boyhood—or even since the 1920s—the possibility of writing his own version of a hunting 'accident' grounded in hidden motives, the case for a purely benevolent view of Margot's motives (along with a lofty ironic view of life's mischances) might be put to its well-deserved rest."

Fortunately, I was wise enough to begin the next paragraph with the statement that, given our disputatious nature as academics, "I don't for a

moment believe that will happen." Actually, I did hope that it would happen, or at the least, that it would quiet things down for a good long time;
but—*Bango*—seven years later I hear from restlessly benevolent Nina
Baym, whom I would now like to answer through the following open letter:

August 24, 1991

Dear Nina Baym:

I have just finished reading your Macomber essay for the third time, in
preparation for an open answer to it, and must confess that I think it is a
terrific essay. You make the best and most persuasive case I have ever seen
for the "purely benevolent view," and against my own characteristic male
resistance and denial I have to admit that I admire and like it and agree
with most of what you say and with most of your reasons for saying it.
Your case for the importance of the lion's point of view over the first half
of the story, and its continuation through Margot's point of view for the
rest of the tale, seems to me incontrovertible; and that you make it in
behalf of the story's readers, not its author, seems to me also a refreshingly
welcome change, including as it does those resisting women readers and
their brothers, as Judith Fetterley might call them, for whom standard
male readings in the past have had no place.

In some ways I count myself among those resisting readers. I assume
you sent me a copy of your manuscript because you thought so too, or at
the least because you found me redeemable or persuadable. You must have
noted, that is to say, my obvious regret in the essay on which you base
your salutation that Hemingway was *loco* enough to want us to enjoy
Wilson's humiliation of Margot at the end, his continuation of the power
struggle with her slain husband, his awareness of her mixed feelings, and
his conscious cruelty nonetheless in affixing her with the revenge motive
and dismissing her better impulses. I will come back to the issue of
Margot's mixed feelings later, because you do not allow for them in your
essay; but for the moment I want to focus on my own redeemability as one
who does not happily accept the author's chauvinism in this story as an
exemplary male model. In my new Hemingway book, for instance, I further suggest that, in a world where men are more likely to kill women than
be killed by them, Hemingway may well be projecting onto Margot his
own vengeful feelings. I also suggest that "the story proceeds on false or
contradictory premises, established by the guide, which Hemingway here
and elsewhere underwrites" (239). I then cite the tale's fallacious premise

"that courage acquired on safaris—the courage to dominate and destroy," can be equated with "the constructive courage required in homes, in domestic relations, where grown men often prove evasive, one might well say cowardly, whatever their frontier performances" (240). Also, like you, I reexamine the guide's story, his willingness to hire himself out, as it were, as my lady's fucker, his status as a bachelor and a hired stud who confines himself to minor put-downs and pointedly believes that "women *are* a nuisance on safaris" because they set men against each other. I note also, in this vein, his ultimate reduction of the transferable male courage he posits into the courage to *leave* difficult women, not to live with them as equals.

Of course, my point is that Hemingway all too sadly sides with him on the principle of renewable and transferable manhood and any number of related matters; and though he stands a little to one side of him throughout the story, and shows us more than the guide encompasses, he uses him nonetheless to make his concluding points about the hidden meaning of the shooting "accident." I further place this story as representative of the hardening of the author's outlook during the 1930s, and therefore not easily equitable with those sympathetic stories of the 1920s, "Cat in the Rain" and "Hills Like White Elephants," which you rightly cite as indicating an early concern for women in the face of "male self-involvement and self-aggrandizement" (112). Whatever our differences, however, I think you make some devastating points about Wilson's "cannon," his blunderbuss for ensuring the deaths or disablings of recalcitrant animals; and, perhaps more to the point, you seem to me brilliantly right about Hemingway's capacity to get across Margot's point of view as an extension of the lion's, so that even though he never enters her thoughts extensively, her voice becomes a powerful focus for all things questionable in the male hunting code. As when, for instance, she makes those three telling objections:

> "I want to see you perform again. You were lovely this morning. That is if blowing things' heads off is lovely."
>
> "It seemed very unfair to me . . . chasing those big helpless things in a motor car."
>
> "You're both talking rot. . . . Just because you've chased some helpless animals in a motor car you talk like heroes."

Not a hunter myself, nor likely to become one, I have always secretly shared that view of "male bonding and blood sports," to use your own ethnocentric labels for these matters. The evidence, new and old, that Hemingway himself drew the line at shooting elephants, that he killed animals chiefly to keep from killing himself, that he self-satirized his own vainglory as a hunter and sometimes even balked at his own male demands, suggests further that he well understood how a woman might feel about big-game hunting. He has given us in Margot a more powerful critique of his own macho standards than we have previously seen, or have even been able to see, and your reading deserves full credit for making that critique so incontrovertibly evident.

My problem now is how to disagree with you without falling into the traps set in your essay for those who use male authority to set women straight or keep them down, or who cut off discussion with that old male shibboleth of the single correct reading of a story. Let me object then chiefly that your reading turns the tale upside down: you not only open the tale to resistant women readers and their brothers, you destroy it for everyone else, including Hemingway. Or as a deconstructionist might put it, your marginal reading is now not only central: it envelopes the text. I would like a more balanced resolution myself, and accordingly invoke a helpful observation from D. H. Lawrence's *Study of Thomas Hardy*: namely, that "every work of art . . . must contain the essential criticism on the morality to which it adheres." The beauty of that observation is its implication that the morality will be balanced and tempered by the criticism; it will be challenged and tested by it rather than destroyed or displaced; and the work of art will itself be strengthened by containing both the tested morality and the challenging critique. My problem then is to demonstrate how your reading challenges and tests the tale's morality without altogether displacing it.

Let me begin with your marvelous bit of hubris about what Margot knows. You proceed fairly enough as you explain how the lion's point of view on the hunt and slaughter "is transferred to Margot Macomber":

> She registers Macomber's cowardice, Wilson's brutality [with his slaughtering cannon], and the interdependence of the two as epitomized in the lion's fate. She also recognizes that the animals in the wild are not true adversaries or antagonists, because they are so massively overpowered by the men's technology—their guns, their cars. The safari as she sees it is a sham, its participants hypocrites. Wilson, who makes his living by manipulating the appearances of mortal danger for the titillation of his clients, is anxious to suppress her point of view, and he appears to succeed at the story's close. (114)

I am impressed, I confess, by the way you prepare here for your view of Margot as framed or trapped, like the lion, between her husband's cowardly and Wilson's bullying ways. I have no quarrel with your perception of that dilemma. However, when you later review the story of the lion, you make a few questionable statements yourself. Let me quote the crucial sequence to illustrate my several points:

> She comes to hate hunting when she sees what it consists of. She sees that Macomber, with Wilson and his gun behind him, is never in any real danger. And she sees that what is a matter of life and death for the animal becomes a wasteful war game for men. The story quietly endorses her judgment by giving the lion himself the last word on his wounding and death.
>
> That was the story of the lion. Macomber did not know how the lion had felt before he started his rush, nor during it when the unbelievable smash of the .505 with a muzzle velocity of two tons had hit him in the mouth, nor what kept him coming after that, when the second ripping crash had smashed his hind quarters and he had come crawling on toward the crashing, blasting thing that had destroyed him. Wilson knew something about it and only expressed it by saying "damned fine lion." (120)
>
> Macomber knew nothing about the lion. Wilson knew something, but a good deal less than he thought; Margot knew almost everything. But Margot does not recognize, it seems safe to say, that she too in relation to these men, is in the situation of the lion—imaged as dangerous, but in fact helpless. I am not saying that Margot "should" have let the buffalo kill her husband. . . . (119)

I interrupt at this point because a glaring contradiction has just occurred. You have said that Margot, who knows almost everything, knows that her husband is never in any real danger with Wilson and his gun behind him. Yet, jumping to the buffalo incident, you raise the question of Margo's letting the buffalo kill her husband; and like Warren Beck and the many who follow him, with all of whom you side, you insist that Margot in shooting at the buffalo "when it seemed about to gore her husband" was acting to save him from the perceived threat that his life was in real danger. Well, I was going to save that point for last; but since I am anxious to pursue it let me now suggest that if Margot knows almost everything, and you as a 1990s feminist know a good bit more, you both forget at this point that big-game animals supposedly have no chance. In fact they do; they are dangerous animals, and those who hunt them do so at some risk to life. If Wilson uses a cannon to cut down the risk to his clients, or, if you will, the risk of losing them, that is not the same thing as titillating clients with the false appearance of mortal danger. Wilson may arrange the killings to satisfy his clients' male vanities as conquering heroes; that is a well-made point. However, the danger remains because Wilson cannot guarantee results, neither for himself nor his clients nor the hired native help—though in fact he does seem to have brought down the buffalo that threatened Macomber in this instance, without help from the forgetful Mrs. Macomber.

God help me, I am writing like a snotty male authority. Let me try to deliver my other points with more equanimity. I agree that the odds are greater against lions and buffaloes than those who hunt them, and hopelessly greater against Margot in this story; and I hope that you will now agree in turn that the risks with lions and buffaloes for male hunters are much greater than their risks with women. For unlike female lions, whose privileged male partners sit around all day while they hunt for the family, women are not deadlier than the privileged males of their species. I use the word "privileged" advisedly since I am now going to jump to a related issue: I am now going to argue that Hemingway's interest in the risks of hunting has something to do with lost male privileges based on the lost male functions—provision of basic foods, protection from wild marauders—that originally justified those privileges; and that such an interest makes for a different kind of sympathy for the lion than yours or mine or Margot's—the kind that Wilson does indeed know something more about than either Macomber or his wife because Wilson, like the man who created him, believes that brave privileged males are an endangered species. It is Wilson, in this light, and not the quietly endorsing story, who has the last word on the "damned fine lion"; like other code figures, he has trained himself to think ahead, and to give careful consideration to how his beloved opponents feel; and as the size of his cannon implies, he knows a great deal more than you think he does about the male lion's desperate power.

As these last thoughts indicate, I am now going to try to defend Hemingway's lifelong interest in big-game hunting. You have ruled out the author in your own approach in favor of female student responses that are "not constrained by the need to anchor an interpretation of the story to known (or supposedly known) facts about Hemingway's life or to reigning interpretation," and you have taken your title "Actually, I felt sorry for the lion" from what one such student unconstrainedly said in a class transcript, a threatening remark that an apprentice male teacher then crushed by admonishing "Now you sound like Margot" (119-20, 468). Fair enough. It seems to me a real advance in literary history and culture to restore Margot's intelligent voice to the story's spread of speakers: the narrator, Macomber, Wilson, and that all-important lion, which you and two previously benevolent male critics take as the story's real "standard of true bravery" (118). It is here, however, with this multiplicity of competing voices, that your own unfairness begins. You bring to the story and the classroom new feminist insights into cultural dilemmas that assuredly belong there; but you also suppress what seem to me the real cultural dilemmas embattled male chauvinists like Hemingway were coming from in granting the narrator, Wilson, and Macomber, and the lion they variously perceive, their tempered and tested places in your own acknowledged pantheon of competing voices.[1] My problem, then, is to restore a sense of those old cultural dilemmas. To do that I have to say that the author who created these characters was a nostalgic defender of the lost American frontier, that like Teddy Roosevelt and other big-game hunters he saw Africa as an extension of that concept, that his lifelong love affair with the Michigan woods around his summer home, his father's idea of training him as a frontier scout, his mother's attempt to affirm that idea while at the same time instilling in him her own turn-of-the-century feminist gentility, are all relevant to that multiplicity of voices to which Margot's has just been so validly and valiantly restored, and to their unconstrained classroom and critical presence.

Well, I have taken some time and trouble to establish my position. Now let me quickly make my several points. First, as I long ago argued, Hemingway wrote a number of stories that go beyond his familiar position of stoic endurance of wasteland conditions to affirm the value-possibilities of what I call his private imaginative frontiers: bull-rings, boxing rings, racetracks, ski runs in Austria, guerrilla camps in Spain, fishing and hunting grounds in Michigan, France, Spain, and Africa. In his Rousseauistic eyes these various arenas could be corrupted by social intrusions and often were; he seldom presented them in pristine states of nature. However, he always presented them as involving risks to life and gangrenous limb, even in "Big Two-Hearted River," where fishing the swamp will involve the risk of death; and he always presented those risks as endemic to private states of mind, imaginative apprehensions of perilous conditions on his designated frontiers. "The Short Happy Life of Francis Macomber" is one of those stories, remarkable for its Rousseauistic attempt to judge a corrupt modern marriage by frontier actions that reveal its hidden quality and direction: Macomber's cowardly flight from the lion as the story begins, Margot's accidental killing of her husband at the end—events that explain how and why husband and wife are *both* to blame for the failure of their marriage. His cowardice leads, that is to say, to her initial infidelities; she then grows to like her power—or her "illusion of power," as you nicely put it—and resents his newfound bravery as likely to disrupt it. The resentment leads to a buildup of hostile feelings that the narrator demonstrably underwrites,[2] and that can be legitimately said to deflect her aim when she tries to save Macomber from the apparent threat of death. In the Marryat essay I cite that familiar Freudian idea—"there are no accidents"—by which subconscious feelings may be said to affect all conscious actions. I speak elsewhere of the attempt Hemingway was making in the 1930s to

compete in method and effects with psychological writers like Joyce and
Faulkner in stories like "Macomber" and "The Snows of Kilimanjaro,"
and of his stylistic attempts to overcome his usual difficulties in depicting
women and their "deep or complex inner conflict[s]" through frontier situations like those of charging buffaloes. There is no room in your approach,
apparently, for such complex treatment of Margot's inner feelings at this
closing point in the story, or even for the relevant existence of her mixed
reactions: she is revealed as purely innocent and praiseworthy because she
shot at the buffalo, and the only basis for thinking otherwise is provided
by an unreliable witness who is trying—as you argue in the wake of
Kenneth Lynn (1987) and his unacknowledged source, Ann Greco
(1972)—to blackmail Margot so as to protect himself from legal prosecution for hunting animals in cars. Apparently it is alright to guess at
Wilson's hidden motives in this final scene, but not at Margot's. I think, in
all fairness, that we have to guess at both, and at Hemingway's as well,
since there is good reason to believe that Wilson functions here as
Hemingway's carefully chosen hit man.

He was attracted to Wilson's hardened but pliant point of view, that is
to say, because he wanted someone other than himself to level flat blue
machine-gunner's eyes at Margot and blast her with a verbal cannon. He
had promised Pauline at the end of *Green Hills of Africa* to reproduce the
appearance of a man they both admired, their African guide, Philip
Percival, in a story. Philip was a married British man with strong views
about American women, but Hemingway made him a bachelor in the
story because he admired loners, men without women, "the remains of
the lone trapper and cowboy," as D. H. Lawrence writes so perceptively
of Nick Adams. When you speak in your essay of "the fraternity of white
hunters" who devise the hunting laws that Wilson breaks, you understandably misconceive the private nature for Hemingway's loners of the
hunting code. Such marginal men do what they themselves imagine to be
ethical, with slight regard for legal prohibitions; they make up their own
moral conditions and try to live up to them. Thus, when Margot interestingly accuses Wilson of shooting animals from cars, and he points out her
error—"No one shot them from cars"—she switches to the more accurate
charge—"I mean chase them from cars"—and he answers: "Wouldn't
ordinarily. . . . Seemed sporting enough to me though while we were
doing it." You quote this passage without explicating what "sporting"
might mean: the implied answer seems to be taking the risks involved of
driving a car at high speeds over rough terrain, that like a charging lion
or buffalo is likely to maim or kill you. Since Macomber knows those civilized risks, motor cars make the risk of hunting big-game animals more
familiar to him, in Wilson's staccato list of reasons for Macomber's new-

found bravery that you now include while questioning Wilson's tactics with his clients.[3] You understandably also go astray now in your estimate of what constitutes bravery as you make your impressive argument about megaguns, with which, as you say, Wilson kills or prepares for killing every single animal that is killed in the story. It is the risk of death, and the overcoming of the fear of death, not the vainglory of actual killing, that makes for bravery in Hemingway's hunting/fishing stories.

That is why Hemingway's narrator tells us sympathetically that Macomber, when he woke at night frightened by the lion's roar, did not know the Somali proverb that "a brave man is always frightened three times by a lion; when he first sees his track, when he first hears him roar and when he first confronts him." That is also why Wilson feels better about Macomber when he says he wants to try to "fix it up on buffalo" after his public cowardice with the lion; and why he is so moved by Macomber's fearless elation with the buffalo that he brings out with embarrassment "this thing he had lived by," the lines from Shakespeare— "By my troth, I care not; a man can die but once; we owe God a death and let it go which way it will, he that dies this year is quit for the next"—lines that Margot, feeling her exclusion from this diffident male bonding and its intimate literary sanction, soon calls rot.[4] Finally, that is why the lion cannot be the story's "true standard of bravery." As I laboriously show in my essay on another Percival, *Percival Keene*, Hemingway shares Marryat's belief that "men are naturally cowards"; they need incitement to overcome the fears of shame and death that beset them, and to acquire what Marryat calls "courage positive . . . an active restless feeling" that seeks out danger and finds opportunities for engaging it. Lions are accordingly disqualified; they are not natural cowards; men are; and men have invented bows, arrows, spears, and guns, even megaguns, to give themselves sufficient advantage in confronting much more physically powerful animals to overcome the fears and hazards of that old survival struggle.

It is the shakiness of that acquired courage, and the private imaginative states of mind needed to achieve it in functionless modern times, that the excluded Margot further undermines with her hostile questions and comments, and that she aborts so tragically by shooting illegally and unethically from the car with her manly Mannlicher, in Hemingway's terrible parody of female interference in men's business. That she does so, in your admirably quixotic view, in a sudden selfless effort to save Macomber from becoming a man like Wilson, I sincerely doubt; it seems to me enough that she wants Macomber to live in the face of those deep-felt and understandably vengeful sympathies with charging lions and buffaloes that deflect her aim.

Well, I have run on unconscionably, and can only nod in passing at Hemingway's undercutting jealousy and envy of, as well as supportive admiration for, his guide to heroic frontier behavior, and at his own elected abortion of male happiness through that dubious "accidental" ending and its spurious affixing of ultimate blame on subconsciously vengeful female saviors;[5] and I must also forgo such minor matters as your textual misreading of the guide's supposed bungling of his own business with the wounded buffalo, and such major matters as a summary of the supportive case for the guide's admirable character.[6] I would like to say, however, in conclusion, that your critique of the hunting code is also Hemingway's critique, and that it hedges his bets—not on the shaky frontier existence of male courage—but on its transferability to those even more hazardous domestic regions in which we natural cowards are forced to confront our own abusiveness, our own greater gender propensity for violence, evasiveness, and betrayal. As Hemingway well knew but could not often admit.

Sincerely yours,
Mark Spilka
2 September 1991

NOTES

1. In footnote 4 (468) you invoke Bakhtin's theory of "multiple and competing voices" as applicable to this text. In a recent letter to me, however (16 October 1991), you acknowledge your failure to include Macomber's independent voice in that pantheon—which raises, among other questions, the interesting problem of how to read the irony of his "short happy life" in the title phrase in the light of your views about other "voices." More intriguing still, for a biographical critic like myself, is Hemingway's apparently strong sympathy with a man he had himself cuckolded, Grant Mason, the rich husband of Hemingway's beautiful if aging mistress, Jane Mason. It seems likely that the Macombers are based on this couple, who also modeled for the unhappy Bradleys, Tommy and Helene, in *To Have and Have Not*. Such precedents would also seem to support Hemingway's apparently tolerant view of Wilson's "windfall" philosophy about sex with female clients in "Macomber." It seems to me, in other words, that Hemingway has a personal stake in all these competing voices. Not surprisingly, one way or another he inhabits all his characters.

2. "'You've gotten awfully brave, awfully suddenly,' his wife said contemptuously, but her contempt was not secure. She was very afraid of something." These are the narrator's comments, not Wilson's, and though you may want to appropriate them for your generous view of Margot's supposed

fear that Macomber will become a man like Wilson, that fear would scarcely involve insecurity about contempt.

3. Pauline Hemingway's diary entries for the African safari with Ernest in winter 1933-34 tend to confirm this reading. She describes how cars were routinely used by their guide, Philip Percival, in pursuing large animals, but how shooting from cars was considered unethical. Thus, on 4 January 1934, while the hunting party pursues elands by car, a male and female lion are spotted on a nearby hill:

> We went toward them but they instead of retreating advanced inquiringly on the car, the lioness going to one side, the lion to the other. It had been agreed that I was to shoot at this lion and I was pushed out in the face of the advancing super lion.
>
> I took aim and was about to fire when my dear Mr. P said for Christ sake don't shoot the lioness. Can I be shooting the lioness, I thought, and turned to look at the lioness . . . then resumed beading [the] lion. While this was going on Charles was trying to get out of the car in full view of the lions, which certainly would have spooked them *and E was in the car unable to aid his wife should the lion charge.* I shot standing up . . . and missed. . . . [The] lion . . . disappeared into the donga and was never heard of again. [Emphasis added.]

4. In *Hemingway's Quarrel with Androgyny* I note how these lines from Shakespeare had become "a permanent talisman" for courage for Hemingway when a young British officer wrote them out for him during his convalescence from wounds in a Milan hospital in World War I (359-60). That he assigns the same lines to the British Wilson strikes me as an incontrovertible supporting argument for his essential admiration of Wilson and his strong affirmation of Wilson's role in this diffident bonding scene. See also the textual support in Wilson's lines: "He was very embarrassed, *having brought out this thing he had lived by,* but he had seen men come of age before and it always moved him. It was not a matter of their twenty-first birthday" [emphasis added].

5. In her African safari diary, Pauline more than once expresses her admiration for Percival—"Mr. P is a darling—most attractive man on African continent"—and spends much time alone with him while Ernest and their friend Charles Thompson are off hunting with native guides. Ernest's imagination of her possible infidelity and his consequent resentment of her attraction for Percival is one obvious source for this story that supports your reading. On the other hand, his rigging of a short happy life and ambiguous death for Macomber supports mine.

6. You claim that Wilson's "mistake" about the death in the brush of the first bull Macomber shoots is one "which the skillful hunter he is supposed to be would not have made," and that it lulls the group into false security that allows the wounded bull to make its later deadly charge. Yet Wilson is

immediately troubled about that bull; and when his gun-bearer later examines the bull's blood spoor and says something to Wilson in Swahili—obviously that the bull is or must be dead—Wilson merely translates
exuberantly for the others: "He's dead in there." Then, on going further
forward, the gun-bearer wildly indicates his hematological mistake—not
Wilson's—while crabbing fast sideways out of the brush with the bull
charging after him. As for Wilson's admirable virtues, besides his generous
response to Macomber's newfound courage, already mentioned, and a sexual talent you ignore that leaves Margot looking younger the next day,
"more innocent and fresher and not so professionally beautiful"—he is
furious with himself for not noticing Macomber's earlier fear and sending
him back to his wife, which suggests a healthy measure of self-critical
acuteness; and he further displays what Saul Bellow elsewhere calls "an
economy of imagination" for his appointed tasks, which, along with carefully planning ahead and knowing his beloved opponents, also includes a
strong personal sense of order, beauty, health, dignity, moral courage on
the frontier, and that disinvolvement from emotional consequences elsewhere that characterizes Hemingway's stoic heroes.

WORKS CITED

Baym, Nina. 1990. "Actually, I Felt Sorry for the Lion." *New Critical Approaches to the Short Stories of Ernest Hemingway*. Edited by Jackson J. Benson. Durham: Duke University Press.

Beck, Warren. 1955. "The Shorter Happy Life of Mrs. Macomber." *Modern Fiction Studies* 1 (November 1955). Reprinted 21 (Autumn 1975) along with the author's long-delayed response to my 1960-61 critique of his position.

_____. 1976. "Mr. Spilka's Problem: A Reply." *Modern Fiction Studies* 22 (summer).

Bellow, Saul. 1953. "Hemingway and the Image of Man." *Partisan Review* 20 (May-June).

Greco, Ann. 1972. "Margot Macomber: 'Bitch Goddess' Exonerated." *Fitzgerald-Hemingway Annual*.

Hemingway, Ernest. 1987. "The Short Happy Life of Francis Macomber." *The Complete Short Stories of Ernest Hemingway*. New York: Scribner's.

Hemingway, Pauline. 1933-34. African Safari Diary, Winter 1933-34. Stanford University Library.

Lawrence, D. H. 1936. *Selected Literary Criticism*. Edited by Anthony Beal. New York: Viking Press.

_____. 1936. "Study of Thomas Hardy." *Phoenix: The Posthumous Papers of D. H. Lawrence*. Edited by Edward D. McDonald. New York: Viking Press.

Lynn, Kenneth S. 1987. *Hemingway*. New York: Simon and Schuster.

Spilka, Mark. 1990. Appendix A and "Tough Mamas and Safari Wives." *Hemingway's Quarrel with Androgyny*. Lincoln: University of Nebraska Press.

_____. 1984. "A Source for the Macomber 'Accident': Marryat's *Percival Keene*." *The Hemingway Review* 3 (spring).

_____. 1960-61. "The Necessary Stylist: A New Critical Revision." *Modern Fiction Studies* 6 (winter).

_____. 1976. "Warren Beck Revisited." *Modern Fiction Studies* 22 (summer).

HEMINGWAY'S "TODAY IS FRIDAY" AS A BALLAD OF THE GOODLY FERE

WARREN BENNETT

"TODAY IS FRIDAY" IS A STORY that has received little critical recognition, and the problem with the story, according to Arthur Waldhorn, is "not one of irreverence but of irrelevance" (Waldhorn 1972, 89). The story, however, is not irrelevant, and the approach here is to see Hemingway's purpose in "Today is Friday" as similar to Ezra Pound's purpose in his "Ballad of the Goodly Fere," which is the masculinization of Jesus of Nazareth, and to demonstrate that "Today is Friday" contributes to an understanding of Hemingway's code hero or exemplar figure.

Hemingway was certainly aware that in art Jesus has been predominately portrayed as rather effeminate. His body is not muscular, but smooth, narrow shouldered, and slim; his head is not heavy boned, but small boned and finely formed, the face narrow, the nose straight and thin, and the eyes are large and soft; his hair is not trimmed at the neck, as the hair of the disciples is portrayed, but falls below the shoulder; his beard, however, is short and carefully clipped, as the beards of the disciples are not. In the crucifixion scenes, Jesus' body is never naked, with male genitalia, as was the case in Roman crucifixions, because the execution was intended to be not only an agonizing punishment but also a humiliation (Myers 1987, 246).[1] In short, Jesus appears harmless, and pitiful. Literature deals with Christ indirectly, and one of the most ideal young Christians is little Lord Fauntleroy, with his hair arranged in shoulder-length curls, and dressed in a black velvet suit, a lace collar, and a neck ribbon. For a young man to be a Christian, that is, to use Christ as a role model or exemplar, he must be a "proper gentleman." This general attitude is especially clear in Mark Twain's *Huckleberry Finn*, when Huck decides to flee westward to the territories rather than be adopted and "sivilized," that is, Christianized, by Aunt Sally.

Ezra Pound's response to an effeminate Jesus is set forth in the "Ballad of the Goodly Fere," although the provocation for the poem came from a source other than art or literature.

203

> I had been the evening before in the "Turkish Coffee' cafe in Soho. I had
> been made very angry by a certain sort of cheap irreverence which was new
> to me. I had lain awake most of the night. I got up rather late in the morning
> and started for the Museum with the first four lines in my head. . . .
> (Carpenter 1988, 118)

The poem was written in April 1909. Fleet Street rejected the poem
"because its portrait of Jesus seemed too daring" (Carpenter 1988, 118),
but it was nevertheless published by Ford Madox Hueffer in the *English
Review* in October 1909, and it was reprinted in Pound's collection,
Exultations which came out on 25 October 1909.

Pound's approach to Jesus is through a first-person eyewitness
account: "Simon Zelotes speaketh it somewhile after the Crucifixion"
(Pound 1976, 112).[2] To Zelotes, Jesus was a rugged, powerful, active
man associated with the hard men and mean life of the seaman. He was a
"lover of brawny men/O' ships and the open sea," his "mates" "drank his
'hale' in the good red wine," and the "scorn of his laugh rang free." "No
capon [castrated] priest was the Goodly Fere," and "No mouse of the
scrolls" was he. Jesus was "Like the sea that brooks no voyaging/With
the winds unleashed and free." He was a "master of men" who could
"cow a thousand." He was a man who said, "I'll go to the feast . . .
/Though I go to the gallows tree," and a man who said, "Ye shall see one
thing to master all/Tis how a brave man dies on the tree." "He cried no
cry when they drave the nails/And the blood gushed hot and free." "If
they think they ha' slain our Goodly Fere/They are fools eternally"
(Pound 1976, 112-13).

When "Today is Friday" is approached from this angle, it becomes
another of Hemingway's stories that is concerned with the code hero or
the exemplar. The story may lack the artistic ambiguity of Hemingway's
best works, but the story is of some importance to Hemingway's primary
concern: "I did not care what it was all about. All I wanted to know was
how to live in it" (Hemingway 1970, 148). "Today is Friday" is
Hemingway's assessment of the degree to which Christ is a true exemplar
figure for modern man. The strategy is to retain historical fact but impose
modern perception upon those facts. The story's drama form, the modern
language, the admiring soldier, the objective soldier, the sick soldier, the
Hebrew (rather than Roman) barman, and the women at the crucifixion,
can then be evaluated in more significant terms.

Hemingway, like Pound, approaches the question of Jesus' true identity
through an on-the-scene, eyewitness account. In contrast to Pound, however, the drama form enables Hemingway to establish a broader objectivity and to use contrasting tensions: the tension of the three points of view

expressed by the Roman soldiers, the tension between the conduct of the Hebrew wine-seller and the conduct of the Hebrew Jesus, and the tension between the conduct of Jesus' male disciples and the conduct of Jesus' female disciples.

The modern language of the piece has been disconcerting, as Paul Smith has pointed out in his *Reader's Guide to the Short Stories of Ernest Hemingway*. The responses to it range from Carlos Baker's dismissal because the dialogue resembles "a locker-room discussion among high-school sophomore football players" (Baker 1988, 169) to Sheldon Grebstein's view that the dialogue "method verges on self-parody" (Grebstein 1973, 114-15). Both complaints are open to question. Baker fails to take into account the fact that soldiers are most often young and tend to talk as young men talk in the locker room. Grebstein's self-parody charge is questionable because Hemingway had written only eighteen stories before "Today is Friday" and Grebstein does not indicate which piece Hemingway is parodying. In terms of Hemingway's strategy, it seems certain that Hemingway was intentionally, and therefore legitimately, trying to show that one of the most important events in history was still relevant to his own times. The bold use of a name such as "George" (271) for the Hebrew wine-seller indicates that Hemingway was deliberately trying to metamorphose a historic event in Jerusalem, blurred or obscured by antiquity, into a more modern world drama. In the process, Hemingway's primary concern was not to render the literal speech of Roman soldiers, but to render the rhetorical brevity of soldiers experiencing subconscious guilt, and to render the timelessness of the way a "brave man" meets pain and endures death in an unmerciful world.

Turning to the characters, it is historically doubtful that the Roman centurions would have frequented a Hebrew wine-seller rather than gone to the Roman "Jerusalem officer's club." Consequently, Hemingway's strategy seems to be to establish a correlation between the Hebrew George and the Hebrew Jesus. The second soldier smiles at George and tells him, "You're a regular Christer, big boy" (272), and he makes another comparison when he says, "George is a kike just like all the rest of them" (273). George, like Jesus, is also characterized as a Hebrew healer. Just as the Hebrew Jesus healed the servant of the Roman centurion at Capernaum (Matt. 8:5-13), the first soldier says about George, he "fixed me up fine the other day" (271). The purpose seems to be to establish that Jesus was just as helpful and cooperative with the Romans, just as apolitical and innocent as George, in spite of the criminal charge posted on the cross above his head: "King of the Jews." Finally, Hemingway gives George, and consequently Jesus, a degree of superiority over the Roman soldiers. George gives of his wine freely and helps the Romans in whatever way he can, but the Romans do not pay. George asks, "You couldn't let me have a little something on account, Lootenant?" (273), to which the second soldier replies, "What the hell, George! Wednesday's payday" (273). This is against Hemingway's code. In *The Sun Also Rises*, Jake says about Brett Ashley, "I had been getting something for nothing. . . . You paid some way for everthing that was ever good" (Hemingway 1970, 148), and when Pedro Romero, the bullfighter, walks out on Brett the "woman who ran the hotel would not let me [Jake] pay the bill. The bill had been paid" (Hemingway 1970, 243) by Pedro Romero. The Romans do not pay. Jesus paid.

Hemingway's use of *three* Roman soldiers, a trinity of soldiers, instead of one soldier, enables him to establish through repetition three descriptions of the cruelty of Roman crucifixion and the fact that it was a horrible way of dying. The first soldier says, "I was surprised how he acted" (272) and repeats six times, "he was pretty good in there today" (272, 273). The third soldier says, "The part I don't like is the nailing them on" (272), and the second soldier says, "It isn't that so bad, as when they first lift 'em up. . . . That's when it gets 'em" (272). The use of three centurions also enables Hemingway to present three separate responses to Jesus during the agony of his crucifixion and death. The first soldier, modeled on the Biblical centurion who says, "Truly this was the Son of God" (Matt. 27:54), admires Jesus for the dignity with which he "acted," and he makes it clear that Jesus stayed on the cross and suffered, not helplessly, but by an action of the will: "He didn't want to come down off the cross. That's not his play" (272). The first soldier recognizes that prolonged physical agony can be worse than death and he believes in mercy killing: "You see me slip the old spear into him? . . . It was the least I could do for him" (273). The third soldier has also recognized Jesus' dignity and courage, and he says, "He was all right" (272). The second soldier, in contrast to the first soldier, is an arrogant scoffer and calls Jesus a "false alarm" (272). Three views of the same man, from the first soldier's recognition and admiration of an exemplar, to the third soldier's simple recognition of exceptionally, to the second soldier's ridicule instead of recognition.

Finally, the three soldiers provide an ironic contrast between the dignity, will, and physical stamina of the vaunted Roman occupation forces and the dignity, will, and courage of the Hebrew Jesus under the heel of oppression. When Jesus was offered wine with myrrh (Mark 15:23) before he was put on the cross, a palliative to lessen the pain, he refused. He suffered the lengthy agony of crucifixion cold sober by choice. The centurions, on the other hand, afterward resort to alcohol and are a *"little cock-eyed"* (271). The weakness of the third soldier is the primary focus in this regard. In contrast to the torture of the crucifixion in which he has participated, he complains that he has a "gut-ache" (271). The second soldier suggests that he has been drinking the native water, but the first soldier has had trouble with his gut too, and he says, "George fixed me up fine the other day" (271). Two things are happening simultaneously here. First, Hemingway's strategy to give one of the centurions a "gut-ache" was a deliberate decision because the street euphemism for dignity, will, and courage is to "have guts." Jesus had guts. The Roman centurions have lost their guts for soldiering and crucifixions. Second, when the second soldier says the third soldier is sick because he has been "out here too long" (273), the third soldier says, "No, it ain't just that. I feel like hell" (273). The third soldier, in crucifying the "gutsy" Jesus, has lost his Roman stomach. He does not have a gut-ache because of the water but because he has watched "how a brave man dies on the tree" (Pound 1976, 113), and he now "feels like hell" (273).

The most significant irony in the story, however, is the role played by the women. The scene where the first soldier and the second soldier discuss the women who are present at Jesus' crucifixion comes late in the story:

1st Roman Soldier—You see his girl?

2d Soldier—Wasn't I standing right by her?

1st Soldier—She's a nice-looker.

2d Soldier—I knew her before he did. [He winks at the wine-seller.]

1st Soldier—I used to see her around the town.

2d Soldier—She used to have a lot of stuff. He never brought her no good luck.

1st Soldier—Oh, he ain't lucky. But he looked pretty good to me in there today.

2d Soldier—What become of his gang?

1st Soldier—Oh, they faded out. Just the women stuck by him.

2d Soldier—They were a pretty yellow crowd. When they seen him go up there they didn't want any of it.

2d Soldier—Sure, they stuck all right. (273)

There are three important factors in this scene. First, there is sexuality; second, there is that important element in Hemingway: luck; and third, there is the courage and bravery of Jesus' female disciples in contrast to the cowardly male disciples.

In the matter of sexuality, Hemingway is stressing Jesus' image as a male. "His girl," to whom the second soldier refers, is probably the Biblical prostitute, Mary Magdalene.

[She] stood at his feet behind him weeping, and began to wash his feet with tears, and did wipe them with the hairs of her head, and kissed his feet, and anointed them with the ointment (Luke 7:38).

In this passage, Jesus' divine portion has transformed Mary Magdalene's sexual cynicism into adoration. Hemingway, however, recognizes that since Jesus was "fully human," he must have had a sexual nature by necessity. Given Jesus' humanness and his male sexuality, and given Mary Magdalene's sexual profession, the second soldier quite reasonably assumes that Jesus has had a sexual relationship with her. "I knew her before he did," he says, then "*winks*" (273) at the Hebrew wine-seller. The sexuality in this short scene is intended to further the masculinization of Jesus as a figure whose appearance and behavior make other men view him as an exemplary man among men. In Ezra Pounds words, "No capon [or castrated] priest was the Goodly Fere" (Pound 1976, 113).

The second factor of importance is the reference to "luck" (273), because luck in Hemingway's world is crucial. An individual can attempt to make the best of a given situation according to a standard or a code, but the individual can never control the external circumstances, and the individual's downfall or death may therefore be universe-inflicted. When an individual effort and the external circumstances converge, then the individual has luck and success. If the external circumstances do not converge with the effort, even though the effort in itself is worthy, the individual has no luck and may appear to be a failure, a loser. An example of the individual without luck is Manuel Garcia in "The Undefeated." As Joseph DeFalco has pointed out, the story "approximates the motif of crucifixion and redemption in the Christ story" (DeFalco, 1963, 201). In "The Undefeated" there are six incidents that have to do with luck. When Retana says, "I thought they'd killed you," "Manuel knocked with his knuckles on the desk" (183). When Manuel says, "I don't like to substitute for anybody," "He tapped with his knuckles on the table" (184). When Manuel is at the *barrera* waiting for the "next third," he has a "heavy sense of apprehension" (197). When Retana's man says, "that's where he's going [to the hospital] damn quick," Zurito says, "Knock on that. . . . Knock on the wood" and Retana's man "knocked three times on the *barrera*" (200). In the infirmary, Manuel says, "I was going good. . . . I didn't have any luck. That's was all" (204). Significantly, Hemingway employs the strategy of using judges in "The Undefeated" just as he does in "Today is Friday." Retana, Retana's man, the second-string reporter, and the crowd, all misjudge Manuel. Zurito, however, recognizes the validity of

Manuel's words, "I didn't have any luck" (204), and he does not cut off Manuel's pigtail. Manuel has fought with dignity, will, and endurance, and in his death he has gone undefeated.

In "Today is Friday," the three soldiers are employed as judges. The second soldier says, "he never brought *her* no good luck," and the first soldier admits, "Oh, he ain't lucky" (273). The first soldier, like Zurito, recognizes the importance of luck, knows that Jesus was crucified, not because he had it coming, but because he was unlucky, and he pays Jesus tribute by insisting that Jesus was undefeated because "he looked pretty good to me in there today" (273).

The third factor of importance is the role of the women in the story, because the women have judged Jesus correctly, or they would not be standing by him at the crucifixion. The multitude who cried "Crucify him" (Mark 15:13), the Roman soldiers who scourged him, his own disciples, and the second and third soldiers in George's bar have all misjudged Jesus. They judge him, as the second soldier says, a "false alarm" (272), a false exemplar, and his death is misinterpreted as defeat and failure. His "girl," however, and the other women have recognized his exemplary qualities even before his trial and before the crucifixion. "Just the women stuck by him," "The women stuck all right," "Sure, they stuck all right" (273). His "gang" of male disciples "faded out," and in doing so they became a "pretty yellow crowd" (273). In contrast, the women face some risk, and their recognition of Jesus' dignity and fortitude prompts them to courageous loyalty.

In "Today is Friday," Hemingway is dramatizing his own unique perception of the importance of Jesus of Nazareth. Jesus was a heroic figure of exemplary qualities, a man of dignity, will, and endurance. As such, he becomes a code hero or exemplar. Hemingway's employment elsewhere of the figure *imitatio Christi*, such as Steve Ketchell in "The Light of the World" or Santiago in *The Old Man and the Sea*, can be most accurately understood through the focus Hemingway provides in "Today is Friday."

NOTES

1. The clothing of crucifixion criminals was given as spoil to the Roman soldiers. Jesus' garment, for which the Roman soldiers cast lots, was not a "coat," which is the English term used in the King James Bible (John 19:23), but a "tunic" (Myers 1987, 1023), or as the Jerusalem Bible translates the passage, "His undergarment."
2. For the convenience of the reader, Pound's entire poem is provided here.

"The Ballad of the Goodly Fere"
Ezra Pound

(Simon Zelotes speaketh it somewhile after the Crucifixion)
Ha' we lost the goodliest fere o'all
For the priests and the gallows tree?
Aye, lover he was of brawny men,
O' ships and the open sea.
When they came wi' a host to take Our Man
His smile was good to see,
"First let these go!" quo' our Goodly Fere,
"Or I'll see ye damned," says he.
Aye, he sent us out through the crossed high spears,
And the scorn of his laugh rang free,
"Why took ye not me when I walked about
Alone in the town?" says he.
Oh we drank his "Hale" in the good red wine
When we last made company.
No capon priest was the Goodly Fere
But a man o' men was he.
I ha' seen him drive a hundred men
Wi' a bundle o' cords swung free,
When they took the high and holy house
For their pawn and treasury.
They'll not get him a' in a book I think
Though they write it cunningly;
No mouse of the scrolls was the Goodly Fere
But aye loved the open sea.
If they think they ha' snared our Goodly Fere
They are fools to the last degree
"I'll go to the feast," quo' our Goodly Fere
"Though I go to the gallows tree."
"Ye ha' seen me heal the lame and the blind,
And wake the dead," says he.
"Ye shall see one thing to master all:
"Tis how a brave man dies on the tree."
A son of God was the Goodly Fere
That bade us his brothers be.
I ha' seen him cow a thousand men.
I ha' seen him upon the tree.
He cried no cry when they drave the nails
And the blood gushed hot and free,
The hounds of the crimson sky gave tongue
But never a cry cried he.

I ha' seen him cow a thousand men
On the hills o' Galilee,
They whined as he walked out calm between,
Wi' his eyes like the gray o' the sea.
Like the sea that brooks no voyaging
With the winds unleashed and free,
Like the sea that he cowed at Gennesaret
Wi' twey words spoke' suddenly.
A master of men was the Goodly Fere,
A mate of the wind and sea,
If they think they ha' slain our Goodly Fere
They are fools eternally.
I ha' seen him eat o' the honey-comb
Sin' they nailed him to the tree (Pound 1976, 112-113).

WORKS CITED

Baker, Carlos. 1988 [1969]. *Ernest Hemingway: A Life Story*. New York: Scribner's.

Carpenter, Humphrey. 1988. *A Serious Character: The Life of Ezra Pound*. Boston: Faber and Faber.

DeFalco, Joseph. 1963. *The Hero in Hemingway's Short Stories*. Pittsburgh: University of Pittsburgh Press.

Grebstein, Sheldon. 1973. *Hemingway's Craft*. Carbondale: Southern Illinois University Press.

Hemingway, Ernest. 1987. *The Complete Short Stories of Ernest Hemingway*. The Finca Vigía Edition. New York: Scribner's.

_____. 1970 [1926]. *The Sun Also Rises*. New York: Scribner's.

Myers, Allen C., et al., eds. 1987. *The Eerdmans Bible Dictionary*. Grand Rapids: William B. Eerdmans Publishing Company.

Pound, Ezra. 1976. [1926]. "The Ballad of the Goodly Fere." *Collected Early Poems of Ezra Pound*. Edited by Michael John King. New York: New Directions Books.

Smith, Paul. 1989. *A Reader's Guide to the Short Stories of Ernest Hemingway*. Boston: G. K. Hall.

Waldhorn, Arthur. 1972. *A Reader's Guide to Ernest Hemingway*. New York: Farrar, Strauss and Giroux.

"The Ballad of the Goodly Fere" by Ezra Pound from Ezra Pound: *Personae*. Copyright © 1926 by Ezra Pound. Reprinted by permission of New Directions Publishing Corp.

LOVE AND DEATH IN HEMINGWAY'S SPANISH NOVEL

PAUL SMITH

GEORGE PLIMPTON, WHO CALLS himself a "participatory journalist," once had the temerity to ask Ernest Hemingway about "the significance of the white bird that sometimes turns up in your, ah, sex scenes." Hemingway bristled at the question and dared Plimpton to say he could do any better. Later during dinner the question still rankled the writer: he stood up from the table, raised his fists, and reduced the participatory journalist to tears with a left hook—"while Miss Mary picked at her salad." A rich anecdote: the great writer's deep nerve touched; the writer's wife, who knew how it was, intent on her salad; and the journalist weeping for having asked the perspicuous question.

He may have deserved that left hook. The question, after all, implied that Hemingway was either inept when he wrote about sex—what Plimpton dismisses as "the 'earth moves' and all that business"—or that he was indifferent to the contemporary lexicon of the act of love. There were Joyce and Lawrence before him, and in the 1930s, Henry Miller; but next to them, as Plimpton says, Hemingway was "all thumbs."[1]

Biographers have argued that the influence of Oak Park religiosity and Scribnerian scruples forced Hemingway to double-space to signify an orgasm and to suggest a postcoital sigh with "Then, afterwards"—and they are right. But so is Plimpton, and his disingenuous question about the white bird is interesting because it raises another. How could a writer whose goal was "the real thing, the sequence of motion and fact that made the emotion,"[2] stray so far into the often jejune prose of the love scenes in his Spanish novel? Unless, of course, it was not the actual things he was after there, but something else, something more elemental; and among those that mattered most to him were love and death, so often merged in his fiction that they seem one.

In 1960 Leslie Fiedler was the first to note that the act of love was "the symbolic center" of Hemingway's fiction—but Fiedler seemed personally affronted by that fact.[3] Perhaps that distaste led him to ignore Kenneth

Burke, who, while barely noticing Hemingway, had brilliantly illuminated
his fiction in *A Rhetoric of Motives* ten years earlier. Burke's anatomy of
the ways of dying—*active* killing, *self-reflexive* suicide or sacrifice, or the
passive being killed—informs the dramatic episodes or recollections of
death in *For Whom the Bell Tolls*.[4] Just as Burke argues that the character
of a life is revealed in its "ultimate of endings," invoking the Christian
injunction "to lead the dying life"; so, too, he suggests that an analogous
"ultimate of beginnings"—a creative act, an act of love—may also define a
life; and its secular injunction, we may infer, is to lead the loving life.[5]

With this much from Burke, I will venture that the thematic center of
For Whom the Bell Tolls rests somewhere within a complex analogy
between the ways of death and the ways of love. Robert Jordan is obsessed
with his ultimate ending and how it will define his life—that much is obvious. Beyond—or, more properly, before—that, he must submit, like some
medieval courtier, to an education in the ultimate beginning, the act of
love, and learn how a life may be informed by the human injunction to
lead the loving life. Just as Catherine Barkley leads the dying life to initiate
Frederic Henry into the mysteries of the loving life, so Maria leads the loving life to instruct Robert Jordan in the way to die, and so to define his life
and their transcendent love.

Some may cast Robert Jordan in the role of the experienced lover initiating an innocent girl into the rites of sex, but Jordan is a mere technician
who has read the manual: he knows where the noses go in a kiss, but little
of more moment. It is Maria who brings to their love the sibylline wisdom
of Pilar and enacts it; she is the tutor, he the tyro; and without her subtle
instruction from Pilar, their lovemaking would have been, as Fiedler said,
"the most absurd . . . in the history of American fiction."[6]

How does she love him? Let me count the ways. There are four; and
that the number is *even* is itself *odd*, for one expects three in a fiction so
pervaded with the archetypes of romance.[7]

The first of the four scenes, which—for want of a better term—I will
call a *rebirth*, occurs in chapter 7 (69-73), after midnight of the first day.
Jordan has reconnoitered the bridge and found allies in Anselmo, Pilar,
and of course Maria. However, the scene is troubled, first, by two recollections: The partisans recall Kashkin's talk of "suicide" at the demolition of
the train when they rescued Maria; and then Jordan recalls the suicide of
his own father, a "Republican" who shot himself to avoid torture of a
domestic sort (66). With those two lies or, at best, half-truths about his
participation in the death of Kashkin and his memory of his father's suicide, the motive concealed in his decision not to kill Pablo is implied.
Everything and everyone argues for shooting Pablo; but Jordan refuses, for
some strategic reasons but more so in obedience to the drama of his own

life. Pablo, although an elder figure and a cowardly father in the partisan family, is unlike those in whose death Jordan had been involved, either as an agent as in Kashkin's case or as a surviving child who would feel complicitous in his father's suicide. He may spare Pablo to exonerate his own past, but he jeopardizes his present mission, perhaps on the off chance that Pablo will finally redeem himself, as he does so brutally when he murders his compatriots for their horses.

Maria, innocently believing the lie about the "torture" Jordan's father suffered, absolves him of cowardice by associating his death with her own father's heroism, and she tells Jordan that "you and me we are the same." Then for the first time, Jordan notices that her eyes are "suddenly hungry and young and wanting" (67). This begins a pattern in which the ways of dying—suicide, sacrifice, killing—are associated with, and may initiate, a way of loving, as a way of loving will finally initiate a way of dying.

This first act of love is a rebirth and, in the metaphorical schema of this novel, a "re-flowering" of Maria. Pilar had told her "soon after the train" not only that "nothing is done to oneself that one does not accept," but also that if she "loved someone it would take it all away." When she first spoke of her rape, Jordan was put off. It is only after Maria has told him what Pilar said that he recognizes the significance of their first sexual act (72-73).

She had wished to die at the train and, in a sense, had died—even *had* to die—so that in the first act of love she could be reborn and restored to her original innocence. However, if Pilar's maxim, "nothing is done to oneself that one does not accept," is inscribed as fictive law in this act of love and therefore revokes Maria's rape, may it not also rescind or at least diminish something of Jordan's past? His dark joke about his Republican father's suicide is associated with his participation in Kashkin's suicide to escape torture, not the least because both the private joke about one death and the lie about the other suggest that Jordan, like Maria, "does not accept" what was done to him by the two suicides. This act of love, entangled with varieties of suicide, may be the unexpected one added to the three love scenes typical of romance.[8]

The second love scene—I will call it a *union with the earth*—occurs in chapter 13 (158-61). On a high meadow in the afternoon of the second day, the lovers return with Pilar from their meeting with El Sordo. As Pilar and Pablo were the elders in the wings of the first scene, she and El Sordo are just offstage in this one. Again, Pilar has arranged the event, foreseen its significance, and instructed Maria in its mystery. In this act of love, the physical world seems to respond to the lovers' sudden ecstasy when Jordan "felt the earth move out and away from under them." The ecstatic experience is one of "standing outside" of space: the insistent rhythm of the passage falls on the word "nowhere," and time stands still at the present moment, "now," the word within "nowhere" without "here" (159).

The mystery associated with this event in Pilar's gypsy lore [9] is a mystery of the earth and is revealed in the clear light of day: as Jordan says, "We know nothing about what happens to us in the nights. When it happens in the day though, that *is* something." Though for him time hung on a still moment, the experience is finite, given only thrice in one's lifetime (174-75). This act of love—finite, diurnal, and apportioned—is a mystery that ascends from the natural order of things and so will differ from the last act of love, which descends from a supernatural one.

Any analogy between this act of love and a way of dying would seem to point to a natural death. In the first love scene Maria recalled that she wanted to die when she was raped and now is happy she did not. Here, for the first of two times, she speaks of *la petite mort*, saying "I die each time." For Jordan, it was a bit less than the little death, only "almost" (160). He knows the metaphor, but either he has been denied the experience (which is unlikely) or denies it himself, reluctant to confirm the human truth that associates the act of love and the passion of death.

Since there is no exemplary natural death in this novel, the closest to one may be prefigured in Jordan's long discussion of strategy with El Sordo before the love scene, and in his own long thoughts about the attack after it. As Pablo's cowardice and the memory of Kashkin color the first act of love, so the meeting with El Sordo, the brave and laconic grandfather, colors the second. It is to that wise and doomed old man that Jordan first admits killing Kashkin, and is absolved: "'*Menos mal*,' said El Sordo. 'Less bad'" (149). On the next day El Sordo exemplifies another "less bad" way to die, first feigning suicide and then sacrificing himself to save others. Thus El Sordo's remark that ended their conversation on the tactics of retreat is a resonant one: "We must think much about the manner of our going" (152).[10]

The third love scene—a *union with another*—occurs in chapter 20 (258-64), late in the night of the second day. Although less mysterious than the others, whatever meaning it has is introduced by Maria. She likens the two of them in the snow to "one animal of the forest [since they are] so close that neither one can tell that one [is] not the other," and then she transforms that image into the concept that the two of them "will be one now and there never will be a separate one." When she adds that "I will be thee when thou art not there" (262-63), it is both fitting and ironic that she offers the argument Jordan will use to persuade her to leave him at the end of the novel (463-65).

This third act of love is marked with dialogue that is more mundane than sublime—if not downright domestic. The chapter opens with Jordan

LOVE AND DEATH IN HEMINGWAY'S SPANISH NOVEL   217

preparing a pine-bough bed like a bridegroom, to which Pilar, like a reluctant mother-in-law, contributes a slab she was saving for a shelf. When
Maria comes to this marriage bed as his new wife, the shirt she wore the
night before becomes her wedding shirt, as she transformed the one forest
animal into an emblem of their union. There is even some connubial concern with warming her cold feet, and a postcoital moment when they
almost bicker (260-63).

That moment comes when she admits that "it was not as this afternoon
[but] one does not need to die"; and Jordan, buried in the thought of
death, again feigns ignorance of the metaphor to tease Maria with the
reply, "I hope not." Like his private joke about his father's suicide, his
casual jest iterates a reluctance to identify love and death. He admits that
he knew what she meant; but Maria, in her innocence, asks the pertinent
question, "Then why did you say that instead of what I meant?" His
answer, "I only spoke thus, as a man, from habit," avoids her question;
and Maria, in her wisdom, does not ask it again (263).

That brief dialogue might seem unexceptional had this wedding night
not been darkened by the telling snow or had Jordan's senses not been
soured by Pilar's vivid evocation of the smell of death (chapter 6). Her
impassioned speech gathering the fetors of old brass and swallowed blood,
dead chrysanthemums and the slop of whores, with "the smell that is both
the death and birth of man" (256) was meant to convince Jordan that
Kashkin "smelt of death" (251). When she repeats that claim at the end of
her recital, Jordan dismisses it again with a jest: "If that is true it is a good
thing that I shot him"—but he spoke "gravely" (256).

Lying in bed awaiting Maria, Jordan recalls the old woman's speech as
he smells the pine boughs, "Pilar and the smell of death. This is the smell I
love." Then, as if to clear his head of her fetid litany, he recites his own list
of smells, like clover and sage, Indian sweet grass and the sea (260). He
falls asleep with Maria and imagines that with her body touching his they
are "magically . . . making an alliance against death." Yet he is awakened
in the night by the fear that "she was all of life and it was being taken
from him." Then he kisses her once, puts his pistol within reach, and lies
there "in the night thinking" (264).

This scene of wedded love is the darkest and most prophetic of the four.
For all its sylvan domesticity, it reeks of death; and Jordan awakes on the
first morning of marriage to kill a cavalryman with a shot from his wedding bed.

The fourth and last love scene, in the early hours of the fourth and
last day, is a *union with heaven* (chapter 37, 378-81), and several of the
thematic elements from the earlier scenes recur. Six chapters lead into
this scene (31-36), and this attenuation of the narrative serves both to

juxtapose the final futility of Andres's journey with the lovers' last act of love and to give them the time to recapitulate the brief history of their love.

However, this scene's primary function is to reverse the image of the second love scene: as the earth reflects heaven and the sacred the profane, the second and fourth acts of love mirror one another. All through the night, Jordan has been marking the time on his watch; then "as the hand on the watch moved," they made love and it was "all and always; this was what had been and now and whatever was to come." When they loved the day before on the sunlit earth, "now" was taken from "now-here" to sig- nify a moment out of space; here, as they love on their wedding bed with the "smell of the pine-boughs and the night," they discover "all" there is in "always" (379).

As Jordan experiences this ultimate ecstatic moment, once again it is Maria who tells him what it means. For the first time, however, it is not something she has learned from Pilar's gypsy lore. She speaks of "having been another time in *la gloria*," and he comes to understand what she intu- itively knows. It was not a valorous glory, nor the patriotic *la gloire* of France. *La gloria* "is the thing in the Cante Hondo and in the Saetas. It is in Greco and San Juan de la Cruz, of course, and in others" (379-80). Her one word evokes the *cante hondo* of ancient flamenco music, the "deep song" with its "tragic sense of life," but also the *saeta*, a song of "rever- ence and joy" sung in Holy Week as "invocations to the Virgin Mary."[11] More than this, the word summons up the sacrificial figures of El Greco, stretched on the rack of this life as if to point more precisely to another. At last, it also recalls the poems and commentaries of St. John of the Cross, *The Ascent of Mount Carmel—The Dark Night* and *The Spiritual Canticle*, tracing a path through the "life of divine love" that leads to the "perfect union that will be had in glory."[12]

Maria has learned more from Pilar than Pilar knew, as Jordan has learned more from Maria than she could say (380). Knowing that he is going to die, he learns on that last night that the act of love can, finally, unite him with the divine. In that ultimate act of love, then, he may, at last, come to know how his imminent death may be so blessed.[13]

Four scenes of love inform the novel in a sequence that begins with a symbolic *rebirth*, followed by a mystic *union with the earth*, then a *union with another*, to end with an ecstatic *union with heaven*. Hemingway had his wits about him, certainly, when wrote the second and fourth scenes that bring earth to heaven and heaven to earth. With the first, the rebirth, and the third, the union with another, he may have been less certain; and Leslie Fiedler was almost right when he said that Hemingway's "rejection of the sentimental ending of marriage [in the third scene] involves the acceptance of the sentimental beginning of innocent and inconsequential sex [in the first]."[14] What he missed was the fact that, for whatever reason, the first love scene was hardly inconsequential, but was a necessary rebirth demanded by the aura and scent of death that so pervades the third scene of wedded love.

On the ways of dying and their analogues with the ways of loving, Hemingway's wits were, I think, rather less collected, but the incipient similarities he saw are enough, I believe, to suggest that in *For Whom the Bell Tolls* he tried honestly to show us the necessity of living both the loving and the dying life. Finally, lest we miss his point, he gave us Robert Jordan's thought that when "you get through with this war you might take up the study of women" (176). As Hemingway did.

NOTES

1. George Plimpton, "JFK and Hemingway," *College Literature* 7 (1980): 184-85. Plimpton was wise enough not to ask how that great bird managed to fly "out of the window of [a] gondola" in Ernest Hemingway, *Across the River and Into the Trees* (New York: Scribner's, 1950), 154. The image appears earlier as an "owl in twilight" in Ernest Hemingway, "Fathers and Sons," *The Short Stories of Ernest Hemingway* (New York: Scribner's, 1938), 497.
2. Ernest Hemingway, *Death in the Afternoon* (New York: Scribner's, 1932), 2.
3. Leslie Fiedler, *Love and Death in the American Novel* (Cleveland: Meridian, 1962 [1960]), 304. Fiedler's contempt for Hemingway's work and his disdain for "mere textual analysis" (vii) led him away from the subject and astray in the fiction.
4. In Ernest Hemingway, *For Whom the Bell Tolls* (New York: Scribner's, 1940) they are Anselmo's troubled monologue on killing (43), Jordan's memory of his father's suicide associated with Kashkin's Roman version in which a faithful companion holds the weapon (66-67, 338-39), the sacrifice of El Sordo and of Jordan himself at the end (307-22, 460-71), the deaths remembered in Pilar's accounts of the execution of the Fascists and Finito's last days (98-130, 182-90), and Maria's story of the execution of her parents (350-54). All of these deaths, except for two (El Sordo's sacrifice and Jordan's, the first a model for the other) occur in introspective or retrospective passages, like recursions to mythic memory in an epic
5. Kenneth Burke, *A Grammar of Motives* and *A Rhetoric of Motives* (Cleveland: Meridian, 1962 [1945, 1950]), 537-38.
6. Fiedler, *Love and Death*, 304-5.
7. I think of the novel as a romance as described in Northrop Frye's "Third Essay" in *Anatomy of Criticism: Four Essays* (Princeton: Princeton

University Press, 1957). Gerry Brenner is as persuasive in his original study of the novel as an epic in chapter 3 of *Concealments in Hemingway's Works* (Columbus: Ohio State University Press, 1983).

8. As such, it marks an idiosyncratic displacement of the narrative pattern (Frye, "Third Essay," 136-38) and so demands the reader's close attention, especially the reader whose familiarity with Hemingway's response to his father's suicide may lead him to dismiss Jordan's as the writer's lapse into mere autobiography.

9. Jordan resents her making it into a "gypsy thing" but is intrigued by the idea that it may well be a universal belief: "Nobody knows . . . what mysteries were in the woods . . . that we came from" (175-76).

10. The chapter ends with Pilar's prediction that it will snow; Jordan says "It can't snow," and then, watching the darkening sky "cutting off the tops of the mountains," like El Sordo's, "'Yes,' he said, 'I guess you are right'" (176-77).

11. On the origins and significance of these flamenco musical forms see *The New Grove Dictionary of Music and Musicians*, 20 vols., edited by Stanley Sadie (London: Macmillan, 1980), 3:719, 16:380-81.

12. *New Catholic Encyclopedia*, 17 vols. (New York: McGraw-Hill, 1967), 7:1045-47.

13. If the novel is read as a romance, the last love scene would serve to predict the hero's apotheosis, or as close to one as a writer so imbued with the ironic mode could come.

14. Fiedler, *Love and Death*, 305.

LOVE IN *FOR WHOM THE BELL TOLLS*

HEMINGWAY'S UNDISCOVERED COUNTRY

ALLEN JOSEPHS

THIS ESSAY IS THE FOURTH in a series of four outlining what I think about *For Whom the Bell Tolls*. The first one, biographical in nature, satisfied me that Hemingway's disgust with the politics of the Spanish Civil War led him to invent a war in the novel that did not reflect an accurate picture of the politics of the time. The second, an analysis of the Civil War short stories, proved to me that he could write about the real war when he wanted to, including the politics, and that the writing of these stories, all prior to the writing of *For Whom the Bell Tolls*, served as a purgation of his disgust with the real war and as a warming up for the invented novel.[1]

The third essay, presented at the *For Whom the Bell Tolls* Conference in Moscow in September 1990, was a beginning analysis of the nature of the invention, an attempt to begin to separate the invented foreground action from the historical background action. What was invented? The battle lines, the bridge, the guerrillas themselves, Jordan, María, the cave, and so forth. I concluded that Hemingway wanted to invent, that he consciously chose to tell a story.

At the Moscow conference—nearly a dozen and a half papers on one novel—Professor Charles M. Oliver gave a very interesting paper comparing the language of the first of T. S. Eliot's *Quartets*, "Burnt Norton," to the language of love in *For Whom the Bell Tolls*, what I have eventually come to call the language of ecstasy. "Burnt Norton" is hardly a love scene, but as Oliver pointed out, the language is often similar, especially in its insistence on the *now*, the present. Furthermore, he concluded, "The novel is only superficially about the Spanish Civil War," a conclusion that fit nicely with my own.

Bearing all the above in mind, we arrive at the present topic, *For Whom the Bell Tolls* as Hemingway's "Undiscovered Country." According to Carlos Baker, "The Undiscovered Country" was Hemingway's favorite of twenty-six possibilities for a working title, which is to say, up until he found the quotation from John Donne.[2] "The Undiscovered Country" may not be as good a title as *For Whom the Bell Tolls*, but it is a more explicit description of the novel.

I see four aspects of the undiscovered country. In the first place, Spain itself was the undiscovered country: it was the place Hemingway came to after "they" had ruined Michigan and Italy. It was the undiscovered country until he discovered it—discovered the briefly great trout fishing, the people, the language, and of course *los toros*—and then it became the last good country. Now it was in danger of being taken by the fascists, just as Italy had been. It was Hemingway's psychic allegiance—and Robert Jordan's, by extension—that made the Spanish conflict so important. Angel Capellán, Edward Stanton, and I have elaborated on this psychic allegiance in the past and I do not believe it needs any further elaboration here. Suffice it to say that Hemingway did not go to Ethiopia.

The second aspect is the novelized war as undiscovered country. Hemingway clearly gave up writing about the real war, which was right there under his nose, in order to invent a war on the stage of his imagination. He gave up the *ethos* of the war in order to discover its *mythos*. He deserted the real war—and took his lumps for it from Alvah Bessie and "the ideology boys" and from the Spaniards themselves—in order to discover a "truer" war. What he discovered was—and this is what I outlined in Moscow—new battle lines, guerrillas that did not ever exist in that region, a steel suspension bridge brought perhaps from the Jarama River south of Madrid, and a big cave in granite where there could be no caves. He discovered a Robert Jordan that was no more Robert Merriman by the time Hemingway finished discovering him than he was you or I—after all, most if not all of us, including Merriman and Jordan, are college professors, and I even teach Spanish. He discovered a war, in short, that while not real was truer than real. This was not the Sevastopol he had seen; it was the Borodino he had discovered within. The fate of humanity did not literally hang on that bridge, but figuratively it became as important as the Spartans at Thermopylae.

Love is the third aspect of the undiscovered country and the one I want to treat most in depth here. Therefore, I will skip to the last aspect, death, and then return to love.

Death, I need remind no one, is precisely "The undiscovered country from whose bourn/No traveler returns . . ." that gave rise to the original title.[3] Death, the impending-ness and foreshadowed-ness of death, inform *For Whom the Bell Tolls*, and yet, almost ironically, Robert Jordan does not die, at least he does not die *in* the book. Hemingway cut out the epilogue, which went beyond Jordan's death, and in so doing, left Jordan lying at the end of the novel on the *commodius vicus* (*Finnegan's Wake* came out in 1939) of the forest floor, his heart still beating as at the beginning against the bosom of the Spanish earth. As Michael Reynolds observed in Moscow, "Art stops time—it's the only thing that does." Death, in other words, is held at bay by art and the original undiscovered country remains—in this novel, at least—undiscovered indeed, although always disclosing.

That—art—brings us back to love, love as the undiscovered country. The trajectory of love in Hemingway's work is toward ecstasy. The impossibility of such love runs all through *The Sun Also Rises*. It begins for real—and ends tragically—in *A Farewell to Arms*. Then, in *Green Hills of Africa*, a book not seemingly about love, there appears an important description of ecstatic love: "to have, and be, and live in, to possess *now* again *for always*, for that long sudden-ended *always*; *making time stand still*, sometimes so very still that afterwards you wait to hear it move, and it is slow in starting."[4]

The most revealing phrase, in terms of ecstasy, is, of course, "making time stand still." Time is an important subject in *Green Hills of Africa,* but it is paramount in *For Whom the Bell Tolls*, the three days and nights and the final fourth morning, all determining in their inexorable telescoping the nature of love, of life, of death, in short, of everything in the novel. I know of no more time-obsessed work, and time is the ground for all the undiscovered countries in *For Whom the Bell Tolls*. The ticking, or I suppose I should say the tolling, begins in the book's title.

From *A Farewell to Arms* on, at least, love is a religion for Hemingway. Catherine's famous phrase, "You're my religion," is straight from the rhetoric of courtly love and the literature of passion.[5] María goes a step further and calls their lovemaking *la gloria*. Jordan thinks: "*La gloria.* She said La Gloria. It has nothing to do with glory nor La Gloire that the French write and speak about. It is the thing that is in Cante Hondo and in the Saetas. It is in Greco and in San Juan de la Cruz, of course, and in the others."[6] *Saetas* are mystic religious flamenco songs, usually sung to the Virgin; El greco is a mystic painter; San Juan de la Cruz is a mystic poet whose metaphor for mystical union is sexual. *La gloria*, Jordan is right, does not mean glory—it means heaven. María says she is thankful "to have been another time in *la gloria*."[7] *Estar en la gloria* means to be in heaven, to be out of this world, to be in ecstasy, *in ex-stasis*, out of where one normally stands. It is, in short, sexual mysticism, sacred ecstasy, or what certain Buddhists would call tantric sexuality.

Robert and María make love four times. Only two are detailed love scenes: when the earth moves in the meadow on the afternoon of the second day and in the early hours of the fourth and final morning. María says "another time," after the last love scene, so we can assume that both times are *la gloria*, but the phrase is associated with the second time. Ecstasy, then—the undiscovered country of love—stops time and is a mystic union María and Robert call in perfectly idiomatic Spanish *la gloria*.

However, is that it? Is there nothing new here, no further progression along the path of ecstasy? Hemingway had already told us in *Green Hills of Africa* that lovemaking can stop time, and when Catherine and Frederic become "the same one," are we not dealing with a similar mystical union? There is, I think, at least one more step, one more dimension involved in *For Whom the Bell Tolls*.

What does it mean when the earth moves? Is that a sympathetic response on Mother Earth's part? Is Kali dancing in chthonic or geopathic celebration? Is this the supreme pathetic fallacy, orgasm as earthquake? Or did Hemingway have something less overtly romantic in mind? The fact that the phrase "did the earth move for you?" has become a cultural cliché (like the tip of the iceberg) suggests that at a popular level the description is just corny romance, but Hemingway—ever so sensitive about these matters—surely had more in mind. What?

Phrases from "Burnt Norton" echoed in my mind after the Moscow Conference: "Time and the bell; And all is always now; Quick now, here, now, always." Hemingway doubtless read "Burnt Norton." The phrase that most titillated me was: "At the still point of the turning world . . . at the still point, there the dance is."[8] In terms of *For Whom the Bell Tolls*, I knew what the dance was, but was there a still point?

After Einstein there was no still point anywhere in the universe. The only seeming stillness was constant speed. Lovers lying in a Castilian meadow traveling at the same speed as the rotating earth—that might seem a still point in the turning world. If they stopped, the earth would go right on turning and "move out and away from under them."[9] Of course, it was Einstein. After Einstein there were no longer three dimensions of space and a separate one of time. After Einstein the fourth dimension, the famous fourth dimension, was space-time, no way to have one without the other. So when we come to the passage about "time absolutely still and they were both there, time having stopped and he felt the earth move out and away from under them,"[10] it was only logical; it made perfect sense, relatively speaking. It was a modern ecstasy, an escape for the sexually bonded lovers, however momentary, from the continuum of space-time; not romance, not pathetic fallacy, not even Kali dancing: new physics. Or perhaps romance and religion and relativity. How to know?

Hemingway was certainly aware of Einstein's ideas. In the spring of 1921 Hadley used the phrase in a letter to Hemingway, "an unknown fourth dimension just like ours."[11] As Michael Reynolds comments: "The idea of a fourth dimension was much discussed in those days, for Einstein's theories of relativity turned him into an international figure. . . .

Years later when Hemingway needed a phrase to describe his art, he said he was trying to achieve in fiction a fourth dimension . . . which probably meant the *timeless* quality of great writing."[12]

In a later paper cited by Paul Smith, "Einstein's Train Stops at Hemingway's Station," Reynolds looked at Hemingway's ironic treatment of time and space in the story "Homage to Switzerland," which was written in 1932. As usual, Reynolds has done his homework and he informs us that "from 1922-28, the *New York Times* carried 172 stories about Einstein . . . and almost 100 articles appeared in English and American general periodicals."[13] Hemingway knew his Einstein all right, just the way he knew his Eliot and his Joyce and his Pound and his Gertrude Stein. If by no other way than by osmosis: romance *and* religion *and* relativity.

It turns out that is not such a strange combination, just somewhat advanced for its time, especially in Western culture. The earliest Eastern students of enlightenment found ecstasy through sexuality thousands of years ago. Pound and Joyce were both interested—each in his own way, of course—in the connection, and sexual gurus and mystics such as G. I. Gurdieff and P. D. Ouspensky were common enough in Paris. Ouspensky even talked about a fifth dimension. And Gertrude Stein spoke of the "continuous present," which brings us again to "Burnt Norton" and *For Whom the Bell Tolls*. Sexual ecstasy, sexual mysticism, and sex as religion were very much in the air, and they were only new ideas to the children of intolerant and repressive societies. And I do not just mean Irish Catholicism or Oak Park Protestantism—I mean virtually the entire Western religious tradition. They were not new ideas but they were daring enough at the time.

Hemingway's real stroke of genius was not his participation in this ancient new dance, but the addition to it of relativity. Religion as love, androgyny, unity, sexual ecstasy—these topics fascinated Hemingway all his life, more than we suspected until we read *The Garden of Eden*. But *For Whom the Bell Tolls* has something else—only here does the earth move, a fact that most critics have handled like a hot potato. Hemingway himself never seems to have mentioned it.

The Green Hills of Africa—where he first mentions the fourth and fifth dimensions—provides, by contrast, the proof of Hemingway's stroke of genius: "making time stand still, sometimes so very still that afterwards you wait to hear it move, and it is slow in starting."[14] Time stops, but only in a manner of speaking. The clever near-synaesthesia of hearing it move is only a smoke screen. So is the oxymoronic phrase "sudden-ended always." We are told, not shown. We do not—or I do not—believe it; that is, in Hemingway's terms, we do not experience it at all. He does not make us feel it. It is flat. And flat passion, even flat talk about passion, no matter how poetically couched, is still flat.

For Whom the Bell Tolls, on the other hand, is far from flat. I see the design of the novel as a yoni mandala, a circle, and inside the circle an upside-down triangle, a delta. In the circle from forest floor to forest floor we have the love story of Robert Jordan and María, which is the triangle of romance, religion, and relativity. It is upside-down, a delta, a yoni, because the way in becomes the way out; ecstasy—to be *in la gloria, in* heaven, *in* bliss—and unity—"one and one is one, is one, is one . . ."—come from the union of the sacred and the sexual—one and one is one, one body, one soul. The in becomes the out, the ex of "ex-stastis" and the effect is ecstasy. Real ecstasy, not rhetorical ecstasy. Time stops and of course the earth moves. While they climb the Jacob's ladder of conscious-ness to bliss the world turns. Pilar understands because certain Gypsies preserve some vestigial wisdom from their ancient Indian past, and because a few of them live tantric, intuitive lives.

Intuition is the magic word. Does it matter if the earth really moved? Does it matter if they were really in *la gloria*? Does it even matter if, in fact, Hemingway really had relativity in mind, that is, consciously in mind? Are we supposed to believe Hemingway could really deal in the arcane language of high mathematics? Is not it instead high poetics, high sexuality, and high romance?

Hemingway's invented ecstasy for Robert Jordan and María had gotten it right. Parenthetically I will say that getting it right and then writing it right so that we experience it too, through art, is probably what Hemingway's *fifth* dimension is about. Hemingway plays it on the stage of his imagination and by getting it right—getting the words right, turning it into a kind of poetry in which the rhythm of the words recreates the rhythm of lovemaking—makes it play on the stage of the reader's imagina-tion. The fact that the whole business has turned into a cliché is a partial proof of that transformation.

Not, ultimately, the physics of love, certainly not the mathematics—"one and one is one, is one, is one" does not sound like math. It sounds like poetry. The love scenes continue to fascinate us, haunt us, and remain fixed in our collective imagination because they are above all the poetics of love, a poetics that transcends, appropriately, the very physical reality it pretends to describe—and transcends it without betraying it.

In *The Dancing Wu Li Masters*, Gary Zukav points out some sub-limely elegant similarities between Eastern enlightenment and the new physics. Tantra, he points out, transcends rationality just as the new physics must, as "the profound physicists of this century increasingly have become aware that they are confronting the ineffable." Gary Zukav cites Max Planck, the father of quantum mechanics: "Science . . . means unresting endeavor and continually progressing development toward an aim which the poetic intuition may apprehend, but which the intellect can never fully grasp."[15] This is almost identical to something the Spanish poet Lorca said: "Through poetry man more quickly approaches the edge where the philosopher and the mathematician turn their backs in silence."[16] Zukav concludes that this reaching "the end of science"—that is, rational science—"means the coming of western civilization . . . into the higher dimensions of human experience."[17] That is precisely what I think Hemingway was doing fifty years ago. Putting aside the real war and his own experience, leaving behind the observed and the observable, going beyond the rational, he invented his own undiscovered country. It had diverse aspects but the greatest of these—the one he was most interested in—was love. Hemingway knew, somehow, that the only way to realize love fully and most transcendentally was by going within. The real undiscovered country was the fertile meadow of his imagination. There is where the dance is.

NOTES

1. Allen Josephs, "Hemingway and the Spanish Civil War or the Volatile Mixtures of Politics and Art," in *Rewriting the Good Fight: Critical Essays of the Spanish Civil War*, eds. Frieda Brown, et al. (East Lansing: Michigan State University Press, 1989); "Hemingway's Spanish Civil War Stories, or the Spanish Civil War or Reality," in *Hemingway's Neglected Short Fiction: New Perspectives*, ed. Susan F. Beegel (Ann Arbor: UMI Research Press, 1989).
2. Carlos Baker, *Ernest Hemingway: A Life Story* (New York: Scribner's, 1969), 348.
3. *Hamlet* III, 1.
4. Ernest Hemingway, *Green Hills of Africa* (New York: Scribner's, 1935), 72, emphasis added.
5. Ernest Hemingway, *Farewell to Arms* (New York: Scribner's, 1929), 116.
6. Ernest Hemingway, *For Whom the Bell Tolls* (New York: Scribner's, 1940), 380.
7. Ibid., 379.
8. T. S. Eliot, *The Complete Poems and Plays and Plays 1909-1950* (New York: Harcourt, Brace and World, 1971), 117-22.
9. Hemingway, *For Whom the Bell Tolls*, 159.
10. Ibid., 159.
11. Michael S. Reynolds, *The Young Hemingway* (New York: Blackwell, 1986), 208.
12. Ibid., 209.
13. Michael S. Reynolds in Paul Smith, *A Reader's Guide to the Short Stories of Ernest Hemingway* (Boston: G. K. Hall, 1989), 255.

14. Hemingway, *Green Hills of Africa*, 72.

15. Gary Zukav, *The Dancing Wu Li Masters: An Overview of the New Physics* (New York: Bantam Books, 1980), 313.

16. My translation from Sandra Forman and Allen Josephs, *Only Mystery: Fredrico Garcia Lorca's Poetry in Word and Image* (Gainsville: University Press of Florida, 1992), 69.

17. Zukav, *The Dancing Wu Li Masters*, 313.

SOMETHING IN IT FOR YOU

ROLE MODELS IN *FOR WHOM THE BELL TOLLS*

LINDA PATTERSON MILLER

THE TITLE OF THIS ESSAY, "Something in it for You," derives from a letter that Ernest Hemingway wrote to Sara Murphy while he was working on *For Whom the Bell Tolls*. This letter, with its references to Sara and to Hemingway's novel in process, suggests that Sara and her husband Gerald played a significant role in Hemingway's conception of *For Whom the Bell Tolls*, and it further confirms that Hemingway's relationship with the Murphys figured larger in Hemingway's emotional life and art than his biographers have yet recognized.

Hemingway had met the Murphys in France in 1925, and their relationship quickly intensified during the 1926 "avalanche" winter wherein Hemingway's marriage with Hadley was ending. Both Gerald and Sara gave Hemingway specific advice during that troubled time, and Hemingway never forgot (and probably never forgave) the strong role they played in encouraging his break with Hadley. He was particularly angry at Gerald's fatherly and presumptuous air when he urged Hemingway to cut "cleanly and sharply" at a point when Hemingway was wavering. Gerald told him that Hadley was "miscast" as Hemingway's wife and that Hemingway must, above all, protect his talent—"that thing in you which life might trick you into deserting."[1] Hemingway's remorse and rancor, primarily about Gerald, eventually worked its way into *A Moveable Feast*, wherein he castigated the Murphys as the "understanding rich" who took "the nourishment they needed" and left everything dead behind them.[2] Twenty-five years before the posthumous publication of *Feast*, however, Hemingway's feelings about the Murphys also worked their way into *For Whom the Bell Tolls*—Hemingway's Spanish novel about betrayal and loss and human interconnectedness.

As Hemingway was in the final stages of his manuscript, he wrote to Sara from Cuba (27 December [1939]). "Dearest Sara. Thank you for the lovely letter. I had kept your other letter from France with me always to answer. Had hoped we would all be in France this fall. Then the war—and

229

book still unfinished. Now I will go in the spring when this is done. Am in the last part now." Farther into the letter Hemingway stated: "Must finish this book. With a little luck and a little less being slugged over the head (it's a good tough head though and people liable to find they broke something hitting it) it can be the best one that I have written." Then Hemingway added a surprising, and seemingly offhand, reference to the novel and to Sara. "I put a couple of things in it for you that you may find some time," Hemingway told Sara.[3] Something that Hemingway had put there for Sara, that only she would know? Despite Hemingway's propensity to boast, he seldom told friends he had written things *for* them, and this line should be taken literally. Indeed, when analyzed in light of both textual and biographical evidence, Hemingway's statement to Sara Murphy suggests that Hemingway used both Sara and Gerald as models for Pilar and Pablo.

If imagining the beautiful Murphys of Villa America fame as crude peasant stock requires a willing suspension of disbelief, remember that Hemingway often used real people, thinly disguised, in his fiction, just as he also incorporated insider jokes, sometimes inverting physical realities to get at emotional truths. His portrayal of the Murphys as peasants ironically mocks their monied, elegant lifestyle, as it also reflects their bohemian life in 1920s France—what Hemingway later derided as the "fiesta" concept of life. The Murphys' creative attire and their entertainments on the Riviera—all orchestrated by Gerald—embodied this gypsy-like freedom and flair. At their Villa America and on the Garoupe Beach in Antibes, France, Sara wore flowing skirts with scarves knotted about her waist, neck and head, while Gerald dressed up in invented costumes, his favorite getup comprising a peasant shirt, gypsy pants, rope sandals, and a black cap. Sometimes Gerald provided their guests with "costumes," such as the summer everyone wore red and white striped sailors' shirts that Gerald had discovered in the French market. Although Hemingway drew upon this spirited and colorful Villa America life in order to evoke in Pablo and Pilar the physical dimensions of the Murphys' characters and lifestyle, he primarily captured in Pablo and Pilar the Murphys' psychological complexities, particularly those of Gerald.

In Pilar, one of Hemingway's most powerful and unconventional females, Hemingway portrayed Sara's strength of character. Although Gertrude Stein, with her Buddha-like build and demeanor, bore a strong physical resemblance to Pilar, Pilar's psychological qualities are identifiably Sara's: her intuitive, gypsy knowledge (Harry Crosby described Sara as "sphinx-like but knowing");[4] her immediate understanding of situations and people; her graphic awareness of life's brutalities (two sons dying at the age of sixteen); her forthright talk; her anger. Sara vented her anger at friends, such as Fitzgerald, who exasperated her, just as she cursed a cruel God, raising her fist high as she stalked Park Avenue following her first son's death in 1935.[5] She felt, as she told Fitzgerald, a "sympathetic vibration" to Zelda's inner turmoil, which Sara called Zelda's "violence."[6] Archibald MacLeish believed that Sara's "reticence" comprised "her power of feeling what she had not put in words," and he said as well that Sara was "all woman."[7] In her femininity, however, she exuded a certain masculine power such that she preferred being with men and was to her male friends, including Hemingway, a comrade. Hemingway would tell Sara during the 1930s that he had "no closer friend" than she and that they were "the only two non serious people left."[8] Although Sara was fourteen years older than Hemingway, he was drawn to and married older women. Pilar is roughly Sara's age (48 years) at the time Hemingway was writing the novel, and, like Sara, she is touchy about getting older and, as she says, "ugly." Like Sara, Pilar has a healthy temper, a rich, throaty laugh, a comfortable sense of self, and a no-nonsense demeanor.

If Pilar is a woman of straightforward reliability, however, she has a husband who is neither simple nor trustworthy. When Agustin compares Pilar and Pablo, he could be talking about Sara and Gerald directly. "No Pilar," Agustin said. "You are not smart. You are brave. You are loyal. You have decision. You have intuition. Much decision and much heart. But you are not smart. . . . Pablo I *know* is smart."[9] In that smartness, Pablo is dangerous and, also, as Jordan recognizes, "very complicated." Sara would acknowledge openly that, while she was of the heart, Gerald was of the head. She told Scott Fitzgerald, for example, that "it seems not to matter *nearly* so much what one thinks of things—as what one feels about them."[10] Gerald, however, had an intellectual bent by which he distanced himself from life and tried to organize it. He repeatedly apologized to his friends for being "super-organizational" and agonized over his inability to control life in the end.[11]

From the first moment that Robert Jordan sees Pablo, he knows that Pablo cannot be trusted, for Pablo has turned—on the cause, on others, and, most significantly, on himself. Pablo embodies the betrayal and the uncertainty around which the novel revolves, and he is very much Gerald Murphy as Hemingway had sized him up, as early as 1928. Hemingway believed that Gerald was a liar and a phony because he was not true to himself and consequently not true to others. Hemingway put Gerald to the test in this regard in early 1928, when he confronted him, in an indirect yet patently clear way, about his sexual identity. As Gerald assessed it, Hemingway "was extremely sensitive to the question of who was [a homosexual] and who wasn't," and he had asked Gerald "casually," "I don't mind a fairy like X, do you?" Although Gerald "had never met the man," he said "No." "I have no idea why I said it," Gerald stated later, "except that Ernest had the quality of making it easier to agree with him than not. . . . Anyway, instead of saying I had never met the man I agreed with him, and he gave me a funny look. Afterward I almost wondered whether it had been a trap he laid for me."[12] Gerald knew then that Hemingway had nabbed him in his complicated lies, and he recognized also that Hemingway, at that precise moment, had written him off.

By 1936, Gerald had begun to deal with his ambivalent sexuality, discussing it with Sara, who had called him to task. Previously he had only hinted at a repressed homosexuality when he spoke of a personal "defect," which he would name in 1936 as his "sexual deficiency." He and Sara discussed what they called "topic A" by way of letters as Gerald remained in Manhattan to oversee the family Mark Cross Company while Sara stayed in upstate New York, where their son Patrick lay dying. Gerald recognized in these 1936 letters that, in failing to deal with his sexual and emotional deficiencies, he had betrayed Sara and himself. He told Sara that while she believed in relationships, as she did in life, he was "less of a believer" because he did not "*admire* human animals as much." "I am not as capable (for a fundamental sexual deficiency)," and "I lack the confidence (quite naturally) to command it." "You are luckier than I am," he concluded. "I *fear* Life. You don't."[13]

Although Hemingway would malign both Gerald and Sara in *A Moveable Feast*, he had targeted his rancor at Gerald, and Sara became implicated more by association than for any negative feelings for her that Hemingway harbored. Indeed, the qualities in Gerald that Hemingway distrusted were the very qualities that Gerald and Sara had begun to address in their letters to each other during the spring of 1936. As Gerald tried to understand his own inadequacies and as Gerald and Sara struggled to resolve their marital strains, Sara turned increasingly to Hemingway. Throughout the 1930s, Sara and Hemingway saw each other often, both in Florida and New York, and they also corresponded. Their letters from this period reflect the candor and respect—and the love—that characterized their relationship, and the tone and phrasing of these letters, particularly Sara's, reverberates in the dialogue between Pilar and Jordan in *For Whom the Bell Tolls*. When Pilar says to Jordan, "I speak to you as though I knew you for a very long time," he responds: "It is like that when people understand one another" (36). Then, a little later, he adds: "I like very much your way of speaking." "I try to speak frankly," Pilar states (37-38). In several instances, the cadence and thematic thrust of Sara's 1930s letters to Hemingway can be heard in Pilar's voice, as best summarized when she says to Jordan: "Everyone needs to talk to someone. Before we had religion and other nonsense. Now for everyone there should be someone to whom one can speak frankly, for all the valor that one could have one becomes very alone" (98).

Sara felt particularly alone during 1935 following the unexpected death of their son Baoth (from spinal meningitis) as she continued to tend Patrick, the Murphys' other son, who remained sick with tuberculosis. With Gerald's physical and emotional distance from her during these days only exacerbating her sense of isolation, Sara turned to Hemingway for companionship and some frank talk. She had just received Gerald's letter that acknowledged his sexual inadequacies and his fear of life (16 April 1936) when she left for Key West, Florida, to spend a week with Hemingway on board his *Pilar* (the boat he had commissioned two years before). When she returned to upstate New York, she wrote Gerald a more forthright letter that apparently questioned him about his possible homosexuality. Although this letter has not survived, Gerald's return letter (25 June 1936) makes clear that he had taken a while to respond because Sara's direct question— "a poser"—had caught him off guard. "I've thought about it much," he wrote, "but didn't feel up to answering it." "My ideas on topic A are so bad," he continued, "that even I think so. I'm afraid I've always skulked the question. Wanted to and was aided and abetted, I guess, by family and education." Gerald goes on to quote from his recent reading of Santayana's *Last Puritan*: "'He had been brought up to believe that all women were ladies but not that ladies were women—'etc." "I'm not looking for alibis," Gerald concluded. "Too late, too late. People are defective. Life is defective. My defect though not openly ruinous effects life and people very fundamentally. . . . Unfortunately it gives one a feeling of inferiority." "As for changing," Gerald speculated, "either it's impossible to change any thing so elementary,—or I'm too weak."[14]

Given the content of Sara and Gerald's letters (which speak explicitly of Gerald's emotional and sexual "deficiencies"), and given the timing of these letters (which directly sandwich Sara's visit with Hemingway), it seems clear that Sara did discuss Gerald's "defect" with Hemingway. Such privileged knowledge would have confirmed Hemingway's earlier suspicions about Gerald's unreliability and influenced a couple of years later his portrayal of Pablo as one who lacks *cojones*. The repeated references in *For Whom the Bell Tolls* to Pablo's becoming like an effeminate lover underscore the degree to which he has become, in every respect, a coward.

Although Pablo's self-emasculation runs as a major motif throughout *For Whom the Bell Tolls*, Hemingway's characterization of Pablo draws directly upon Gerald Murphy in many ways, beginning with the opening description of Pablo's round head. Gerald believed that his face was too round, and he joked about his "Irish moonface," which he tried to square off with sideburns and hats—hats that might also disguise his slightly balding head. Hemingway's description of Pablo stresses that "his face was almost round and his head was round" (12), and he refers as well to Pablo's balding head. In addition, Hemingway emphasizes throughout how Pablo's organizational skills, like those of Gerald, characterize him. "Pablo is an organizer," says Pilar, organizing those in the plaza into lines (114). Pablo is also vehemently anti-Catholic, hating priests "even worse than he hated Fascists" (140). Gerald, too, rejected what he saw as the Catholic rigidity and pretense of his upbringing, which he would talk about with friends—these same friends who also came to respect Gerald's moodiness and his underlying sadness. In Pablo's "sullenness there was a sadness that was disturbing to Robert Jordan. He knew that sadness and to see it here worried him. . . . I don't like that sadness, he thought. That sadness is bad. That's the sadness they get before they quit or before they betray. That is the sadness that comes before the sell-out" (15).

Pablo's pattern of behavior throughout the novel—to turn tail and run during moments of crisis, reflects a pattern of behavior that both Sara and the Murphys' friends, including Hemingway, recognized in Gerald. In the face of himself and what he called his "ersatz" nature, Gerald found it easier to avoid friends, such as he did in 1930 when he came to the States for a brief visit. "Gerald is here," Archibald MacLeish told Scott Fitzgerald, "but no one has seen him. . . . Skulks like a shadow."[15] When the Murphys' son Patrick took ill in 1929 with the tuberculosis that would kill him in 1937, Gerald went on a racing cruise and tried to ignore Sara's telegrams imploring him to return. Sara believed that Gerald had reneged on his responsibilities and was consequently betraying himself. Shortly after this cruise, Gerald quit his painting, for which he had gained recognition in France as the best American painter working in the modern manner. He went with Patrick and the family to a sanitarium in Switzerland, where he increasingly turned inward, retreating at one point to a monastery nearby. Here he grew a beard (not unlike Pablo's stubble) and contemplated quitting everything. Gerald's friends had already grown leery of Gerald's mood swings, which could be harsh and immediate, "like the closing of a door," said John Dos Passos. MacLeish noted that, in the end, Gerald did something very Irish—he turned on himself.[16]

That kind of turning on self becomes a major theme in Bell Tolls, one that is reinforced through Pablo's moodiness—unpredictable mood swings from conviviality to gloom not unlike Gerald's, and through the novel's often ironic treatment of sexual inversion. Besides the direct allusions to Pablo's becoming more effeminate and "changed" ("as finished and as ended as a boar that has been altered," Anselmo says [212]), Hemingway gives Pilar and Maria's relationship a lesbian cast (toning down the more explicit homoerotic references in the final manuscript revisions). Although Pilar recognizes that others could misinterpret her physical caressing of Maria, she affirms that she is "no *tortillera* but a woman made for men." "I do not make perversions," she states in clarifying her actions with Maria. "I only tell you something true. Few people will ever talk to thee truly and no women"(169). Indeed, Pilar's frankness in acknowledging all facets of herself, sexually and otherwise, informs her strength of character and stands in stark contrast to Pablo's inability to be true. Hemingway emphasizes throughout that Pilar's solid androgynous nature allows for Pilar's frank acceptance of who she is, "all woman and all ugly." "I would have made a good man," she tells Jordan, "Yet many men have loved me and I have loved many men. It is curious" (108).

After Gerald had quit painting and returned to the business world that he had rejected in 1921, he dubbed himself the Merchant Prince. "I was never happy until I started painting," he confessed years later, "and I have never been thoroughly so since I was obliged to give it up." He questioned "how many aspiring American artists have been claimed by the harmful belief that if a business is your 'inheritance' that it is heresy not to give up all in favor of it." He recognized that "if one *is* to be a painter of note nothing really prevents it. . . . I cannot forget that Ucello suddenly gave up painting in favor of mathematics—but returned to painting after a long lapse."[17] Gerald Murphy never returned to his art, and, like Pablo, he seemed to know that he had betrayed the real work to become a capitalist and to live the good life. Anselmo denounces Pablo for betraying himself and his calling. "Until thou hadst horses thou wert with us. Now thou art another capitalist more" (19). Jordan, though, understands the power of those horses and the strong allure of the good life. "The old man was right," he thought. "The horses made Pablo rich and as soon as he was rich he wanted to enjoy life. Pretty soon he'll feel bad because he can't join the Jockey Club" (20).

Although Gerald had renounced the country club set that he and Sara had left behind in New York during the 1920s, Hemingway seemed to feel that Gerald Murphy embraced that clubbiness once again when he returned to New York and the life of money in 1933. As Hemingway makes sardonic references to Pablo's "Palace of Fear" (218), he simultaneously mocks Gerald's elegant lifestyle, his fear of life, and his personal and artistic betrayal. "But since a long time he is *muy flojo*," Anselmo says of Pablo. "He is very flaccid. He is very much afraid to die" (29). And while he "was a very good man," as Pilar recognizes, he is now "terminated" (35). He was now, as Jordan perceives it, one of those Spaniards who "turned on you. They turned on you often but they always turned on everyone. They turned on themselves too" (148).

To the degree that Hemingway characterized Pablo as a coward who lacks *cojones* and who is, above all, untrustworthy, he was portraying Murphy as Hemingway had come to see him during the 1920s and 1930s; and he was portraying as well the Gerald Murphy who stands at the center of *A Moveable Feast*. In many respects, *For Whom the Bell Tolls* becomes the emotional and thematic predecessor of *A Moveable Feast*, and there are strong parallels between the two works. Note this opening to *For Whom the Bell Tolls* and then hear in it as well the thrust of *A Moveable Feast*:

> The young man, whose name was Robert Jordan, was extremely hungry and he was worried. He was often hungry but he was not usually worried because he did not give any importance to what happened to himself and he knew from experience how simple it was to move behind the enemy lines in all this country. It was as simple to move behind them as it was to cross through them, if you had a good guide. It was only giving importance to what happened to you if you were caught that made it difficult; that and deciding whom to trust. You had to trust the people you worked with completely or not at all, and you had to make decisions about the trusting. (6-7)

This concern with finding the right guide and deciding whom to trust underlies *A Moveable Feast*. To Hemingway's regret, he had trusted "the pilot fish," Dos Passos, and he had followed the guidance of the "understanding rich," under whose charm he "was as trusting and as stupid as a bird dog who wants to go out with any man with a gun, or a trained pig in a circus who has finally found someone who loves and appreciates him for himself alone."[18] By allowing himself to be too easily led by Gerald Murphy during a vulnerable time, Hemingway suspected that he had given in to the good life represented by Pauline's, and the Murphys', money and that he had ultimately betrayed his writing in the process. Gerald Murphy had hit a raw nerve when he cautioned Hemingway in 1926 not to betray that talent that life might trick him into deserting.

Both *A Moveable Feast* and *For Whom the Bell Tolls* are about going into the new, unknown country, determining who the enemy is, and discovering he is yourself when you allow yourself to be duped and to lose hold of the center. Toward the end of *For Whom the Bell Tolls*, Jordan reflects upon the complications of the Spanish fighting wherein there are no clear sides, and issues of trust and confidence assume huge proportions. "If a thing was right fundamentally," he thinks, "the lying was not supposed to matter. There was a lot of lying though. He did not care for the lying at first. He hated it. Then later he had come to like it. It was part of being an insider but it was a very corrupting business" (249). A deleted portion of *A Moveable Feast* acknowledges that if the decisions Gerald Murphy had encouraged Hemingway to make "were wrong," they had all "turned out badly finally from the same fault of character that made them. If you deceive and lie with one person against another," Hemingway wrote, "you will eventually do it again."[19]

When Hemingway read Fitzgerald's *Tender Is the Night* in 1934, he was outraged, for he believed that Fitzgerald had modeled Dick and Nicole Diver after Gerald and Sara without knowing anything about their psychological complexities. Fitzgerald, as such, had romanticized the Murphys, capturing their charm and none of their real character. In writing *For Whom the Bell Tolls*, Hemingway consciously reversed this process, deromanticizing the Murphys in his own revised *Tender Is the Night*. Not coincidentally, Hemingway reread *Tender* as he was at work on his own manuscript, and his famous letter to Fitzgerald upon the publication of *Tender is the Night* in 1934 bears some rereading in light of this essay, for it reveals between the lines something about Hemingway's own use of the Murphys later. "I liked it and I didn't like it," Hemingway wrote.

> It started off with that marvelous description of Sara and Gerald. . . . Then you started fooling with them, making them come from things they didn't come from, changing into other people and you can't do that, Scott. If you take real people and write about them you cannot give them other parents than they have . . . you cannot make them do anything they would not do. You can take you or me or Zelda or Pauline or Hadley or Sara or Gerald but you have to keep them the same and you can only make them do what they would do. You can't make one be another. Invention is the finest thing but you cannot invent anything that would not actually happen.

Then Hemingway added: "You could write a fine book about Gerald and Sara for instance if you knew enough about them and they would not have any feeling, except passing, if it were true."[20]

Hemingway believed he did know enough about the Murphys, and in *For Whom the Bell Tolls*, he wrote that very fine book. As to whether or not Sara discovered Hemingway's use of them in the novel, Hemingway's line to Fitzgerald probably addresses that precisely. If the writer knows enough about the people, and writes them true, rather than inventing them, then the people he has used will not have any feeling, except passing. Sara had been furious over Fitzgerald's use of them in *Tender*, probably because Fitzgerald had made a big deal out of it, telling everybody that the book was about the Murphys. Perhaps Hemingway made that seemingly passing reference in his letter to Sara, that he had put things in the novel for her, to deflect the larger implications of his use of the Murphys.

If Sara did discover the parallels, no specific evidence of her reaction to the book remains. Indeed, her relationship with Hemingway had abated and their correspondence, for the most part, ceased, once Hemingway had married Martha Gellhorn and published *For Whom the Bell Tolls*.

It is interesting to note in conclusion that Pablo and Pilar have made certain accommodations and compromises by the end of the novel. Although Pablo remains a coward in the face of himself, Pilar clearly continues to love him, and she and Pablo leave together for the city with the girl, Maria, between them. After the loss of their sons in 1935 and then 1937, the Murphys, with their one surviving daughter, Honoria, gathered their forces and moved in together in New York City.

NOTES

1. The correspondence between Hemingway and the Murphys is published in Linda Patterson Miller, ed., *Letters from the Lost Generation: Gerald and Sara Murphy and Friends* (New Brunswick: Rutgers University Press, 1991). See Gerald to Hemingway, [6 September 1926], 21-23.
2. Ernest Hemingway, *A Moveable Feast* (New York: Scribner's, 1964), 208.
3. Miller, *Letters*, 244-45.
4. Harry Crosby to Henrietta Crosby, 20 December 1934, in Geoffrey Wolff, *Black Sun: The Brief Transit and Violent Eclipse of Harry Crosby* (New York: Vintage Books, 1977 [1976]), 155.
5. See Honoria Murphy Donnelly with Richard N. Billings, *Sara and Gerald: Villa America and After* (New York: Times Books, 1982), 91.
6. Letter of 20 August [1935] in Miller, *Letters,* 140.
7. MacLeish's poem about Sara, "Sketch for a Portrait of Mme. G____M____," was first published in 1926 and is in MacLeish's *New and Collected Poems: 1917-1976* (Boston: Houghton Mifflin, 1976), 107-9; MacLeish to author, 17 October 1979.
8. Hemingway to Sara, [ca. late December 1940], Miller, *Letters*, 260-61.
9. Ernest Hemingway, *For Whom the Bell Tolls* (New York: Scribner's, 1940), 104.
10. Sara to Fitzgerald, 20 August [1935], in Miller, *Letters*, 139-40.
11. See, for example, Murphy to John Dos Passos, 27 August 1957, unpublished letter in The Dos Passos Papers, University of Virginia. Scott Fitzgerald emphasized these qualities in Dick Diver, the protagonist in *Tender Is the Night* modeled after Gerald.
12. When Calvin Tomkins was beginning to write about the Murphys and life in France in the 1920s, Gerald Murphy and Tomkins corresponded, and Tomkins also conducted several taped interviews. Transcriptions from these interviews, as well as copies of the Murphy-Tomkins correspondence, are in the Murphy Papers (Honoria Murphy Donnelly, East Hampton,

New York). Gerald's statements about Hemingway are drawn from these interviews.

13. Gerald to Sara, 16 April 1936, 18 April 1936, and 26 June 1936, in Miller, *Letters*, 162-64 and 168-69.

14. Gerald to Sara, 26 June 1936, in Miller, *Letters*, 168-69. Although Sara drove down to Florida with John and Katy Dos Passos, she spent six days on board the *Pilar* with Hemingway, as she stated in her follow-up letter to Pauline (who had been away visiting family in Arkansas). See Sara to Pauline, [11 May 1936], in Miller, *Letters*, 164-65.

15. MacLeish to Fitzgerald, 15 September [1930] in *Letters of Archibald MacLeish 1907-1982*, ed. R. H. Winnick (Boston: Houghton Mifflin, 1983), 236.

16. John Dos Passos, *The Best Times: An Informal Memoir* (New York: New American Library, 1966), 146.

17. Quoted in Rudi Blesh, *Modern Art USA: Men, Rebellion, Conquest 1900-1956* (New York: Alfred A. Knopf, 1956), 93-96.

18. Hemingway, *Feast*, 209.

19. *Feast* manuscripts, Hemingway Papers, The John F. Kennedy Library, Boston.

20. Hemingway to Fitzgerald, 28 May 1934, in *Ernest Hemingway: Selected Letters, 1917-1961*, ed. Carlos Baker (New York: Scribner's, 1981), 407. On 25 March 1939, Hemingway wrote to Maxwell Perkins telling him that he had "found Scott's Tender Is the Night in Cuba and sent it over" (to Key West) so that he could read it again. His rereading found much of it "excellent." See Baker, *Ernest Hemingway*, 483.

"ANTI-WAR CORRESPONDENCE"

RESHAPING DEATH IN THE *FOR WHOM THE BELL TOLLS* MANUSCRIPT

THOMAS GOULD

UNLIKE REVISIONS IN HIS earlier manuscripts, Hemingway's revisions in *For Whom the Bell Tolls*, particularly when dealing with the subjects of death and killing, lean toward additions rather than reductions. Throughout the manuscript, he expands by revision nearly every scene that involves violent death, whether in external narrative or internal monologue. These revisions come in two forms: minor additions of specific details in individual scenes, and long inserts that expand the scenes. One effect of these revisions is to illustrate the cruelty and the necessity of death and man's need to shut out all emotional attachment during the revolution. More importantly, these changes create a more vivid, brutal, and realistic picture of war and, consequently, draw the reader into the experience.

The first scene that undergoes extensive revision contains the conversation between Jordan and Anselmo in chapter three. In this scene, as the two men observe the sentry post on the bridge, both agree that killing is necessary. In the first draft, this conversation between the two men is quite succinct, a half-page discussion that briefly mentions Anselmo's preference for hunting animals over killing men and Jordan's belief in the necessity of killing in order to win the fight. In revision, Hemingway expands this brief conversation into eight pages of argument concerning the ethics of killing. This additional material includes Anselmo's recollection of his hunting trophies, his bear story, Jordan's contribution of what American Indians believe about bears, Anselmo's reasons for why gypsies kill, and their discussion of the lack of religion in Spain. These are important thematic elements that will become more apparent as the novel progresses: the homelessness of the guerillas, superstition, killing, and faith themes. Anselmo's distinction between why he kills and why gypsies kill is particularly significant to the killing theme in the novel. He explains that the difference is one of motive: the gypsies kill because they know "there is war and people may kill again as in olden times without a surety of punishment" (MS-63). However, Anselmo and the partisans fight for the cause, so their killing is justified as an act of war. This clarification shows how thin the line is that separates barbarism and nationalism when it comes to killing in the war.

Another section showing considerable revision toward a dramatic sense of death is Pilar's story about the killing of Fascists in her hometown of Avila. Sections of her narrative are heavily revised. Originally, her narration of Pablo's assassination of *guardia civil* members is terse. The first draft reads: "Pablo shot them each in turn in the back of the head with the pistol going from one to another and putting the barrel of the pistol against the back of their heads. Only one put his hands in front of his eyes, and he was the last one and the four bodies were slumped against the wall" (MS-217-18). In revision, Hemingway expands this scene, letting Pilar tell us how each head moved against the gun barrel, how the body shivered. The result is a vivid picture of the cold brutality of one human being toward another. He also adds the paragraph describing Pilar as "weak in the stomach" after the killing of the guards (MS-224). This scene now shows how even a hardened individual like Pilar can be disturbed by war's cruelty. In addition, the author inserts this conversation between two peasants:

> "But I do not think one blow with this will kill a man," and he held his flail in both hands and looked at it in doubt. "That is the beauty of it," another peasant said, "there must be many blows." (MS-Insert-222)

Hemingway also adds more fully detailed descriptions of the killing of the Fascist townspeople. In the case of the killing of Don Benitez, the original draft simply states that he was beaten by the peasants until he fell and then they "dragged him to the cliff and threw him into the river" (MS-225). The handwritten revision in the margin of the manuscript is far more descriptive. It reads: "and the man who had struck him first called to the others to help him and he pulled the collar of Don Benitez's shirt and others took hold of his arms and with his face in the dust of the plaza they dragged him over the walk to the edge of the cliff" (MS-225). The literal details of this incident make it real, a vivid picture in the reader's mind.

In another kind of revision, instead of drawing the reader to a broad view of war, Hemingway deepens the realism of Jordan's thoughts on war's personal tragedy. In chapter seven, Jordan, Pilar, and Maria, on the trail to El Sordo's camp, encounter fellow partisan Joaquin, who relates the story of the murder of his parents by the Fascists. Originally, the scene lasted a scant one-and-a-half manuscript pages. In revision, Hemingway inserts seven pages that not only expand the chapter but also refocus the intention of the scene.

The first draft of the scene contains a brief reflection by Jordan on the tragic realities of death during the revolution. The rest of the passage refers to Pilar's extraordinary storytelling ability. In the first draft, Jordan's reaction to the death of Joaquin's family is concise: "It was just a loss stated, after an action you make a list of casualties, no one can reconstruct the action from that list who has not seen the battle" (MS-264). The rest of the manuscript section is single-mindedly concerned with Pilar's ability to retell, convincingly, a story. All of this material is incorporated into the revised version, where it now plays a minor role compared to Hemingway's typewritten inserts, which dramatically refocus the passage: the revised version retains its praise for Pilar's narrative skills, but here the focus shifts to the suffering of the people during the conflict. Jordan's thoughts now range from the physical suffering and sacrifice of the Spanish peasants to the psychological suffering of the Belgian boy from the Eleventh Brigade. These additions achieve precisely what Jordan admires in Pilar's recollections, the clear image of human suffering in war.

Throughout the manuscript, there are also numerous instances where the author has revised the image of the dead or wounded in graphic detail for better visualization. He adds graphic details to Karkov's story of the wounded Russian soldiers, Anselmo's discovery of Sordo's decapitated men, and Fernando's slow death on the bridge. At every opportunity, Hemingway gives added emphasis to the horror of war.

In chapter eighteen, Jordan remembers Karkov's story of the wounded Russian soldiers. In first draft, the recollection simply reads: "In the event the city should be abandoned, Karkov was to poison them and to destroy all evidence of their identity before leaving the Palace Hotel. No one could prove from the bodies of the three wounded men, who would be found in their beds at the palace, that they were Russians" (MS-429). The remainder of the scene, in the original draft, consists of Jordan and Karkov discussing cyanide. In the margin, the author adds to this scene the horrific details of each soldier's wounds and other cold realities about death, such as "Your nationality and your politics did not show when you were dead" (MS-429). Hemingway emphasizes the results of combat and how, in the finality of death, all men are equal, regardless of allegiances.

The events surrounding El Sordo's hilltop stand offer a number of Hemingway's revisions on death. For instance, Sordo's interior monologue on his impending death is an insert into the manuscript. Before revision, there is no monologue. In the original draft, Sordo receives a wine bottle from a comrade, raises it to his lips, and returns the bottle. Hemingway crosses out this action and inserts four pages that illuminate Sordo's thoughts before he passes the bottle back. This additional material is clearly and cleanly written and appears to be a copied second draft of the original inserts. The emphasis in these pages is upon Sordo's reluctant acceptance of death: "Whether one has fear of it or not, one's death is difficult to accept. Sordo had accepted it but there was no sweetness in its acceptance . . . . If one must die, he thought, and clearly one must, I can die. But I hate it" (MS-Insert-2 and 3-615). Also included in these pages is Sordo's comparison of life and death:

> Dying was nothing and he had no picture of it nor fear of it in his mind. But living was a field of grain blowing in the wind on the side of a hill. Living was a hawk in the sky. Living was an earthen jar of water in the dust of the threshing with the grain flailed out and the chaff blowing. (MS-Insert-3-615)

Prior to revision, the scene's focus is upon Sordo's bravery and his willingness to die for the cause. The inserts shift this focus to now promote life over death. The concrete image of life in contrast to no image for death is precisely the effect Hemingway's revisions supply: death as loss. Also, the additional material serves to humanize Sordo. He is no longer just a soldier, no longer an acceptable casualty of war. On the contrary, he is a man who values life; and his death, like the deaths of all men in war, is a tragedy. Without question Sordo is brave, but he is no martyr. He is merely one of many ordinary individuals caught in an extraordinary situation, but now the death and the man are personalized by Hemingway's revisions.

Hemingway revises to achieve the same deepening sense of loss after the decapitation of Sordo and his men. As the Fascist troops descend from the mountain with the bodies of their own dead strapped to the horses, Lt. Berrendo reflects about what transpired on the hill. Before revision the scene reads: "Then he thought of Julian, and as he rode down into the dark pine forest, leaving the sunlight behind him on the hill, riding now in the quiet dark of the forest, he started to say a prayer for him again" (MS-666-67). In the top margin, Hemingway writes a short but significant additional thought: "Then he thought of Julian, dead on the hill, dead now, tied across a horse in the first troop, and as he rode down . . ." (MS-666-67). This short revision shows a loss that was not as readily apparent in the first draft. The emphasis here is upon the loss of a friend, not just a fellow soldier. Also, the repetition of "dead" points out the finality of death. The loss is permanent. The war has taken his friend, and Berrendo will forever bear the scars of this loss. As with Sordo, Hemingway's revision here enhances the humanity of the soldier. The deaths of these men are tragic losses both for themselves and for the others.

Once the Fascists depart from the hill, Anselmo walks across the battleground on his way back to the rebel cave. The revisions to Anselmo's expe-

rience on the hill stress how the horrifying violence of war can have a chill-
ing effect upon even the most hardened individual. Anselmo's grisly discovery of the headless bodies of his fellow rebels terrifies him. This reaction,
however, is not fully evident in the original draft. The first draft reads: "But
he counted them [the bodies] and then made off for Pablo's hide out.
Walking alone in the dark, with fear in his heart from the feeling the holes
of bomb craters had given him, he put all thoughts of the next day out of
his mind" (MS-670). From this passage, the reader infers that Anselmo is
astonished at the amount of destruction on the devastated hillside. In revision, Hemingway makes some detailed interlinear additions to Anselmo's
experience that significantly alter this conclusion. The passage now reads:

> But he counted those that lay there and then made off across the hills for
> Pablo's camp. Walking alone in the dark, with a fear like a freezing of his
> heart from the feeling the holes of the bomb crater had given him, from them
> and from what he found on the hill, he put all thought of the next day out of
> his mind. (MS-670)

These specific revisions impress upon the reader that the ghastly details
of the scene are what greatly disturb the old man and not the general
destruction. Anselmo earlier states that he fully understands that killing is
a necessary, if undesirable, component of the revolution. This mutilation
of Sordo's men, however, is not an act of war; this decapitation is an act of
barbarism. Anselmo is stunned that man could do this to his fellow man,
even if he is the enemy. Hemingway's revisions to the Sordo episode
expand the grotesque tragedy and human cruelty of war. In this revision,
Hemingway demonstrates his sense that war is not a dignified and noble
affair; war is the violent and oftentimes barbaric infliction of pain by men
upon other men.

The revisions to the last chapter are short additions of a sentence or
two, and they accentuate the physical pain of the wounded rebel and the
awful reality of his condition. During Fernando's conversation with
Primitivo and the gypsy, Hemingway describes the agony of the rebel. The
original description simply reads: "His eyes were shut tight with pain"
(MS-43:39). To this, Hemingway adds "the edges of the lids twitching"
(MS-43:39). The printed text version of "his lips" instead of "the lids" is
either an editorial or typist error or a correction in the galley stage. Either
way, the addition highlights the uncontrollable anguish of a dying man.
Hemingway also adds a description: "He opened his eyes, turned his head
and looked across the bridge, then shut them as the pain came" (MS-
43:40). In revision, Hemingway continues to remind the reader of
Fernando's suffering. After the rebels leave, the author describes the

wounded man propped up against the road bank: "His head was in the shadow but the sun shone on his wound and on his hands that were cupped over it. His rifle lay beside him and there were three clips of cartridges shining in the sun beside the rifle" (MS-43:44). This original description gives little indication of Fernando's terrible state. This restraint drops out in revision. The revised description reads:

> His head was in the shadow but the sun shone on his plugged and bandaged wound and on his hands that were cupped over it. His legs and feet were also in the sun. The rifle lay beside him and there were three clips of cartridges shining in the sun beside the rifle. A fly crawled on his hands but the small tickling did not come through the pain. (MS-43:44)

The additional description here paints a gruesome, tactile portrait of the dying rebel. Hemingway's addition of "plugged and bandaged" reveals that Fernando's wound is so gaping that it must be "plugged" and not merely bandaged. Also, the fly predicts Fernando's fate and signals his separation from the living world. All of Hemingway's descriptive additions to Fernando's suffering remind the reader of the racking pain and hideous truth of his condition.

In the same chapter, Hemingway revises both Anselmo's reaction to the killing of the sentry and his own violent death. In the first one hundred pages of chapter forty-three only a few of the pages are typescript. Manuscript pages 43-43 and 43-44 have only a couple of word or phrase revisions. Furthermore, the second page ends halfway down. All this evidence indicates that these pages are second draft copies of revised material. The first page of the typescript contains Anselmo's reflection on his shooting of the sentry:

> I hated the shooting of the guard and it made me an emotion but that is passed now. How could the *Ingles* say that the shooting of a man is like the shooting of an animal? In all the hunting I have had an elation and no feeling of wrong. But to shoot a man gives a feeling as though one had struck one's own brother when you are grown men. And to shoot him various times to kill him. Nay, do not think of that. That gave thee too much emotion and thee ran blubbering down the bridge like a woman. (MS-43:43)

Anselmo has killed before, but he will never get used to it. Hemingway is stressing to his audience that even though killing is necessary in war, it should not be taken lightly. In order to kill, a man must shut out all emotion and become inhuman because it is an inhuman act to kill one's own "brother."

Finally, Jordan's discovery of Anselmo's dead body undergoes substantial revision. In the original draft, Jordan kneels down, picks up the dead man's equipment, and walks away with no reflection about his dead friend. In revision, Hemingway inserts a page of Jordan's thoughts about the dead man: "He looked very small, dead. Robert Jordan thought. He looked small and grey headed and Robert Jordan thought, I wonder how he ever carried such big loads if that is the size he really was" (MS-43:61). This revision points up the loss Jordan feels and the humanity of Anselmo. Here lay a man, like all other men, reduced in death. Afterward, as Pilar speaks to Jordan, Hemingway inserts another typed page of Jordan's thoughts that sum up the experience of war and loss:

> The anger and the emptiness and the hate that had come with the let down after the bridge when he had looked and seen Anselmo dead were still all through him. In him too was despair from the sorrow that soldiers turn to hatred in order that they may continue to be soldiers. Now it was over he was lonely, detached and un-elated and he hated everyone he saw. (MS-43:62)

Friends lose friends in war. That is the reality of the experience. To Hemingway, the experience of war for the ordinary man boils down to two ingredients: violence and loss.

Throughout the manuscript, the scenes involving death are the most consistently revised. These revisions of death and violence are always additions to the scenes and not reductions. Furthermore, the passages involved are not, as Alvah Bessie claimed, "fruitless and somewhat meaningless disquisitions upon the significance of death and killing" (MS-9). These revisions are integral to the stylistic goal of the novel: to present the experience of war as realistically as possible. By revising the scenes toward fuller and more graphic detail, Hemingway also depicts the true nature of war and the human consequences of death and loss. To his audience, the American public standing at the threshold of World War II, Hemingway's message is clear and striking because of his prose style: war is a violent and tragic assault on the bodies and emotions of all those involved; so do not enter into it lightly or with any misconceptions.

Once we look carefully at Hemingway's revisions, we discover the manuscript revisions are essential to the reader's involvement in the story. The revisions in For Whom the Bell Tolls create a more vivid picture than appeared in the original draft. As a result, one of the strengths of the novel is its ability to draw the reader into the experience through the cumulative effect of expanded realistic details in the narrative. Without the revisions, the picture of war is not as sharp, and the impact of the novel is considerably lessened.

It would be a mistake to limit the scope of *For Whom the Bell Tolls* exclusively to the Spanish Civil War. Certainly, Hemingway's interest in the cause and the Spanish people is genuine; but in 1939-40, when the writing of the novel took place, the "good fight" was all but lost for the Loyalists. As Hemingway predicted, a larger conflict was beginning. The Spanish war was only the "dress rehearsal" for the coming European war. The graphic visual additions to the death scenes reflect what Hemingway said was his "one reason" for going to Spain: to write "anti-war correspondence" to the American people (Baker 1964, 458). World War I had ended twenty years earlier, and Hemingway feared the memory of its horrors had faded from the collective American mind. By presenting the details of war directly to the reader, Hemingway reminded his audience of war's reality and also avoided the impression of editorializing or propagandizing. The combination of Hemingway's detached, reportorial style with revisions that expand narrative images of war shows rather than tells the reader about war. As a result, the audience feels as if they are living the experience as the characters do. This book is not only about the war in Spain, but it is also about the war that began in September 1939, while Hemingway was writing his novel.

WORKS CITED

Baker, Carlos, ed. 1981. *Ernest Hemingway: Selected Letters, 1917-1961.* New York: Scribner's.

_____. ed. 1972. *Hemingway: The Writer as Artist.* 4th ed. Princeton: Princeton University Press.

_____. 1964. *Ernest Hemingway: A Life Story.* New York: Scribner's.

Bessie, Alvah C. 1971. "Review of *For Whom the Bell Tolls.*" *The Merrill Studies in For Whom The Bell Tolls.* Edited by Sheldon Norman Grebstein. Columbus: Merrill. 6-15.

Hemingway, Ernest. 1987. *For Whom The Bell Tolls.* New York: Scribner's.

_____. *For Whom The Bell Tolls Manuscript.* Hemingway Collection. John F. Kennedy Library. Boston, Massachusetts.

Preston, Paul. 1986. *The Spanish Civil War: 1936-39,* New York: Grove.

Reynolds, Michael S. 1976. *Hemingway's First War: The Making of A Farewell to Arms.* Princeton: Princeton University Press.

Svoboda, Frederic Joseph. 1983. *Hemingway and The Sun Also Rises: The Crafting of a Style.* Lawrence: University Press of Kansas.

RECONSIDERING THE TRAVESTY OF HIMSELF

ANOTHER LOOK AT *ACROSS THE RIVER AND INTO THE TREES*

MICHAEL SEEFELDT

INTRODUCTION

No HEMINGWAY WORK WAS as rudely received, as viciously and frequently lambasted, and, at least among his fiction, as forgotten as *Across the River and Into the Trees*.[1] Cousins called it "a bleating boast for a sentimental brute."[2] Kazin said that it "must distress those who have admired Hemingway's work for the past quarter century . . . such a travesty of himself."[3] Cowley concluded, "*Across the River and into the Trees* is a tired book. . . . We still have to wait for his big novel."[4] Young classified it "a pretty bad book . . . the sum of many errors."[5] Yet, *Across the River and into the Trees* (*ARIT*) is the only full-length work he allowed to be published after 1940. It was, the author claimed, his greatest book. Such enthusiasm partnered many other works in development, but here he seemed particularly enamored, and his giddy postpartum behavior in New York with Ms. Ross on its completion is a well-known part of American literary gossip, an at least occasional topic in his own correspondence, and a frequent springboard for many of his contemporary critics.[6] That shoot-phantoming fiasco aside, some writers and critics hailed or defended the work, including Faulkner,[7] Waugh,[8] Paul,[9] and John O'Hara.[10] Charles Poore, in the *New York Times,* cited it as "proof positive that he is still the old master."[11] Tennessee Williams called it the best.

This article will argue that *ARIT* is not the disaster often claimed, but is a poetic, perplexing, timely, and well-constructed allegory. As in Turner's sympathetic essay,[12] it will suggest several directions from which to begin reconsidering the work. First, it will examine *ARIT*'s reception as a function of the limited vision of the time and place of publication. Then it will suggest avenues for exploration of Cantwell's persona more subtle than have usually been pursued. Third, the solidity of structure and its relation to theme and content will be explored, followed, in contrast, by a brief survey of the organic poesy and imagery in the work. Finally, *ARIT* will be

249

placed, as allegory, in an analytical system of chronological periods dividing Hemingway's *oeuvre*. Initially, however, any effort to further explore *ARIT*'s finer qualities must first address the disaster of its appearance.

CONTEMPORARY RESPONSE TO THE WORK

ARIT was better received on the continent than among English-speaking audiences, and not just because of its military judgments. In Germany, especially, where the ages-of-man theme, the medieval heritage, and the experience of personal defeat after war were part of cultural consciousness, *ARIT* fared quite well.[13] A postwar nocturne with self-questioning and memento-mori undertones was consistent with Central European perspectives at the time. Cantwell's bitter pride and cautious craft in daily matters, both in the face of demotion and decline, ring far more consonantly with exhausted postwar Europe than with the youthful jingoism and opportunistic materialism of the untouched States. *ARIT* is a sobering work, and postwar America, self-righteous and cold-war bound, was not sober. Mindless consumerism and heavy-handed marketing, facilitated by infant television, reigned in a nation saturated in three decades of Hollywood pulp. The surface-interior interplay of a Cantwell presented too complex a profile for such a people. Nor would their moralistic narrowness allow an autumn-spring affair the suspension of judgment, much less credibility or respect, that careful study of the work requires. In a moralistic observation of his own, Evelyn Waugh scored the cynicism of the literary set while sympathetically reviewing *ARIT*.

> If we ask why his critics hate him so, I believe we have to see that they have detected in him an unforgivable thing—Decent Feeling. After we look past all the bluster and profanity, we find an elementary sense of chivalry—respect for women, pity for the weak, a love of honor. That is what affronts the fashionable supercilious caddishness of literary types and this is why their complaints are so loud and insistent.[14]

In fact, the work itself is full of tweaks at American narrowness that may have further colored much American critical response. Offhand slaps at revered American (and British) military and governmental leaders and consular figures, at the inanity of its new generation, the vacuous intolerance of its communities, and its lack of appreciation for the romance of old culture abound. Parallel expressions of admiration for German military leaders; affection for the Russian people; musings on the arbitrariness of "the enemy"; respect for centuries of European (especially Italian) art, culture, history and cuisine; and sensitivity to old aristocratic sensibility compile throughout the work. *ARIT* is in fact a paean to a recent enemy's land. Add its earthy irreverence on drinking, marriage, sex, language, patterned conformity, and even bathroom functions, and the potential looms large for other attributes to shape a priori what purports to be informed aesthetic judgment.

Indeed, Hemingway was as much international as American. True, inherent optimism of the frontier pioneer underlies the disillusion that thematically centers most of his work. However, he disliked much in his native land: its lack of artistic soul, its Calvin Coolidgism, its blue-law mentality, its hypocritical claims of freedom and equality. Though he thrice fought fascism, as a participatory correspondent in Civil War Spain, as a reconnaissance leader in the Caribbean, and as an irregular in France during WWII, he did not hesitate to attack even FDR in his work for *New Masses*.[15] Given this, why did *ARIT*, a poetic nocturne, cross-cultural and sentimental, antiwar, and artistic, not at least hit in the antiestablishment sixties? The persistent cross-generational theme—Cantwell constantly "teaching" an eager Renata, as well as learning from her—implies an instinctive need to speak to younger generations. But there is an obvious factor: *The Sun Also Rises*[16] and *A Farewell to Arms*,[17] featuring youthful love and awakening, and *The Old Man and the Sea*,[18] with its unimpeded sentiment, were the featured works in literature classes. Even *For Whom the Bell Tolls*[19] and *A Moveable Feast*[20] were more popular. In addition, the machismo of Hemingway's public persona, with its association with war and killing, affronted "peace and love." The nuance of the conditional relation of his violence to its zeitgeist required historical subtlety and understanding of iceberg values not common in the Aquarian age. Humanitarian, existential, and pantheistic features underlying his images of aged militarists, bullfighters, big-game hunters, or deep-sea fishers were lost on a generation rejecting its own parents' militaristic, practical, rugged-outdoor figures.

Hemingway was an earnest romantic in the realist garb of a previous generation, not a fantasist in new threads. Though a disappointed idealist, he could neither drop out nor escape into fantasy or fanfare. He avoided plumage and disliked losing control à la the experimental drug culture. His poesy was set in spare prose, not hallucinatory fantasy. Though physically and emotionally wounded, he did not believe the ostentatious display of such in art was proper. The struggle of the wounded survivor against the disadvantage, not its display, was his focus. There was no exhibitionist masochism about him, and his personal wounds did not assume the romantic excess of Poe, Van Gogh, or Dostoevsky. Hence the appropriate form and tone represented by the iceberg motif. In an age caught up in emotional immediacy, he was a consistently obdurate Cezanne.

AUTHOR IMAGE AND AUTHOR
CHARACTER CONFUSION

Even by 1950, Hemingway's public image was offensive, both to many of the subgroups comprising the literary world and to the legions of literarily jealous. It is not surprising that the descent of his ever-present, blustering face into the literary parlor for the first time in ten years was roundly greeted with jeers. How many times another clever critic claims that Cantwell is just Hemingway exposing himself is impossible to count. This parade of clichés finds little in American literary criticism to rival it. (Maybe antebellum sleuths sniffing out *Moby Dick* as Melville's muddling decline a century before, or, at the same time, Griswoldists on Poe.) Perhaps Edmund Wilson's "Letter to the Russians about Hemingway," often raised as in Trilling's citation in 1939, formed the mold.

> something frightful seems to happen to Hemingway as soon as he begins to write in the first person. In his fiction, the conflicting elements of his personality, the emotional situations which obsess him, are externalized and objectified; and the result is an art which is severe, intense and deeply serious. But as soon as he talks in his own person, he seems to lose all his capacity for self-criticism and is likely to become fatuous or maudlin.[21]

The pattern was set with Hemingway's critics some years before in Wilson's confident observation, and now its application to treatment of Cantwell as Hemingway and vice versa impeded thoughtful treatment of the book. The superannuation of a man, prefiguring *The Old Man and the Sea*, is seldom mentioned. At least in their persistence critics might have hit on some of the more interesting biographical parallels: the old boatsman's family size the same as Hemingway's father's or the eye injury of the author and Arnoldo's wound. For Hemingway did purge himself of mental and emotional baggage through his imagery and plots, e.g., Catherine Barkley's death at the time of Pauline's difficulty in delivering Patrick, and of course the Adriana-Renata connection. Therefore, a richer approach to the author-character confusion would have been to cite characteristics in the author that also obtain in Cantwell, but were not so easily stereotyped, parodied, or assaulted.

For example, place, origin, and destination are important in the work. Cantwell is a postwar Ishmael not unlike the author. Kazin has seen Hemingway as once among many American authors, including Melville, Twain, and James, who are itinerant in spirit.[22] *ARIT* is about an old midwestern expatriate written by an old midwestern expatriate. Consistent with that origin, Cantwell is a believer in the reward of honest work and practical efficiency and in the ability of the individual involved truly in daily tasks to conduct them well. He is suspicious of modernity and bureaucracy. Accordingly, he is sincere and sentimental in romance, and seeks to make love a singular and lasting event. He has gained his cultural awareness the practical, midwestern way, by self-instruction and real experience, not as an intrinsic component of high birth, eastern urbanity, or Old-World culture. The application of stolid values has carried him through his personal odyssey and linked him with archaic bonds of trust from Old-World Europe, but such values' diminishing utility in the modern age is part of the understanding among those in the Order. That diminishment personally presents Cantwell with as sure a sign of his mortality as do his torsal twinges. A sense of his anachronism parallels his physical plight. He has a broken nose "like a gladiator's in the oldest statues" and regrets the passing of the *Condottieri*. Now the Milanese profiteers and gambling *pescecani* are the future. Even the monumentality of Renata's aristocratic heritage is fading. So not only Cantwell's true and careful modus operandi, but also the unspoken Old-World valor he has come to know among some Europeans are left in subdued, if confidential and undefeated, retreat.

Americanism in the ascendancy also represents the decadent trend. The "ugly Breda works" near Maestre "might have been Hammond, Indiana" (35). San Dona is built up anew "no more ugly than a middle western town" (17). Renata's true profile at the mirror contrasts with American "things of wire and sponge rubber, such as you use in the seats of tanks" (113). Young Jackson, the chauffeur, pales against the Stonewall Jackson of the title's derivation. The youth's patterned, uninterested conformity contrasts with the passioned, heroic risk in the Generals Jackson and Cantwell (both undone by their own military). The chauffeur, Cantwell tells the Gran Maestro, is one of many "sad" Americans, "sad, self-righteous, over-fed and under-trained . . . in our army, they don't even shoot for self-inflicted wounds" (58-59).

Superannuation also redounds in the personalization of the inanimate. The regime-denying boatman's antique craft takes Cantwell reminiscing through the canals, finally to the Gritti dock. "Every move she makes, the Colonel thought, is a triumph of the gallantry of the aging machine" (52). Two worn stakes at the Rio Nuovo chained together but not touching are "like us the Colonel thought. . . . That's us. . . . That's our monument" (46) (his and Renata's, not, as Baker maintains, his and his youth's: Cantwell is not that self-centered).

Things must be put to rest, however. A used Jeep engine will replace the gallant Fiat. The tides had pulled the chains wearing the wood on "our monument." His own monument at Fossalta is a ceremonial burial of old trauma, a foreshadowing of his necessary acceptance of coming death, reverberated in the many reflections on his own burial. His monument combines his blood, his feces, the iron of the weapons that shred through him and his friends, and Italian money, all finally united by the old German Sollingen clasp knife. In the personalized gallantry of the old motorboat, the old chained stakes, and old knife, Hemingway not only marks the lasting reliability of anachronistic objects in their last days, but uses them to reinforce mortality through Cantwell's last days.

EXPRESSIVE CLICHÉ AND CANTWELL AS COMMON MAN

Many critics have noted stylistic weakness throughout *ARIT*. For example, Waldhorn unfavorably contrasts Hemingway's initial description of Renata with that of Brett in *The Sun Also Rises* as lifeless and trite.[23] He characterizes such passages in *ARIT* as "embarrassing." But the personae of the describers must be considered. Jake is young, unfocused, energized, literary. Cantwell, while a culturally self-trained man, is not above simple and common ways of looking at many things, such as honor, love, and beauty. Many critics chortled over the transparency of Hemingway's personal weaknesses in the Cantwell character, when in actuality, the depiction of Cantwell, warts-and-all, makes him a real, an individual character, even an everyman. It is unlikely that he would be as creative as a young journalist either in his use of the language or in his description of an adolescent female with whom he is smitten—it is, after all, his view of her that introduces her to the reader. In fact, some of the hackneyed description of Renata and of their time together ("carefully" and "truly") is perfectly expectable from a moonstruck, sentimental, basic, military man. The dialogue, whether internal with the portrait, or with Renata, *is* basic *and* constant. The narrator never steps out of character. What the author is doing is akin to James Joyce's use of the "Uncle Charlie Principle" as Kenner dubbed it. Werner explains: "In essence the 'Uncle Charlie Principle' states that word choices, syntax, idioms, etc., should be understood as expressions of and implicit commentary on, the most important character in the textual passage in question."[24] Description of Cantwell's actions opens with the adverbs "carefully," "hard," and "steadily" in chapter 1 and closes in chapter 45 with "all right," "carefully," and "well." These refer to simple, mechanical tasks, oaring a boat and shutting a car door. They are consistent with the vestigial pride of a beaten elder: proper effort at least will remain for what it was and is, even through failed outcome and canceled aspiration. Thus Cantwell enters and exits our view. There is no Brett, sleek like a hull; no intimate taxi rides with Brett at the end; no closing ride past the French officer's raised baton. Instead of the sleek hull, here is a Dante-esque barque with a surly Charon struggling through autumnal ice to open the tale; instead of the taxi, a "big Buick . . . the large back seat of this goddamned, over-sized luxurious automobile" (307) serving as a hearse and coffin at the end; and instead of the French raised baton, a bureaucratized American chauffeur ready to put Cantwell's dying order "through channels" to close the tale. Effort is made throughout to balance honor and childlike sentiment (as well as recollection and acceptance), exactly as persona Cantwell would do. The simple, basic, even trite words and concepts, not gymnastic expressions, are his tools. Of course it is embarrassing, but Cantwell cannot step out of character to please critics. The intrusion of a persona who could would violate the solidity and commonality of the central theme—accommodating new love while facing pointless mortality, however gracelessly, simply and alone.

Finally, dialogue among bilingual speakers not fully familiar with each other's tongues is bound to be deliberate and simple, appreciating, even cherishing, basic words. Whether Italian, French, German, or Spanish, Hemingway's environment throughout his adulthood was seldom of his native tongue. The resultant simplicity may appear ridiculous on the surface, but critical treatment of dialogue in Hemingway's last three books published in his lifetime, For Whom the Bell Tolls, ARIT, and The Old Man and the Sea, must take cognizance of the linguistic setting and characters, the problem of transliterated foreign expressions, their deep structure, and Hemingway's experimental use of language. An actual count of foreign terms in ARIT may be surprisingly high.

STRUCTURE IN *ARIT*

When Hemingway was apprenticing himself to Paris in the 1920s, he studied Cezanne in the Luxembourg Museum. Cezanne maintained that all nature could be reduced to basic geometric building blocks: the cone, the cube, and the sphere. Hemingway documented his aspiration to realize Cezanne's purity in his own work, and perhaps nowhere is the influence of Cezanne's basic geometric sense of aesthetic construction as apparent as in ARIT. Many have discussed the beauty of the closed-circle composition. Beginning with the duck hunt, it circles through the previous couple days and back to the duck hunt to end it all. There are other structural considerations as well, however, and one is struck by the repeated craft in their symmetry and parallelism. These considerations will be discussed in several parts: (1) a proposed five-act symmetric division of Cantwell's last weekend; (2) other recurrent structural devices, especially the use of contrasts and parallels and the counterbalance of characteristics in the protagonists;

(3) the recurrent triadic motif; and (4) the four authorial modes of communication in the work.

To consider the last first, virtually all of the novel is conveyed through Cantwell. Three of Hemingway's four modes of communicating to the reader center on Cantwell: actual dialogue with others; internal dialogue with himself; internal reflection, including contextual descriptions through his eyes. Outside Cantwell, only a few external descriptions of events, most notably as end pieces in the first and last pages constitute the fourth mode. Others have written of these modes, but it may be of interest to note how relentlessly the internal dialogue drives the mental climax of the character throughout. This is a book about a man come through the ages of man to realize the last act, the solitary act among acts, his own death; and the use of internal dialogue and internal reflection to convey it is structurally and psychologically true. Its strongest forerunner, "The Snows of Kilimanjaro,"[25] depends on the rhythms of progressive alternation, and less on axially symmetric geometry.

Just as the emphases among those modes is consistent with *ARIT*'s solidarity theme, story analysis yields structural parts consistent with thematic content. The work is like a double-circular, symmetric, five-act drama. Figure 1 presents these five "acts," and figure 2 orchestrates them in this double-circular structure. The circle arcs from solitude to approach to unification, loops back internally through separation to solitude and back to approach and reunification, and finally loops out again through separation to the ultimate solitude in death. The first act deals with solitary reminiscence and approach to Renata. It extends through the first eight chapters, which may be seen as scenes. Act Two, extending from chapters nine through fourteen, may be titled "With Renata." This is the beautiful but false climax.

Act Three, in which the Colonel is alone "at home" in the hotel room with the portrait, in his proxy death sleep, and alone in the morning at his natural functions and on his *solitaire ambulante*, covers chapters fifteen through twenty-three. It is the hump, the bridging act, like the bridges of Venice across the river, between the symmetrically arranged first and fifth outer acts, approaching and departing Renata, and the second and fourth inner acts, being with her. Symbolically consistent and foreshadowing the end, he must tell her in Act Three she cannot be with him for that time. Act Four, with Renata again, extends from chapters twenty-four through forty. Here most of the retrospection and expunging occurs, some while Renata sleeps.

The last act, spanning chapters forty (which crosslinks the fourth and fifth acts, touching back to the former after opening the latter) through forty-five, depicts his departure from Renata and from Venice, back

FIGURE 1

Structure in *ARIT*: The Five Acts

I.   The Approach (Ch. 1-8)
II.   With Renata (Ch. 9-14)
III.   Alone Again (Ch. 15-23)
IV.   Rejoined with Renata (Ch. 24-40)
V.   The Departure (Ch. 40-45)

FIGURE 2

Structural Analysis of *ARIT*, by Acts

APPROACH (Act 1)

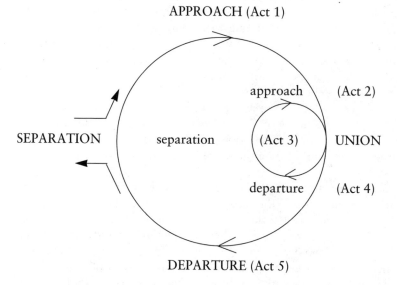

DEPARTURE (Act 5)

through the duck hunt again. On this she also cannot accompany him. In chapter forty, the first scene, prefiguring the death, opens with the coffin-like "He was in the sunken oak hogshead" (278). After the flashback to the previous act, it returns in chapter forty-one with the self-admonition: "Now don't think of her . . . . because it won't do you any good, boy" (288) and closes with "The shooting's over" (294). Consistent with the superannuation theme, the story's last scene is given to the channelized chauffeur, Jackson. The fifth is the shortest, quickest act, like life and death. Still, in that brief span it comes round on remaining details: deciding what to leave for Renata (versus what to take from her); following through for the old boatman in the canal; and resolving the opening conflict with the contrary boatman. This last takes a poignant twist as the boatman's attitude emerges as a true, if indirect, consequence in his personal war losses, at the hands of the Colonel's metier, making the boatman a compelling character in his Italian surliness when set against the accommodating, mindless American, Jackson.

The internal structure of the individual acts repeats the external structure. Act Two, for example opens with approaching Renata (approaching Harry's) in chapter nine, then primarily focuses on union with Renata, and closes in chapter fourteen, after a thought of returning to Harry's: "But I think I'll go home." This perfectly parallels the basic structure of the story—approach, union, departure. Act Three, the solitary internal interlude between the Renata-union sections depends fittingly on the appropriate modes: internal dialogue, dialogues with the portrait and with the lonely porter, and the *solitaire ambulante*. It symmetrically reverses the outer edges of Act Two by beginning with going home (departure), separation from Renata, and ending with going out to her (approach). Structurally, Act Three is a minicircle in reverse within the larger five-act circle. Even in Act Four, concentric with the three middle acts, they are out together, return to the hotel (home), and go out together again. Like a microcosmic version of the entire central Act Three, midway in Act Four Renata sleeps in the hotel room, and her sleep separates her from the Colonel during some of his most significant exorcising reminiscences, just as his sleep and solitude and her innocent sleep have separated them in the central act.

The use of contrasts and parallels also abounds in the work. For contrasts there are the old and the modern, the American and the European, the two Jacksons, the two boatmen, the lovers themselves. Parallels include the two generals' (Cantwell's and Jackson's) injured hands, their being undone by internal bodily failure, their joint victimization by their own army, There is the identification of the old Cantwell with old machines—the Fiat engine in the boat, the elevator at the Gritti, the balky locks and keys. Renata's definitive "no's" to Cantwell regarding formal commitment for their romance, quite contrary to the criticism that Renata is merely a convenient noncharacter for Hemingway's machismo, are mirrored in his "no's" regarding her intended gifts to him and her coming with him.

Indeed, the structural balance is further maintained in contrasts between the protagonists themselves: his age and her youth; his beaten ugliness, her beauty; his bitterness, her emollient; his experience in love and war, her *naiveté* in both; his itinerancy, her rooted aristocracy; his New-World commonness, her Old-World wealth; his teaching her to deal with life, her helping him to face death. There is balance in Cantwell himself. Many have written of him as a bitter Hemingway striking out at everyone, but this ignores the reverential in Cantwell. There are balanced and often parallel dislikes and likes in the man. For Montgomery there is Rommel. For Sinclair Lewis there is Red Smith or Shakespeare. For Fascist dandies there are the wounds of the fisherman's hands and Cantwell's own crooked walk. For men in armor there are the foot soldiers. For those giving orders from above there are those wounded in war. For artificial women from Texas there are the tall, striding Venetian beauties. For profiteers there are honest workers. The list goes on: such recurring parallels and contrasts, and there are many, occur in a rhythm that adds to the poesy of the book and structurally tightens in details the fitted larger structure of the work.

Other structural consistencies abound as well. Most significantly, the triangle, the artistic compositional motif of the Renaissance in Venice, reverberates in triadic patterns throughout. This includes the double triad in Cantwell's approaching, being with, and departing from Renata, again approaching, being with, and departing; the three ages of man; the three lost battles; the three lost battalions and commanders; the three lost wives; the three last days; the three final strikes to the heart. The triadic structure also recurs in minor manifestations: the three key Italian positions in WWI, the cook who performs thrice on his fiftieth birthday, the three schools of French military thought (but I cannot be sure there are *three* love acts in the gondola, as many allege). Three is a sacred number in the Church, appropriate for Catholic, Renaissance Venice. This and other structural devices provide left-brain balance to the poetic tone and allegorical nature of the work, just as the geometric sets off the organic in Cezanne's composition to create a universal whole.

POESY AND IMAGERY

It is only appropriate that *ARIT* centers around Venice. The fantastical city on the sea carries with it the warlike tradition, the artistic wonderment, and the antiquated reference fitting to the tone and theme of the work. Conveyance by water is consistent with both the title and the implicit references to the River Styx and to Dante's barque. As in Thomas Mann's *Death in Venice*,[26] the city of impressionistic light and color is rendered autumnal gray. The cold wind from the mountains and the domination of departing day, dark dawn, and nighttime hours set a tonal context for the *totentanz* theme. The intensity of the contrast between the colorful city of summer and the autumnal, nocturnal images meshes with the intensity of Cantwell's emotion as he encounters his reborn ("renata") love in the face of the end. Elegiac and somber as the whole is, the brutality of the cold wind in the face, the hotel windows open onto winter's approach, the drinking and sleeplessness are all necessary in their behemence to absorb Cantwell's ruddy crudity and emotional pressures as he faces that end. Here the past violence of Venice and of the *Condottieri*, the war setting, the corruption reflect the heartlessness of fate before Cantwell's fatal heart.

Throughout the work though, the pitch of imagery rises repeatedly, not only to reinforce fatality, but also to sharpen the beautiful in life. *ARIT* is rich in poetic imagery, and if the inhospitable rain in *A Farewell to Arms* finds a fit replacement in the cold sea-wind from the mountains and beyond, the contrasting appreciations of the sensuous in life are also present. Hemingway's imagery is everywhere. An analysis of its full use must begin with such categories as will be given brief treatment here: nature, the senses, and the arts.

From "Big Two-Hearted River,"[27] through *The Sun Also Rises* and *Green Hills of Africa*,[28] to *Islands in the Stream*,[29] the water and tree-hills images set up this death-title. The landscape and structure of nature in Cezanne corresponded with Hemingway's need for aesthetic and mental order, and he used nature often. Often, it is his central characters' solace or bonding site, retreat, and metaphorical referent for their developing philosophy. While Nick flees to the Upper Peninsula and Jake to the Irati to balm their inner torment, in *ARIT* the walk to the marketplace, replete with the jumble of life-celebrating images and proletarian banter, constitutes Cantwell's benediction to life as he awaits death, celebrated, ironically, in reverence for the visually rich, dead animals.

Natural imagery abounds in *ARIT*: the wind, the ice, the cold, the dark, the water, the moon, the trees. The wind whips from "somewhere else" beyond the "high mountains" (152), bringing the ducks south to their death. It "hits" Cantwell. It drives unrelentingly over the gondola lovemaking. It blows the women's beautiful hair. On his *solitaire ambulante*, Cantwell wishes he could issue "wind-proof coats to everyone" (184). The moon fills the lobster, and under the moon the *pederastes* batter the pretty portrait painter. Cantwell would like to be buried near "the tall, great trees" (35). Renata's mother wants to move where she can live out her life near trees. Crossing the river, like breaking the ice on the hunt, takes Cantwell to his death, just as riding up the canal under the Venetian bridges symbolizes stages in a man's life. While the wind lashes the lovers' faces, Cantwell's ruined hand searches for Renata's sex, "the island in the great river with the high steep banks"(153).

The sensual abounds as well. The work is replete with tasteful tastes, the icy, right drinks, the best chosen foods. Much has been made of this in attacking Hemingway as decadent. However, it is often Renata, under Cantwell's tutelage, whose indulgence is celebrated. Her lobster dinner, her big breakfast, her sexual response, her sound sleeping: life will remain to her. While Cantwell has been able to provide her most of these last learned indulgences, in a curious twist, he misses Bobby, who runs off before receiving his well-earned reward of the best sausages. Hemingway uses sound—Renata's voice is like Casals's cello—but he paints most freely with color. True to the elegaic tone, his palette is restrained: Grays, greens, blacks. Grays predominate: Besides Degas's grayest grays of nature, the water, the sky, the hair and steel eyes of Cantwell. Green is traditionally the color of life, but here, in unusual manifestation: the full lobster, Renata's gems, the grass fed by war dead. Black is frequently cited: the barges, the gondola, the hitching posts, the trees with no leaves moving in the wind, Renata's sweater, the ebony pin. However, death can come "with the great white-hot, clanging roar we have lived with" (219). Color, like nature, is a key poetic tool in *ARIT*.

The work is also rich in artistic and literary referents. The former especially heighten its painterliness. We find the sensuality of Titian's women, the somber gray of Degas, the Renaissance solidity and power of Giotto, Tintoretto, Michelangelo, Piero, and Mantegna. The anonymous Dutch painters celebrated in detail the things shot and eaten, rendering in their object-orientation a material, secular flavor to the swan-song marketplace benediction of Cantwell's morning walk. Literary figures are also present. Sinclair Lewis, as a book-guided tourist, is ridden throughout in an unpleasant overkill of literary satire (though Renata, as with food, sex, and sleep, is the sustained indulger here). Dante, befitting the work's theme and setting, appears. Blake (a painter-poet), Browning, Byron, Whitman, Wasserman, Rimbaud, and Verlaine make cameo appearances. Significantly, Francois Villon, the vagrant medieval Parisian outlaw, crafts the unifying theme, set ironically against Cantwell's disgust with the past: "Ou sont les neiges d'antan? . . . Dans le pissoir . . ." (112).

The poetic tone set by such rich imagery in Hemingway's spare syntax both runs within the confines of the strong geometric structure described above and is punctuated by the linear progression of the clockwork of Cantwell's cardiovascular episodes. Similarly, a last tight metronome symbolic of life events is suggested by Baker in his analysis of the sequence of various bridges along the canals.[30]

ARIT AS ALLEGORY

Perhaps the work most influential on Hemingway was the Bible, *the* allegory in his Oak Park heritage. From it he drew titles (*The Sun Also Rises*), themes (*The Garden of Eden*),[31] plots ("This Must be Friday"),[32] and symbolism (*The Old Man and the Sea*). During the same time, major

allegory-prone forerunners in the existential age also appeared or were res-
urrected: *Billy Budd*[33] and a *Moby-Dick*[34] and Melville revival; Kafka's
The Metamorphosis;[35] Nietzsche's *Thus Spoke Zarathustra*;[36] even
Freudian symbolism. All of these are first and foremost allegorical literature. In his own work, the beauty, challenge, and staying power of a
Hemingway story reside in his obdurate adherence to simple poesy of style
and continuity of the story line. Then, the poesy so often associated with
allegorical prose and the singularity of each story event lead the reader on
the allegorical iceberg-study to realize the allegorical, subsurface meaning
and moral concept. The irony of a concrete, craftsmanly, publicly crude,
self-made man engaged in the triad between antiromantic gesture, poetic
sensitivity, and spiritual allegory is key to the Hemingway mystique. In his
later life, he shifts from concrete reality to generalized allegory. No one
misses it in *The Old Man and the Sea*, but the immediate sibling of that
work and partner to it as high allegory, *ARIT*, is just as representative,
allegorically, of the life journey.

Further, now in retrospect, one may argue for a loosely quadripartite
division in Hemingway's work throughout his life: (1) The Poetic-
Romantic years (the twenties); (2) the Realist years (the thirties and early
forties); (3) the Allegorical years (1946-54?); and (4) the Revisitation
years, the apparently less creative, illness-ridden years after the African
plane crashes (1954-61). The divisions overlap a bit, but it is clear where
ARIT belongs in this scheme, and its thematic coverage of the three ages of
man corresponds well with the author's three productive work divisions:
youth, adulthood, and maturity. At the same general time as *ARIT*, he was
speaking of his great trilogy (including material in *Islands in the Stream*
and *The Old Man and the Sea*) and was working on *The Garden of Eden*,
which, with *Across the River and Into the Trees* and *The Old Man and the
Sea* makes a triad of representatives of this allegorical era. *Islands in the
Stream* may be seen as a bridge between the realist and allegorical years. *A
Moveable Feast*, the second African novel, and *The Dangerous Summer*[37]
may represent the "Revisitations" category (of *The Sun Also Rises*, *Green
Hills of Africa*, and *Death in the Afternoon*,[38] respectively. In *Across the
River and Into the Trees*, however, though elements of revisitation are pre-
sent in Hemingway's reworking of previous settings (*A Farewell to Arms*
especially), revisitation is only a mechanism in service of the larger superannuation theme and the allegorical whole.

In summary, properly examining *ARIT*'s intentions and recognizing its
qualities depend on the approach allegorical works require. At the same
time, removing the work from the bias of the time of its first appearance,
critiquing the Cantwell and Renata personae more carefully, studying the
structure of the work—its geometry, parallels, and contrasts—and

enjoying its poesy constitute some of the starting points for reconsideration. The past ease with which many critics and echoing novices have relegated *Across the River and Into the Trees* to the bottom of the novels published during the author's lifetime should not continue so blissfully unchallenged.

NOTES

All references to quotes taken from *Across the River and into the Trees* use pagination based on the Scribner Library of Contemporary Classics publication, and correspond with the original edition.

1. Ernest Hemingway, *Across the River and into the Trees* (New York: Scribner's, 1950).
2. Norman Cousins, "Hemingway and Steinbeck," *Saturday Review of Literature* 33 (28 October 1950): 26-27.
3. Alfred Kazin, "The Indignant Flesh," *The New Yorker* 26, 19 September 1950, 113-18.
4. Malcolm Cowley, "Hemingway Portrait of an Old Soldier Preparing to Die," *New York Herald Tribune Book Review* 27 (10 September 1950): 1, 16.
5. Philip Young, "Reviews in General: *Across the River and Into the Trees,*" *Tomorrow* 10 (November 1950): 55-56.
6. Lillian Ross, "Profile," *The New Yorker* (13 May 1950).
7. William Faulkner, "Faulkner to Hemingway," *Time* 56, 13 November 1950, 6.
8. Evelyn Waugh, "The Case of Mr Hemingway," *Commonwealth* 53 (3 November 1950): 97-98.
9. Elliot Paul, "Thanks to Ernest," *Providence Sunday Journal*, 10 September 1950, vi-8.
10. John O'Hara, "The Author's Name is Hemingway," *The New York Times Book Review*, 10 September 1950, 1, 30.
11. Charles Poore, "Books of the Times," *The New York Times*, 7 September 1950, 29.
12. W. Craig Turner, "Hemingway as Artist in *Across the River and into the Trees*: A Reevaluation," in *Hemingway, A Reevaluation*, edited by Donald R. Noble (Troy: Whitston, 1983), 187-203.
13. Wayne E. Kvam, *Hemingway in Germany* (Athens: Ohio University Press, 1973), 118-32.
14. Evelyn Waugh, "The Case of Mr Hemingway," 98.
15. Ernest Hemingway, "Who Murdered the Vets?" *The New Masses* 16, no. 12 (17 September 1935): 9-10.
16. Ernest Hemingway, *The Sun Also Rises* (New York: Scribner's, 1926).
17. Ernest Hemingway, *A Farewell to Arms* (New York: Scribner's, 1929).

18. Ernest Hemingway, *The Old Man and the Sea* (New York: Scribner's, 1952).
19. Ernest Hemingway, *For Whom the Bell Tolls* (New York: Scribner's, 1940).
20. Ernest Hemingway, *A Moveable Feast* (New York: Scribner's, 1964).
21. Edmund Wilson, "Letter to the Russians about Hemingway," in "Hemingway and his Critics," by L. Trilling, *Partisan Review* 6 (Winter 1939).
22. Alfred Kazin, "Hemingway the Painter," in *An American Procession* (New York: Knopf, 1984.)
23. Arthur Waldhorn, *A Reader's Guide to Hemingway* (New York: Farrar, Strauss and Giroux, 1972), 182.
24. Craig Hansen Werner, *Dubliners: A Student's Companion to the Stories* (Boston: Twayne Masterwork Series, 1988), 46.
25. Ernest Hemingway, "The Snows of Kilimanjaro," *Esquire*, August 1936.
26. Thomas Mann, *Death in Venice* (New York: Random House, 1970).
27. Ernest Hemingway, "Big Two-Hearted River," in *In Our Time* (New York: Boni and Liveright, 1925).
28. Ernest Hemingway, *Green Hills of Africa* (New York: Scribner's, 1935).
29. Ernest Hemingway, *Islands in the Stream* (New York: Scribner's, 1970).
30. Carlos Baker, "The River and the Trees," in *Hemingway: The Writer as Artist*, 4th ed. (Princeton: Princeton University Press, 1972), 264-88.
31. Ernest Hemingway, *The Garden of Eden* (New York: Scribner's, 1986).
32. Ernest Hemingway, "This Must Be Friday," in *Men Without Women* (New York: Scribner's, 1927).
33. Herman Melville, *Billy Budd and Other Stories* (New York: Penguin, 1986).
34. Herman Melville, *Moby-Dick; or the Whale* (New York: Penguin, 1986).
35. Franz Kafka, *The Metamorphosis* (New York: Schocken Books, 1968).
36. Wilhelm Friedrich Nietzsche, *Thus Spoke Zarathustra* (New York: Penguin Books, 1978).
37. Ernest Hemingway, *The Dangerous Summer* (New York: Scribner's, 1985).
38. Ernest Hemingway, *Death in the Afternoon* (New York: Scribner's, 1932).

THE SUSPENDED WOMAN IN THE WORK OF ERNEST HEMINGWAY

ROBERT E. GAJDUSEK

IT MAY PROVE VALUABLE to glance at a group of metaphors that Hemingway has used with some consistency throughout his work. For want of a ready name, let them be called metaphors of "feminine arrest."

In a wonderful but neglected short story, "Alpine Idyll,"[1] Hemingway carefully prepares the reader throughout for his deftly carved metaphor, one that appears to be at once grotesque and perverse. The wife of Olz, the seemingly crude peasant from the high mountains, has died in the winter, and since she cannot be buried in the iron-hard frozen, ice-covered ground until the spring, when he will be able to take her body down to softer ground and sanctified burial in the churchyard in the valley, Olz places her body in the woodshed where, for lack of space, it is propped up against the wood. During winter nights, when he goes out to the shed to get wood, he finds no place convenient to hang his lantern and he apparently callously hangs it from the lower jaw of his wife's mouth. The deformation this gradually creates over time and the very act itself are used, in the story, to shock and awe those in the fiction who finally learn of it; and the story's readers share their shock. Part of Hemingway's focus is carefully kept on the dead woman in a state of frozen suspension, removed from processes of decay and immune to rot. That she, so used, becomes a source of light for the male, is a necessary part of the metaphor.

Catherine, in *A Farewell to Arms*, dies on the biological wheel[2] that she cannot remove, it being part of the biological "trap"[3] that Frederic considers their lot, and not even his fictional assumption of morning sickness the morning after her announcement of her pregnancy can take that cross, the wheel on which she is to be martyred,[4] from her. The idyllic days spent in the high frozen heights above Montreux are at last ended when three days of rain[5] confirm the thaw and break in the weather. As Frederic and she descend to the waters of Lac Leman, it is the beginning of an unarrestable progress toward a birth/death due to love, echoing against the suggestion of a birth/death due to war in the first chapter of the novel, the former as

265

Catherine dies in childbirth, the latter as the soldiers going toward deaths in battle seem to be big with child. Life—that had apparently been suspended or arrested at the cold great heights in the Swiss Alps where they had lived and celebrated Christmas, or divine birth based on immaculate conception—is seemingly set once more in motion by the thaw, and Catherine moves toward her inevitable death within a biological birth process down below. Catherine's wheel is, however, halted at last when, after her death, Frederic's last conception of her is of her as a statue, this in seeming opposition to the cyclical rains of process that enclose the narrator in the novel's last words. It is almost as though Frederic's image of Catherine effectively takes the biological wheel off her and arrests her in an aesthetic immortality, as frozen into an "object" as Olz's wife. We might posit that Catherine, as the "statue within the mind," has been the bearer of light against darkness/death for Frederic/Hemingway and has demanded her own story, the work of art that is the novel we have read that Frederic was by guilt impelled to write. It is Joseph Flora who has well argued that in "an Alpine Idyll" Nick, as auditor of the story of the frozen suspended wife, is learning how to gather his materials for his own creative work.[6]

These two plots suggest that heights remote enough to arrest decay or process, rot and decay itself, and freezing and thawing,[7] as they are related to the suspended state in which a woman might be held, are intricate metaphors that relate to the creative process itself and the role of the woman as Muse within the imagination. This suggestion leaves room for the speculation that the fear of "consequences," or avoidance of pregnancy, or attempts to outwit natural creative birth process, appear with great frequency throughout the Hemingway canon and are related to sacrifices made to the creative process. Early in Hemingway's work, the imagination of the creative artist seems duped into believing that it needs either the woman set apart (as possible Muse) or a free space unprejudiced by complicating bonds with the earth. I say "duped" because Hemingway as a mature artist mocks these attitudes, knowing that the risk of death and "consequences" is what defines the bravery of the true torero or artist, even as it defines for him whether a man is a man. However, in Hemingway's early work "The End of Something," he studies how it is the fear of going with Marjory—which is spelled out as the fear of "consequences," or pregnancy, in the following story, "the Three-Day Blow,"—that is answered by the artificial, largely verbal, and adolescent abstract male world of Nick and Bill. This latter story focuses distinctly on the distance Nick and Bill have taken themselves from the sources of their language and imagery as they relate to life through literature and the abstract tales and legends of others while they drink the father's spirits. These stories of the puerile fears of youth set up a pattern that following stories like "Cross Country Snow," "Cat in the Rain," "Hills Like White Elephants," and even "Soldier's Home" extend to more seemingly mature protagonists, stories where fertility-avoiding males try to maintain absolute controls, either by imposing artificial or sterilizing situations or states of suspension on their women or by attempting to distance themselves in states of abstraction from the fear of consequences. Hemingway carefully studies the vapidity of such boy-men, and the attendant dilemmas of their women. The insulated, storm-protected house of "The Three-Day Blow," where the boys drink the father's spirits by the fire while shutting out nature and the wet and shutting themselves away from Marjory, is a compelling paradigm of the antisepsis of the life-fearing male.

The wife of "Cat in the Rain" is held in a state of expatriate suspension by her careless husband, detached from friends, associates, things familiar or known, and initially out of contact with the rain, the cycles of life, potential pregnancy, or her own nature or growth. This suspension is carefully judged in the story a product of the husband's domination of the bed with the book as he advises her to choose a similar strategy of insulated life avoidance through the abstract word. The wife's willingness to expose herself to getting wet as she descends for the sake of the kitty is a sign of her desire to break out of the aridity and sterility and also the abstractness of her suspended state. In "Hills Like White Elephants," the conversation between the girl and the young man again carefully focuses upon their detachment from familiar life, and on their insulation and expatriate isolation. They are suspended in a foreign medium where sights, ideas, spirits, and "letting in the air" are abstract devices, and where abortion, or frustration of the cycle of life, is the male obsession. Mr. and Mrs. Elliot, in the story of that name, also expatriates suspended in such an environment, will have as their major problem the begetting of a child, while Mr. Elliot alternatively strives to beget his poems. The detached husband in "Cross Country Snow" considers his own state of suspension in skiing while contemplating the necessary process to which he must return as he descends to those lower valleys that will mean normal life patterns and acceptance of his wife's pregnancy. In each case, the male who yearns for detachment or arrest of the natural cycles of decay—as does Harry in "Snows of Kilamanjaro"—is one who in life avoidance gives himself to high artificial or abstract verbal or literary alternatives, and the woman, who by virtue of his detachment is frequently a victim of suspension or of arrested natural process, is one thwarted or thwarting in her desire for or state of pregnancy, or one who reminds him of the biological love/death that life means. Life as art or life as process are the alternatives. Colonel Cantwell, in Across the River and Into the Trees, carefully considers the living/dying girl who is Renata against and in contradistinction to the "unmaneuver-able" image of herself in the painted portrait that she gives him. The alternative Renatas are (1) an abstract immortality established on a reality-denying fictional base, and (2) the warm, if compromised, girl.

Images of arrested life, seemingly frozen in time within an immortality that dispenses with the cycles of time, are everywhere studied in Hemingway's works, and they are usually seen in opposition to and against the eternally turning wheels of process—rot—and time. Catherine, as seemingly stone statue, is carefully placed against the birth process that cannot separate itself from death and the falling rain, just as, at the beginnings of "The End of Something" and "Big Two-Hearted River," the white stones of the foundations of the earlier lost worlds of the mill and Seney are seen against second growth, the renewing green, and the life of nature. Brett, in *The Sun Also Rises*, a story of expatriate suspension, is a woman who can't seem to stop anything. She is the goddess-icon at the center of the whirling dance, and is studied in relation to Jake, the would-be writer who tries to stop the room from wheeling by fixing his eyes upon the word, this in a novel where the momentary arrest of the cycle—the policeman's raised baton brings the taxi wheels to a halt—is the last image of the novel. Brett's exclamatory marker is "rot!" and she leaves a trail of ashes behind her; this suggests that as Hemingway studies the pull of the woman toward Circean cycles, he creates the necessary dephallization of Jake as a poetic device to avoid consequences and enable him to avoid cycles and to achieve the immortality of stasis. The novel is really a handbook of devices and rituals to enable a state of arrest for the male, to be achieved through rituals of synthesis, whether through the fishing cameraderie rituals of Burguete, where time seems temporarily suspended; through those of the torero, who knows how to cross over, so that two can become one—as Jake cannot—into the territory of the "other" without loss to the self; or in the ordering and cleansing rituals of San Sebastian. It would take a longer paper than this is to show how these rituals are equivalent psychic achievements to those of the art of the artist.

The lost or denied mother is frequently in Hemingway's works a statement of the maternal creative principle being denied or replaced by the male. *Torrents of Spring* offers Diana's anecdote of how she lost her mother. It is an elaborate paradigm of the operation of the creative process, and as it tells how a French General assumed the "lost" mother's place in her bed, Hemingway is studying how a man can fictively and at risk take over the reproductive/creative role of the mother. The cost, of course, is the forever lost mother, but, as Hemingway observes, "The general . . . always seemed to us like a pretty brave man" (107).[8] Another lost mother is sketched in "The Doctor and the Doctor's Wife," as the mother, in that story screened off behind drawn blinds, is denied and turned from by both son and husband; and the same denial is implicit in the direction finally taken by Krebs, in the interest of truth, in "Soldier's Home." It is not without profound meaning that Hemingway's early work details—in such works as "On the Quai at Smyrna," "Indian Camp," chapter 2 of *In Our Time*, and in the ending of *A Farewell to Arms*—a vivid sense of horror and trauma that attends those who attend upon the biological birth process. The distance between biological birth and immaculate conception seems that between nature and spirit, between time and immortality; and the son or potential father figure who strikes for immortality as a replacement for his implication in the biological birth process names the creative artist who, in abstract media, himself becomes begetter/creator.

All kingdoms where time seems stopped are finally exemplified in the remote heights of Kilamanjaro, where the leopard lies undecaying, heights sought by the imagination of the dying unfulfilled artist. We should remember, however, that it was in Hemingway's early *Torrents of Spring*—whose very title speaks of the emergence from the suspension stasis of winter, as the thaws of spring create release to life for a would-be writer, Scripps, who is learning his trade—that Hemingway had first elaborately studied the relations between biological and aesthetic creativities and impotence. In *A Farewell to Arms*, Catherine had too glibly seen high frozen Switzerland, an island out of war, away from "consequences," as a place where there were "no rolls"; and for a while, before the thaws of spring, when the cycles reasserted themselves, it was that for her, but with the resumption of seasonal cycles, the descent to the waters is necessary. There are obviously no rolls, no cyclical decay processes, on that square top of Kilamanjaro, and none in time that can break the figures on any Grecian Urn from their state of immortal arrest: "forever wilt thou love and she be fair."[9]

In *The Forest Lovers*, whose plot situation Nick reflects upon in "The Three-Day Blow," the sword placed erect between the sleeping lovers that keeps them apart is the device that operates only as long as the male principle is erect and there are no rolls: if the sword falls over, you can "roll right over it." In *The Sun Also Rises*, the road to hell is "paved with unbought stuffed dogs" because neither a stuffed dog, nor a taxidermically mounted trophy, nor a hard-boiled egg—placing life as they do in states of suspension—will permit the rolls that life process demands.[10] Artificial or mythic ways to circumvent natural biological process, like immaculate conception, order much of Hemingway's work, and it is carefully a Christmas story that is told in "God Rest You Merry, Gentlemen" as the boy, in pursuit of a life-transcending purity and yearning for a state of suspension within what are to him the demeaning cycles, seems to emulate Jake Barnes as he fatally dephalluses himself.

This extended elaboration should make the patterning of *The Garden of Eden* more visible. In the original Eden, the penalty for transgression, or the eating of the forbidden fruit, was removal from the Edenic state of suspension; it meant expulsion into that world of decay and process where Adam and Eve were gifted with biological birth and death and Eve was to bring forth her progeny in pain. David's story, which he finally is able to write, attempts to tell of a state of innocence before his own fall and his subsequent losses, and it seemingly can be told only by means of David's detachment from life during which he perfects his craft. That detachment suspends Catherine and keeps her in an expatriate malaise where trying new cities and hotels and beaches and drinks, like a trying on of new hats, seems an artificial series of excitements that have no real contact with reality around them. David and Catherine have few friends, and the only person introduced intimately in their life is a "pick up," Marita, chosen for experimentation. Catherine, here named like the protagonist of *A Farewell to Arms*, is the uneasy victim of the need for a biological creativity whose frustration is her undoing. She is the wife of "Cat in the Rain," driven toward an ultimate craziness by her suspension from any significant activity or identity. Unable to abstractly create—she can neither write nor paint—yet jealous of the dedication and success her husband has found in his art, she chooses to impose unnatural patterns upon real living flesh and to become, like God, a creator in the real.

The original holograph manuscript in the Kennedy Library makes abundantly clear that Hemingway's first conception of the novel was hard focused upon Catherine's rage at her frustrated motherhood, which she says is David's doing. Her sterility she there declares his fault—the result of his gonorrhea or syphilis when young—and that first version places the source of their dilemma as a couple squarely on their biological infertility. Marita, in the holograph version, when she enters into relationship with David, quickly presents herself as the fertile alternative to his sterile relationship with Catherine, and her lovemaking with David is fully focused on the begetting of a child.

The motivations in the holograph help us to understand underlying patterns in the novel as published. We can see that the pregnancy/fertility concern that Hemingway has intricately explored in many other works, as early as the stories of *In Our Time*—and that is part of a ubiquitous metaphor in which process and childbearing, and decay and death are placed in dialectical balance or struggle with abstracting heights, whether of art/word or expatriate disengagement—although stripped from the published version of *The Garden of Eden*, is still the other side of the state of suspension and arrest in which Catherine finds herself. The elephant hunt that is at the center of David's creativity, the story he needs to tell and has never told, has to do with his complicity in the destruction of the great white elephant that he really loved. In "Hills Like White Elephants," the white elephant, an unwanted gift, is certainly the unwanted child whose abortion is the unstated subject of conversation. If we imagine for a moment that the elephant might remain somewhat similarly coded in *The Garden of Eden*, then David's tale is, on one level, the tale of the way he participates in a "father's" killing of an unwanted child. It seems an almost mimetic act that Catherine then styles her destruction of David's manuscript as the killing of a child.

Throughout the holograph David's abstract creativity as artist is opposed to Catherine's sterility as childbearer, or aesthetic creativity is balanced against biological fecundity, and maternity is seen as compromising or competing with the male artist's art. Catherine accurately then labels David's writing as practicing solitary vice in a wastebasket filled with clippings. Such onanism, or spilling of seed upon the ground, rather than with potency into her womb, is the source of her growing rage; his art, in her image of it, is a waste, and it supports, as she sees it, a vanity. In *For Whom the Bell Tolls*, Robert Jordan, seemingly sexually denied Maria for the night, momentarily allows himself abstract and imaginative fulfillment, after having rejected Maria's offer to help satisfy him. As he does so, he thinks about Onan, who spilled his seed on the ground. Asking himself, "whatever happened to Onan?" he concludes that we never heard any more about him; and the unstated conclusion is that there is no immortality to be had by that route. Before the chapter ends, Jordan has affirmed his ethical position, that he will not accept self-satisfaction without the satisfaction of his partner, that only through mutually fulfilling sex is there any true and lasting immortality to be had. In *The Garden of Eden*, the opposing poles, as Catherine initially sees it, are either feminine biological fulfillment, or a feminine state of suspended arrest from process as a result of the male's dedication to his art. When David finally detaches himself from Catherine and begins to write, he creates a hunger; he satisfies it as he eats not only his own eggs, but Catherine's eggs as well. That they have been getting cold is his justification. At the detached and high abstract state in which creativity takes place, however much Catherine and David may be creatures of the Riviera, giving themselves to the sun and the waters, *her* eggs have been getting cold.

The suspended woman in Hemingway's work is then not unlike the leopard on Kilamanjaro; in an unnatural place, in a condition of suspension from natural process, and integrally related in her dilemma to the artist's desire to find fulfillment on the square sun-struck top of the

Mountain of God. Yes, it does seem as though Hemingway's artists sought a woman who would be willing to accept for their sake the unique conditions that their art might impose upon them. The wife in "Cat in the Rain" or the girl in "Hills Like White Elephants" are exemplary. It also seems that, unlike many, Hemingway was fully aware of the costs of such an art, and that he labored throughout his lifetime to come to terms with the dilemma created by that cost; that he strove to find aesthetic means to declare his guilt and a way whereby the woman might be spared that price. That the men in "Cross County Snow," "Hills Like White Elephants," and "Cat in the Rain" are mocked is patent. In "On the Quai at Smyrna," the story Hemingway carefully later added to be the real introduction to *In Our Time*, the mothers with dead babies at their breasts are the paradigm for the suspended and arrested women who follow in the stories. The male attempt to take those dead babies away is the attempt to outwit such suspension, a result of male dialectics, and to return process to its normal cycles.

The Garden of Eden, I would imagine, is an unfinished novel, as Keats's "Hyperion" is an unfinished poem, because it could not be completed. Nothing in the holograph version of *The Garden of Eden* warrants the promising ending of the published version, or even an aesthetically satisfying conclusion to David's dilemma, for the extraordinary exploration for alternatives to the cost of the creative process has not been successful, though Marita is offered, but only in the published version, as a satisfactory solution. Hemingway knew, and his story shows that he knew, that there is no good place for the woman who is the cost of an artist's art. A story like "Get a Seeing-Eyed Dog" is a superlative example of a story in which the creative artist well sees the penalty his art exacts in his wife's suspension as she is tied to him in a dependency and sterility that he carefully evaluates. In Keats's "Eve of St. Agnes," the lovers abandon the frozen castle, fleeing from that suspended state into the southern storms, where they are forever lost to us. They have exchanged their images as statues in art—Catherine's final state in *A Farewell*—for love and life, and they are finally devoured and obscured, as most things outside of art are, by time. They could not accept dying into life upon the urn, nor could the Catherine of *The Garden of Eden*; and Hemingway—who, I affirm, never could accept the role of the martyred scapegoat victim, whether as a Christ absolving us of our sins or as the wife in "Cat in the Rain"—repeatedly exposed the victimization. Catherine, in *A Farewell to Arms*, may have become, to Frederic, a statue, but that she is drives Hemingway as artist into his confessional self-laceration. He repeatedly excoriates himself for the dilemma of suspension he, as seemingly life-careless, abstract-oriented male, casts upon his consort, and I think it is important to note that the husbands in "Cat in the Rain," "Out of Season," and "Cross Country Snow" were modeled on Hemingway himself. A story like "After the Storm" becomes unbearably poignant as the suspended woman clearly seen floating behind glass ambiguously seems somehow to be the treasure that the protagonist so desperately needs to recover and also the sacrifice permitting the accessibility of that treasure. As he batters at the round porthole with his useless pole, the sexual and mythic dimensions of the painful quest suggest themselves.

If one is interested in extending the self-reflexive concern for the creative process of the work being written that saturates the Hemingway canon, one might be impelled to see dephallused Jake as the suspended man aware of the cost of his detachment. However, his attempt to master that seemingly unarrestable wheel, to stop the room from wheeling, is somewhat similar to Frederic's attempt in *A Farewell to Arms*, by taking Catherine to the heights of Switzerland and finally viewing her as a statue, to master the fact of the destructive cycles by which she is slain. The suspension of the woman becomes in such a case ambiguously charged with meaning: it may be a knowing illustration of the way the woman becomes a sacrifice to art, and yet it may be the only way the author can mythically attempt to protect her from the destructive aspects of the cycles of life that of course lead to inevitable death. Either way, the suspension exists within a work of art, and the message—whether "In my rhyme you live" or "life is the cost of art"—is an artist's sensitive perception.

NOTES

1. See my article, "'An Alpine Idyll': The Sun-Struck Mountain Vision and the Necessary Valley Journey," anthologized in Susan Beegel's collection, *Hemingway's Neglected Short Fiction: New Perspectives* (Ann Arbor and Tuscaloosa: UMI Research Press and University of Alabama Press, 1989).

2. Catherine in *A Farewell to Arms*, and later Catherine in *The Garden of Eden*, are carefully named after the saint whose icon is the wheel on which she was martyred. Both novels study the biological wheel of pregnancy that is the dilemma for both women, one who attempts to find absolutes—"always," "forever," words or immortalities—to replace death, time, and the biological trap; the other who attempts to take over the role of the male.

3. The biological "trap": in *A Farewell to Arms*, after Catherine tells Frederic she is pregnant, he remarks, "You always feel trapped biologically" (133). Toward the end of the novel, as Frederic forsees Catherine's death in childbirth, he thinks to himself, "This was the end of the trap" (303). *A Farewell to Arms* (New York: Scribner's, 1957).

4. Crucifixion on the wheel rather than the cross is a frequent Hemingway inversion: we see it in Catherine's death at the end of her nine-month cycle, in *A Farewell to Arms*, in a scene like "a drawing of the Inquisition" (308); and in *To Have and Have Not*, in Harry's dying, while he "hung against the wheel" (173). *To Have and Have Not* (New York: Scribner's, 1962).

5. Hemingway delights in forcing birth against death in "On the Quai at Smyrna," "Indian Camp," and *A Farewell to Arms*, so he frequently places the three days between Christ's death and his Easter resurrection against an imagery of Christmas. In *A Farewell to Arms*, snow comes "three days before Christmas"; but, later, after three days of rain, which should in the religious symbolism be answered by spiritual transcendence of death in resurrection, they descend instead to biological process and biological death. The suggestion seems to be that Nature outwits God, that the cycles of natural process, for Hemingway, take precedence over spiritual powers. That is essentially the meaning of *A Farewell to Arms*: its ironies everywhere announce the ineffectuality of the word, prayer, or God as they try to go against "life."

6. See Joseph M. Flora, "'An Alpine Idyll' is the story of the coming into being of a story," in *Hemingway's Nick Adams* (Baton Rouge: Louisiana State University Press, 1982), 209.

7. A master's thesis, written at San Francisco State University in 1978 by Susan Ormandy Simons, "A Grand Illusion: The Motif of Mountains and Snow in Hemingway's Fiction," well studies the relations between freezing, thawing, and flow in Hemingway's work.

8. Ernest Hemingway, *The Torrents of Spring* (Harmondsworth, England: Penguin Books, 1964), 107.

9. John Keats, "Ode On a Grecian Urn."

10. "Let's roll," commands Colonel Cantwell to his driver, Jackson, in *Across the River and Into the Trees* (30); "We'll roll," commands Frederic Henry to his ambulance drivers in *A Farewell to Arms* (193). In both instances the actual directions being taken are toward the beloved and also toward possible death. *Across the River and Into the Trees* (New York: Scribner's, 1950).

STEPPING INTO THE LABYRINTH

FIFTEEN YEARS OF HEMINGWAY SCHOLARSHIP

KELLI A. LARSON

THE NOTION THAT ALL good writing is travel writing is certainly not new to Hemingway aficionados, who explore the world with one of this century's greatest travel guides without ever leaving the comfort of their armchairs. From the bullrings of Pamplona to the cafes of Paris, Hemingway's books convey the reader along inner journeys spanning time and space; enabling them to discover and rediscover not only their world, but themselves in the process. In compiling the most current annotated bibliography on Hemingway scholarship, I have learned that good criticism, too, invites the reader on a journey—a mental exploration driven by mutual curiosity, leading both critic and reader to a deeper understanding of the text under consideration; preparing both, as more sensitive travelers, for future journeys with Hemingway. The very best criticism over the past fifteen years has followed this course and includes all areas of scholarship, from textual studies to biography. Unfortunately, as with any large endeavor involving literally thousands of authors, editors, and publishers, a goodly portion of these critical journeys have led frustratingly to dead ends, while still others have made us feel as though we've never left home.

Unified efforts such as the establishment of the Hemingway Collection at the Kennedy Library in Boston in the mid-1970s and the founding of the Hemingway Society in 1980 have provided the necessary impetus and direction for the recent renaissance that has occurred in Hemingway studies. With hundreds of notes, articles, and books published worldwide each year, the need for such centralized organization is greater than ever as scholars struggle to keep abreast of the field without succumbing to information overload. If we have indeed created a Frankenstein's monster in

Reprinted from *The Hemingway Review* 11, no. 2 (spring 1992): 19-24, by permission of the journal and the author.

terms of sheer volume, we have also given that monster legitimacy and permanency in establishing such organizations, and therefore share in the responsibility of management. Periodic reviews of the literature like those performed annually by *American Literary Scholarship*, though adding to the quagmire of Hemingway studies, should be encouraged, for they provide an invaluable service in tracking new trends and ensuring that significant scholarship does not become lost in the overflow.

Probably the most vital work done in the last decade and a half concerns preservation of primary materials like that under way at the Kennedy Library. However, the preservation of primary resources through biography is also of monumental importance. With each passing year, our access to those who actually knew Hemingway, who lived with him, loved him, and despised him, diminishes. Multivolume biographies by Michael Reynolds and Peter Griffin, other partial biographies focused on particular time periods such as Norberto Fuentes's *Hemingway in Cuba*, and numerous memoirs by wives, sons, lovers, and war buddies are critical to our understanding of the author, achieving a level of personal insight beyond the scope of biographical studies that will be written just two decades from now. This is not to imply that our current race against the ding dong of doom is not without its own inherent limitations. Relying on opinions and remembrances clouded by the passage of time is, at best, a risky endeavor. Even those memoirs compiled through contemporaneous journals and diaries have been reinterpreted and edited decades after the fact. Still, at the risk of sounding callous, the importance of gleaning all that these "primary sources" have to offer grows more critical with each passing day. For example, while touring Hemingway's boyhood home in Oak Park during the 1990 Chicago MLA convention, many of us were surprised at the lack of firm knowledge concerning the house's downstairs layout at the time of the Hemingways' occupation. Contacting a friend or acquaintance of the family, or Carol Hemingway (the only surviving child), would clear up such confusion.

Along with the many biographies appearing in the past fifteen years have been a number of studies, some of them bordering on the sensational, purporting to reveal the "man beneath the myth." Perhaps it is not surprising that a man of Hemingway's popular stature should be subjected to such analysis, especially when one considers the extent to which Hemingway himself created and perpetuated the legendary myths that surrounded him. However, what bothers me as a bibliographer is the sheer repetition of such studies—seemingly oblivious to the existence of their predecessors. These studies also serve as a warning to the rest of us who believe we are engaged in legitimate and worthwhile scholarship. As long as Hemingway continues to hold the interest of both the literary and non-literary public, "schlock" will be published simply because it deals with the larger-than-life figure of Hemingway—a man who created and lived beyond the imagination of most of us and therefore continues to hold our fascination. Problematic areas such as this one, however, could provide future scholars with opportunities for discovery, provided they alter the focus of their inquiry. For example, redirecting attention in the opposite direction—to the theoretical, cultural, sociological, and psychological underpinnings of Hemingway's mass appeal—has yet to be fully explored.

The repetition found in Hemingway scholarship over the past decade and a half is both astounding and disturbing. Admittedly, the sheer volume of criticism produced annually creates difficulties in keeping abreast of all the latest advancements in the area. However, a number of purported new studies point to, rest squarely upon, or steal shamelessly from classic explorations by authors such as Carlos Baker and Philip Young—without so much as a passing footnote, let alone the coauthor designation they deserve. Perhaps the Hemingway code and wound theory have pervaded our culture to the extent that they now fall under the realm of public domain, so that contemporary scholars are no longer obligated to acknowledge or even recognize their origins. As noted above, these "overdone" areas can be transformed into opportunities for discovery, if scholars simply redirect their focus. In a few recent innovative studies, critics have begun to apply the code to both texts and characters previously dismissed as "codeless," with interesting results. For example, in "Catherine Barkley and the Hemingway Code: Ritual and Survival in *A Farewell to Arms*," Sandra Whipple Spanier argues for a reversal of the orthodox interpretation of Henry as code hero. Instead, Spanier suggests that Barkley's honor and courage mark her as the true Hemingway hero/mentor, who then must teach the code to Henry.

In addition to the countless repetitive studies in the past decade and a half are those that, while not actually replicating or duplicating previous criticism, still manage somehow to break no new ground or advance no new thesis regarding the author or his writing. These include, for example, the numerous articles and notes devoted to straightening out the confusion behind Margot's shooting at the buffalo in "The Short Happy Life of Francis Macomber" and the waiters' dialogue in "A Clean, Well-Lighted Place." Whether Hemingway intentionally left the waiters' exchange ambiguous or an error was made during the writing or printing stages of the short story has been the focus of over a dozen studies in as many years. Within the broader scope of the Hemingway canon, these singularly narrow preoccupations seem rather trivial for both the critics who write them and those optimists like myself who continue to read them, one after another—hoping against hope that this will be the one to offer a final solution, thus theoretically cutting off the impetus behind having to write or read any more of them.

The number of dead-end and repetitive studies wrongly suggest that the Hemingway canon has finally been exhausted. In truth, judging by the quality of numerous articles and books produced on the author in the last decade and a half, we are now in the midst of a Hemingway renaissance. New generations of scholars are breathing new life into texts once thought critically eviscerated—new insight garnered through new approaches. Hemingway scholars are now discovering that only the surface has been scratched, due to our strong historical reliance upon conventional methods of analysis such as biographical and thematic studies, and close textual readings. In the past, many of us were reluctant to apply more contemporary theoretical apparatus to Hemingway's writing, thus implying that his work was unable to withstand the rigorous critical scrutiny that such frameworks demand. As the 1980s drew to a close, however, we were gladly proven wrong as a number of Marxist, deconstructionist, semiotic, and psychoanalytic studies emerged—demonstrating that new avenues for exploration are limited only by our imaginations, critical tools, and departmental travel budgets.

Clearly the most analyzed novel of the last fifteen years is *The Sun Also Rises*, with *A Farewell to Arms* and *For Whom the Bell Tolls* bringing up a distant second and third. Since *The Sun Also Rises* has long been considered stylistically and creatively superior to the others, the attention focused on this text is not surprising. Of course, we must not overlook another important factor behind this novel's procurement of the lion's share of critical attention—its popularity in the classroom. The novel's accessibility to students of today makes it a familiar inclusion on college and university syllabi across the country. By teaching the novel, and thereby engaging in a re-examination and re-evaluation of it, we partake in the initial stages of literary analysis. Eventually we arrive at new ways of thinking about the text, which we, in turn, share with colleagues via criticism. Inexplicably, this cyclical phenomenon has not occurred with *The Old Man and the Sea*. Despite widespread use at both the college and high school level, it remains a distant fourth in the critical ranks, receiving less than one third of the attention directed toward *The Sun Also Rises*.

Our recently renewed interest in Hemingway's non-fiction may reverse the trend of long neglect experienced by those full-length works of the 1930s, *Death in the Afternoon* and *Green Hills of Africa*. Together with *To Have and Have Not*, the combined coverage of these three is considerably less than the scant portion alloted to *The Old Man and the Sea*. Bredahl and Drake's *Hemingway's Green Hills of Africa as Evolutionary Narrative: Helix and Scimitar* is certainly a step in bringing one of these texts out of obscurity and into the critical light. Focusing upon both the authorial and environmental "creative energies" in the book, Bredahl and Drake redefine the conventional categories of fiction and autobiography in their ascription of the work to a genre by itself, thus introducing new directions in the analysis of Hemingway's nonfiction. It is also hoped that the publication of Reynolds's and Griffin's multivolume biographies will encourage further our intellectual curiosity regarding both this undervalued period in Hemingway's life and the works created from it. A complete understanding of the author requires a comprehensive view of his life's writings beyond the aesthetic value we attach to individual eras or texts. In short, these neglected periods present wide-open opportunities for future scholarship.

Studies of Hemingway's short fiction have also increased considerably over the past decade and a half. Not surprisingly, those oft-anthologized few attracted most of our attention, with "The Short Happy Life of Francis Macomber" narrowly edging out "Big Two-Hearted River," "Hills Like White Elephants," and "A Clean, Well-Lighted Place" in the critical stakes. This trend may eventually reverse itself as diligent scholars continue to unearth "new" finds and attend to the overlooked items composing Hemingway's short fiction canon. Two important full-length investigations focusing on the short stories appeared in 1989, Susan Beegel's *Hemingway's Neglected Short Fiction: New Perspectives* and Paul Smith's *A Reader's Guide to the Short Stories of Ernest Hemingway*. Smith devotes a chapter to each of the fifty-five short stories published during the author's lifetime—from "Up in Michigan" to "A Man of the World," including brief discussions of their respective composition, publication, sources, and important criticism. Beegel's is a collection of essays on Hemingway's lesser-known short stories, designed to bring them into the canon. Sadly, as Beegel points out in her introduction, "to date, we lack a carefully researched and edited text that collects and arranges in chronological order of their composition all of Hemingway's efforts in the genre, both previously published and otherwise." Unfortunately, a significant portion of Hemingway's short fiction remains either unpublished or uncollected and thus virtually inaccessible to critics, students, and the general reading public. Perhaps even more disturbing, however, is Beegel's contention that a goodly portion of accessible works suffer from critical neglect because of their failure to meet our critical expectations. In struggling to reconcile a writer's works within our own literary sensibilities, dismissing or undervaluing texts because they do not fit prescribed patterns of theme or style does a disservice to both author and critic. Hemingway's posthumous writings, though questionably edited, also fail to conform, thus underscoring the need for a revisionist reading of the

author's oeuvre—revision beginning less with the individual texts themselves than with our own preconceived notions about those texts.

The truly difficult task of re-evaluating the multi-dimensional nature of
Hemingway's art has been eased considerably by the availability of many
of the author's manuscripts at the Kennedy Library. Focusing on both
Hemingway's evolution as a writer and on the writing process itself, a
number of seminal studies have emerged over the past decade that trace
the transformation of jotted notes into finished art. At this point, however,
we stand upon the threshold of discovery. The construction of a comprehensive view of Hemingway's stylistic development, evolving aesthetic, and
philosophy of composition not only presents new directions for study, but
will also establish the theoretical framework necessary for a fresh examination of the entire Hemingway canon, seeming oddities and all.

Despite their broad range of subject and approach over the past fifteen
years, the driving force binding Hemingway scholars together has been the
desire to know more fully one of this century's greatest authors. Having
placed myself in the unenviable position of criticizing the critics—a role
that Hemingway enjoyed over the course of his life, it seems only fitting
that I conclude this overview with a visionary assessment of the future
direction of Hemingway studies in the closing decade of the twentieth century. Can one accurately detect and predict trends and areas of discovery
likely to occupy the minds and imaginations of such a diverse body of
scholars? Probably not, but it is hoped that the recent resurgence of interest in the conventional essay form as an intellectual exercise of the mind—
that is, as a tool of critical inquiry—will have a great impact upon our
future literary dialogues.

To employ the essay in the exploratory process itself, as an experiment
in making sense of things that puzzle, rather than as a firm thesis or argument being developed, is a challenge to those of us who submit our essays
to editors as though they were miniature tanks, tightly constructed and
heavily fortified against attack with impeccable logic and documentation.
Such daring, placing emphasis on idea generation during the transmission
of meaning, may in the end not only stimulate and refine critical debate,
but also help us to overcome our predisposition of thought regarding
Hemingway's art. Clearly, to let our authoritative guard down as we
explore what these texts really say to us is a risky endeavor; but
Hemingway, a man who lived life on the edge, would surely have appreci-
ated such a methodology.

WORKS CITED

Beegel, Susan F. 1989. *Hemingway's Neglected Short Fiction: New Perspectives*. Ann Arbor, Michigan: UMI Research Press.

Bredahl, Carl A. Jr. and Susan Lynn Drake. 1990. *Hemingway's Green Hills of Africa as Evolutionary Narrative: Helix and Scimitar*. Lewiston, New York: Edwin Mellen Press.

Fuentes, Norberto. 1984. *Hemingway in Cuba*. Translated by Consuelo Corwin. Secaucus, New Jersey: Lyle Stuart.

Griffin, Peter. 1985. *Along With Youth: Hemingway, the Early Years*. New York: Oxford University Press.

_____. 1990. *Less Than Treason: Hemingway in Paris*. New York: Oxford University Press.

Reynolds, Michael. 1986. *The Young Hemingway*. New York: Blackwell.

_____. 1989. *Hemingway: The Paris Years*. New York: Blackwell.

Smith, Paul. 1989. *A Reader's Guide to the Short Stories of Ernest Hemingway*. Boston: G.K. Hall.

Spanier, Sandra Whipple. 1987. "Catherine Barkley and the Hemingway Code: Ritual and Survival in *A Farewell to Arms*." *Ernest Hemingway's A Farewell to Arms*. Edited by Harold Bloom. New York: Chelsea. 131-48.

INDEX

A

Across the River and Into the Trees: as allegory, 249, 262; artistic and literary figures in, 261; color in, 261; contrasts and parallels in, 258-59; critical reception in, 249, 250, 251, 254, 263; four modes of communication in, 256; imagery in, 259-61; metaphor of feminine arrest in, 267-68; structure in, 255-59

Adams, George,* 31, 40

Adams, Henry (Dr.),* 21, 29, 31, 32, 33, 34, 40, 41-43, 53-56, 96-97

Adams, Nick*: in "The Battler," 19-20, 34, 89; in "Big Two-Hearted River," 19, 25, 26, 67, 77-89; in "The Doctor and the Doctor's Wife," 32; in "The End of Something," 67, 68, 89; in "Fathers and Sons," 34, 91-100; in "Indian Camp," 21, 29-30, 31, 34, 37, 40-44; in "The Killers," 18; in "The Last Good Country," 20, 75n. 14; in "The Three-Day Blow," 68-71, 89; in "Three Shots," 30; in "A Way You'll Never Be," 89

"After the Storm," 273

"Along with Youth," 25

"Alpine Idyll," 265

Anselmo,* 214, 219n. 4, 241, 243, 244-45, 246

Arroz y tartana (Ibanez), 150

Ashley, Brett,* 129, 130, 131, 132, 133-34, 146-47n. 14, 181, 206, 268

Aymo,* 170, 173

B

"Ballad of the Goodly Fere, The," 203, 204, 210-11n. 2

Barker, Lewelys, 118

Barkley, Catherine,* 120, 158-65, 168-69, 171, 173, 178-80, 182, 187nn. 16, 17, 214, 223, 265-66, 268-69, 272-73, 273n. 3

Barnes, Jake,* 129-35, 136n. 15, 137-38, 141-42, 144, 181, 206, 268, 273

Barton, Bruce, 49

Barton, Rev. William, 49, 51

"Battler, The," 15, 19-20, 30, 34, 89

Bay View Association, the, 17, 21

"Big Two-Hearted River": counterpoint technique in, 30-31; fictionalized Michigan in, 15, 19, 21, 24; influence of Hemingway's war wounding on, 78-82; metaphor of feminine arrest in, 268; nothing theme in, 77-90; swamp in, 89, 195; as symbolic of end of Hemingway's youth, 23, 25-27; symbolism in,

---

* fictional character

283

T

Tabeshaw, Billy,* 32
Tabeshaw, Eddie,* 32
"Tale of Orpen, The," 179, 180, 181
"Ten Indians," 31
Third Congregational Church of Oak
  Park, the, 49-50, 51
"This Must be Friday," 261
Thompson, Charles, 199n. 5
"Three-Day Blow, The": counterpoint
  technique in, 31, 34; metaphor of
  feminine arrest in, 266, 267, 269;
  real-life basis of, 65-66, 68-71;
  swamp in, 89
"Three Shots," 29, 30, 31
"Today is Friday," 203, 204-9
To Have and Have Not, 123, 198n. 1,
  274n. 4
Torrent, The (Ibanez), 150
Torrents of Spring, The, 13, 15, 75n.
  14, 120, 268, 269
"Train Trip, A," 123, 124, 125n. 10
"Twa Corbies, The" (anonymous bal-
  lad), 109, 125n. 8
Twysden, Duff,* 140

U

Uncle George.* See Adams, George
"Undefeated, The," 152, 208-9
"Undiscovered Country, The," 221
"Up in Michigan," 39, 61

V

Villon, Francois, 261
von Kurowsky, Agnes, 167, 174-75n.
  16

W

Walker, Al, 23
Waugh, Evelyn, 249, 250
"Way You'll Never Be, A," 82, 89, 90,
  123
Williams, Tennessee, 249
Wilson,* 190, 191, 193, 194, 196-97,
  198n. 1, 199-200n. 6

Z

Zurito,* 208-9